A LEGAL HISTORY OF ROME

D1602102

Roman law is one of the most remarkable and enduring contributions to civilization: many of the familiar norms which regulate our social and economic lives in the Western world originated in ancient Rome, and the Roman legal institutions comprise a vital part of the background of several contemporary legal systems. A study of Roman legal history also provides valuable insights into the origins and progress of law as a social and cultural phenomenon. Knowledge of ancient Roman law therefore constitutes an essential component of a sound legal education as well as the education of a student of history.

This book equips both lawyer and historian with a complete history of Roman law, from its beginnings *c.* 500 BC through to its rediscovery in Europe, where it was widely applied until the eighteenth century.

Combining a law specialist's informed perspective of legal history with a socio-political and cultural focus, it examines the sources of law, the ways in which these laws were applied and enforced, and the ways the law was influenced and progressed, with an exploration of civil and criminal procedures and special attention paid to legal science. The final chapter covers the history of Roman law in late antiquity and appraises the move towards the codification of law that culminated in the final statement of Roman law: the *Corpus Iuris Civilis* of Emperor Justinian. Throughout the book, George Mousourakis highlights the relationship between Roman law and Roman life by following the lines of the major historical developments.

Including bibliographic references and organized accessibly by historical era, this book is an excellent introduction to the history of Roman law for students of both law and ancient history.

George Mousourakis teaches legal history and comparative law at Niigata University, Japan, and at the University of Auckland, New Zealand. He practised law in Greece, obtained his MJur and PhD in the UK, and has taught law at universities around the world. As well as his work on legal history and comparative law, he has published extensively in the areas of criminal law and jurisprudence.

A LEGAL HISTORY OF ROME

George Mousourakis

Routledge
Taylor & Francis Group

LONDON AND NEW YORK

First published 2007
by Routledge
2 Park Square, Milton Park, Abingdon, Oxon OX14 4RN

Simultaneously published in the USA and Canada
by Routledge
270 Madison Ave, New York, NY 10016

Routledge is an imprint of the Taylor & Francis Group, an informa business

© 2007 George Mousourakis

Typeset in Garamond by
Book Now Ltd, London
Printed and bound in Great Britain by
Antony Rowe Ltd, Chippenham, Wiltshire

British Library Cataloguing in Publication Data
A catalogue record for this book is available from the British Library

Library of Congress Cataloging in Publication Data
Mousourakis, George.
A legal history of Rome/George Mousourakis.
p. cm.
Includes bibliographical references and index.
1. Roman law–History. 2. Civil law–History. 3. Rome–History. I. Title.
KJA147.M685 2007
340.5'409–dc22
2006100344

ISBN10: 0–415–40893–8 (hbk)
ISBN10: 0–415–40894–6 (pbk)
ISBN10: 0–203–08934–0 (ebk)

ISBN13: 978–0–415–40893–6 (hbk)
ISBN13: 978–0–415–40894–3 (pbk)
ISBN13: 978–0–203–08934–7 (ebk)

CONTENTS

CONTENTS

PREFACE

From the vantage point of history, Roman law is one of Rome's most remarkable and enduring contributions to civilization. In no other field of human endeavour have the Romans a greater claim to lasting fame than in the creation of a sophisticated legal system that constantly adapted itself to an ever-changing and developing society. The Western world derived from Roman law most of the basic norms and institutions concerning the organization and regulation of socio-economic life that are essential for guaranteeing the ideal that we refer to as the 'rule of law'. As Roman law constitutes an important part of the intellectual background of contemporary law, the study of its history is a valuable component of a sound legal education. Without the knowledge derived from such study it is impossible to fully understand the evolution and functioning of contemporary legal systems and institutions rooted in Roman law. From the perspective of the historian of civilization, the study of Roman legal history can provide valuable insights into the origins and progress of law as a social and cultural phenomenon.

The history of Roman law is divided into two periods. The first period spans more than a thousand years, from the formation of the city-state of Rome to the codification of Justinian in the sixth century AD. The second period, although beginning in the sixth century, did not really become important until the eleventh century, when Roman law was 'rediscovered' in the West and made the object, first of academic study and then, in the course of time, of far-reaching reception in large parts of Continental Europe. The present work focuses on the history of Roman law in antiquity. It examines the nature and development of law-making and the sources of law, the mechanisms whereby the diverse sources were effectuated, and the way each legal source influenced the progress of the law. Special attention is accorded to the development of Roman legal science, which emerged as the most productive element in Roman legal life by the end of the first century BC. And since the Romans tended to shape their legal rules in terms of procedural techniques, rather than in terms of general and abstract norms, the book also explores the evolution and main features of civil and criminal procedure, and elucidates the implementation of legal judgments. The last chapter of the book covers the history of Roman law in late antiquity and appraises the move towards the codification of law that culminated in the final statement of Roman law: the *Corpus Iuris Civilis* of

Emperor Justinian. In analysing institutional change in the legal system of ancient Rome, the present work combines the perspectives of legal history with those of social, political and cultural history, giving full weight to non-legal factors and historical events that prompted or contributed to that change. Since Roman legal history is too long to treat as a whole, it has been divided into a number of shorter periods. For each period there is first a discussion of the political and socio-economic situation at the time, then the sources of law and the administration of justice during the period under consideration are examined in some detail. The end of the book lists the bibliographical references for further reading, together with the titles of the studies and research that formed the basis of this work.

The book has been written primarily for students whose course of studies encompasses Roman law, legal history and comparative law. It is also designed to provide an accessible source of reference for students and scholars of ancient history and the classics. As long as it is remembered that the book is not devised as a thorough elaboration of the complexities of substantive Roman law, and is therefore likely to be used in conjunction with other, more detailed materials, it has a place in rendering Roman legal history more accessible to readers in many diverse fields of legal and historical learning.

The impetus for this book emanated from a series of lectures that I delivered in undergraduate courses at the University of Auckland and the University of Queensland from 1997 to 2006. I should like to thank my colleagues and students for their encouragement and constructive criticism when the themes of this book were discussed in class and seminar presentations. I am also greatly indebted to Professor A. Bürge and Dr J. Platschek of the Leopold Wenger Institute at the University of Munich, Professor C. Baldus of the University of Heidelberg, Professor B. Sirks of the University of Frankfurt and Professor W. Sadurski of the European University Institute, who all enabled me to spend several months in Europe as a research scholar and to access the libraries and facilities of their Institutions. My thanks also go to my colleagues and students at Niigata University for their cooperation and support during the final stages of this project. I must also tender my thanks to my research assistant, Miss L. Stroud, who read the final draft and saved me from a number of errors and obscurities, and to my publishers for their courteous assistance in the realization of this project.

ABBREVIATIONS

Bruns, *Fontes*   *Fontes iuris romani antiqui*, ed. C. G. Bruns, Tubingen 1909, repr. Aalen 1969
C.   *Codex* of Justinian
C. Th.   *Codex Theodosianus*
D.   *Digest* of Justinian
FIRA   *Fontes Iuris Romani Anteiustiniani*, I–III, ed. S. Riccobono, J. Baviera and V. Arangio-Ruiz, Florence 1940–43, 2nd edn, 1968
G.   *Institutes* of Gaius
Girard, *Textes* *Textes de droit romain*, ed. P. F. Girard and F. Senn, 7th edn, Paris 1967
Inst.   *Institutes* of Justinian
MGH   *Monumenta Germaniae Historica*
Nov.   *Novels* of Justinian
SZ   *Zeitschrift der Savigny Stiftung für Rechtsgeschichte*
P. Oxy.   *The Oxyrhynchus Papyri*, ed. B. P. Grenflell, A. S. Hunt, *et al.*, London 1898
PS   *Pauli Sententiae*
UE   *Tituli ex corpore Ulpiani* in FIRA II, 261–301
XII T.   *Twelve Tables*

INTRODUCTION

The history of Roman law in antiquity spans a period of more than a thousand years. Initially, the law of a small rural community, then that of a powerful city-state, Roman law became in the course of time the law of a multinational empire that embraced the entire Mediterranean world. During its long history, Roman law progressed through a remarkable process of evolution. It advanced through different stages of development and underwent important transformations, both in substance and in form, as it adjusted to changes in society, especially those changes derived from Rome's expansion in the ancient world. During this long process the interaction between custom, enacted law and case law entailed the formation of a highly sophisticated system that evolved from layers of different elements. But the great bulk of Roman law, especially private law, was the product of jurisprudence, not legislation. This unenacted law was not a confusing mass of shifting customs, but an enduring tradition developed and transmitted by specialists, initially the members of the priestly college of the pontiffs and, in later times, the secular jurists. In the final phases of this process, when law-making was increasingly centralized, this law, together with statutory law, was compiled and then codified. The codification of the law both completed the development of Roman law and formed the means by which Roman law was subsequently disseminated to the modern world.

Roman history is traditionally divided into three major periods that correspond to Rome's three successive systems of political organization: (i) the Monarchy, from the founding of Rome in the eighth century BC to 509 BC; (ii) the Republic, from 509 BC to 27 BC; and (iii) the Empire, from 27 BC to AD 565. The republican era is subdivided into two phases: the early Republic, from 509 BC to 287 BC, and the late Republic, from 287 BC to 27 BC. The imperial era is likewise subdivided into two parts: the early Empire or Principate, from 27 BC to AD 284, and the late Empire or Dominate, from AD 284 to AD 565. According to one approach, Roman legal history follows these divisions as the various legal institutions adapted to the type of government in power. But Roman legal history may also be divided into periods by reference to the modes of law-making and the character and orientation of the legal institutions that prevailed in different epochs. In this respect, the following phases are distinguished: (i) the archaic period, from the formation of the city-state of Rome to the middle of the third century BC; (ii) the pre-classical period, from the

1

middle of the third century BC to the early first century AD; (iii) the classical period, from the early first century AD to the middle of the third century AD; and (iv) the post-classical period, from the middle of the third century AD to the sixth century AD. The archaic period covers the Monarchy and the early Republic; the pre-classical period largely coincides with the later part of the Republic; the classical period covers most of the first part of the imperial era, known as the Principate; and the post-classical period embraces the final years of the Principate and the late Empire or Dominate, including the age of Justinian (AD 527–65).

Although the above divisions facilitate the study of Roman law, one must recall that Roman law evolved gradually and therefore no distinct lines separate the different stages of its development. The sources of law were, in varying degrees of strength from period to period, all present and in force at the same time, and in diverse ways qualified the influence of each other.

1

THE MONARCHY AND EARLY REPUBLIC: THE HISTORICAL, SOCIAL AND CONSTITUTIONAL BACKGROUND

The origins of Rome

Archaeological evidence indicates that the territory of Rome was not permanently inhabited until around 1000 BC. The first people who settled around the Tiber valley and the area that became Rome were the Latins and the Sabines, two of the Indo-European peoples referred to collectively as Italians. These groups drifted down from the North across the Alps into the Italian peninsula at the end of the second millennium BC. The people of Latium, as this area was later called, were divided into several independent groups organized in separate communities, but all considered themselves members of the same broader family with largely common interests.[1] The Latin culture and conditions of life displayed very little change until the late seventh century BC. In this period the people of Latium encountered the Etruscans, who occupied the neighbouring territory of Tuscany, and later the Greeks and the Carthaginians.

Unlike the Latins, the Etruscans were a city-dwelling people. Their fortified cities, situated on hilltops and other easy-to-defend positions, formed strong political and commercial centres. Each city was politically independent and, until the sixth or early fifth century BC, was governed by a king chosen from among a few noble families. Although in later years the kings were replaced by annually elected magistrates, the Etruscans' social and political organization remained predominantly aristocratic in character. Economic life was based on agriculture, cattle-rearing, industry and commerce. The Etruscans were also a powerful maritime people and through sea-trade they established contacts with other Mediterranean peoples, such as the Greeks and the Phoenicians. The Greek influence on their culture is reflected in their art and architecture, and is evidenced by the thousands of tomb inscriptions they left behind. These inscriptions indicate that the Etruscans adopted a Greek alphabet (probably from the Greek city of Cumae in Campania) before the end of the seventh century BC.

Towards the end of the seventh century BC, the Etruscans initiated their territorial expansion in Italy by conquering neighbouring Latium. The occupation of Latium launched the urbanization of the rural communities settled in the area around the river Tiber that later evolved as the city of Rome. By the middle of the sixth century BC, the Etruscans had gained control over a large territory extending from the Adriatic coast in the east to the Alps in the north, and from the Arno river to the bay of Naples on Italy's western coast. But the Etruscan domination of Italy was brief, largely due to the rigidity of their aristocratic system of government that thwarted the peaceful assimilation of subject populations, and the lack of an effective political alliance between the Etruscan city-states to secure their territorial gains. In the late sixth century BC, the Etruscan power dwindled rapidly following a series of military setbacks and armed revolts of subject populations. Despite the decline of Etruscan power, the Etruscan culture prevailed in productive and influential form for several centuries.

From as early as the eighth century BC, Greek colonies were established on the shores of southern Italy and Sicily. The colonists retained their contemporary culture and systems of government, but each colony was an independent city-state owing no political allegiance to its mother city in mainland Greece. The presence of the Greek element in Italy stimulated the cultural and political development of other Italian communities. It was largely through the Greek cities that the Etruscans and, later, the Romans, came into contact with the more advanced civilizations of the eastern Mediterranean.

According to Roman tradition, Rome was founded in 753 BC by Romulus, a descendant of the Homeric hero Aeneas. Archaeological evidence confirms the presence of several settlements from the ninth to the seventh century BC in the area where Rome was established. These settlements were probably transformed into a city under Etruscan influence in the seventh century BC. The strategic importance of the site compelled the Etruscans to drain the marshy land between the hills and build temples, reservoirs and a city wall. Under an Etruscan ruling elite, the various groups in the area were unified into a single community and organized according to the Etruscan system of political organization. Despite the Etruscans' role in the formation of Rome and the influence of their civilization on early Roman culture, the Romans and their social institutions remained predominantly Latin in character.

Early Roman society

Similar to other Indo-European communities, the early Roman society was strongly patriarchal and conservative in nature. This pattern remained a distinctive feature of the Romans during most of their history. Obedience to authority, perseverance and keeping faith in unsettled times when it seemed propitious to do so were the ideals that characterized the early Romans' outlook on life.

The cornerstone of Roman society was the household (*familia*), a closely knit unit distinguished by its social and economic cohesion. The head of the family (*pater familias*) had absolute control (*patria potestas*) over all persons, irrespective of their age, and all property in his household.[2] He also performed the sacred rites of the household and, as a judge, inflicted punishments for breaches of the customary norms governing family life. Within the family he was the only person who possessed any rights in private law.

Families claiming descent from a common ancestor formed a broader social group, the *gens* or clan. The *gentes* played a central role in the earliest period of Roman history as they performed most of the social, religious and economic functions that were only later gradually assumed by the state. Each *gens* was distinguished by its own name (*nomen gentilicium*), celebrated its own religious rites (*sacra gentilicia*), held meetings and passed resolutions that were binding on all its members. The *gentes* did not play a direct role in Roman politics during the Republic, but the ruling families of Rome relied upon clan solidarity as a key element for advancing their social and political influence.[3]

The clans assumed the role of patrons for a motley class of people, the clients (*clientes*), whose members had a position of complete personal dependence on the clans to which they had attached themselves. The individual or clan members that accorded these people protection were termed, in relation to their clients, *patronus* or *patroni* respectively.[4] Notwithstanding their inferior status, the clients were free persons in the eyes of the law. A client and patron relationship was hereditary on both sides and based on reciprocity of socially prescribed duties and obligations. Thus, a patron was expected to protect his client's life and bodily and moral integrity, monitor his financial interests, advise him on legal and other matters and act as his representative in the courts of law (in which a client could not appear alone). In return, a client was expected to support his patron on all occasions and advance his interests by every material or moral resource in his power. Any breach of the trust enshrined within the client–patron relationship entailed was strongly condemned by custom and public opinion as contrary to established social and religious norms. The client system was an extremely important element of Roman society that played a diverse and essential role throughout Roman history.[5]

Another distinctive feature of early Roman society was the division of the population into two classes: the aristocrats or patricians, who increasingly asserted economic, social and political predominance, and a heterogeneous group of commoners or plebeians.[6] The early patrician aristocracy formed a closed order in society with clearly defined privileges based on birth and the ownership of landed property. The members of this class enjoyed all the rights of the Roman citizenship – only they were Roman citizens in a full sense (*cives optimo iuris*) – and monopolized all political power by controlling the senate, the popular assembly and the various state and religious offices. The plebeian class constituted the great majority of Rome's population and was mainly composed of small farmers, labourers, artisans and tradesmen. Although its members were Roman citizens, they did not initially enjoy the public rights (*iura publica*) of the Roman citizenship, such as the right to hold public office (*ius honorum*), whether political, military or religious.[7] Of the private rights (*iura privata*), the plebeians enjoyed the right of acquiring, holding and transferring property (*ius commercii*). But it appears that they did not possess the right to contract a regular Roman marriage (*ius connubii*) and thus intermarriages between plebeians and patricians were forbidden.[8]

5

During the early republican era, the plebeian class continued to grow, while the old patrician aristocracy rapidly declined in numbers. Although the gap between the rich and the poor generally expanded, several plebeian families acquired considerable wealth and, from a position of strength, began to challenge the patricians' monopoly of political power. For nearly two centuries after the establishment of the Republic, Rome's internal history was marked by the struggle between the two classes. During this contest (designated 'the struggle of the orders'), the plebeians gradually removed all obstacles to their political emancipation and secured equality with the patricians regarding civil rights. However, the plebeians' success only erased a specific political division and, overall, did not affect the more fundamental division between the rich and the poor. After the struggle of the orders, the meaning of the term '*plebs*' gradually changed. During the last century of the republican era this term did not denote a politically distinct social group, but simply the whole mass of lowly and poverty-stricken citizens in contradistinction with Rome's new nobility of wealth and office.[9]

Economic conditions

In early Roman history, economic life mostly revolved around cattle-rearing and agriculture. Indeed, for many centuries the cultivation of land was viewed as one of the most important activities for a Roman citizen. It seems more likely that, initially, the pasture-land remained largely undivided while the arable land gradually became open to private ownership. However, there is little agreement among historians over the scope of the institution of private property or the process of its introduction into early Roman society.[10] Under the influence of the Etruscans, the Romans later developed an interest in commerce and industry that was precipitated by the transformation of their settlements into a city-state. Payment for the various products was initially made in kind (probably in timber, salt, cattle and such like), as coinage was not introduced in Rome until the later fourth century BC. Instead of coins, the early Romans often used in their transactions pieces or ingots of bronze (*aes*), whose value was determined according to their weight.[11] After the introduction of a written alphabet in the fifth century BC, the Romans began to record their customary rules relating to property and to draft legal documents for certain economic transactions, testaments and wills.

The political organization of the regal period

According to Roman historical tradition, a succession of seven kings had governed Rome in the first two and a half centuries after the city's establishment.[12] The office of king (*rex*) was not hereditary but elective; moreover, although technically the king was supreme warlord, priest and judge, his authority was limited by the clan organization and the characteristic Roman habit of eliciting advice before action. As the chief priest of the state, the king acted as an intermediary between the community and its gods, and exercised general supervision over all matters relating to public worship.[13] In times of war, as commander-in-chief of the army, he called the people to arms and led them in the battlefield. Moreover, as the supreme judge of the community, the king had jurisdiction over all matters in both public and private law.[14] In executing these tasks the king would usually seek cooperation from the heads of the leading families. The royal power appears to have significantly expanded in the late seventh and sixth centuries BC with the introduction, under Etruscan influence, of the principle of *imperium* or supreme command.

The Roman kings turned for advice to a council of clan elders or senate, which probably represented the collective opinion of the patrician class.[15] The members of the senate (*patres, senatores*) were appointed by the king from among the heads of the patrician families. Besides functioning as the king's advisory body (*regium consilium*), the senate was also entrusted with the task of governing the state during the period between the death of a king and the election of another (*interregnum*) through a succession of senators acting as temporary kings (*interreges*). Moreover, the king would often, for convenience, delegate the management of state affairs to the senate, but the senate was bound to act within its limited authority granted by the king. As the scope of the senate's authority was not prescribed officially, the extent of a king's power greatly affected the degree of influence this body exercised.

Since the state's success ultimately depended on the cooperation of the citizenry, the king and his council found it expedient to inform the people of important decisions and therefore occasionally convoked a gathering called the curiate assembly (*comitia curiata*).[16] This assembly was composed of the thirty *curiae*, or wards, into which the whole citizen body (*populus Romanus*) was divided.[17] Its functions probably had a largely religious nature and included the inauguration of the king and the election of priests. The assembly also met to consider important matters concerning the entire community, such as the declaration of war or the conclusion of peace and the admission of a new clan. Strictly speaking, the curiate assembly had no legislative power but its most important function was the formal sanctioning of the laws proposed by the king. Moreover, a newly elected king acquired his *imperium*, or supreme command, by a special law issued by this assembly – the *lex curiata de imperio*. Although ostensibly the assembly had a passive political role during the regal era, the idea that political authority rested ultimately with the Roman people as a whole had great importance in the development of Roman political theory.

According to Roman historians, the military and political organization of Rome underwent an important change during the reign of King Servius Tullius (*c.* 578–535 BC). The Roman army was enlarged and new battle tactics were introduced to improve its effectiveness.[18] The reformed army was organized, further, into centuries or groups of a hundred soldiers. In order to recruit and equip these units, the entire citizen body was divided into five classes on the basis of wealth and each class supplied a set number of centuries (a total of one hundred and ninety-three centuries existed). The first class, comprising the wealthiest citizens, those who could equip themselves with horses and heavy armour, provided most of the centuries. On the basis of this division of citizens into classes and centuries, a new political body was formed over time, the centuriate assembly (*comitia centuriata*), which replaced the curiate assembly as the chief political body in the state.

According to Roman tradition, the kingship ended with the expulsion of the Etruscan King Tarquinius Superbus (Tarquinius the Proud) in 509 BC, but the circumstances surrounding its demise are uncertain. Apparently, the fall of the Monarchy was devised by the patricians who, chafing under high-handed foreign monarchs who did not respect their prestige (*dignitas*) or their advice, led a movement that wrested control of the state from the king. The uprising was probably inspired by similar movements in neighbouring cities and precipitated by the general weakening of the Etruscan power in Italy.

The coming of the Republic

The ousting of the Etruscan dynasty launched a new phase in Roman history, known as the Republic (from *res publica* or commonwealth). During the early years of this period the patrician class appeared as the sole beneficiary of the political revolution that entailed the establishment of the Republic. The patricians possessed absolute control over the government of the state; they also monopolized the priestly functions and, in an age when religion, custom and the as yet unwritten law were indistinguishable, they interpreted custom and 'found' laws in their own interest. On the other hand, the plebeians were denied access to state offices and remained, both socially and economically, subordinate to the patricians.

However, the patricians' monopoly of political power was soon challenged by the plebeians who, defining themselves as an independent order, pressed for political equality. Prominent plebeians resented their exclusion from office and membership in the senate, the only means for attaining prestige. Poorer plebeians, constantly threatened with bankruptcy by the military demands imposed on them by the state, focused on improving living conditions and securing protection from the arbitrary power of the patrician magistrates.[19] The patricians, whose power ultimately depended on plebeian cooperation in fighting Rome's wars, found themselves under increasing pressure to make political concessions and gradually gave in, although not without considerable resistance, to the plebeian demands. Territorial expansion and improved debtor legislation alleviated the worst forms of economic distress and, gradually, leading members of the plebeian class elected to the new offices in the growing state were admitted to the senate. By the middle of the third century BC a precarious equilibrium between the classes was established and a new nobility composed of both patrician and wealthy plebeian families dominated the Roman state. Landmarks in this process embrace the introduction of the *tribuni plebis*, plebeian officials acting as spokesmen of the plebeian class and protecting its members against arbitrary acts of patrician magistrates (*c.* 494 BC); the promulgation of the Law of the Twelve Tables, the first written statement of Roman law (*c.* 450 BC); the removal of the prohibition against intermarriage between patricians and plebeians by the *lex Canuleia* (445 BC); the Sextio-Licinian Laws (*leges Liciniae Sextiae*), which appear to have recognized the plebeians' right to hold the consulship, the highest office of the state, by providing that at least one of the two consuls elected each year should be chosen from the plebeian class (367 BC);[20] and the introduction of the Hortensian Law (*lex Hortensia*), which decreed that the enactments of the plebeian assembly (*plebiscita*) had the full force of laws binding on all Roman citizens, including patricians, whether or not these enactments were subsequently approved by the senate (287 BC).

As noted before, the plebeians' success in the struggle of the orders and the elimination of the political division between the two classes did not entail the eradication of social and economic inequalities. Instead, a new type of nobility (*nobilitas*) emerged in the place of the old patrician aristocracy. The political rights generated by the plebeians' success in the struggle of the orders allowed wealthy plebeian families access to the highest offices of the state that secured membership in the nobility.[21] In the course of time, the Roman government was monopolized by a few patrician and plebeian families who provided almost all the high magistrates and members of the senate. Thus, the fundamentally aristocratic character of the Roman state did not change. What changed was the constitution of the aristocracy in power: the old patrician aristocracy was replaced by a new and exclusive patricioplebeian nobility based on wealth and office-holding.

The Roman expansion in Italy

Rome's social and political development during the early republican period was directly related to her steady expansion throughout Italy. By the end of the fifth century BC, Rome with the cooperation of the Latin League had suppressed the threat posed by the marauding mountain tribes and conquered a large part of Etruria. But in 390 BC Rome suffered a serious setback, when invading Celtic tribes from Gaul defeated the Romans and their Latin allies and captured the city. The invaders were finally bought off with gold and withdrew, but the Gallic occupation survived in the Romans' memory as a great tragic event of their early history. In the years that followed, Rome consolidated her earlier conquests and continued her territorial expansion. In 338 BC the Romans defeated the Latins, who attempted to break free from Roman domination, and dissolved their alliance. In 295 BC, after a long struggle, they subdued the powerful Samnite tribes of Central Italy. Like the Latins and the Etruscans, the Samnites were gradually incorporated into the Roman state through their admission to the Roman citizen body. The rapidly growing power of Rome provoked conflict with Tarentum, the most powerful Greek city of Southern Italy. In 280 BC the Tarentines and their allies summoned the aid of King Pyrrhus of Epirus. Although Pyrrhus won several victories over the Romans, he was eventually expelled from Italy in 275 BC and Tarentum was forced to surrender in 272 BC. Like the other Greek cities of Southern Italy, Tarentum became a Roman ally and agreed to supply Rome with naval forces in return for military protection. By 264 BC the Romans had achieved political control over the Italian peninsula that was secured through the creation of a dependable and remarkably flexible system of federation.[22]

The republican constitution

The republican system of government was based on three interrelated elements: the magistrature (*magistratus*), the assemblies of the Roman people (*comitia*) and the senate (*senatus*). The latter element appears to have predominated as, in practice, the approval of the senate was a necessary condition for the efficient functioning of both the magistrature and the assemblies.

The senate

During the Republic, the senate (*senatus*) played a pivotal, stabilizing role in Roman political life. This derived from the prestige and influence of its members and the relative stability of its constitution. Its resolutions (*senatus consulta*) were not legally binding but they possessed special authority in the eyes of the Romans. They were perceived as a reflection of the accumulated experience and wisdom of the ruling aristocracy, whose members were engaged as political, religious and military officers of the state. Moreover, since the magistrates' term in office was limited in time, the senate, as a permanent body, exercised a strong influence on them and, despite internal conflicts, it was capable of pursuing long-term policies with continuity and consistency.

At the beginning of the republican period the senate was composed of three hundred members, chosen exclusively from the patrician class. Leading plebeians were admitted to it after the passing of the *leges Liciniae Sextiae* in 367 BC. The senators were selected first by the consuls and, from 443 BC, by the censors (*censores*). Initially, the criteria for the selection of senators were not stipulated by law but mainly derived from custom. However, the discretionary power of the censors in preparing the senators' list was limited after the passing of the *lex Ovinia de senatus lectione* in the late fourth century BC. This statute probably confirmed existing practice in directing the censors to select new senators from among the most prominent citizens. In reality this meant that the senators were chosen from among those who had occupied the highest offices of the state. Although the senate did not function as a legislative body, resolutions passed by the assemblies of the people could not acquire the full force of laws without their subsequent ratification by the senate (*patrum auctoritas*). The *lex Publilia Philonis* of 339 BC provided that the senate's approval had to be issued in advance (i.e. before a proposal was put to the vote of the people). Furthermore, the *lex Maenia* (early third century BC) stipulated that candidates for the highest offices of the state had to be approved by the senate before their formal election by the assembly. Although these enactments entailed many cases where the granting of the senate's approval was a mere formality, the senate exercised a strong influence on legislation, for neither the magistrates nor the assemblies could easily disregard its opinion when discharging their functions. Moreover, the senate had complete control over foreign policy. It received envoys of other states, conducted negotiations with foreign powers, appointed ambassadors (*legati*) from its own ranks, concluded treaties and alliances and intervened in disputes between cities in alliance with Rome. The senate appears to have had the ultimate responsibility of declaring war and concluding peace, although in principle this power belonged to the people. Within the senate's province also fell various duties relating to the administration of public finances, such as establishing the budget assigned to each magistrate, managing public lands (*ager publicus*) and imposing a special taxation (*tributum*) to cover war expenses. The senate, assisted by the pontiffs and other priestly colleges, also exercised supervision over the state's religious affairs and addressed matters relating to public morals. In times of crisis, it could declare a state of emergency by passing a special resolution (*senatus consultum ultimum*) that authorized the consuls to apply any extraordinary measures deemed necessary to avert the danger.

The magistrature

Many modern historians adopt the view that the fall of the Monarchy entailed the transfer of the king's power to two supreme magistrates who acted as heads of state, while the senate sustained its function as a mainly advisory body.[23] A more recent theory claims that the government of the infant Republic was most likely controlled by the senate, from whose ranks one or more functionaries were appointed when necessary for addressing urgent state matters.[24] The institution of the magistracy (*magistratus*) appears to have acquired a more definite form after the introduction of the *leges Liciniae Sextiae* in 367 BC.

The most important offices of the state during the Republic were the consulship (*consulatus*), praetorship (*praetura*), censorship (*censura*), aedileship (*aedilitas*), quaestorhip (*quaestura*) and dictatorship (*dictatura*). These offices were augmented by the tribunate (*tribunatus*), although the tribunes were not formally regarded as magistrates. The category of higher magistrates (*magistratus maiores*) comprised the consuls, praetors and censors, while the aediles and the quaestors were regarded as lower magistrates (*magistratus minores*). Magistrates elected at regular intervals for a fixed term were termed *ordinarii*, whereas those appointed only under special circumstances and for specific purposes were called *extraordinarii*. The former category embraced the consuls, praetors, censors, curule aediles, quaestors and tribunes. Extraordinary magistrates were the dictator and the *interrex*.[25] In principle, any free-born Roman citizen could be a candidate for public office. No special knowledge or ability was formally required and, until the passing of the *lex Villia Annalis* in 180 BC, no specific law prescribed a minimum age of eligibility for magistrates. It was recognized as a general norm, however, that a person could not be appointed to the highest offices of the state without first progressing through the lower ones – a process referred to as *cursus honorum*.[26]

The magistrates' main duties encompassed the implementation of the decrees issued by the people and the senate, and the administration of the laws. The term *potestas* denoted the executive power possessed by every magistrate as soon as he was elected to office. By virtue of this power, a magistrate could execute the various duties and responsibilities of his office. In exercise of his *potestas*, he could issue executive orders (*ius edicendi*) and employ any coercive or punitive measures considered necessary for the enforcement of his orders (*ius coercendi, coercitio minor*). Besides the *potestas* attached to all state officials, the highest magistracies (the consulship, praetorship and dictatorship) were accompanied by a special power known as *imperium*.[27] Only magistrates with *imperium* could assume command of an army, convene and preside over the assemblies of the people (*ius agendi cum populo*), summon and preside over the senate (*ius agendi cum senatu*), and celebrate triumphs after victory in battle (*ius triumphandi*). Moreover, only these magistrates had the full power of *iurisdictio*, i.e. the power of prescribing the legal principles for determining legal disputes,[28] and could impose severe penalties for violations of their orders, including capital punishments (*ius coercendi, coercitio maior*).

The Roman magistrates' tenure of office was limited to one year, with the exception of the censors who were appointed for eighteen months, and the dictators whose term in office did not exceed six months. The principle of annuality served as an important constitutional safeguard against the danger of abuse of power, which a long term in office could entail.[29] Besides annuality, another important principle governing the institution of the magistrature was collegiality (*collegium*): the same magistracy was held by at least two persons,[30] each with equal *potestas* and, regarding the higher magistrates, equal *imperium*. The principle of collegiality was designed as a barrier against abuses of power by state officials. Thus, a magistrate could not enforce a decision or order without the consent or acquiescence of his colleague. A magistrate could prevent the execution of a decision of his colleague either in advance (*prohibitio*) or after its publication (*intercessio, ius intercessionis*).

The highest executive office of the state was held by two annually elected officials initially called *praetores* or *iudices* and, probably after the enactment of the *leges Liciniae Sextiae* (367 BC), *praetores consules* or simply *consules*. The consuls were elected by the assembly of the centuries (*comitia centuriata*), which was convened for that purpose by one of the highest magistrates. Originally, the consuls' powers were very broad but in later years, especially after the *leges Liciniae Sextiae* and the introduction of the praetorship and other offices, some of their duties were transferred to other magistrates. As bearers of *imperium domi*, the consuls were in charge of the government at home and exercised control over all other state officials.[31] They convened the senate and the assemblies, presided over them as chairmen and introduced matters for senate discussion and legislative proposals for assembly voting. In addition to ensuring that the decisions of the assemblies and the senate were properly executed, they had responsibility for maintaining law and order in the city and could impose penalties for civil disobedience. Moreover, as bearers of *imperium militiae*, they acted as commanders-in-chief of the army, with the authority to recruit troops, appoint officers and distribute the spoils of war. Before the introduction of the praetorship in 367 BC, they governed the administration of justice in relation to both civil and criminal matters.

In crises that threatened the security of the state, each consul had the right to appoint (with the senate's approval) a special magistrate, the dictator, in whose hands all state power was concentrated. During his term in office the dictator could introduce any measures he deemed necessary without obtaining the consent of any other state organ or the approval of the senate. But the dictator's power was limited by the expectation that he would resign immediately upon resolution of the emergency situation or fulfilment of the task he was appointed to tackle. In any event, a dictator could not remain in office for more than six months and this rule was apparently engaged without exceptions.[32] During the early republican period, when the constant wars between Rome and her neighbours posed a real threat to the city, the Romans often resorted to appointing dictators as a means of tackling emergency situations. After the Roman conquest of Italy and the subjugation of Carthage at the end of the second Punic war (201 BC), the institution of the dictatorship appears to have fallen into abeyance. During the later Republic, in a great emergency (*ultima necessitas*) the senate could pass a special decree (*senatus consultum ultimum*) that armed the consuls with additional powers and authorized them to initiate any extraordinary measures for averting the danger.[33]

The praetorship was introduced in 367 BC and initially the office only admitted members of the patrician class; from 337 BC the plebeians were also eligible. The new magistracy acquired the duties of the consuls relating to the supervision of civil litigation (*iurisdictio*) in disputes between Roman citizens.[34] In the middle of the third century BC, an additional praetor was appointed (*c.* 242 BC) in response to the escalating population of foreigners (*peregrini*) living in Rome and their flourishing transactions with Romans. This praetor supervised litigation in disputes between foreigners (*iurisdictio inter peregrinos*), and between foreigners and Roman citizens (*iurisdictio inter cives et peregrinos*). The new praetor (*praetor peregrinus*) was distinguished from the original official who had jurisdiction over disputes involving only Roman citizens (*iurisdictio urbana*) and was thus termed *praetor urbanus* or *praetor urbis*. As the Roman territory expanded, two further praetors were appointed in 227 BC and these were supplemented by two more in 197 BC. These officials were appointed as governors of the newly formed Roman provinces overseas (*praetores provinciales*). Under Sulla (early first century BC), the number of praetors in Rome was increased to eight. Among these praetors, the *praetor urbanus* and the *praetor peregrinus* continued to supervise the administration of the civil law in Rome and Italy,[35] while the remaining six (*praetores quaesitores*) served as chairmen of the newly established criminal courts (*quaestiones perpetuae*).[36]

Like the consuls, the praetors were elected annually by the assembly of the centuries (*comitia centuriata*). As holders of *imperium*, they could assume military command and had the right to summon and propose measures to the senate and the assembly of the people (*comitia tributa*). As elaborated previously, the praetors had the full power of *iurisdictio* – the power to prescribe the rules governing legal proceedings and declare the principles of law on the basis of which disputes were resolved. Connected with this power was their right of issuing binding regulations or edicts (*ius edicendi*). The edict issued by a praetor upon assuming office specified the principles he would observe in enforcing the law and the conditions under which he would allow prosecutions and suits. It was designed to retain validity throughout his year in office and thus was called 'continuous edict' (*edictum perpetuum*). If occasions arose, the praetor could issue additional edicts at any time during the year (such an edict was termed *edictum repentinum*). Although each praetor's edict was valid only during his own term, it was customary for a newly elected praetor to incorporate into his own edict the bulk of his predecessor's edict, making only limited alterations.[37] Over time, the praetorian edict emerged as a most important factor in the development of Roman private law and provided the basis for a distinct source of law known as *ius praetorium* or *ius honorarium*.

During the earliest period of the Republic, the census – the registration of citizens and their property for the purposes of determining their class and amount of property tax to pay – was administered by the consuls. In 443 BC, this task was assigned to a new magistracy – the censorship. Initially, two censors were appointed exclusively from the patrician class; after the enactment of the *lex Publilia Philonis* in 339 BC, plebeians were also eligible.[38] In the late fourth century BC, the censors were entrusted with the additional tasks of compiling the roll of the senators (*album senatorium*) and filling vacancies in the senate.[39] Moreover, the censors were responsible for collecting the Roman public revenues (*publica*).[40]

Although the censors belonged to the *magistratus maiores*, they did not possess *imperium* but were invested with only *potestas*. Nevertheless, the censorship was regarded as one of the most important state offices and its holders were not subordinate to the other magistrates. In the course of time, the censors acquired the right to scrutinize the public and private conduct of citizens when administering the census, and identify those whose behaviour violated generally accepted moral norms. Thus, they were recognized as overseers of public morals and upholders of the moral standards of society (*regimen morum, cura morum*).[41] In the last century of the Republic, the office of censor was stripped of most of its powers and, during the closing years of this period, it appears to have fallen into abeyance.

The aedileship was created in the middle of the fifth century BC. Initially, the assembly of the plebeians (*concilium plebis*) appointed two aediles as exclusively plebeian officials (*aediles plebis*) to serve as assistants to the tribunes. Under the *leges Liciniae Sextiae* of 367 BC, two additional aediles were appointed and designated as *aediles curules*.[42] The latter were elected by the assembly of the tribes (*comitia tributa*) from both the patrician and the plebeian classes. Although they ranked above their plebeian colleagues, the aediles curules performed mainly the same tasks. These included the maintenance of public roads and buildings, the retention of public records, the supervision of water and grain supply, and the organization of certain public games. Moreover, they were entrusted with police duties in the city of Rome and had criminal jurisdiction over cases involving minor offences. An essential function of the aediles was the supervision of activities in the marketplace. In their capacity as market officials they issued edicts (*edicta*) regulating the sale of goods and ensured that the prices charged were reasonable, and that the measures and weights used complied with the prescribed standards. The edicts of the aediles and the limited civil jurisdiction these magistrates exercised in the marketplace played an important role in the development of the Roman law of sale.

As an ordinary magistracy, the quaestorship was established in the middle of the fifth century BC. Initially, two quaestors were appointed by the consuls exclusively from among the patricians. Since 421 BC, four quaestors were elected by the assembly of the tribes (*comitia tributa*) from both the patrician and the plebeian classes. Two quaestors remained in Rome to serve as public treasurers (*quaestores urbani* or *aerarii*), while the other two (*quaestores militares*) accompanied the consuls in military campaigns and performed the duties of quartermasters in charge of supplies, the payment of troops and the distribution of war booty. Around the middle of the third century BC the number of quaestors was increased to eight.[43] Besides supervising the public treasury (*aerarium*), the quaestors were assigned a diversity of other tasks, such as collecting public revenues derived from taxation and other sources, financing public projects and directing criminal proceedings before the *comitia*.[44]

The tribunate was introduced in 494 BC as an exclusively plebeian office. Originally, two tribunes were appointed but their number was subsequently increased to five and, around the middle of the fifth century BC, to ten. These officials were elected by the assembly of the plebeians (*concilium plebis*) under the supervision of one of the tribunes in office. Free-born Roman citizens who were members of a plebeian family by birth or adoption were eligible for the office of tribune. As leaders of the plebeians, the tribunes had the right to convene and preside over the plebeian assembly (*concilium plebis*) and to submit bills to it. In the course of time, they acquired the right to intervene on behalf of any plebeian who sought their assistance (*ius auxilii*) and to veto the acts of patrician magistrates that they considered detrimental to the interests of the plebeian class (*ius intercessionis*). The office of tribune was inviolable; if a tribune was assaulted or impeded in the execution of his duties, the perpetrator could be declared an outlaw.

When the political differences between the patrician and plebeian classes disappeared in the early third century BC, the tribunes were regarded as magistrates for all the Roman people. In the course of time they acquired the right to convene and preside over the assembly of the tribes (*comitia tributa*) and the senate (*ius agendi cum senatu*), and to submit proposals to them. By the end of the second century BC, persons who had held the office of tribune were admitted as members of the senate. Thereafter, the tribunes were no longer chosen by the assembly of the plebeians (*concilium plebis*) but were elected by the assembly of the tribes (*comitia tributa*), and even patricians could be candidates. During the socio-political crisis of the later Republic, the tribune's power of veto emerged as a powerful weapon often utilized by the senatorial aristocracy. This group frustrated legislative initiatives detrimental to their interests by winning over one or more tribunes and inducing them to use the veto against the rest. Even though the tribunate lost a great deal of prestige in the closing years of the republican period, it prevailed during the Empire to furnish an important basis for the first emperors to legitimize their power and secure control of the state.

The assemblies

During the Republic the curiate assembly persevered but, as a political body, was superseded by the new assemblies formed after the military and political reforms of the late sixth and early fifth centuries BC: the assembly of the centuries (*comitia centuriata*) and the assembly of the tribes (*comitia populi tributa*). Another type of assembly was the *concilium plebis*, the assembly of the plebeians. The assemblies could only meet to discharge their functions when formally summoned by a higher magistrate.[45] In all Roman assemblies voting was conducted by units or groups rather than individuals. Thus, in the assembly of the centuries (*comitia centuriata*) decisions were reached by considering the number of centuries that voted in favour of or against a proposal; the vote of each century was determined by the majority of the individual voters it comprised. In the *comitia curiata* and the *comitia tributa* issues were resolved by the majority of the *curiae* and *tribus* respectively. However, the assemblies differed from each other with respect to composition, powers and scope of competence.

The main function of the *comitia curiata* during the Republic was to grant the power of *imperium* to the supreme magistrates of the state, i.e. the consuls and the praetors, following their election by the assembly of the centuries.[46] Moreover, the competence of the curiate assembly embraced the confirmation of certain ceremonial acts of private law, such as public testaments and adoptions.[47] At the end of the Republic the functions of the curiate assembly were so purely formal that its meetings were no longer attended by the citizens but only by the thirty representatives of the *curiae*.[48]

Rome's principal legislative assembly, the *comitia centuriata*, consisted of the citizens organized on a timocratic basis into classes and centuries (groups of a hundred citizens).[49] There were five classes in all, each comprising a set number of centuries. The assembly's decision on any submitted proposal was determined by the majority of the centuries.[50] However, the system was far from democratic as the first class, comprised of the wealthiest citizens, supplied most of the centuries and thus could outvote the other four classes in the assembly. This was the case notwithstanding the fact that the first class represented a much smaller section of the citizen body than the other classes. This inequality pertaining to the political rights of citizens mainly derived from the fact that in ancient city-states these rights were customarily determined by reference to a citizen's contribution to the defence of the state.[51]

The most important political function of the centuriate assembly was the election of the supreme magistrates of the state (*magistratus maiores*), i.e. the consuls, praetors and censors. Legislative proposals were submitted to the assembly by the higher magistrates of the state. A proposal, after its approval by the people, became a law (*lex*).[52] Private members bills were not permitted, as the magistrate alone could select the motions presented for voting. Moreover, the people could only accept or reject a proposal introduced by a magistrate, without prior debate or the possibility of amendment.[53] The assembly also functioned as a court of justice to hear appeals against sentences involving death and other severe punishments imposed by magistrates (*provocatio ad populum*). Since the early Republic, the judicial powers of the magistrates were increasingly restricted by legislation and this entailed a definite recognition of the assembly's criminal jurisdiction. Thus, the assembly emerged as the regular court of justice for the investigation and punishment of the most serious crimes.[54]

The *comitia tributa* was the assembly of the Roman citizens organized into groups according to their place of residence. According to Roman tradition, at the end of the regal period the city was divided into four districts or urban tribes (*tribus urbanae*), and the remaining Roman territory into sixteen rural tribes (*tribus rusticae*). As the territory of Rome grew with the annexation of neighbouring regions, the rural tribes gradually increased to a total of thirty-five in 241 BC.[55] The tribes served as the basic administrative units for the registration of the citizens and their property, as required for collecting property taxes, raising military levies and other purposes.[56] Shortly after the tribal system was introduced, the tribes began to hold informal meetings to discuss matters of local or general interest. These meetings assumed the standing of regular *comitia* in the early fifth century BC. As indicated before, each tribe in the tribal assembly had one vote that was determined by the majority of its members and the assembly's decision was established by the majority of the tribes. The rural tribes, mainly comprised of the affluent farmers and large landowners, outnumbered the urban ones (despite the fact that the latter contained a much larger number of citizens); thus, the wealthier citizens exercised the most influence in the assembly.

The tribal assembly possessed the important political function of electing the lower magistrates of the state (*magistratus minores*), such as the aediles and the quaestors. Another task of this assembly was voting on laws proposed by higher magistrates, although generally these laws were less politically important than those enacted by the centuriate assembly. However, the relatively uncomplicated proceedings in the tribal assembly often inspired the senate, in emergencies or for expediency, to request magistrates to submit bills to this assembly rather than the *comitia centuriata*. Finally, the *comitia tributa*, acting as a popular court of justice, heard appeals against sentences imposed by magistrates (*provocatio ad populum*).[57]

The assembly of the plebeians (*concilium plebis*) was created in 471 BC, following the recognition by the Roman senate of the plebeians' right to hold meetings to elect their leaders (the *tribuni plebis*) and discuss matters concerning their class interests.[58] The plebeian assembly passed resolutions (*plebiscita*), which originally had no binding effect outside the plebeian class. After the plebeians' success in the struggle of the orders, the *plebiscita* were recognized as having the full force of laws and were thus binding on both patricians and plebeians alike.[59] Besides its legislative functions, the *concilium plebis* acted as a court of justice to hear cases involving violations of the plebeians' rights.[60] Like the assembly of the tribes, the plebeian assembly was organized on a tribal basis.[61] A simple majority of tribes established the decision of the entire assembly, while the vote of each tribe was determined by the majority of its members. But whereas the assembly of the tribes was originally convened and presided over by a consul or a praetor, the plebeian assembly was summoned and presided over by a tribune of the plebs.

The formal distinction between the *concilium plebis* and the *comitia tributa* was retained until the close of the Republic. However, after the middle of the third century BC the differences between the two bodies, regarding their composition and the laws they enacted, were very few in practice. This mainly emanated from the elimination of the political division between the patricians and the plebeians, and the rapid increase of the plebeian population following the social and economic changes engendered by Rome's expansion.[62] Thus, during the later Republic three legislative assemblies existed in Rome and were comprised of mainly the same people, whose decisions were binding on all citizens: the *comitia centuriata*, *comitia tributa* and *concilium plebis*. The last two assemblies were organized in the same way and essentially performed similar functions, although they were summoned and presided over by different magistrates.

2

THE MONARCHY AND EARLY REPUBLIC: THE SOURCES OF LAW

Introduction

The fabric of the entire legal system in the earliest period of Roman history, encompassing the city's formation to the fifth century BC, was mainly composed of customary norms designated *mores maiorum* (the ways of our ancestors). Some norms were regarded as components of the human sphere, while others derived their binding force from their supposed divine origin. However, the early Romans did not establish a clear distinction between secular law (*ius*) and divine law (*fas*).

Priestly officials were entrusted to enforce the religious duties as prescribed by the norms of *fas*. These officials independently discharged their task by devising and administering coercive practices. Essentially, the Roman priests were state officials responsible for the religious branch of public administration.[1] The most important religious body was the college of the *pontifices*. According to Roman tradition, King Numa Pompilius established this college in the late eighth century BC.[2] As guardians and interpreters of the divine law, the pontiffs exercised general supervision over a wide range of matters associated with public religion, set the rules governing the conduct of religious ceremonies and rituals (*ius sacrum*),[3] and punished those who committed offences against the norms of *fas*. Behaviour that violated the rules of divine law was referred to as *nefas*, and regarded as disruptive to the harmonious relationship between the community and its gods. The Romans believed that such behaviour could invoke the wrath of the gods and entail misfortune for the entire community. The violation of a rule pertaining to *fas* rendered the offender impious and the ensuing punishment was expiatory in character: its purpose was to heal the condition of collective impurity and thus to restore the state of harmony (*amicitia*) between the community and the gods.

Conduct that caused no harm to others was regarded as consonant with *ius*, the body of man-made norms governing human relations. Any behaviour that violated these norms was termed *iniuria*. Originally, the term *ius* (plural, *iura*) denoted that which is due in human relations – the rightful power of a community member to act in a certain manner vis-à-vis his fellow citizens. It referred to a course of conduct that the community would take for granted and, in that sense, endorse. Thus, a person who appropriated an object, entered upon land, ejected or imprisoned another individual may in so doing be exercising *ius*. The community had a general awareness of the circumstances when such acts would be construed as *iura* and these were established by custom. The existence of a *ius* was determined by securing, probably through ordeal, the sanction of the gods. At this stage, the exercise of *ius* had no connection with state organization and thus *ius* was defined as any instance of approved self-help. After the consolidation of the early Roman state and the establishment of a formal system of justice, *ius* denoted the rules or norms capable of enforcement with the consent of those responsible for safeguarding and maintaining the norms governing community life. Thus, the holders of *imperium* had the essential functions of pronouncing the *ius* and assisting those with rights to obtain their entitlements through formal channels. The earliest form of legal procedure was the act whereby a person who possessed or claimed a *ius* against another requested a jurisdictional magistrate to both confirm his *ius* and enable its exercise by effectively suppressing an opponent's resistance. Roman law developed primarily as a private law that was devised as a system of rights or claims bolstered by causes of action and specific procedural remedies. When Roman legal thinking evolved to perceive the various protected powers as a system, the term *ius* resembled our modern meaning of the word 'law' in a broad sense: the entire system of norms by which the rights and concomitant powers of community members are defined, protected and enforced.

Although from an early period the Romans distinguished between the human and divine orders,[4] the two spheres of *ius* and *fas* occasionally overlapped. The link between *ius* and *fas* is evident from the fact that certain types of behaviour involving a gross breach of faith[5] originally related to *ius* but were deemed particularly reprehensible as they were also interpreted to violate *fas*. In the archaic period, the notions of *ius* and *fas* were also linked through the king who, as head of the state, dealt with matters pertaining to both human and divine law. Moreover, until as late as the second century BC the interpretation of the norms of *ius* was governed by the college of the pontiffs, who acted as custodians of both the divine and the secular law. They alone were acquainted with the technical forms employed in creating the typical transactions of private law, and were entitled to present advice and authoritative opinions on questions of law. As members of the Roman ruling class, the pontiffs represented a unique combination of socio-economic power with religious and political authority. This blend of economic and political power with religious authority provided a sufficient legitimation of their judicial authority.

As Roman legal thinking developed, *ius* or law in a broad sense was construed to embody a strong normative element, reflecting the relationship between law and justice (*iustitia*).[6] In this broad normative sense *ius* is not the same as morality nor as positive law; rather, it is right law, or positive law as it ought to exist in light of what morality and justice ordain.[7] *Ius*, as defined above, was distinguished from *lex* (plural *leges*). The latter term signified a law created by a competent legislative organ of the state in conformance with a prescribed procedure. During the Republic the term *lex* was used to denote a statute enacted by a popular assembly and created in a form directed to all citizens. However, in fact and often in form, the statute imparted general directions to jurisdictional magistrates.[8] A *lex*, which by definition pertained to a specific type of legal relationship, drew upon *ius* but was not identified with it. The normative principles of *ius* that determined the question of lawfulness or unlawfulness were not reducible to the body of formally enacted laws. These principles were regarded as pre-existing and transcending the enacted law, which merely prescribed the method for implementing *ius* under certain circumstances. Unlawfulness was defined primarily in relation to *ius*, for an unlawful act was deemed to encroach upon the principles of *ius* that informed the particular legislative enactment encompassing the act. From this viewpoint, the word *iniuria* signified any infringement of the law comprised of an act performed '*contra ius*'. Furthermore, the application of a *lex* was typically strict, as an act or dispute was tackled according to the letter of the law without reference to the circumstances of the individual case. On the other hand, the norms of *ius* were construed as flexible and thus adaptable to the circumstances of each particular case. Whereas the implementation of a *lex* was based on formal criteria, the implementation of *ius* was anchored in its intrinsic rightness.[9]

A characteristic feature of early Roman law was its extreme formalism, indeed ritualism, manifesting the religious origin and character of many legal rules and institutions. In this context, formalism denotes not only the need for compliance with the forms or rules of procedure characteristic of any legal system, it also emphasizes form in every part of the legal system; the casting of all legal acts into an unchangeable form where successful completion depends on strict adherence to a set ritual engaging certain words or gestures. Archaic Roman law is perceived as formalistic because legal acts, that is, acts that effected or intended to effect changes in the legal relations of individuals, were accomplished with a complicated array of forms. Further, an individual electing to assert a claim at law against another had to mould the claim within the scope of a particular limited cause of action expressed by means of a strictly prescribed formula – the slightest mistake would entail loss of his case. Interpretation might stretch the meaning of certain words, but the words themselves were immutable: only claims adapted in concordance with the words were possible. This form of procedure offered no opportunity for modifying the issue based on the objections issued by the defendant, who could only admit or deny the plaintiff's claim. This system displays an important feature of Roman legal thinking: its *normativity*. For the Romans, the law consisted of rules similar in manner to their religion. The rules of law, consisting of fact–decision relationships, could not be argued for – similarly, a minister of religion was unable to present a rational justification for his prophesies. In each case the link between the facts (the judicial proof, the flying bird) and the decision (an interpretation of the law or a statement concerning divine law – *fas* and *nefas*) remained an inexplicable norm. This perspective emphasizes the *irrational* aspect of archaic decision-making.

The traditional law of archaic Rome was termed *ius Quiritium* because Roman citizens were addressed by the name *Quirites* in the *comitia*. In later eras this law was referred to as *ius civile* or civil law: the legal order of the Roman citizenry (*cives Romani*). In a broader sense, the term *ius civile* denoted the law peculiar to a particular state or political community.[10] Like most archaic peoples, the Romans observed the personality of the laws principle, whereby each person lived by the law of their community. Thus, the Roman *ius civile* was the law that applied exclusively to Roman citizens, and the term *ius civitatis* denoted the legal rights to which only Roman citizens were entitled.[11] There were two kinds of rights: public rights (*publica iura*) and private rights (*privata iura*). The principal public rights embraced membership and voting in the popular assemblies (*ius suffragii*), access to political office (*ius honorum*), the right to serve in the army (*ius militiae*) and the right to appeal from a magistrate to the assembly against sentences involving death or the loss of personal freedom or citizenship (*ius provocationis*). The most important private rights encompassed the right to contract a regular Roman marriage (*ius connubii*), the right to acquire and transfer property according to law (*ius commercii*), the right to create a will or inherit under a Roman will (*ius testamenti factio*) and the right to legal recognition in the courts of law. An individual entitled to all the rights of the citizenship was designated *civis optimo iure*.[12] From an early period, communities affiliated with Rome were granted limited rights under the Roman *ius civile*. The members of these communities occupied an intermediate position between Roman citizens and foreigners.[13] The term *peregrinus* signified any free person who was not a citizen of Rome.[14] Initially, foreigners living in Rome had no rights under Roman law.

The Roman *ius civile* emanated from several sources: custom, legislation, administration of justice and constructive interpretation of existing rules by the jurists.

Customary law and the laws of the kings

The formation of the Roman city-state probably derived from a gradual process whereby several neighbouring clans (*gentes*) coalesced to form a larger political entity under a common head, the king (*rex*). From a legal standpoint, the establishment of the *civitas Romana* may be attributed to an arrangement resembling a treaty (*foedus*) between the various *patres gentium*. Naturally, the framework of the new political entity was akin to that of the pre-existing *gentes*. The emergence of the *civitas* invoked the necessity for a system of law to govern the entire community. However, so long as the gentile organization remained more or less intact, this legal system would refrain from regulating relations between members of the same clan as this was the function of that clan's law. The legal system would confine itself to directing relations between members of different clans as well as the structure, functions and activities of the organs within the *civitas*. Moreover, its rules governing inter-gentile relations were based essentially on the pre-existing inter-gentile customary law that developed while the clans were still independent. One might perhaps say that the earliest phase of Roman history is marked by a fundamental dualism: the *gentes* on the one hand and the *civitas* on the other. However, Rome evolved politically as a unitary state when the gentile organization declined and the sense of unity among the population intensified. The initially diverse customs of the different *gentes* underwent a process of assimilation that engendered a common body of norms, designated *mores maiorum* (the ways of our ancestors), for governing the whole community. As the family organization replaced the earlier gentile organization, the customary rules formerly applied by the *civitas* to regulate inter-gentile relations were mainly wielded to manage inter-family relations.

The unwritten customary norms governing early Roman society emanated from traditional usages of the community and the cases generated from disputes presented to the clan patriarchs or the king for resolution. Many norms originated in the remote past, while others emerged later, during the formative years of the Roman state. As noted, knowledge of the customary norms was handed down as tradition in noble families and was preserved by the college of the pontiffs, who acted as custodians and interpreters of the law. As Roman society continued to grow both in numbers and complexity, the role of custom as the principal source of social regulation gradually diminished, for the customary norms, often vague and limited in scope, could not provide the certainty that a more intricate system of social and economic relations required. But the state expansion and emergence of legislation did not eliminate the role of custom. Many laws that the state enacted and enforced through its organs derived from or sanctioned existing customary norms. Further, custom prevailed as an important component in the interpretation and application of the law. Custom furnished the basis of the essential part of the clan and family organization, many of the rules governing private institutions, such as property, contracts and inheritance, and some basic rules governing public institutions, such as the senate, the popular assemblies and the magistracy.

It is unknown when legal rules began to be formally enacted and stipulated in writing. According to the jurist Pomponius and other authors, a function of the people's assembly (*comitia curiata*) during the Monarchy was to vote on the laws proposed by the king. It must be recalled that in the archaic period, legislation in the modern sense and as the Romans understood it in their politically mature eras, was practically unknown. The law was mainly construed as a sacred custom and thus not subject to change by direct legislative means. The role of the *comitia curiata*, like that of the assembly of a *gens*, was in all likelihood a passive one, limited to approving (or disapproving) proposals of an extraordinary nature submitted by the king. Pomponius describes the state of the law during this period as featuring a series of laws, referred to as *leges regiae*, which supposedly emanated from some of the early kings.[15] According to Roman tradition, these laws were collected and recorded at the end of the regal era by Sextus Papirius, a *pontifex maximus*. The *ius Papirianum*, as this collection was known, if it ever existed, is lost to us, but a number of rules ostensibly promulgated by kings have been preserved in the works of later Greek and Roman historians. Some modern commentators remark that these authors' accounts of the so-called 'laws of the kings' were probably based on observations on their own contemporary law and therefore are not very reliable. Others assert that the *leges regiae* were not real laws, but were declarations of certain norms with a religious-juridical character composed by the kings and publicly announced during an assembly.[16] The surviving fragments of the *leges regiae*, as far as they are authentic, attest to the close connection between law and religion that marks the nature of archaic law. Some of these early rules had fallen into disuse by the time the Law of the Twelve Tables was introduced in the middle of the fifth century BC.

The law of the Twelve Tables and the emergence of legislation

The earliest document of Roman law and the first true legislation was the *Law of the Twelve Tables*, which dates from the middle of the fifth century BC. This legislation emerged from the struggle between patricians and plebeians. The Roman historical tradition, enveloped by ambiguity, records the events leading to its enactment: in 462 BC Terentius Harsa, a tribune of the plebeians, requested that the rules of customary law be recorded and made publicly available to halt its arbitrary application by the patrician magistrates who controlled the administration of justice. After eight years of strife, the patricians conceded and the senate dispatched a three-member commission to Greece to study the laws of the famous Athenian lawgiver Solon, and those of other Greek city-states.[17] Upon the commission's return, the senate decided to suspend the constitution and entrust the government to an annually appointed board of ten magistrates (all of them patricians). In addition to their governmental functions, these magistrates were to be assigned the special task of drafting a written code of laws (*decemviri legibus scribundis*).[18] The new centuriate assembly appointed the commission in 451 BC and its members were invested with supreme political power (*imperium*). In 450 BC the decemvirs produced a series of laws inscribed on ten tablets (*tabulae*). These laws were considered unsatisfactory, which prompted the election of a second commission of ten men (now incorporating some plebeians) to complete the work.[19] In 449 BC two further tablets of laws supplemented the existing ten and, after it was ratified by the assembly, the work was published under the name *lex duodecim tabularum*. According to Roman tradition, the second decemviral board refused to resign after completing their legislative work and endeavoured to retain their office by ruling as tyrants. Eventually, however, they were deposed following a popular revolt and the constitutional order of the Republic was restored. The desired publicity of the new laws was secured by exhibiting them, inscribed on boards or tablets (probably wooden), in the Forum. It is believed that the original tablets perished during the Gallic invasion of *c.* 390 BC, but their contents were reconstructed from memory and fresh tablets were created.

The traditional record of the events leading to the enactment of the Law of the Twelve Tables is embellished with myths and legends; it contains several inconsistencies and anachronisms. In modern times, the queries over the origin and nature of the decemviral legislation have generated much controversy. However, the main outlines of the tradition regarding the legislation are still accepted by most historians as substantially authentic. Some scholars have challenged the historicity of the second decemvirate and argued that the work of the original commission was probably completed by the consuls of the following year. Moreover, historians contend that the dispatch of a commission to Greece is highly unlikely and, even if such a mission existed, it may have visited only Greek cities in Southern Italy. The influence of Athenian law is contested on the grounds that at the time of the codification the Romans had no direct contacts with states outside Italy.[20] Further, it is noted that legal life in the leading commercial centres of the times, such as Athens and Syracuse, was remote from the legal conditions of the primitive agrarian community in Rome. The preserved fragments of the Law of the Twelve Tables reveal scant material that could be directly traced to a Greek influence, although certain parallels with the laws of other early societies can be observed.[21] As noted, these facts do not exclude the possibility that a degree of cross-fertilization with the Greeks of Southern Italy occurred.[22]

The original text of the Law of the Twelve Tables is lost. The preserved slivers of its content consist of quotations and references included in the works of later lawyers, historians and grammarians. By referencing or reproducing parts of the Law of the Twelve Tables, these writers modernized them in language and consciously or subconsciously adapted them to the conditions of their own times.[23] The precise quantity of missing text is unknown, as is the arrangement of the original provisions of the Law of the Twelve Tables. Thus, the reconstructions by modern scholars that draw on various juridical and literary sources are largely hypothetical.[24]

The Law of the Twelve Tables is a highly casuistic, case-oriented (in contradistinction to generalizing, principle-oriented) piece of legislation. It reflects the life of a fairly primitive agricultural community and integrated well with the system of customary unwritten law existing at that time. It could not have been an all-encompassing codification for, although quite detailed in some respects, it was far from complete. Rather, it restates and clarifies in writing customary solutions to particularly recurrent, important or controversial questions of law. Most of the preserved provisions canvass matters of private law, such as family relations, succession and wills, property, contracts and torts. Special attention is given to matters of procedure in court actions and enforcement, as in this area the unskilled parties to a dispute, usually plebeians, could be misled by those conversant with the law. Some provisions address issues in criminal law and sacral law, while only two provisions relate to constitutional law.[25] The provisions of the Twelve Tables are couched in the form of terse commands and prohibitions, exhibiting a rhythmical cadence that must have facilitated memory retention. But the wording is often abstruse and grammatically ambiguous, and the actual legal principles underlying the various provisions were not elaborated as they were probably assumed. This is hardly surprising in view of the unwritten conventions by which the archaic community of the Romans functioned.

Even though archaic in form and thought, the Law of the Twelve Tables contains elements indicative of a legal system that had advanced considerably beyond its original, primitive stage. For example, uncontrolled self-help was restricted with the establishment of orderly forms of procedure; in some cases, private vengeance was limited by the principle of retaliation and in others replaced by public punishment. Of particular importance for the subsequent development of the law were the rudiments of interorgan controls to prevent excesses in the administration of justice. Thus, the right of appeal to the assembly of the people (*provocatio ad populum*) against capital punishments meted out by magistrates was recognized, and it was rendered unconstitutional to propose a law inflicting penalties or disabilities only upon a particular person. Considered from a political angle, the most notable achievement of the Law of the Twelve Tables was vindicating the state authorities' monopoly over all acts of judicial administration. Regarding the legal matters essential for daily life, the decemviral legislation produced a common body of law for all citizens, regardless of their patrician or plebeian status. As a result, predominantly patrician institutions were rendered both accessible and applicable to the entire community. Citizens and magistrates alike were subject to the sovereignty of the law and the members of the plebeian class were no longer exposed to the vagaries of customary rules administered by patrician magistrates. At the same time, the process towards the secularization of the law accelerated: conduct patterns formerly shrouded in religious ritualism were rationalized by general rules of substantive and procedural law in a written form, and thus ascertainable by all people. As the law was now publicized, it began to lose the immutable quality of a religious mystery, becoming conventional, human and therefore subject to change.

For a thousand years, the Law of the Twelve Tables remained the only attempt by the Romans to comprehensively record their laws. This first attempt ushered in the history of Roman law as discernible today and for a thousand years it formed the basis of their whole legal system, despite changes in their social, economic and political conditions.[26] The perpetuation of the currency and validity of the Law of the Twelve Tables was feasible as it embodied norms that were constantly modified and extended through legislation and interpretation by trained jurists; thus, it was adaptable to the changed conditions in later eras.

After the enactment of the Law of the Twelve Tables, the legislation created by the assembly of the people evolved as a generally acknowledged source of law. However, in contrast to the role of legislation in the Greek city-states, Roman legislation remained underdeveloped. Controversy still prevails as to the extent (or the exact time) it was deemed legally viable to modify the ancient *ius civile*. The Romans' disinclination to apply legislation derived from their conservative attitude towards law and the deeply rooted conception of the merits of their ancient customs, reinforced by the special position accorded to the Law of the Twelve Tables. It was not easy to frame statutes in a way that avoided infringement of these established norms, especially in the field of private law. Therefore, the necessary reforms were fashioned in an indirect manner by means of interpretation. Accordingly, statutes remained relatively rare and dealt only with certain special matters. In constitutional crises, legislation was wielded by the conflicting parties to advance their position or used as a means to effect a political compromise. Statutes were enacted, for instance, to incorporate in the constitution the gains forged by the plebeian movement and to create new magistracies. In matters of social concern, legislation was occasionally relied on to instigate reforms or merely to appease the populace. Some legislation had a hybrid character displaying a political basis and also elements that affected the private relations of citizens – this embraced specific laws relating to civil procedure, marriage, debts and testamentary benefits.[27]

Laws could only be passed by the citizens of Rome gathered in an official assembly. As elaborated in the previous chapter, the Roman popular assemblies existed in two forms: those including all citizens, who voted either according to wealth (*comitia centuriata*) or tribe (*comitia tributa*); and the assembly of the plebeians (*concilium plebis*), which excluded the patrician upper class from its membership. Originally, legislative measures proposed by a consul were regularly submitted before the *comitia centuriata*. Eventually this assembly, presumably because of its cumbersome nature, was seldom convened for the purposes of legislation. Thus, practically legislative measures proposed by higher magistrates were presented to the *comitia tributa*. Statutes (*leges*) enacted by the *comitia centuriata* and the *comitia tributa* were binding on all citizens, i.e. on both patricians and plebeians alike as these classes were represented in the assemblies. The resolutions issued by the assembly of the plebeians were referred to as *plebiscita* and were initially only binding on the plebeians. Since the enactment of the *lex Hortensia* in 287 BC, at the latest, the *plebiscita* were considered as complete laws binding on the entire citizenry.[28] Thereafter, the *concilium plebis*, convened under the presidency of a *tribunus plebis*, was the most active legislative body. The great majority of the *leges* that we can observe in records were, strictly speaking, *plebiscita*. According to Roman tradition, the laws passed by the *comitia centuriata* and, presumably, the *comitia tributa* could not come into force until the senate issued approval (*auctoritas patrum*). However, the reversal of this rule in 339 BC by the *lex Publilia* dictated the acquisition of the senate's sanction before the proposed legislation was submitted to the assembly.[29] After 287 BC, the same rule applied to the resolutions of the plebeian assembly. Although these changes appeared to liberate the popular assemblies from senatorial control, in reality the senate ordinarily exercised substantial control over the legislative activities of the assemblies through its influence on the magistrates. The senate's discussion of all legislative proposals prior to their presentation to the people was a regular constitutional practice. Although a magistrate was not, in principle, compelled to accept the senate's judgment, he would normally defer to its authority. It is only in times of political crisis and internal disorder that we find legislative proposals carried in the teeth of senatorial opposition.

Interpretation and the origins of jurisprudence

The interpretation of the law as a source of the Roman *ius civile* originates from the early archaic period and probably emerged soon after the Law of the Twelve Tables was enacted in the middle of the fifth century BC. After the introduction of this legislation, the population mass and intricacy of Roman society proliferated. Thus, the old rules proved increasingly inadequate for fulfilling the requirements of social and commercial life. But the Romans did not respond to the need for legal change by replacing the Law of the Twelve Tables with fresh legislation. As noted, the Romans were conservative and extremely careful in their approach to legal matters. They were attached with great tenacity to the Law of the Twelve Tables, which they considered as the foundation of their legal system. Although legislation introduced

27

some new rules, interpretation was the chief means of changing the law (especially in the field of private law). Through skilful interpretation of the provisions of the Twelve Tables and later statutes, the Roman jurists filled the gaps in the law and also succeeded in infusing the old rigid rules with new substance, thus adapting them to changed conditions. As archaic formalism excluded any change in the letter of the law, these jurists endeavoured to derive new law by extending the meaning of the words within existing legal provisions beyond their literal sense, and thus produced effects that advanced beyond their original purpose.

As a close link existed between religion and law in the archaic period, the college of the pontiffs governed the interpretation of the law and its deriving actions for more than a hundred years after the Law of the Twelve Tables came into force.[30] As the guardians of all written tradition and ritual techniques, the pontiffs alone knew all the laws, the forms of actions and documents, the court calendar and the authoritative opinions their predecessors had rendered in the past. Although the laws were openly displayed and legal proceedings occurred in public, the interpretation of the terse language of the Twelve Tables and subsequent statutes would be difficult even for those citizens who could actually read them. Moreover, the rules of procedure and the technical forms prescribed for litigation were not publicly available. Thus, private citizens had to consult the pontiffs to obtain advice on whether specific rules of law applied to their particular case and the correct procedure in litigation. Only the pontiffs were endowed with the highly specialized knowledge necessary to command the formalistic and traditionalistic *ius civile*.

The influence of the pontiffs on legal development was also connected with their role in the administration of justice. As noted earlier, the Romans construed the term *lex* as a formal act of the people that required or permitted a magistrate to enforce a *ius*, which was demanded in a particular way by a particular procedure. In the archaic period, the principal method for obtaining a *ius* was the *legis actio* (literally, an action based on the law) – a ritual procedure that was conducted orally and divided into two distinct phases. The first phase (*in iure*) originally proceeded before a pontiff or, according to some scholars, a consul. This official determined on the basis of the applicable law whether the plaintiff could initiate legal action and, if so, its required form. After the enactment of the *leges Liciniae Sextiae* in 367 BC, this task was entrusted to the praetor.[31] In the second phase (*apud iudicem*) a private judge (*iudex*), appointed by both the pontiff or magistrate and the relevant parties, considered the evidence and decided the case within the frame set by the pontiff or magistrate. In the *in iure* phase of the proceedings the plaintiff had to couch his claim in set words, and the defendant also replied in set words – this formed the actual *legis actio*. If a party used the wrong *legis actio* or departed from the set form, his claim was rejected. The pontiffs possessed knowledge of the word forms that could be admitted as efficacious.[32] They could expand or restrict the scope of a *legis actio* by construing it broadly or narrowly as required by the relevant case. Despite the emphasis that archaic law attached to the letter of the law and the forms of action based on it, there was a tendency to permit a slightly greater degree of freedom in legal proceedings than was allowed in purely religious ceremonies – at least in the era when the *legis actio* emerged as a definite form of procedure.

As elaborated, an important part of the pontiffs' work was imparting practical expression to the provisions of the Law of the Twelve Tables and subsequent enactments. In performing this task the pontiffs extended or restricted the scope of a legal rule and, on occasion, introduced entirely new rules under the guise of interpretation to address new situations. A well-known illustration of law-making through interpretation is the method devised for releasing a son (*filius familias*) from his father's control (*patria potestas*). As Roman society developed in complexity, cases emerged where a son's absolute dependence on the father regarding his legal position had to be overcome so as to sustain the healthy functioning of economic life. Originally, the power of the *pater familias* over his children (and also over his grandchildren and more remote descendants) entailed complete control over them. Only the father had any rights in private law – he alone was entitled to own property and own all the acquisitions of the subordinate family members. As economic conditions changed, this rigid system could not be absolutely sustained in practice. The problem was resolved by the constructive interpretation of a certain clause of the Twelve Tables that was apparently designed to protect a son against a father who misused his power. A father could consign a son to another person for money on the understanding that the son obtained manumission upon completion of work for that person. Following the manumission, the son returned automatically into the *potestas* of his father and the sale process could be repeated. Table IV. 2 limited this right of the father by stating that if a father sold his son three times, the latter acquired freedom. The pontiffs seized this provision and engaged the pretence of interpretation to introduce the rule that if a father completed a fictional threefold sale of his son to another person, the son after the third alienation and manumission gained released from the *patria potestas* and become *sui iuris* (in control of his own affairs).[33] This example displays how a legal provision was utilized to achieve a purpose quite different from that originally contemplated by the legislator and how, through interpretation, a new norm was created as required by altered conditions.[34] While the pontiffs retained their monopoly in legal matters, it was mainly through their interpretations that innovations in the field of private law could be effected. At the same time, the pontiffs' activities as interpreters of the law forged the groundwork for the subsequent development of Roman legal science.

According to Roman tradition, the pontifical monopoly of legal knowledge ceased after the publication by Gnaeus Flavius, secretary (*scriba*) to Appius Claudius (a prominent patrician who was appointed censor in 312 BC), of a collection of formulas and ritual words that were recited in court when litigation took place (*ius civile Flavianum*). Shortly afterwards, he also published the calendar of the days (*dies fasti* and *dies nefasti*) scheduled for legal proceedings in the courts.[35] Although any alert citizen must have known a great deal of the information embodied in the *ius Flavianum*, it was now rendered official and the jurisdictional magistrates could no longer refuse what all the people would know to be the law. The disclosure of the procedural rules was followed by the enactment of a *lex Ogulnia* (*c.* 300 BC), by which the plebeians were admitted to the priesthood. As a result, Tiberius Coruncanius became the first plebeian *pontifex maximus* (head of the pontifical college) in *c.* 254 BC. He introduced the innovation of offering public legal instruction and advice for using the *legis actiones* to all those consulting him on the subject.[36] Thereafter, an increasing number of leading Roman citizens adopted the practice of proffering legal advice without being members of the pontifical college. The pontiffs' exclusive retention of the technical knowledge of law waned and this knowledge became an ingredient in national culture. The law captured the intellectual fascination of people and those engaged in the law (*iuris periti, iuris prudentes, iuris consulti*) had considerable distinction. In later times, the functions of these jurists were classified as pleading (*agere*), advising (*respondere*) and conveyancing (*cavere*): they guided litigating parties as advocates, evaluated whether an individual in a particular factual situation had a valid claim in law and drafted the texts employed in legal practice, such as the *formulae* used in lawsuits and memoranda of transactions that could prompt future litigation. The services of these men, who were also actively engaged in public affairs, were equally demanded by jurisdictional magistrates embroiled in doubt and by litigants aspiring to assert a claim. Around 200 BC one of these jurists, Sextus Aelius Paetus Catus, consul in 198 BC, published a book containing the text of the Twelve Tables, the interpretations of its rules by the pontiffs and secular jurists and a list of the legal forms employed in the *legis actio* procedure.[37] This work, known as *Tripertita* (i.e., tripartite exposition of the law), marks the beginning of Roman legal literature and the transition from the unsystematic approach of the earlier jurists to a new approach that may be termed scientific. Thereafter, the development of Roman legal thinking was moulded by the influence of Greek and Hellenistic science that began to infuse Rome from the end of the third century BC.

3

THE MONARCHY AND EARLY REPUBLIC: THE ADMINISTRATION OF JUSTICE

Civil procedure

Roman private law was closely connected with the law of civil procedure, otherwise recognized as the law relating to actions. In a sense, the law of actions may be construed as the most important part of the law. This mainly derives from the fact that the early jurists, the shapers of the *ius civile*, were concerned not so much with the formulation of general principles regarding the rights and duties of individuals, but with establishing the factual circumstances under which an aggrieved person should be granted a legal remedy. In other words, unlike modern lawyers, who tend to emphasize rights and duties, and regard remedies as merely their procedural shell, the Roman jurists attached significance to remedies rather than to rights, to forms of action rather than to causes of action. Thus, the law as a whole had little import for the Romans unless a recognized form of action existed whereby an individual could enforce a claim. As the evolution of Roman private law was greatly influenced by the development of legal procedure, the study of procedural law can illuminate the framework that cultivated substantive private law.

As noted previously, the early Romans used the term *ius* to denote a right or a form of conduct approved by the community. Before the formation of the state there was no comprehensive system of rules or remedies designed to assist an aggrieved person with the enforcement of his rights. The obvious course for an aggrieved person was self-help, for example, by forcibly evicting a trespasser or reclaiming property he was wrongly deprived of by another person. A general awareness existed of the circumstances where such demonstrations of hostile power were *iura* and this was established by custom. The development of the state was accompanied by the formation of rules that required the person aspiring to wield self-help to show actual infringement of his rights, and establishing this proof often necessitated a judicial decision. Only then was the wronged party allowed to execute the decision by means of self-help. The holder of *imperium* had a principal function of declaring the *ius* or identifying rights. In the earliest times, this function of identifying the *ius* was probably undifferentiated from the magistrate's other functions. The exercise of his power to issue commands, which could be drastically enforced, assisted the aggrieved party in obtaining the *ius* that was declared as their entitlement. Therefore, if a person possessed or claimed a *ius* against another and secured that person's appearance before the magistrate, he could have both his *ius* confirmed and its exercise protected by the suppression of any resistance. Initially, the magistrate's law-finding activity must have been a relatively simple task as the circumstances where a *ius* was recognized were mainly presumed. But as social and economic conditions changed, magistrates were confronted with unfamiliar claims and forms of *ius*. We may surmise that they denied support for such cases, unless the new *ius* was adapted to resemble a recognized form. In the course of time, a more sophisticated system of rules and principles developed to provide remedies for a variety of infringements on the rights of Roman citizens.

The Roman law of procedure is generally distinguished by three stages of development: the period of the *legis actio* procedure, the period of the formulary system and the period of the *cognitio extraordinaria*. The *legis actio* procedure was used during the Republic, the formulary system featured in the second century BC to the third century AD and the *cognitio extraordinaria* prevailed during the Empire.

The *legis actio* procedure (literally, an action based on the law) is the earliest form of Roman legal procedure known to us. Its origin is not quite clear. It probably derived from the practice established by custom where contested claims were voluntarily submitted to arbitration, and must have been in habitual use before its formal adoption. We may assume that at some time a *lex* required or permitted a magistrate to enforce a *ius* that was demanded in a particular way, and this procedure was consequently termed *legis actio*. The *legis actio* was essentially a ritual and, as such, was elaborated by the pontiffs. It was conducted orally and divided into two stages. The first stage (*in iure*) proceeded before a consul (or a pontiff) and, after the enactment of the *leges Liciniae Sextiae* (367 BC), before the praetor.[1] The second stage (*in iudicio, apud iudicem*) proceeded before a citizen appointed as the judge (*iudex*) by the magistrate and the parties concerned.[2] In certain cases two or more judges were appointed and thus designated as *recuperatores*.[3]

Whenever a Roman citizen wished to raise a dispute and institute legal proceedings against another, he first had to approach a magistrate endowed with the power of *iurisdictio*. This magistrate would determine whether the case was sufficiently strong for referral to a judge for trial and, if so, stipulated the appropriate procedure. This formed the first phase of the *legis actio* procedure, called *in iure*, as the magistrate declared the law (*ius*) applicable to the case.[4] However, the case was only heard if both the plaintiff and the defendant were present at the opening of the proceedings *in iure*.[5] According to the Law of the Twelve Tables (T. 1. 1.), the plaintiff could forcibly compel an absent defendant to appear before the magistrate. However, this action was averted if the defendant produced a guarantor (*vindex*) who would assure their appearance in court at a fixed later date. When both parties appeared before the magistrate, the plaintiff had to pronounce his claim in a set form of words attended by equally formal ritual acts prescribed by law for the relevant case. The defendant had to reply by also employing a mandated combination of words and gestures. The magistrate finally intervened in a prescribed manner so that the case might be sent for trial. The *litis contestatio* (joinder of issue)[6] formed the final act in the proceedings *in iure* as it established the disputed issue. The most important effect of the *litis contestatio* precluded the plaintiff from instigating a fresh action against the defendant for the same claim.

The use of a formula with the solemn enunciation of prescribed formal words to request a magistrate to exercise his power on one's behalf was an ancient, deeply rooted practice among the Romans, who attached great importance to the efficacy of ceremonial acts in most communal activities. As the *legis actio* was essentially a ritual any mistake, even a trivial one, was necessarily fatal. This is illustrated by a case reported by the jurist Gaius where a man sued another for chopping down his vines. The aggrieved party lost his suit because he used the words 'vines' (*vites*) instead of 'trees' (*arbores*) as prescribed by the Law of the Twelve Tables (T. 8. 11.).[7] As previously elaborated, the pontiffs had knowledge of the formulas a magistrate would be likely to accept as efficacious. It was a customary practice to consult the pontiffs for some formula even before the *legis actio* became a well-defined and established system.

Five different types of *legis actiones* are mentioned in the sources: the *legis actio sacramento*, the *legis actio per iudicis arbitrive postulationem*, the *legis actio per condictionem*, the *legis actio per manus iniectionem* and the *legis actio per pignoris capionem*.[8] The first three were applied to resolve a dispute, while the last two were used to enforce the execution of a judgment.

The *legis actio sacramento* (action in the law by oath) was the earliest and most important of the *legis actiones*. Gaius describes it as *generalis* (of general application),[9] since it applied to any case where no other action was provided by law. This action could be used to enforce either a real or a personal right and was thus referred to respectively as *legis actio sacramento in rem* (action in the law by oath for a real right) and *legis actio sacramento in personam* (action in the law by oath for a personal right).[10] The name of this *legis actio* derives from the fact that originally both litigant parties had to confirm the justification of their claim in the particular dispute under oath and before witnesses. Each party exhibited proof of their good faith by depositing a wager or stake (*sacramentum*) consisting of a monetary sum.[11] The successful party in the subsequent trial retrieved his *sacramentum* whereas the failed party forfeited his *sacramentum* to the authorities who used it to fund religious ceremonies (*ad sacra publica*).[12]

In a *legis actio sacramento in rem* the property in dispute (or a token of the object if it was immoveable) was presented before the magistrate and each party asserted ownership over it by performing certain symbolic gestures and pronouncing prescribed formal words. An altercation then ensued between the parties over their respective titles, and each party supported their assertions by issuing an oath with a monetary sum staked on the outcome (*sacramentum*).[13] An important note is that an issue was not created by assertion and denial, but by the two parties asserting contradictory rights. The magistrate then produced an interim decision assigning possession of the disputed object to one of the parties and demanding security from him.[14] After establishing the question at issue (*litis contestatio*), the *iudex* was nominated to try the case and the *in iure* phase of the proceedings was thus completed.[15]

The *legis actio per iudicis arbitrive postulationem* (action in the law by application for a judge or arbiter) was employed in specific cases where a law had authorized it and was applicable when a claim emerged from a verbal contract (*sponsio/stipulatio*)[16] or it was necessary to institute an action for the division of a common estate or inheritance (*actio familiae erciscundae*). Under a *lex Licinia* (an early republican statute of unknown date) this *legis actio* could also be engaged in cases involving a claim directed at the division of joint property (*actio communi dividundo*).

When the parties appeared before the magistrate, the plaintiff stated the cause of his action (e.g. *ex sponsione*) and called upon the defendant to reply. If the defendant denied the plaintiff's claim, the latter requested the magistrate to appoint a *iudex* or an *arbiter* to decide the case. It seems that a *iudex* was appointed in cases involving claims invoked by verbal agreements, while cases concerned with the division of joint property were determined by an *arbiter*. In comparison to the *legis actio sacramento*, the *legis actio per iudicis arbitrive postulationem* had the advantages of relative simplicity and no risk to the unsuccessful party of forfeiting a *sacramentum*.[17]

The *legis actio per condictionem* was introduced by the *lex Silia* (*c.* 204 BC) for actions directed at the recovery of a fixed sum of money (*certa pecunia*). It was extended by the *lex Calpurnia* (probably passed early in the second century BC) to encompass claims involving other definite objects (*aliae certae res*).[18] As in the case of the *legis actio per iudicis arbitrive postulationem*, its application was restricted to cases stipulated by legislation. However, the *condictio* as such was an abstract action as the formal words employed in respect thereof omitted reference to a cause of action. The *condictio* was a personal action that could be employed in a variety of cases, such as *mutuum*,[19] *stipulatio certa*,[20] *contractus litteris* (written contract) and *furtum* (theft). It also applied to cases of unjust enrichment when one person dishonestly acquired a benefit from another's property (*ex iniusta causa*) or without any legal justification (*sine causa*).

In a *legis actio per condictionem* the plaintiff declared his claim (i.e. the defendant owed him a certain amount of money or a specific object) and then invited the defendant to acknowledge or deny it. If the defendant denied the plaintiff's claim, the latter 'gave notice'[21] to him to appear before the magistrate after thirty days for the appointment of a *iudex*.

In contrast to the proceedings *in iure*, no formal rules governed the second phase of the procedure that occurred before the *iudex* (*apud iudicem, in iudicio*).[22] During this phase the judge (*iudex*) conducted the trial based on the evidence produced within the frame established by the magistrate.[23] The judge had no restriction in assessing the evidence and adhered only to certain general rules (for example, it was recognized that the plaintiff assumed the burden of proof).[24] After observing the litigants' pleas (*causae coniectio* or *collectio*), hearing their witnesses and advocates[25] and investigating the matter, he pronounced a verdict orally in the presence of both parties. Before delivering his judgment, the judge could consult anyone he chose or seek the advice of a council appointed by him (*consilium*) when necessary, which was usually composed of persons with legal knowledge. No appeal to a higher authority against the judge's verdict was possible, because by accepting the *iudex* through the *litis contestatio* both parties agreed in advance to submit to his verdict.[26]

The *legis actio per manus iniectionem* (action in the law by the laying on of a hand) differed from the aforementioned *legis actiones* that were designed for dispute resolution. It applied to the execution of a judicial decision with a focus on the person of the judgment debtor and not his property.[27] According to the Law of the Twelve Tables (T. 3. 1. and 2.), the *legis actio per manus iniectionem* could be engaged against the party condemned (*iudicatus* or *damnatus*) by the *iudex* at the end of the *in iudicio* phase of the proceedings and who had failed to discharge his debt within thirty days after the relevant decision, as well as against the party who acknowledged his debt in the *in iure* phase (*confessus pro iudicato habetur*).[28] If the condemned person refused to settle his debt or failed to produce a guarantor (*vindex*),[29] he was assigned by the magistrate to the creditor as his prisoner for sixty days. During this time, the creditor proclaimed the debt sum on three successive market days (*nundinae*).[30] On the third occasion, if no one elected to release the debtor by paying the debt he was reassigned to the creditor. The latter could then sell the debtor into slavery across the Tiber river (*trans Tiberim*) or even, in early times, slay him.[31]

The *legis actio per pignoris capionem* (action in the law by the seizure of a pledge) was also designed for the execution of a judicial decision. However, it was dissimilar to the *manus iniectio* as it was a remedy directed at the property of the debtor.[32] This action enabled a creditor in specified cases to obtain a pledge from the property of the debtor without applying to a magistrate for a judgment.[33] In the cases where this form of execution applied, the creditor had to adopt a prescribed procedure that engaged a set form of words (*certa verba*) declared in the presence of witnesses; thus, the relevant procedure was regarded as a form of statute process.[34]

The *legis actio* procedure gradually fell into disfavour, as its archaism and exaggerated formalism rendered it unsuitable for the needs of a rapidly advancing society. The progressive complexity of social and economic life induced the praetor to devise new forms of action and new procedural *formulae* to accommodate *ad hoc* controversies arising from novel socio-economic situations. This prompted the development of a flexible form of procedure, known as formulary (*per formulam*) procedure, which predominated during the late Republic and the Principate. After the formulary procedure acquired legislative recognition by the *lex Aebutia* (second century BC), a plaintiff could choose whether to use the new or the old *legis actio* procedure. Although most claimants selected the formulary procedure because of its advantages, the two types of procedure were used conjunctively until the end of the first century BC when the *legis actiones* were formally abolished by the *leges Iuliae iudiciorum publicorum et privatorum* of Augustus (*c.* 17 BC).[35]

Criminal law and criminal justice

In the earliest period of Roman history, criminal law did not exist as an ordered body of rules bolstered by sanctions and administered by regular courts of justice.

As in other primitive societies, many acts that are now treated as offences against the state and prosecuted by public authorities were regarded as private wrongs that presented the injured party with a rightful claim to seek vengeance on the wrong-doer. However, certain wrongful acts that directly threatened the state's existence and security, such as treason (*perduellio*)[36] and homicide (*parricidium*: the unlawful killing of a free man)[37] were punished as offences against the general community from a very early period. These offences were too grave to be atoned for by pecu-niary compensation or, in fact, by any penalty short of death. Besides the aforesaid wrongs, the early law regarded certain violations of religious norms as crimes liable to provoke the gods' wrath against the entire community; this was only averted by the appropriate punishment and atonement for the violations. As these crimes were primarily directed against divine law, the pontiffs as guardians and ministers of state religion exacted the penalty. As a rule, the punishment imposed entailed sacrificing the offender to the deity concerned (*consecratio capitis*) and the confiscation of his property for religious uses (*consecratio bonorum*).[38] Such punishment was expiatory in character; it served to restore the harmony between the community and its gods (*pax deorum*) by eliminating the state of collective impurity created by the commis-sion of the offence. An array of individual behaviour constituted sins that were expiated in the same way: the patron who wronged the client whom he was bound to protect, the son who mistreated his father, the man who removed a neighbour's landmark or destroyed his corn by night, the thief of sacred objects dedicated to the gods, the witness who gave false testimony and the person who used witchcraft and incantations. Soon after the establishment of the Republic, if not earlier, the sacri-fice of the offender was replaced by the milder penalty of outlawry and the confiscation of goods. As this penalty involved the exclusion of the offender (referred to as *sacer homo*) from the community and from the protection of human and divine law, anyone could kill the offender with impunity; his killing was regarded as a sacrifice to the deity he had sinned against.

As state organization evolved, especially after the Law of the Twelve Tables was enacted, private vengeance was supplanted by retaliation through orderly state-supervised procedures. All injurious acts committed against private persons (*delicta privata*), except the most serious offences, were redressed at the injured party's initiative by means of a civil action (*actio poenalis*) that endeavoured to obtain compensation from the perpetrator as expiation of the act.[39] At the same time, an increasing number of secular offences were treated as public crimes (*crimina publica*) but some offences also exhibited religious influences.[40] However, the list of recognized public crimes only started to resemble a modern system of criminal law in the late Republic.

According to Roman tradition, in the Monarchy era the king, who possessed all jurisdiction in principle, was accustomed to delegating his criminal jurisdiction in cases of treason to a pair of judges (*duumviri perduellionis*) who were specially appointed for each occasion, and in cases of murder to a pair of standing judges called *quaestores parricidii*. Regarding the capital sentences pronounced by either of these pairs of judges, the king had the discretion to allow an appeal to the people (*provocatio ad populum*), and could endorse their judgment on whether the offender should be killed or freed.[41] However, it is impossible to ascertain the entire truth in the traditional account.[42]

After the establishment of the Republic, jurisdiction over the major secular crimes was vested in the consuls. The authority to adjudicate (*cognitio*) derived from their right of supreme coercion (*coercitio maior*) included in their *imperium*.[43] If a case of treason (*perduellio*) arose, the consuls nominated two judges (*duoviri perduellionis*) to conduct the inquiry and pronounce the sentence.[44] In cases of murder (*parricidium*) the two quaestors acted as judges and in this capacity were designated *quaestores parricidii*.[45] The jurisdiction of the curule and plebeian aediles encompassed cases involving offences against the public order or public morals, and contraventions of statutory enactments. Originally, only a magistrate could instigate a charge against an individual and criminal proceedings had an entirely inquisitorial nature. As soon as the commission of a crime captured a magistrate's notice, he had the responsibility to initiate an investigation of the case and embark on procuring any necessary evidence.

According to Roman tradition, the *lex Valeria*, a statute passed in the first year of the Republic, stipulated that a Roman citizen could not be slain pursuant to a magistrate's sentence without a right of appeal to the people (*provocatio ad populum*). The Law of the Twelve Tables and subsequent legislation confirmed this rule that a capital sentence[46] pronounced by a magistrate could not be executed unless on appeal it had been ratified by the people.[47] A provision of the Twelve Tables (T. 9. 4.) rendered the *comitia centuriata* (therein referred to as *comitiatus maximus*) uniquely competent to deal with appeals against capital sentences. On the other hand, appeals against pecuniary sentences were tackled by the *comitia tributa* or the *concilum plebis*, depending on whether the relevant sentence was pronounced by a magistrate of the *civitas* or the *plebs*.[48] However, we may observe after the enactment of the Law of the Twelve Tables the invariable practice of magistrates *cum imperio* of refraining to pronounce a sentence that could be challenged on appeal to the people. The reason is that only the assembly of the centuries had authority to impose a death sentence once a person was declared guilty of a capital offence.[49] Accordingly, criminal jurisdiction was exercised by magistrates alone only in cases involving less serious offences.[50]

The rules concerning appeals and the restrictions imposed on the magistrates' judicial powers by legislation entailed the exercise of criminal jurisdiction by the Roman people in important cases during most of the republican period.[51] The procedure adopted in trials before the people (*iudicia populi*) is only discoverable in the descriptions of writers from a later date and a great part remains obscure. Sources reveal that the magistrate who resolved to impeach a citizen, after duly summoning the accused, held a trial (*anquisitio*) in (at least) three successive *contiones* (informal public meetings). During these meetings he investigated the case and determined matters of fact and law based on the produced evidence.[52] If the accused was found guilty, the magistrate issued an order summoning the appropriate assembly to meet on the expiry of the regular interval of three market days (*trinum nundinum*).[53] When the assembly congregated on the appointed day, the magistrate presented a motion in the form of a bill (*rogatio*) for confirmation of the verdict and sentence. In response to this motion and without any preliminary debate, those in favour of confirmation voted '*condemno*' while those against it voted '*absolvo*'.[54] If the majority in the assembly was in favour of condemnation, the presiding magistrate pronounced the sentence.[55] A notable feature of Roman legal procedure was the right of the accused to flee Rome as a voluntary exile at any time before the assembly's final vote. Selection of this option entailed the enactment of a decree of outlawry, or interdiction from water and fire (*aquae et ignis interdictio*). This practically meant banishment accompanied by loss of citizenship and property. The individual declared an *interdictus* was deprived of legal protection and, if he returned to Rome without permission, could be killed by anyone with impunity.[56]

4

THE LATE REPUBLIC: THE HISTORICAL, SOCIAL AND CONSTITUTIONAL BACKGROUND

Rome's expansion in the Mediterranean world

After resolving her internal political issues and consolidating the constitution, Rome focused on foreign affairs. The third century BC is marked by Rome's wars with Carthage, a great maritime power governed by an oligarchy of merchant families.[1] Initially, the Romans maintained good relations with Carthage, but shortly after Rome's subjugation of the Greek city-states in Southern Italy this precarious coalition turned into open rivalry. The First Punic War erupted in 264 BC when Rome, fearing that a threatened Carthagenian conquest of Messina in Sicily might be a prelude to an attack on mainland Italy, assisted that city and thereby clashed with Carthage. The war ended with victory for Rome in 241 BC. As a result, Rome acquired her first overseas provinces (Sicily, Sardinia and Corsica) and asserted her position as a flourishing international power. In the following years, a resurgent Carthage sought to recover the lost ground by embarking on a programme of military expansion in Spain under Hamilcar Barca and his son, Hannibal, leaders of the Carthaginians who craved revenge on Rome. The Romans attempted to curb the Carthaginian expansion by treaty, but conflict ensued after Hannibal's attack on one of Rome's Spanish allies in 219 BC. In 218 BC a large expeditionary force led by Hannibal was dispatched to attack the Romans in Italy. Despite the initial successes of her armies, Carthage was eventually overwhelmed by the Romans in 201 BC. The political and commercial supremacy of Carthage dissolved and she was reduced to the position of a client-state of Rome. As a result of her victory in the Second Punic War, Rome established herself as the dominant power in the western Mediterranean.

Shortly after the subjugation of Carthage, Rome embarked on another series of wars, this time in the Greek East. To fathom the reasons for her actions, one must consider the political conditions of the Hellenistic world in the third century BC. After the empire of Alexander the Great disintegrated, a complex state system emerged in this highly civilized, cosmopolitan world. It consisted of three great powers, Ptolemaic Egypt, the Seleucid Empire of Syria and Macedonia, and several smaller states, such as Athens, Rhodes and Pergamum. The ambitions of Syria and Macedonia to extend their influence at the expense of smaller states in the region presented Rome with the opportunity to enter the scene of Hellenistic politics, first as a guarantor of the existing balance of power and, subsequently, in pursuit of her own imperialistic designs. Rome's decision to interfere in Greek affairs was also prompted by the realization of the commercial advantages of imperialism, even though economic rather than political motivations were initially far less important.

During the protracted wars fought between 200 and 146 BC, the Romans eventually realized that sustained peace could only be created if their involvement in the East entailed the direct annexation of the besieged territories. However, they initially withdrew their expeditionary forces following their victories over Macedonia (197 BC) and Syria (188 BC), and granted the Greek city-states and leagues the freedom to govern themselves; they even declared themselves liberators of Greece and protectors of Greek freedom (196 BC). As their influence expanded, the Romans perceived themselves as patrons and the Greeks as clients who had to pursue policies congruent with Roman interests. The Roman interference in Greek affairs was deemed intolerable and prompted some disgruntled states to form an alliance with Macedonia's new king, Perseus, who was a self-proclaimed champion of the Greek interests against Roman intervention. To prevent the expansion of Macedonian influence in Greece, Rome declared war on Perseus in 171 BC. Following Perseus's defeat in 168 BC, the Macedonian kingdom was carved into four separate republics. In 148 BC, after a short-lived revolt, the republics were dissolved and Macedonia transformed into a Roman province. Finally, the dissolution of the Achaean League and the sacking of Corinth by the Romans in 146 BC engendered Rome's domination of the entire Greek world. However, unlike Macedonia, Greece was not organised as a Roman province. The Greek city-states were compelled to form treaties of alliance with Rome and the whole country was consigned to the supervision of the governor of Macedonia. The same year marks the end of the Third Punic War (149–146 BC), which resulted in the complete destruction of Carthage and the annexation of her territory as part of the Roman province of Africa.

In 133 BC the rich kingdom of Pergamum (situated in the north-west part of Asia Minor) was gifted to Rome under the will of its last king, Attalus III. The province of Asia was created from the kingdom of Pergamum in 129 BC. Moreover, after Rome's victory in the war against Jugurtha, ruler of the North African kingdom of Numidia, in 105 BC, further territories were added to the Roman province of Africa. In 88 BC Rome embarked on a series of wars in the East against the king of Pontus, Mithradates IV the Eupator. The King had declared himself liberator of the Greeks and launched a campaign designed to expel the Romans from Asia Minor and Greece. Although for a time Roman power in the East seemed doomed, Mithradates was finally defeated in 63 BC. Rome regained control of Greece and a continuous belt of Roman provinces was created along the coasts of the Black and Mediterranean Seas from northern Asia Minor to Syria and Judaea.[2] Behind these provinces to the East, Rome's sphere of interest was safeguarded through a band of client states, which formed a buffer zone against the powerful Parthian Empire. This phase of Roman expansion ended with the conquest of Gaul by Julius Caesar (58–53 BC) and the annexation of Egypt by Octavian in 30 BC.

Internal developments during the late Republic

The organization of the Roman state displayed no major changes during the Punic wars and the wars in Greece. Although in theory democratic, Rome continued to be governed by a few powerful patrician and plebeian families – an oligarchy that developed in the closing stages of the struggle of the orders, when office holding ceased to be a prerogative of aristocratic birth. Since the Roman senate mainly consisted of members from leading families who had served as magistrates, this new nobility was identified as the senatorial class (*ordo senatorius*).[3] The chief source of the senatorial families' wealth was landed property, as senators were precluded by custom and law from engaging in commerce and industry. Notwithstanding their internal divisions, the members of this class were united in their determination to exclude outsiders from high office and prevent any single statesman from gaining control of the state.

In this period, two interconnected trends characterized Roman political life: the mass of Roman citizens scattered in colonies throughout Italy increasingly failed to exercise their political responsibilities; and the senate completely dominated the people's assemblies. The Roman successes during the wars of expansion enhanced the senate's prestige and reinforced its pivotal position in Rome's political system. The magistrates and the assemblies exhibited their readiness to follow its lead and, although only popular assemblies had the constitutional right to enact legislation, senatorial resolutions (*senatus consulta*) were regarded practically as possessing the force of laws. Moreover, even though the actual ratification of treaties or declarations of war fell in the province of the *comitia*, the senate usually carried matters so far that there was nothing for the *comitia* to do but grant their assent.

Over the second century BC, Rome became an important commercial centre and all kinds of private businesses were established to provide services and manufactured goods. The proliferation of economic activity is evidenced by the development and widespread use of currency, and the establishment of financial institutions in Rome and other Italian cities.[4] Rome's increasingly sophisticated economic life required enterprising men to direct her trade, undertake the construction of public works, manage war contracts and collect taxes.[5] This entailed the emergence of an important new class of merchants and entrepreneurs, which were known as the equestrian class (*ordo equester*).[6] An active and visible minority within the equestrian class acquired their wealth by entering into contracts with the Roman state for the collection of public revenues. The Roman revenues were derived partly from lands and other forms of state-owned property, and partly from taxes paid by the citizens of Rome or her subjects in Italy and the provinces. These contractors, referred to as *publicani*, assumed the risk and expense for exploiting the state's assets and paid an annual fixed sum to the Roman state treasury.[7] The wealth and influence of this class of businessmen grew rapidly as Rome's territory and revenues expanded. Although excluded from the aristocracy and basically non-political, the equestrians were inevitably drawn into politics whenever the senatorial oligarchy threatened to infringe on their economic prerogatives.

In the social hierarchy, the position below the *equites* was occupied by the upper classes of the various communities in Italy and the provinces, whose members tended to loyally support Rome and adopt the Roman culture and lifestyle. Lower down in the social hierarchy were the members of the lower middle class: the small landowners in the country, and the artisans and small traders in the cities. The same broader class also comprised most of the urban and rural proletariat, whose chief means of support was the grants obtained from the state or from the wealthy families to which many of its members had attached themselves as clients. As Rome's urban proletariat was susceptible to political manipulation and prone to violence, it came to constitute a serious threat to political stability, especially during the last century of the republican era.[8]

The most vulnerable group in society were the slaves (*servi*). In the early republican period a relatively small number of slaves lived in Rome; but from the mid-third century BC the slave population expanded rapidly and, by the end of the Republic, slave labour was the predominant factor in economic life. Numerous foreign slaves were transferred into Italy during Rome's wars of expansion.[9] Another major source of slaves was the large slave markets of the East, such as that on the island of Delos in the Aegean.[10] As the children of slave families were slaves by birth, the slave population burgeoned. Thus, by the end of the republican period, it is likely that more than one-third of Italy's entire population consisted of slaves. The living conditions of slaves varied considerably, depending on their personal skills, education and place of work.[11] In general, urban slaves were treated better than rural slaves and were more frequently released from slavery.[12] However, the vast majority of slaves, especially those working on the large estates, lived in misery and were treated harshly by their masters.[13] After his liberation a slave was labelled *libertinus* (freedman) and theoretically had all the rights and obligations of a Roman citizen.[14] However, in reality, freedmen and their descendants were regarded as socially inferior by those with no slaves in their ancestry and were virtually excluded from all the important offices of the state.[15] Nevertheless, many freedmen successfully earned a steady living through their involvement in trade, industry and the arts; some even gained access to positions of power, especially in the last century of the Republic and during the Principate.[16]

An important social and economic development during this period was the gradual decline of the yeoman class that Rome depended on for its economic system and military strength. This development was precipitated by Hannibal's invasion during the Second Punic War that devastated and depopulated large areas of Italy, and by the subsequent wars in the East. Farmers recruited to fight for many years returned to discover their homesteads and fields neglected. As traditional cereal agriculture was no longer profitable (corn and wheat were now imported in large quantities from overseas), these farmers encountered increasing difficulties in re-establishing themselves. Some enterprising farmers shifted to other products to more easily secure sales in overseas markets, such as olives and grapes, or turned to cattle-rearing. However, the great majority of small proprietors could no longer hold their own against the senatorial estate-owners and were forced to sell or abandon their farms. They drifted to the cities, which in the long term offered them limited employment opportunities. The senators were eager to increase their hold-ings by buying up farms at bargain prices, cultivating waste or public lands and exploiting the mounting flood of war-provided slave labour that emerged as a deci-sive factor in the economy. Gradually, whole districts were turned into large cattle-ranches and plantations (*latifundia*) owned by a few absentee landlords and worked by slaves or tenants. During the late second century BC, thousands of land-less and poverty-stricken people from all over Italy moved to Rome where they joined the growing urban proletariat of the city. The transformation of a large part of the Roman citizen body into a group later designated the 'Roman mob' had profound effects on social and political life; it was one principal cause of the crisis that induced the weakening and final collapse of the republican system of gov-ernment.

Rome's expansion also had far-reaching repercussions on the cultural develop-ment of Roman society. Rome emerged from cultural backwardness as a result of the Greek influence in the third century BC. This influence increased as Rome's political involvement extended beyond Italy to the Greek East and became perma-nent.[17] Greek civilization significantly infused every aspect of Roman culture, including religion, education, art and science.[18] Particularly influential were the two great schools of Hellenistic philosophy, Epicureanism and Stoicism. As these schools were primarily concerned with offering rules of life, they accorded well with the practical tendencies of the Roman character and attracted many adherents, especially among Rome's educated upper classes. Stoicism, in particular, appealed to the Romans' sense of duty and it formed an important and positive force in society. Its appeal also emanated from the fact that it best reflected the cosmopolitan ideas of the times.[19] At the same time, however, the introduction of Greek models had an erosive effect on the traditional values that forged the unity of the Roman society. Greek morals were more lax and sophisticated than those of the Romans, and their sudden introduction into this new world of wealth, power and uncertain standards provoked moral confusion. The weakening of the old value system established by a tradition-conscious upper class ultimately destabilized the social cohesion, and was one factor that precipitated the socio-political crisis that marks the closing years of the republican period.

The crisis and fall of the Republic

As the second century progressed, Rome's military successes overseas tended to obscure the deficits of the republican constitution. The constitution was originally designed for the government of a small city-state and was inadequate for fulfilling the organizational and administrative requirements of the vast and intricate Roman state that evolved. The ruling senatorial aristocracy was riven by internal divisions and corrupted by the ruthless exploitation of vast human and material resources in the provinces. As the ideological underpinnings of the republican regime crumbled with the weakening of the traditional value system, this group confronted greater hurdles in achieving satisfactory solutions for the acute socio-economic, political and military problems generated by Rome's expansion. The republican system of government failed to achieve the centralized and cohesive control desperately required to tackle the growing social unrest at home and dangerous large-scale rebellions in Italy and the provinces. This failure aggravated political instability and enabled ambitious political and military leaders to attain absolute power. These leaders secured their power by manipulating the senate, magisterial offices and the popular assemblies, and by gaining the support of discontented social groups demanding diverse reforms. As a result, the outward forms of the traditional republican constitution were retained but distorted by forces alien to the traditional framework. The weakening of the traditional constitutional structure was accompanied by an increasingly violent internal strife, both between rival factions and individuals within the ruling classes, and between the aristocracy and various disadvantaged groups. These circumstances degenerated into an almost permanent state of civil war, which prompted the erosion and final disintegration of the republican system of government.

A major cause of the crisis was the decline of the free peasantry and the deepening schism between the growing urban and rural proletariat on the one hand, and the land-owning senatorial aristocracy on the other. A connected element was the growing inability of the state to recruit enough yeoman legionaries to fight its wars and a noticeable lapse in military discipline and morale. Only drastic reform could rebuild the yeoman class, and thus bolster Rome's military manpower and reduce unemployment. In the decade following 133 BC the campaign for reform was embraced by two brothers from the liberal wing of the senatorial oligarchy, the plebeian tribunes Tiberius and Gaius Gracchus. When Tiberius Gracchus was elected tribune in 133 BC, he introduced a bill in the assembly of the people which stipulated that no Roman citizen could hold more than 500 *iugera* (about 300 acres) of state-owned land (plus half that amount for each of up to two sons). The large landowners, who were tenants of the state, had to return tracts of excess land and this freed land would then be allocated in small portions to Rome's landless citizens.[20] It must be noted that this measure and the law subsequently enacted concerned only state-owned land. They did not remove private property nor limit the amount of private land that a citizen could own. Although several senators supported the bill, Tiberius adopted dubious tactics in creating the law. The impression conveyed was that he endeavoured to acquire power for himself by basing his actions purely on the will of the people, thus bypassing the senate.[21] The senate's resentment against him intensified when he took the unprecedented and arguably unconstitutional step of announcing himself as a candidate for the office of tribune for a second year running. In the violent clashes that erupted on the election day in 132 BC, Tiberius and many of his supporters were killed by a large group of senators and their followers. With the death of Tiberius the senate regained control of the state and a special court was established to try for treason those who had aided Tiberius in his more radical undertakings.[22]

Nine years after Tiberius' assassination, his brother Gaius Sempronius Gracchus endeavoured to promote the reforms. One of Gaius' first actions after he was elected tribune of the people in 123 BC was to introduce legislation designed to protect himself and his supporters against future prosecution.[23] Moreover, in an attempt to secure the support of the powerful equestrian class, Gaius instituted measures that strengthened the equestrians' position at the expense of the senators.[24] As a result, the equestrians were for the first time recognised as a distinct order in the state (*ordo equester*) and emerged to play an active role in political life. Although Gaius' extensive programme of reforms, especially his land laws, was more successful than that of his brother, it failed to achieve its ultimate goals – a failure for which Gaius paid with his life in 121 BC. After Gaius' death the senate recaptured control of the state and most of his introduced measures were repealed or drastically modified. The actions and ultimate fates of the Gracchi brothers constituted a watershed in Roman political life. The reforms they initiated highlighted the links between the problems of landholding, poverty, the military, and the extension and retention of the empire. However, the constitutional issues they raised were more important than their programme of reforms. Their attempts at circumventing senatorial authority by relying on the support of the popular assembly and the equestrians provoked a violent political conflict. This affected the equilibrium of Roman society and launched a chain of events that eventually destroyed the republican regime and engendered one-man rule.[25]

The political upheavals in the century after the Gracchi largely emanated from the struggle between two factions: the *populares* and the *optimates*. The *populares* represented the radical reformers and included several ambitious senators who, with the support of the people's assembly, sought personal political aggrandizement by challenging their fellow oligarchs and championing the cause of various discontented groups in the state. The *optimates* (literally, 'the best'), who represented the majority of the senators, defended oligarchic control of the state, and were opposed to any radical changes. However, neither group can be described as a political party, in a modern sense, for their activities were not guided by established political principles or policies but, rather, by the personal interests and ambitions of their aristocratic leaders and their followers.[26] After the age of the Gracchi, a series of crises ensued, prompted by essentially political challenges by individuals against the rule of a reactionary governing elite. The senate met these challenges ineptly and, as the people's assemblies were quite unrepresentative and demoralized, real leadership was captured by whoever could forcibly gain control of the state.

The next important challenge to the oligarchy occurred ten years after the death of Gaius Gracchus, when the senate was held responsible for a series of military setbacks in the wars against King Jugurtha in Numidia (North Africa) and the Germanic tribes of Cimbri and Teutones in Gaul. In 107 BC Gaius Marius, the new leader of the *populares* and a man of considerable military ability, was elected consul and dispatched to Africa to command the army. Marius' success in terminating the Jugurthine War (105 BC) and his subsequent victory over the Cimbri and Teutones (102–101 BC) greatly increased his popularity and political influence – this entailed an unprecedented and continuous tenure as consul for five years (104–100 BC). But Marius' victories were far less significant than the changes he introduced to the organization of the Roman army, whose strength had been undermined by the declining numbers in the class of small property holders – traditionally the army's main source of recruits. Ignoring the usual methods of levy, he formed a professional army consisting largely of volunteers drawn from Rome's proletariat. These troops saw him, rather than the senate, as responsible for their benefits in the form of regular pay, the distribution of war booty and an allocation of land on completion of service. In this way, the great 'vassal armies' of the later Republic emerged and were used by subsequent generals to advance their own careers. The old type of citizen army could never become a factor in political strife, since its members perceived themselves as citizens in the service of the state. The new professional army, on the other hand, was conceived to render its support to a popular commander against any party in the state, and even against the state itself.

A decade of turmoil followed Marius' emergence on the political scene that culminated in the so-called Social or Italian War (90–88 BC) – a successful uprising by Rome's allies in Italy for the attainment of complete Roman citizenship. It was during the Social War and another war fought in the East against Mithradates VI the Eupator, king of Pontus, that Lucius Cornelius Sulla, a member of the *optimates* and Marius' arch enemy, attained prominence. After several years of civil war between Sulla and Marius, the latter was defeated and the senatorial party was restored to power. The senate appointed Sulla as dictator and he engaged the task of reorganizing the state. His first act was to eliminate all his political and personal opposition, using the novel device of proscription – the posting of lists of undesirable persons whom anyone was at liberty to assassinate. He then introduced a series of constitutional reforms devised to safeguard the privileges of the senatorial class and curb the power of the tribunes and the popular assemblies.[27] However, in the years following Sulla's abdication (79 BC) and death (78 BC) most of his measures were overturned and, by 70 BC, the *populares* were again the dominant power in Roman politics.

After the end of Sulla's regime, the civil warfare between the senate and the forces of the opposition resumed both in Italy and the provinces. The situation was further exacerbated by the outbreak of a large-scale slave rebellion in Italy (73–71 BC), the renewed threat of Mithradates in the East (74 BC) and the growing menace of piracy in the Mediterranean. During these turbulent years a new leader emerged in Rome, Gnaeus Pompeius Magnus (Pompey the Great), a successful general who was elected to the consulship with the support of the *populares* in 70 BC. In a series of military campaigns Pompey eliminated the scourge of piracy (67 BC) and won a decisive victory over Mithradates and his allies (63 BC). As a result of these successes, the Roman possessions in Asia were enhanced by two new provinces: Syria and Bithynia. Pompey organized the political administration of the new provinces and secured Rome's eastern frontiers by creating a buffer zone of client states. He then returned to Italy, where the struggle between the *optimates* and the *populares* continued unabated.[28]

Upon his return Pompey disbanded his army, as the law required, and requested the senate to provide land for his army veterans and ratify his arrangements in the East, but his requests were opposed by the majority of senators. Thereupon he formed a coalition (known as the First Triumvirate) devised to divide up the power and bypass the senate (60 BC). Two influential senators joined this coalition: Marcus Licinius Crassus, Pompey's co-consul in 70 BC and victor in the war against the slaves (71 BC); and Gaius Julius Caesar, a relative of Marius and then governor of Spain. In the following year Caesar was elected to the consulship and appointed governor (*proconsul*) of Gaul in 58 BC. His conquest of Gaul was completed after a series of successful military campaigns against the local Celts and invading Germanic tribes. But Caesar's growing power was regarded with unease by both the senate and his two partners in the Triumvirate. The renewal of the coalition in 56 BC only delayed the oncoming crisis, which became unavoidable after the death of Crassus in the war against the Parthians in 53 BC.[29] In the civil war that erupted in 49 BC, Pompey joined forces with the senate against Caesar and his supporters but a year later his army was defeated in a decisive battle in Greece.[30]

Caesar's victorious emergence as the undisputed master of Rome prompted an energetic mobilization of his dictatorial powers to reform the state in a direct and radical manner. Many projects testify to his tireless energy, such as a new enlargement of the senate to 900 members, the acceleration of colonization and urbanization outside Italy, the reorganization of the administration of the provinces, the granting of the Roman citizenship to army veterans and provincials, extensive building schemes and the reform of the calendar. Caesar's style of exercising authority featured an open disregard of the republican traditions and often the brutal assumption of the powers he required. Even though many of his reforms were radical, his style of governance generally invoked a great deal of opposition from the senate. Many senators construed him not as an upholder of the republican order, but as a usurper and tyrant. A conspiracy was formed that entailed the assassination of Caesar in the Senate House by a group of senators in 44 BC. Caesar's assassination was justified by the leaders of the conspiracy as an act aimed at restoring freedom (*libertas*). But the freedom demanded by the group was by no means a democratic freedom for all Romans. It was freedom according to the traditions and interests of the senatorial aristocracy – freedom for the governing class to practise politics once more according to the forms of the oligarchic state.

After Caesar's death the chief contenders for the leadership of the Caesarian party were the consul Mark Antony, Caesar's closest associate, and Gaius Julius Caesar Octavianus, his teenaged grandnephew, personal heir and adopted son. It was not long before the rivalry between the two men resulted in armed conflict. Octavian, with the support of the senate and Caesar's veterans, defeated Antony's forces in a battle in northern Italy. But the senate's plans for resuming control of the state were frustrated when Octavian made peace with Antony and marched with his army on Rome, where he enforced his appointment to the consulship (43 BC). In the same year, Octavian, Antony and Lepidus (Caesar's master of the horse) formed the Second Triumvirate at a conference near Bologna. This coalition intended to secure for the participants the unlimited powers requisite to 'restore the republic' (*tresviri reipublicae constituendae*). The formation of the Triumvirate was followed by a reign of terror that instigated the death of numerous senators, including Cicero. A last stand against the rule of the Triumvirs was made by the senate in Greece, but it ended in failure when the republican army led by Caesar's assassins was defeated by the combined forces of Octavian and Antony at Philippi (42 BC).

After their victory the Triumvirs divided the empire among themselves. Antony assumed control of the eastern provinces, Lepidus acquired Africa and Octavian ruled over Italy and the West. Shortly after the division of the empire, and while the civil war was continuing, the old antagonism between Octavian and Antony resurfaced. A decisive turn of events occurred in 37 BC when Octavian eliminated his republican opponents in the field and removed Lepidus, thereby becoming sole ruler of the West. Antony, on the other hand, made the fatal error of allying himself politically and personally with Cleopatra, the Greek queen of Egypt. Antony's decision to join forces with Cleopatra and allocate her parts of the empire that formerly belonged to Egypt alienated popular sentiment in Rome. Octavian quickly exploited the situation by denouncing his rival as the tool of a foreign monarch. In 32 BC Octavian persuaded the senate to declare war on Egypt and, a year later, his army defeated the combined forces of Antony and Cleopatra at Actium (an island off the west coast of Greece). In the following year Octavian invaded and conquered Egypt, which became a Roman province under his direct control.[31] Soon after his return to Rome, Octavian appeared before the senate and proclaimed his intention to relinquish his extraordinary powers and restore the republic to the senate and the people of Rome (27 BC). This shrewd move earned him a reputation as the restorer of the republic and, at the same time, legitimized his *de facto* control of the state. The senate and the assembly, in return, bestowed upon him a range of powers and titles that placed him in a unique position. Armed with these powers, Octavian, now known by the honorary title Augustus, emerged to surpass all other magistrates in authority and was designated *princeps civium Romanorum*, 'the first of the Roman citizens'. From the word *princeps* arose the term 'Principate', which evolved to describe the new form of government established by Octavian for the empire.[32]

5

THE LATE REPUBLIC:
THE SOURCES OF LAW

Introduction

We observed in the previous chapter that the later Republic witnessed Rome's rise as the dominant power in the Mediterranean world. This era featured Rome's territorial expansion and transformation from a small, closed, agrarian community into a commercial empire. Its archaic system of law, imbued with religious and ritualistic elements, was rigid in its application. Thus, it was bound to become stationary and habitually unresponsive to social change. Under the new socio-economic conditions that materialized in an increasingly complex society, it was vital to modify and extend the scope of the law. In response, Roman law broke through the barrier of formalism and was secularized and internationalized. It formed a highly flexible system that could constantly adapt to the requirements of social and commercial life.

The most important factors in this development encompassed the nascent contacts with other cultures and the increasingly intricate economic relations between Roman citizens and foreigners (*peregrini*). As the granting of Roman citizenship had not kept pace with Rome's expansion, an increasing mass of foreigners residing in Roman territory did not have Roman citizenship and therefore lacked access to the Roman *ius civile*.[1] A foreigner could not easily engage in legal transactions and, if aggrieved by another person, could not defend himself or prosecute a claim before the authorities of the city[2] unless he secured personal protection from a community member. The development of foreign trade and the proliferation of foreigners living in Rome prompted the need to formulate rules applicable to disputes between foreigners, and between foreigners and Romans. This entailed the emergence of a new body of law that was Roman in origin and nature, but lacked the formalism and rigidity of the *ius civile*. This body of law was designated *ius gentium* (the law of nations) and originated from the edicts of the *praetor peregrinus*, the new magistrate charged with jurisdiction over cases involving foreigners.[3] To a lesser extent, this law was also moulded by the edicts of the provincial governors whose jurisdiction embraced disputes between provincial Roman citizens and local community members, and occasionally cases concerning only foreigners. Attending to disputes involving people of diverse national backgrounds would have been difficult without employing rules based mainly on common sense, expediency and fairness, which were confirmed by general and prevalent usage among many communities.⁴ In contrast to the old *ius civile*, the *ius gentium* was characterized by its simplicity, adaptability and emphasis on substance rather than form. In this way, the *ius gentium* became one of the main channels whereby enlightened contemporary thinking, including Greek ideas and ethical principles, could infiltrate the system of Roman law.

However, this change of attitude did not entail relinquishment of the ancient principle concerning the restricted applicability of the Roman *ius civile*. As the office of the *praetor peregrinus* materialized, it induced a division in the law. The rights (*iura*) of citizens were recognized and protected before the old tribunal of the *praetor urbanus*, the magistrate in charge of the administration of the Roman domestic law. These rights were distinguished from those recognized and protected before the tribunal of the *praetor peregrinus*, the magistrate charged with jurisdiction over aliens. The rights within the province of the old tribunal were enforced by means of a *legis actio* and in accordance with the express terms of the Law of the Twelve Tables and subsequent legislative enactments. The other distinct rights were enforced through legal remedies introduced by the *praetor peregrinus* at his discretion and by virtue of his *ius edicendi*, the right to issue orders or administrative regulations that derived from his *imperium*. The peregrine praetor obviously enjoyed greater liberty than did his urban colleague, as no law limited his operations. Thus, when formulating remedies he could consider the new needs created by the ever-changing social and economic conditions. But where did he acquire the ideas that provided the basis of his solutions?

Although little information exists on the methods employed by the peregrine praetor in performing his functions, we may surmise that he adopted the *ius civile* when applicable to the relevant case. Moreover, the customary norms common to many nations must have been relevant to determining whether or not a claim was founded on *ius*. For example, a magistrate could easily fathom that many nations transferred titles to land and property by mere delivery and payment, and not by the formal methods familiar to Rome. This entailed an increasing recognition by jurisdictional magistrates of the validity of informal agreements or consensual contracts based on good faith (*bona fides*) in commercial transactions – contracts where Romans and foreigners alike could engage.⁵ However, an important fact to note is that when a magistrate addressed a dispute involving foreigners he had to bear in mind that his solutions must accord with what was considered proper and reasonable from a Roman citizen's viewpoint. Thus, the *ius gentium* might be described as a complex system of generally observed customs and rules embodying elements which the Romans regarded as reflecting the substance of *ius*, or law in a broad normative sense – in other words, 'that which was good and fair' (*bonum et aequum*).⁶

When an appeal was presented to the *praetor peregrinus*, the primary basis for legal redress was the magistrate's sense of what was right and equitable. The absence of any rigid rules in the procedure implemented by the peregrine praetor created sufficient elasticity for its adjustment to the demands of the relevant case. For that reason, not only foreigners but also Roman citizens increasingly relied on it as a means of resolving legal disputes. In time, however, the elastic technique of the peregrine praetor was adopted by the urban praetor when deciding cases between citizens that fell outside the scope of the existing positive law. At the same time, elements of the *ius gentium* entered the province of domestic Roman law (*ius proprium Romanorum*) through the urban praetor's edict. The transition to a more flexible system of procedure acquired legislative recognition with the *lex Aebutia* (late second century BC), although the recognition most likely occurred long before the enactment of that law. As a result of this development, the urban praetor was no longer bound by the old statutory forms of action (*legis actiones*) and had freedom to devise new remedies and corresponding procedural formulae to tackle *ad hoc* controversies engendered by novel socio-economic circumstances. Such measures were not restricted to the application of the laws in force, but could be used to modify or replace existing law. Although in principle neither praetor had legislative authority, they actually created new law by extensively engaging their right to regulate the forms of proceedings accepted in court. A new body of law emerged that incorporated the norms of private law derived from the edicts of the praetors and other magistrates: the *ius praetorium* or *ius honorarium* (because it proceeded from the holders of offices – *honores*). The *ius honorarium* did not conflict with the existing *ius civile* but functioned conjunctively by supporting, correcting and complementing it.[7] In this respect, it is often compared to English equity. However, unlike English common law and equity the *ius civile* and the *ius honorarium* did not operate as two separate systems administered in different courts, but were regarded as two sides of the same legal system.

The praetors were not solely responsible for the creation of the *ius honorarium*. Like all other magistrates, they were primarily soldiers and administrators whose duties often far surpassed in importance their legal activities. Generally, they were not legal experts and were essentially uninterested in the intellectual and scientific development of the law. This prompts the question of who demonstrated the techniques to them for producing the required legal innovations. As one might expect, responsibility for these advances is mainly attributed to the jurists (*iuris consulti* or *iurisprudentes*) who imparted advice on which the magistrates usually relied for formulating their edicts. The activities of the jurists essentially consisted of presenting of opinions (*responsa*) on difficult points of law to jurisdictional magistrates, judges and litigating parties, framing the formulae used in legal proceedings and drafting memoranda of transactions that could lead to future litigation. Their *responsa* were collated into books and, over time, an enormous mass of legal literature emerged to furnish the basis for the development of Roman law in the ensuing centuries.

After the introduction of the Law of the Twelve Tables, custom (*consuetudo*) ceased to operate as a direct source of law. However, it prevailed as a component in the formulation of the norms of positive law as found in the *leges*, the *edicta* of the magistrates and the interpretations of the jurists.[8] Thus, many forms of action devised by the praetors to address situations not covered by the existing *ius civile* reflected customary norms endorsed by public opinion and actually observed by the people (*opinio necessitatis*).[9] Similar considerations informed the jurists when formulating their *responsa*.

The edicts of the magistrates

As elaborated previously, an established principle of Roman law declared that the higher magistrates of the state (consuls, praetors, censors, aediles and others) had the authority to issue edicts (*edicta*) within their field of competence (*ius edicendi*). Diverse kinds of such edicts were formed: some merely gave public notice of certain facts, others contained orders that required the compliance of citizens and others delineated a programme of policy that a magistrate intended to pursue. In the field of Roman private law, important edicts were issued by the jurisdictional magistrates, especially by the praetors, aediles and provincial governors.

The praetor's edict was designed to provide some measure of certainty in the administration of justice and it enumerated the principles which the magistrate intended to employ in discharging his duty.[10] This edict was issued at the beginning of each successive praetor's year of office and was later called perpetual edict (*edictum perpetuum*) as its validity was intended to subsist throughout the magistrate's term of office. The praetor might issue further edicts during the year when certain occasions arose.[11] Theoretically, a newly elected praetor was free to introduce any measures he deemed appropriate, but in time an expectation surfaced that he would absorb most of his predecessor's edict and only initiate limited alterations. The portion of the *edictum perpetuum* that was retained from year to year was referred to as *edictum tralaticium*. No legal obligation was imposed on the praetor to abide by the directions elaborated in his edict as this was simply assumed. However, the collapse of good government in the closing years of the Republic dictated the enactment of the *lex Cornelia* (67 BC) that forbade the praetors' departure from their *edictum perpetuum*.

As observed earlier, a citizen could obtain remedies from the praetor by means of a *legis actio* and in conformity with the express terms of a statutory enactment. There also existed the possibility of appealing to the praetor for aid during an emergency in accordance with the terms of the edict. The edict equally created important limitations and extensions that the praetor declared to observe when granting a *legis actio*. But what was the source of the praetor's power to initiate measures in concord with principles not provided by the law in force at the time? The *ius* obtained through the methods provided by the praetor rested wholly on his *imperium*. This denoted the absolute authority, in military and civil matters, inherent in the higher magistrates of the state. We must recall that this *ius honorarium* did not initially resemble a system and the praetor, at best, only had the power to deny an action based on the law (*legis actio*), even if all forms were observed, if he thought that the granting of such an action was morally unacceptable. The *ius honorarium* only started to develop as a distinct system supplementary to the existing *ius civile* when the office of the *praetor peregrinus* emerged in the middle of the third century BC.

With the progressive complexity of socio-economic life, the praetor gradually recognized that new needs could be better satisfied by engaging a different method for administering the judicial powers entrusted to him. Thus, he began to devise novel remedies and procedural *formulae* to protect rights and interests that fell outside the scope of the existing *ius civile*. This process inspired the creation by the praetor of a new system of procedure known as the formulary or *per formulam* procedure.[12] The praetor availed himself of this procedure to recognize and enforce claims arising from novel socio-economic relationships that had no basis in the *ius civile*.[13] It must be assumed that innovations in the substantive law were gradual and organic. Whenever possible, a new *formula* was integrated into the system of actions recognized by the *ius civile*. In other cases, the praetor emancipated himself entirely from the positive law by instructing the judge to decide the case on the basis of the factual situation, thus in essence functioning as a law-maker. The praetor's edict contained model *formulae* for each promised remedy and for those that already existed to enforce the traditional *ius civile*. However, new remedies could be granted by the praetor at any time after the publication of the edict. The new remedies and relevant *formulae* were usually embodied in the edict published by his successor in the following year. In this way, the *formulae* used in specific types of cases became relatively fixed and the collection of established *formulae* was constantly augmented by new *formulae*.[14] As previously noted, the enactment of the *lex Aebutia* in the late second century BC was the turning point in the development of the formulary system. This law recognized the right of the praetor to invent new *fomulae* to deal with claims not covered by the traditional *ius civile*.

But how did the praetor choose which rights to protect? The main basis for this choice appears to have been the new social and ethical values generated by the conditions of the times. These values materialized in appropriate guidelines that emphasized the importance of fairness and honesty in business practices, accorded preference to substance over form in transactions and refused to uphold obligations arising from promises elicited by fraudulent means. An important factor was the growing role of contractual good faith (*bona fides*) as a legal concept relating to the enforcement by legal means of what had previously been viewed as merely social or moral obligations.[15] The classical jurists used the term *aequitas* (equity) when referring to the basis or the qualifying feature of praetorian measures granted on a case-by-case basis and promised in the edict.[16] There are two ways to understand the connection of equity with positive law: first, *aequitas* may be construed as the substance and intrinsic justification of the existing legal norms; second, it may be conceived as an objective ideal that the law aims to effectuate and which determines the creation of new legal norms and the modification of those that do not conform with society's sense of justice or fail to accomplish the requisite balance in human relations. This second understanding of *aequitas* served as the basis of the innovations produced by jurisdictional magistrates and jurists. However, according to classical jurists, what has positive force is not *aequitas* as such, but *ius*, or law in a broad sense. Thus, until *aequitas* is transfused into a positive norm it remains confined to a pre-legal sphere. Once this transfusion has occurred, *ius* has notable significance while *aequitas* exists as the matrix.[17] The incorporation of equity into the administration of the law is attributable to the praetorian edict and the interpretations of the jurists. This redressed the formalism and rigidity of the traditional *ius civile* and enabled the creation of new law that could fulfil the needs of a changing society.

It is germane to present a few examples to illustrate the techniques engaged by the praetor for surmounting the difficulties arising from the rigidity of the *ius civile*.

The idea that legal obligations could materialize from anything other than a strict form was strange to the original structure of Roman law established in the Law of the Twelve Tables. Such obligations could only arise from transactions executed in a few solemn forms and rites that had a predominantly public and partly sacred character. Consider *stipulatio*, for example. This formal transaction consisted of a solemn question posed by one party to the other as to whether the latter would render specific performance, followed by a solemn affirmative answer from the other party. This exchange of question and answer created an actionable obligation of the answering party under the *ius civile*. Circumstances could exist that made it unfair for the creditor to enforce the transaction. However, no remedy was provided by the *ius civile* in such a case. If the parties had observed all the prescribed formalities, the validity of the contract could not be questioned. To rectify the situation, the praetor could use his own authority to include an additional clause (*exceptio*) in the relevant *formula* that enabled the defendant to render the plaintiff's claim ineffective by showing grounds for denying judgment in the plaintiff's favour. When the *exceptio* was based on the allegation that the plaintiff had acted fraudulently (*dolo*), it was designated *exceptio doli*.[18] Granting exceptions was an ingenious device that enabled the praetor to deliver appropriate relief in individual cases without questioning the validity of the relevant legal rule. Thus the *exceptio doli* left the principle of the *stipulatio* intact, i.e. the obligation to act as one had promised by responding in a particular way to a specific question posed. The *form* of the transaction still created the legal obligation, although the recognition that intention had priority over form was implicit in accepting the *exceptio doli*.

An important distinction in the early Roman law of property existed between *res mancipi* and *res nec mancipi*. *Res mancipi* included land and buildings situated in Italy, slaves and draft animals, such as oxen and horses. All other objects were *res nec mancipi*. The ownership of *res mancipi* could be transferred only by means of a highly formal procedure called *mancipatio*.[19] If a *res mancipi* was transferred to someone in an informal manner, the transferee did not acquire title under the *ius civile*.[20] In such a case, if the transferee lost possession of the property he could not recover it from the person with the current holding. While retaining possession of the property he could be challenged by the transferor who remained the lawful owner (*dominus*). As economic relations grew more complex and formalism declined, the strictness of the law proved detrimental to many legitimate interests. To rectify the situation, the praetor intervened and placed the transferee in the factual position of a civil law owner. The property was then regarded as *in bonis* (hence the concept of 'bonitary' ownership) and such a 'bonitary' owner could acquire true ownership by *usucapio* (i.e. through lapse of a certain period of time).[21] If the bonitary owner lost possession of the property, he could recover it by means of the *actio Publiciana*.[22] This action was granted to all *bona fide* possessors in the process of acquiring ownership by *usucapio*, and was based on the fiction that the period required for obtaining the property by *usucapio* was completed. If the original owner endeavoured to claim the property, the bonitary owner could raise the defence of *exceptio rei venditae et traditae* (defence of a property sold and delivered by *traditio*),[23] or the *exceptio doli*. The praetor engaged these devices to create a new type of property right that supplemented those recognized under the traditional *ius civile* and this generated a considerable improvement in the Roman law of property.[24]

The law relating to intestate succession was another area where important changes were engendered by praetorian edicts. The sequence of intestate succession under the old *ius civile* was entwined with its family system. The Law of the Twelve Tables provided that in the first instance only *sui heredes* were entitled to inherit, i.e. those persons who fell under the *potestas* of the deceased and who became *sui iuris* at his death. These included the wife who was married *cum manu* to the testator[25] and his children (both natural and adopted). The estate of the testator accrued to all the *sui heredes* and they were compelled to inherit whether interested or not.[26] If no *sui heredes* existed, the deceased's estate transferred to the nearest agnatic relatives (*proximi agnati*). Under the social and economic conditions of the later Republic, the earlier importance of the institution of *patria potestas* faded and thus the rules governing intestate succession proved increasingly inadequate to meet practical requirements. The main defect of the old system was that emancipated children and the *sui iuris* spouse were excluded from succession. To ameliorate this problem the praetor introduced a series of edicts by which he granted certain persons, who otherwise could not inherit, possession of the inheritance (*bonorum possessio*) and accorded them preference over those who were heirs under the *ius civile*.[27] To ensure execution of the *bonorum possessio* decree, a *bonorum possessor* not in actual possession of the estate could obtain the praetor's grant of an *interdictum quorum bonorum* that commanded the holder of the estate to transfer it to the *bonorum possessor*. The latter could then acquire ownership of the estate in one year by means of *usucapio*. Although the praetor could not render anybody a civil law heir, as he was not a legislator, he could place an individual in the position of an heir with virtually the same result. This method enabled the praetor to develop a new system of intestate succession that finally superseded the original system under the traditional *ius civile*.

The above examples present a sketch of the techniques used by the praetor to invent not merely supplementary but often superseding *iura* that galvanized the development of the *ius honorarium*. The descriptions expose two interrelated characteristics of the Roman legal system: a pervasive dualism, perhaps even a dialectic relationship between old and new, and a tendency towards gradual adaptation. There is the dualism between *ius civile* and *ius honorarium*, between an adherence to past forms and an admirable ingenuity in designing ways to address new situations and problems. This system is even more remarkable as both the aspects of respecting the past and adapting to the new were combined in the praetor. The praetor used all his creativity to construct devices that tackled the problems arising from novel socio-economic circumstances, and also acted as a guarantor of the basic forms and principles of the old law. Such a system seemed to satisfy the people's desire to believe that things remained the same as long as they were ascribed the same labels. It created the comfortable illusion that nothing had really changed.

The reluctance to abandon the fundamental principles of the traditional legal system is aptly illustrated by the institution of the *patria potestas*, which was recognized by the Romans as a characteristic element of their system. Despite the enormous inconveniences generated by this institution, it survived until as late as the fourth century AD. Devices were designed to mitigate its unwanted consequences in a new era that no longer required a family structure based on the traditional *patria potestas*; yet, these devices did not affect the essence of that institution. Although several aspects were modified, like the power to prevent the marriage of a daughter, it had a longevity that virtually resembled that of Roman law. The practice of the praetor of granting exceptions to defendants illuminates the same tendency for observing the old rules. Granting exceptions was a cautious device that retained the essence of the rules, while providing relief in a particular case or type of case. Indeed, classifying a particular case as exceptional would appear to confirm the validity of the relevant rule. Similarly, the use of fiction helped the victim of bad faith or error in cases where the requirements of strict law were not fulfilled. However, it did not diminish the validity of the legal principles that applied under the old *ius civile*. For example, the fiction of a completed *usucapio* in the *actio Publiciana* did not affect the basic principles of the *ius civile* relating to the acquisition of ownership over *res mancipi*. Fictions and other praetorian devices facilitated the cautious and gradual adaptation of the rules insofar as this was deemed necessary, but did not appear to change any elements on the normative level. On closer observation, it is not difficult to discern that these devices produced important changes to the law. This evokes the Hegelian idea that a change in quantity may lead to a change in quality. Although the form of this change suggested that only a minor detail of a rule was affected, a major principle of the Roman *ius civile* was actually rendered ineffectual or set aside. The relationship between the *ius civile* and the *ius honorarium* (or between law and equity) clearly exhibits the Romans' commitment to the two notions of stability and change, of preservation of the past and efficient adaptation to new needs.

The practice of issuing edicts prevailed throughout the late Republic and early Empire. During the Empire, the praetorian initiatives were increasingly rare and Emperor Hadrian ordered the jurist Salvius Iulianus to compose a final form of the praetorian and aedilician edicts (*c.* AD 130).[28] As a result, the content of the praetorian and aedilician edicts became crystallized as established law and the position of the praetor as a source of law ceased.[29] Thereafter, the *ius honorarium* could only develop through the juristic interpretation of the maxims and institutions elaborated in this final *edictum perpetuum*, or by imperial initiatives. The republican forms of procedure were gradually replaced by new methods of administering justice in concord with the existing political conditions. This prompted the withering of the distinction between *ius civile* and *ius honorarium*, and the two bodies of law became inextricably fused.

Legislation

As elaborated previously, during the Republic three politically effective assemblies operated in Rome: the *comitia centuriata*, the *comitia tributa* and the *concilium plebis*. Each assembly performed electoral, judicial and legislative functions.[30] Originally, only the laws (*leges*) enacted by the *comitia centuriata* and the *comitia tributa* were binding on all citizens, while the resolutions of the *concilium plebis* (*plebiscita*) were only binding on the plebeians. However, in 287 BC the socio-political developments associated with the struggle of the orders provoked the declaration that *plebiscita* were binding on all citizens by virtue of the *lex Hortensia de plebiscitis*.[31] After the enactment of this law, the *concilium plebis* gained importance and gradually became the legislative assembly *par excellence* while the *comitia centuriata* remained the senior elective assembly. As the great majority of the statutes enacted after 287 BC were passed by the *concilium plebis* on the proposal of a tribune of the plebs, the *plebiscita* were commonly referred to as *leges*.

The citizens passed statutes presented by a magistrate empowered to convene and preside over a popular assembly (*ius agendi cum populo*).[32] The magistrate's proposal was called *rogatio legis* and the resultant laws were identified as *leges rogatae*.[33] Custom and eventually law dictated that the full text of the proposed measure must be posted twenty-four days before its formal submission to the assembly (*promulgatio, promulgare rogationem*). During this interval, the magistrate could hold informal meetings of citizens (*contiones*) where speeches in favour and against the measure were delivered. Throughout this period the proposing magistrate remained in charge of the measure, and did not alter the text unless persuaded to do so.[34] Once the bill was presented to the assembly it could not be modified; the assembly could either accept (*iubere rogationem*) or reject the bill as a whole and in the precise form it was delivered by the magistrate. A bill that was passed (*rogatio lata est*) became a *lex* following a formal announcement of the assembly's decision (*renuntiatio*) by the presiding magistrate. After their passing, laws were inscribed on tablets of wood, copper or stone and retained in the state treasury (*aerarium populi romani*) under the supervision of the *quaestors*.[35] According to tradition, a law passed by the people could not come into force until it was approved by the senate (*patrum auctoritas*).[36] This rule was reversed by the *lex Publilia Philonis* of 339 BC, which stipulated that the *patrum auctoritas* must be issued before, not after, a legislative proposal was submitted to the people. Thereafter, laws usually had immediate effect following the formal announcement of the assembly's decision endorsing the magistrate's proposal.

A statute was composed of three parts: (i) the preamble (*praescriptio legis*) that embodied the name of the magistrate who had proposed it (and after whom it was named), the place and time of its enactment, and the name of the century (*centuria*) or tribe (*tribus*) that had cast the first vote in the proceedings;[37] (ii) the text of the law (*rogatio*) that was usually divided into sections; and (iii) the ratification of the law (*sanctio*). The *sanctio* specified the penalties that would be imposed if the law was violated and stated the rules governing the relation between the new statute and earlier and future legislation.[38] A distinction was drawn between 'perfect laws' (*leges perfectae*), 'imperfect laws' or laws without any sanction at all (*leges imperfectae*) and 'less than perfect laws' (*leges minus quam perfectae*). Acts performed in violation of a perfect law were deemed null and void.[39] The infringement of an imperfect law, on the other hand, did not affect the validity of the relevant act.[40] Similarly, when a less than perfect law was violated, the act itself remained valid but the transgressor was liable to punishment. Laws containing unrelated or superfluous provisions were designated *leges saturae* or *per saturam* and were forbidden under early law. The *lex Caecilia Didia* of 98 BC renewed this prohibition.

In the republican period the enactment of private law rules by formal legislation was exceptional. Changes in this field were effected primarily by means of praetorian action and the new procedure of the *formula* revealed new opportunities. The great majority of the statutes passed during this period pertained to matters of constitutional and criminal law, or immediate political concerns such as the distribution of land, the granting of extraordinary honours and release from debt. As a whole, legislation was employed to deal with specific problems rather than to establish the rules and principles governing social policy or constitutional arrangements in a comprehensive and permanent manner. It served the purpose of adapting the structure of the government and law to changed socio-political and economic conditions; legislation was never engaged to radically alter this structure. Statutes were enacted, for example, to create new magistracies or to define the nature of public crimes and the procedures for dealing with them. In the field of private law, statutes were relied on as a means of supplementing or limiting private *iura*, or instigating changes in civil procedure when juristic interpretation or magisterial action were deemed unable to produce the desired effect. For instance, legislation was employed to introduce new *legis actiones*, such as the *legis actio per condictionem*,[41] or to extend the scope of existing ones.[42]

Besides the *lex Aebutia* noted earlier, a number of other important statutes relating to private law were enacted during this period. The *lex Aquilia*, a plebiscite probably passed in 286 BC, prescribed the general rules of liability for unlawful damage to property and obliged the wrongdoer to pay a fine to the owner.[43] The *lex Atinia* (probably enacted in the second century BC) excluded stolen objects (*res furtivae*) from *usucapio* (the acquisition of ownership through possession of an object for a certain prescribed period of time). The *lex Laetoria* (passed early in the second century BC) aspired to protect persons under twenty-five years of age from fraud. The *lex Cincia de donis et muneribus* (204 BC) prohibited gifts in excess of a certain (unknown) amount, with the exception of those in favour of near relatives and certain privileged persons. The *lex Voconia* (*c.* 169 BC) imposed limitations upon the testamentary capacity of women. The *lex Falcidia* (40 BC) specified the amount of legacies that could be bequeathed.

The role of the senate in the legislative field should be clarified. As noted, under the republican constitution the senate had no direct power of legislation. Its main function was merely to act as an advisory council to the magistrates, who were the executives of the state. However, in practice, the senate exercised substantial control over the legislative functions of the assemblies by virtue of its influence over the magistrates. Ordinarily, the senate thoroughly discussed the drafts of legislative proposals before their presentation to the people and, if necessary, amended these drafts in accordance with the views of the senate's majority. This finally approved draft would then be incorporated in a resolution (*senatus consultum*) advising the magistrate concerned to submit it to the assembly, whose subsequent action virtually amounted to nothing more than a formal ratification of the terms of the *senatus consultum*. Although magistrates had the liberty to ignore the senate's advice,[44] they would normally defer to that authority. They entertained a deep loyalty and respect for this body of which they were part. The few magistrates who were less compelled to effectuate the senate's wishes had to ponder the short life of their own authority and the dependence of their future careers on their colleagues' goodwill. Another factor to consider was that they might be rendered criminally accountable for abuse of office after their year had expired and face a jury composed of the very men they had affronted.[45]

In the last century of the Republic, when the Roman state was embroiled in a political and administrative crisis and the influence of the assemblies declined, it sometimes happened that a legislative proposal sanctioned by the senate was not presented to the people, but immediately entered into force. Moreover, the senate at times assumed the power to declare statutes null and void based on some alleged irregularity or violation of an established constitutional principle.[46] As the government transformed into the bureaucratic administration of a world empire during the first century AD, the mode of creating law by vote of the people gradually discontinued. The legislative function passed to the senate, whose enactments acquired the full force of laws. Thus, in practice, statutes and senatorial decrees were accorded parity as sources of law. This rendered the *senatus consultum* an important vehicle of legislation, although it seems unlikely that any specific constitutional action was implemented to equate *senatus consulta* with *leges*.

The jurisprudence of the late Republic

As elaborated previously, in the earliest period of Roman history knowledge of the law and the rules governing legal procedure was confined to the college of the pontiffs, whose members were recruited solely from the patrician class. After the Law of the Twelve Tables was enacted (*c.* 450 BC) and the system of *legis actiones* emerged, the authoritative interpretation of statutory law and the conduct of the actions at law remained within the province of the pontiffs. The pontiffs sustained their role of presenting opinions to jurisdictional magistrates and litigants on questions of law.[47] Gradually, an increasing number of *nobiles*, members of Rome's wealthy senatorial class, engaged in furnishing legal advice without being members of the *collegium pontificum*. By the end of the second century BC, secular jurists (*iurisprudentes* or *iuris consulti*) had supplanted the original interpreters of the law. These jurists were largely responsible for the development of Roman legal science. They responded constructively to new intellectual developments, particularly the influx of Greek science and philosophy, which occurred around the same time as these jurists appeared. The jurists also evaluated the changed socio-economic and political conditions. The deriving analyses inspired Roman law's most characteristic features: its pragmatism and flexibility, as well as its clearness and intellectual superiority to any previously known body of rules. It is important to note that the contributions of the jurists are not evenly distributed over the whole field of law; private law and civil procedure patently dominate, whereas many areas of public law were never the object of the same intensive analysis and constructive development.

In the later republican period, the political and economic power of the old patrician nobility markedly diminished as the scepticism towards the old state religion concurrently increased. As usual, materialistic and ideological aspects were combined to form at least a seemingly unitary explanation. The legitimation of the legal authority of priestly jurisprudence did not vanish, but there was some very symptomatic criticism. Quite obviously, a new method of legitimation had to be devised, and the answer was clear. As Cicero declared: *ius civile in artem redigendum*.[48] The reference to a scientific method was engaged as the basis for the legitimation of the authority of legal science.

Scholars generally endorse the assertion that since the second century BC Greek philosophy exercised a strong influence on the Roman elite that encompassed the jurists. There is also agreement that the intellectual methods and tools created by Greek science within the framework of logic, grammar and rhetoric became indispensable elements in the education of men from the upper classes in Rome. However, discord exists over the more precise question as to how the evolution of Roman legal science and Roman law was definitely influenced by the Greek theory of the formation of scientific concepts. The theory of science prevailing in that era embraced two principal models: (i) the model of system building *per genus et differentiam specificam* (the Aristotelian classification); and (ii) the rhetoric model, known as 'topical' argumentation, where Aristotelian syllogism was inferred from premises (*topoi*) that were considered acceptable, true or plausible by a certain audience. Romanists have intensely debated the impact of these two models. Many scholars believe that these scientific models had considerable importance, but they did not significantly alter the general perspective of the jurists' activities.[49] Other scholars argue that either model may be used as a general explanatory scheme for the Roman lawyers' methodology.[50]

One might contend that many elements that were earlier construed as expressions of Greek influence must be classified as ideological *loci communes*, i.e. very general dicta that were 'in the air' and that cannot be interpreted as expressions of a real and serious exchange of thoughts. The same cautious judgment must attach to many statements previously quoted to prove that the methods of Greek science were consciously and systematically employed by the Roman jurists. With a few exceptions, the leading jurists belonged to the senatorial aristocracy and were actively involved in social and political life. Rhetoric and some notions of both logic and grammar were routine elements of a Roman gentleman's education. However, expert knowledge and 'professional' work in these fields were not matters for gentlemen but for schoolmasters, frequently Greeks, slaves or freedmen. The chief tasks of the Roman aristocracy were located in statecraft and law. The practice of a lawyer did not imply the use of flawless logical conclusions, the sophisticated methods of interpretation invented by grammarians or the stratagems of orators. It meant exercising mature judgment and practical wisdom to tackle problems arising from individual cases, while considering the position adopted by earlier jurists in similar past cases.

There are two types of juristic method: the *empirical* or *casuistic* and the *deductive*. The Roman jurists were typical representatives of the former method. When dealing with legal problems, they resorted primarily to topical rather than axiomatic argument. If a legal rule or concept is formed by logical reasoning from basic principles or axioms, it invokes axiomatic argument. Topical or problem reasoning, on the other hand, occurs when one proceeds from the case to identify the premises that would support a solution, and then formulates guiding principles and concepts as a basis for attaining a solution. The rules and concepts devised in this manner are not rigid and inviolable but are subject to change, depending on the circumstances of the relevant case. Moreover, it is generally believed that the Roman jurists reached their conclusions intuitively. This intuitive grasp of the law is attributed to the Romans' innate sense for legal matters, and to the jurists' experience with the everyday practice of the law.

It seems correct to say that one should not envisage Roman jurisprudence as the model of a systematic or axiomatic theory. At the same time, one should not construe it as a merely pragmatic, unprincipled case law or believe that Roman decision-making was based solely on free and creative intuition. Indeed, a unique quality of Roman legal science is that it did not stop at a purely pragmatic and precise casuistry. The greatest achievement of the Roman jurists was their ability to extend beyond the accidental elements of the relevant case to illuminate the essential legal problem as a *quaestio iuris*. By means of the dialectical method[51] adopted from the Greeks, the jurists learned to divide juridically relevant facts into *genera* and *species*. They defined these facts and distinguished and categorized juridical concepts. At the same time, they were aware of the logical syllogism (or reasoned conclusions) and learned to construct legal concepts in a deductive manner. Moreover, familiarity with Greek philosophical ethics inspired awareness of the sociological function of law. As a result, the jurists attached more emphasis to arguments based on equity and other general guiding principles.[52] Naturally, the jurists required time to assimilate and fully engage the new intellectual methods and tools. It is quite likely that the relevant thought process varied with the individual problem as well as with the individual jurist. Under these conditions, legal science and literature were gradually moulded from their original raw material: the interpretations of laws and legal remedies that were honed by practical experience and sorted and recorded. In this way, the conclusions of a new science were reduced to common denominators. Further, the literary presentation of its professional knowledge was gradually rationalized and systematized. The effect of systematization is easily observed when appraising the social impact of the systematic efforts of the Roman jurists. It is clear that the tendency towards systematization not only allowed them to present their casuistic approach in a more simple and elegant manner, but also helped them to alter their decision-propositions. An improvement of a system implies the possibility of forming *better* decisions. Thus, one can understand the importance of the systematic thinking of Roman lawyers. A change of methodology was part of their efforts to formulate better decisions. The improvement in decisions was connected with the requirement for integration in the growing empire and its consequent socio-structural changes.

The republican jurists were mainly absorbed with presenting opinions on questions of law posed by private citizens, jurisdictional magistrates and judges (*respondere*), providing assistance to litigants with special attention to preparing the forms necessary for filing a suit, and also presumably briefing the orators who would act as advocates (*agere*), and drafting legal documents, such as contracts and wills, designed to preserve a person's interests in legal transactions by protecting them against certain eventualities (*cavere*).[53] The consultative activities of the jurists were related to the leadership provided to the people by the aristocracy. Thus, the jurists received no remuneration for their work as they considered it their duty to assist the citizens who consulted them with legal problems. Although legal science did not become a profession for earning a living, it provided an outlet for wealthy and educated citizens aspiring to distinguish themselves in social and political life. As the jurists acquired respect and honour through their activities, they could extend their influence among fellow citizens and, by widening the circle of their friends and dependants, win their way to high political office. This especially pertained to those jurists who did not enjoy inherited power and prestige as members of noble Roman families.[54]

Undoubtedly, the most important activity of the jurists was formulating (*responsa*) on points of law. A praetor might consult a jurist for advice on matters relating to the drafting of his edict and, especially, on whether new types of remedies should be available to afford relief under certain circumstances. Similarly, judges and advocates often relied on the advice of jurists for dealing with difficult legal and procedural issues. As the settling of disputes was an extremely technical process, the role of the jurists in litigation became increasingly important.[55] The opinions of prominent jurists had great authority, but no actual binding force. Initially, these opinions were delivered orally but over time they were reduced to writing. Since the second century BC, leading jurists produced collections of *responsa* that had been devised and applied in practice. These collections were designed to facilitate the administration of justice, which in Rome was not organized by the state. Although very few of the *responsa* created by republican jurists survive, it is surmised that in many cases they simply proposed the application of a specific legal norm when the circumstances alleged were proven to the judge's satisfaction. If the jurist concluded that the matter could not be resolved on the basis of an existing rule, he fashioned a new rule of law that could then be ratified by the verdict of a jurisdictional magistrate.[56] As noted, the jurists are credited for essentially adapting Roman law to new conditions and this particularly encompasses the development of the rules and institutions constituting the *ius praetorium* or *ius honorarium*. Besides exercising an indirect influence through their *responsa*, many jurists played a direct role in shaping the principles enforced by the magistrates. This role derived from their sitting on the *consilium*, the advisory council that surrounded the magistrate. Moreover, some leading jurists had a direct opportunity for implementing their own ideas as they were holders of magisterial office or members of the senate, the powerful constitutional body advising the magistrates.

Besides the practical activities outlined above, the jurists were occupied by two further tasks that were instrumental in the development of the law: the education of those aspiring to enter the practice of law, and the composition of legal works. Legal education in Rome had a largely practical orientation; there were no theoretical or academic legal training or educational institutions where law was formally taught.[57] On completion of his basic education, a young man would join the household of a jurist as an apprentice. He would follow his master on daily business and observe him imparting legal advice, drafting legal documents and assisting clients in legal proceedings.[58] Students were often invited to discuss difficult points of law and formulate arguments in favour of or against solutions proposed by earlier jurists (*disputatio fori*). Over time, the jurists combined the teaching of law (*docere*) with the writing (*scribere*) of commentaries or treatises on different branches of the law. Moreover, juristic opinions were collated into books and, gradually, a large body of legal literature materialized. As stated earlier, the emergence of legal literature is associated with the influence of the Greek culture and science on the Roman aristocracy that embodied the jurists. Unfortunately, only a few remnants of the writings of the republican jurists were preserved. Thus, there is scant accurate information on the relevant intellectual processes and achievements of individual jurists. Many jurists are known to the modern world simply by name.

A prominent jurist of the later republican period was Quintus Mucius Scaevola, *pontifex maximus* and consul in 95 BC. Scaevola is declared to have been the first jurist who endeavoured to systematize the existing law in a scientific fashion.[59] Unlike earlier jurists, he did not confine himself to the discussion of isolated cases or questions of law. Rather, he made great efforts towards a higher level of generalization and ventured to introduce more definition and division. In his comprehensive treatise on the *ius civile*, he assembled related legal phenomena and principles under common headings. He also distinguished the various forms of appearance of these broader categories. For instance, he first defined the general features of possession, tutorship and so on, and then described their various individual forms (*genera*) existing in the legal system.[60] He also seems to have written a book that featured brief definitory statements (*horoi*) indicating the decisive factual moment (*horos*) of a certain legal consequence or decision.[61] While earlier jurists often seemed to merely list examples when attempting to establish the meaning of a word, Scaevola invented a more general approach.[62] His work was an important step forward as it introduced a scheme of law conceived as a logically connected whole alongside the collections of precedents and isolated legal rules. It should be noted that Scaevola, like other leading jurists of his time, was influenced by the Stoic philosophy. Compared to rival schools, the Stoics placed far greater emphasis on definitions and classifications, analysis and systematizing that pertained to human concerns rather than abstract mathematics. Scaevola is also attributed with formulating certain standard legal clauses and presumptions, such as the *cautio Muciana* (a promise by a legatee that he would return the legacy if he acted against the attached condition)[63] and the *praesumptio Muciana* (the presumption that all the property a married woman possessed was furnished by her husband, until the contrary was proved). As governor of the province of Asia, Scaevola also composed a provincial edict (*edictum provinciale*) that was used as a model by other provincial governors. Scaevola's work had enduring influence and commentaries on it were still being written as late as the second century AD.

Other distinguished jurists of the later republican period included the following: Manius Manilius, consul in 149 BC, whose work *venalium vendendorum leges* ('conditions of sale for things capable of being sold'), mainly elaborated model *formulae* relating to contracts of sale;[64] M. Porcius Cato Censorius, consul in 195 BC and censor in 184 BC, whose work *de agricultura* ('On Agriculture') comprised forms and precedents for drafting agrarian contracts; the latter's son, M. Porcius Cato Licinianus, who authored a celebrated treatise on the *ius civile* (*de iuris disciplina*);[65] M. Junius Brutus, praetor in 142 BC, who wrote books on the *ius civile*;[66] Gaius Aquilius Gallus, praetor in 66 BC, who introduced the action and exception of *dolus* (a term that merges the ideas of fraud, abuse of right and the general concept of tort)[67] and the *stipulatio Aquiliana*;[68] C. Trebatius Testa, a friend of Cicero's, whose work on the *ius civile* was highly regarded by the classical jurists;[69] P. Alfenus Varus, consul in 39 BC, who produced an extensive work (*Digesta*) in forty books;[70] Servius Sulpicius Rufus, consul in 51 BC, whose writings included an important commentary on the praetorian edict;[71] and P. Rutilius Rufus, consul in 105 BC, who devised the bankruptcy procedure described by Gaius (*actio Rutiliana*).[72] Only a few scattered and fragmentary traces of these jurists' works survive through the writings of jurists from the classical period embodied in the Digest of Justinian.[73]

6

THE LATE REPUBLIC: THE ADMINISTRATION OF JUSTICE

Civil procedure: the formulary system

As elaborated in Chapter 3, the earliest form of civil procedure in Roman law was the *legis actio*, so called because the only actions allowed were those created by statutes (*leges*), or closely adapted to the language of statutes by the pontiffs. Under the changed socio-economic conditions of the late Republic, the *legis actio* system gradually fell into disfavour. This mainly derived from its exaggerated formalism and the prominence of a new and more flexible system: the formulary (*per formulam*) procedure. The formulary procedure was probably first introduced by the *praetor peregrinus* as a way of dealing with disputes involving foreigners. Its application was subsequently extended to cases where both parties to a dispute were Roman citizens and the *legis actiones* were not available under the *lex Aebutia* passed in the second century BC. The reform of civil procedure was completed by the *leges Iuliae iudiciorum publicorum et privatorum* of Augustus in 17–16 BC.[1] One of these laws abolished the *legis actio* procedure, except in cases that fell within the jurisdiction of the centumviral court and in certain cases involving a threat of damage to another person's property (*damnum infectum*).[2]

Under the new system, the praetor was free to go beyond the strict letter of the law and accept or refuse a claim on the grounds of what he deemed right and equitable. He did not accomplish this by introducing new legal rights (as indicated earlier, the magistrates had no legislative powers). Rather, he granted the claimant an action and promised to grant a remedy if the facts forming the basis of the claim were validated in the subsequent trial. As in Roman law a right was regarded as a legal right only if it was enforceable by a recognized process of law, by introducing new remedies the praetor was actually creating new legal rights. The praetor's extensive use of the right to regulate the forms of proceedings accepted in court enabled him to eliminate or reduce the unwanted effects of the antiquated rituals attached to the old *ius civile*. At the same time, he created a supplementary body of law based on common sense, expediency and fairness, the *ius honorarium* or *ius praetorium*, capable of supporting ethical and technical change.

The formulary procedure derives its name from the *formula*, a written document containing an exposition of the dispute between litigants and instructions from the praetor to the judge (*iudex*) assigned to try the case. In contrast to the *legis actio* procedure, where the plaintiff selected the relevant *legis actio* at his own risk, the magistrate at the request of the party concerned issued the formula in the formulary procedure. When it was requisite to introduce a new *formula* to address hitherto unfamiliar facts, the praetor did so by issuing the appropriate decree in his edict. Thus, he established various *formulae* that were moulded by the nature and circumstances of the dispute, and each had its own wording. The forms of action connected with these *formulae* were termed *actiones honorariae*, i.e. actions derived from the *ius honorarium*.[3] The vast majority of the *actiones honorariae* were praetorian creations, although several important actions were created by lesser magistrates such as the curule aediles. The *actiones honorariae* were distinguished from the *actiones civiles*, i.e. the actions originating from the *ius civile*. Several *actiones civiles* were established by legislation, whereas others crystallized from the creative activity of the jurists. When a *formula* pertained to an *actio civilis*, it was designated *formula in ius concepta*, in contradistinction to a *formula in factum concepta* that related to an *actio honoraria*.[4]

The principal forms of action employed by the praetor to deal with cases not covered by the existing law were the *actiones in factum*, the *actiones utiles* and the *actiones fictitiae*. An *actio in factum* (action based on the facts of a particular case) was an 'ad hoc' new action granted to an aggrieved person in a case where neither the *ius civile* nor the praetorian edict were useful and the case situation justified the furnishing of a remedy on equitable grounds. When such an action was allowed, the actual facts of the case were incorporated into a new formula (*formula in factum concepta*).[5] An *actio utilis* ('adapted' or 'analogous' action)[5] was devised by the praetor to tackle a case not covered by the existing law that was analogous to another case with an available legal remedy. Consider the following example: under the *lex Aquilia* (early third century BC), an action was available in a case where a person caused injury to another by directly attacking *vi et armis* the latter's body or property. But the statute did not encompass cases where the injury was caused indirectly, such as when an animal was frightened off a precipice by shouts. However, in such a case the praetor could grant an action (*actio utilis quasi ex lege Aquilia*) to the injured party by adapting the *actio legis Aquiliae*.[6] Related to the *actio utilis* was the *actio fictitia* (action based on a fiction), which enabled the praetor to extend the operation of an existing action by using a fiction, so that a particular case not covered by the relevant action was placed within its scope. The relevant *formula* instructed the *iudex* to assume that certain facts were present or absent in the presented case, depending on the circumstances of the particular case. For example, if the parties to a dispute were not citizens of Rome, they could access certain actions of the *ius civile* (e.g. the action for theft: *actio furti*) through the addition to the relevant *formula* of the phrase 'as if they were Roman citizens'. Another example of an *actio fictitia* is the *actio Publiciana*. As mentioned earlier, this action enabled a person to reclaim a *res mancipi* when they had acquired it in an informal manner (e.g. by mere *traditio*) and lost possession. Even though they had not yet obtained title, this action was available if they proved that the property was acquired under conditions that placed them in the position of acquiring ownership by *usucapio* (i.e.

by remaining in undisputed possession of the property for a certain period of time). This action was an *actio fictitia* as it fictitiously presumed the completion of the period of *usucapio*.[7]

The formulary system featured an important division of actions that had a correlation with the judge's discretion: the division between *actiones stricti iuris* and *actiones bonae fidei*. In actions *stricti iuris* the relevant *formula* had to be strictly construed and the judge could only consider the matters it contained. This category embodied actions based on unilateral contracts, such as the *stipulatio*[8] where the promisor was bound to the precise object promised.[9] On the other hand, the actions *bonae fidei* presented the judge with a greater latitude of discretion, whereby he could take into equitable consideration all facts relative to the case whether or not these were stated in the *formula*. This power was granted by the praetor through appending the clause *ex fide bona* (in good faith) to the *formula*. In *bonae fidei* actions the judge could scrutinize the true intentions of the parties. He could consider any equitable defences, even if these were not expressly pleaded, as the *formula* in these cases instructed the judge to ascertain what the defendant ought to do or give *ex bona fide* and to condemn accordingly. Actions *bonae fidei* encompassed those arising from real or consensual contracts, such as *emptio venditio* (sale), *locatio conductio* (hire), *mandatum* (mandate) and *societas* (partnership). During the later republican period, contracts where the parties' obligations were determined according to the requirements of good faith emerged to play an essential part in economic life.[10]

The *formula* as such was composed of various clauses or sub-divisions, but not all had to exist in every *formula*. According to Gaius, the clauses that normally appeared in a formula were the *demonstratio*, the *intentio*, the *condemnatio* and the *adiudicatio*.[11] In addition, the appointment of the judge (*nominatio iudicis*) was always inserted at the commencement of each *formula*. The *demonstratio* usually appeared at the beginning of the *formula* (directly after the appointment of the judge) and constituted a concise statement of the facts or circumstances on which the claim was based. This part of the *formula* always began with the word '*quod*': inasmuch (e.g. 'inasmuch as the plaintiff deposited a silver table in the care of the defendant . . . ').[12] Next appeared the *intentio* that formed the most important part of the *formula* as it set forth the precise claim or demand of the plaintiff. It started with the phrase '*si paret*' or '*quidquid paret*': 'if it appears', 'whatever it appears'. Depending on whether or not the object of the claim was clearly identified, an *intentio* could be determined (*certa*) or undetermined (*incerta*). An example of an *intentio certa* would read as follows: 'If it appears that the defendant ought to pay the plaintiff the sum of 1,000 sestercii . . . '. On the other hand, an *intentio incerta* would be worded in this manner: 'whatever it appears that the defendant ought to pay to the plaintiff . . . ' In actions relating to the enforcement of a personal right (*actiones in personam*), the *intentio* contained the names of both the plaintiff and the defendant. In actions pertaining to the enforcement of a real right (*actiones in rem*) only the name of the plaintiff appeared (e.g. 'if it appears that the slave belongs to Aulus Agerius in accordance with civil law . . . '). The third part of the *formula* was the *condemnatio*, which delegated to the judge the power to condemn or acquit the defendant. It is significant that the *condemnatio* was always directed at an amount of money (*condemnatio pecuniaria*), which might be determined (*certa*) or undetermined (*incerta*). In the latter case, the judge was authorized to use his discretion in specifying the amount of money owed.[13] The *condemnatio* was replaced by the *adiudicatio* in actions relating to the division of common property (*actio communi dividundo*), or the division of property among co-heirs (*actio familiae erciscundae*), or the determination of the boundaries of land (*actio finium regundorum*). The *adiudicatio* was a component of the *formula* that authorized the judge to effect a division and to determine an award.[14] It was usually worded in this style: 'whatever part ought to be adjudged to any one of the parties, do you, judge, adjudge it.' A *formula* always included an *intentio* and a *condemnatio* (or *adiudicatio*). Exceptionally, actions concerned with preliminary matters upon which a subsequent lawsuit depended (*actiones praeiudiciales*) only included an *intentio* and not a *condemnatio*. For example, a patron seeking to sue his freedman for failing to perform his duties could initiate a preliminary action to determine whether the defendant was actually a freedman. Such an action was not concerned with the condemnation of the defendant but with simply providing an answer to the question raised.[15]

Besides the standard clauses outlined above, a *formula* occasionally contained additional clauses such as reservations (*praescriptiones*) and one or more defences (*exceptiones*) and counter-defences (*replicationes*) raised by the defendant and the plaintiff respectively. The *praescriptio* was an extraordinary clause that a litigant could elect to have inserted in the *formula* (directly after the appointment of the judge and before the *intentio*) when he wished to precisely limit the extent of the claim. Two kinds of *praescriptiones* were distinguished: the *praescriptio* in favour of the plaintiff (*praescriptio pro actore*) and the *praescriptio* in favour of the defendant (*praescriptio pro reo*). A *praescriptio pro actore* was applied, for instance, in a case where the plaintiff sued for an instalment of a debt while retaining his right to sue at a later date for further instalments. The *praescriptio* in such a case recited: 'let the action be only for such things as are already due'.[16] A *praescriptio pro reo* was applied, for example, when the defendant wished to express the reservation that a decision in the present case would have a prejudicial effect on the determination in a more important case (*praescriptio praeiudicii*). However, this form of *praescriptio* fell into disuse from an early period and was replaced by the *exceptio*. The latter was a clause in the *formula* inserted by the defendant before the *condemnatio* which contained an assertion that there were circumstances supporting a defence against the plaintiff's claim. For example, a defendant might assert that he owed the sum claimed by the plaintiff but a special agreement entailed the plaintiff assuming the obligation not to sue for the money. In such a case, the defendant's objection would be inserted into the *formula* as a negative condition: the judge may condemn the defendant 'if there has not been an agreement that the plaintiff will not bring an action'. Depending on their period of operation, exceptions were divided into peremptory or perpetual and dilatory or temporary.[17] A peremptory (*peremptoria*) exception could be invoked without a time limitation (*exceptio perpetua*). If a party failed to raise such an exception during the preparation of the relevant *formula* due to mistake, they could later seek the insertion of an exception into the *formula*.[18] Dilatory or temporary defences, on the other hand, could be raised only within a limited period of time or under certain circumstances.[19] Exceptions were further divided into exceptions based on the *ius civile* (*exceptiones civiles*),[20] and those developed from the praetor's activity (*exceptiones honorariae*).[21] Significant among the *exceptiones honorariae* was the *exceptio doli* that emerged from the claim that the plaintiff had acted fraudulently (*dolo*). Another notable exception in the same category was the *exceptio metus causa*, the defence based on duress. The term *exceptiones utiles* referred to exceptions that the praetor had formulated on the basis of other exceptions located in the *edictum perpetuum*. *Exceptiones in factum*, on the other hand, were new exceptions granted by the praetor in response to claims not covered by the exceptions already recognized.[22] The plaintiff could reply to the defendant's *exceptio* by denying the facts that produced the defence, or by raising his own counter-defence against it. For example, the plaintiff might deny the defendant's claim that the former had promised not to institute an action against him by asserting that this promise had subsequently been revoked, or was limited to a specific time period. The plaintiff's counter-defence (*replicatio*) was also inserted into the relevant *formula* as an additional condition.[23] The defendant could respond to the plaintiff's *replicatio* by raising a further *exceptio*, now termed *dublicatio*. This sequence of responses would proceed until each party's case was thoroughly stated.[24] All the exceptions and counter-exceptions were inserted into the relevant *formula*. However, it appears that *exceptiones* were used less frequently due to the proliferation of the *actiones bonae fidei*, i.e. actions where good faith was explicitly taken into consideration.

Envisage a case presented to the praetor where the defendant had promised by a verbal contract (*stipulatio*) to pay the plaintiff 5,000 denarii, but failed to do so. In such a case, the plaintiff could initiate an action against the defendant known as *condictio certae pecuniae*. The *formula* for this action was elaborated in the praetorian edict and proceeded as follows:

> Let X be the judge. If it appears that the defendant ought to pay to the plaintiff 5,000 denarii, let the judge condemn the defendant; if this does not appear, let the judge absolve him.

In this type of case, the judge was instructed simply to examine whether the plaintiff's claim was true or not. The defendant could deny the promise to pay the plaintiff 5,000 denarii as a matter of fact or, if he admitted the existence of the promise, claim that he was no longer bound by it due to the presence of an exceptional circumstance. He might argue, for example, that the plaintiff had later informally agreed to absolve him of the debt. Pursuant to the *ius civile*, such an informal agreement did not invalidate the initial promise, yet the praetor could grant the defendant a plea that thwarted the plaintiff's action (*exceptio pacti*). In this event, the defendant's defence would be incorporated in the *formula* as a further condition:

> Let X be the judge. If it appears that the defendant ought to pay to the plaintiff 5,000 denarii and if there was no agreement between the plaintiff and the defendant that absolved the latter from the debt, let the judge condemn the defendant; if this does not appear, let the judge absolve the defendant.

As stated earlier, the *formulae* for actions *bonae fidei* encompassed the clause *ex fide bona* (in good faith) as a supplementary condition. For example, consider a case where the plaintiff claimed that through a contract of sale (*emptio venditio*) he sold the defendant an ox, but the latter failed to pay the price. In such a case, the plaintiff could be granted an action (*actio venditi*) based on the following *formula*:

> Let X be the judge. Inasmuch as the plaintiff has sold the defendant an ox, which matter is the subject of this action, whatever it appears that the defendant in good faith ought to give to or do for the plaintiff, let the judge condemn the defendant to give or do; if it does not appear, let the judge absolve him.

The course of the formulary procedure

Like the *legis actio* procedure, the procedure *per formulam* was divided into two distinct stages: before the magistrate (*in iure*) and before the judge (*in iudicio, apud iudicem*).

The procedure in iure

Prior to the commencement of the procedure, the plaintiff announced his intention to institute an action against the defendant (*editio actionis*). The announcement was issued extrajudicially and informally to notify the defendant of the claim and the type of intended action. Therefore, it presented him with an opportunity to settle the case out of court. In the next step, the plaintiff formally summoned the defendant before the court (*in ius vocatio*). A defendant refusing to appear with the plaintiff before the magistrate could be compelled to participate, even forcibly. This was averted if he could enlist someone to act as surety for him (designated a *vindex*) and hence ensure the defendant's appearance *in iure* at a fixed later date.[25] In later times, the defendant could dispense with using a *vindex* and simply issue a formal promise (*vadimonium*) that he would appear in court.[26]

When the parties appeared before the praetor, the plaintiff made a declaration regarding the nature of his claim and the evidence he proposed to present (*editio actionis*). He also requested the praetor to grant an appropriate action (*postulatio actionis*). The praetor refused to furnish an action (*denegatio actionis*) if he concluded from the evaluation of the facts that the plaintiff's claim did not sustain a proper cause of action or that the parties were not contractually capable.[27] However, he would indicate a willingness to grant an action (*dare actionem*) when he thought that legal protection should be provided.

The attention then focused on the defendant, who could either deny the plaintiff's entire claim or request an amendment thereof by means of a *praescriptio* or *exceptio*.[28] If he acknowledged the claim (*confessio in iure*) the proceedings ended as the defendant was already considered condemned (*confessus pro iudicato habetur*).[29] This rule, established by the Law of the Twelve Tables,[30] applied where the plaintiff's claim involved payment by the defendant of a fixed monetary sum (*aes confessum*). However, if the plaintiff's claim did not specify the debt, an immediate execution was impossible and proceedings then continued based on an *actio confessoria*. This action applied where the defendant had already admitted liability and it was designed to determine the amount of money that he ought to pay the plaintiff. If the defendant remained passive (*indefensus*), he had to forfeit the object claimed (*res indefensa*) in the case of an *actio in rem*, or accept the possible attachment of his estate (following the praetor's issue of a *missio in possessionem*) in the case of an *actio in personam*.

If the defendant elected to defend the case, the next steps were: the appointment of the judge, the formulation of the issues in dispute by means of an appropriate *formula* and the praetor's order to institute a *iudicium*. As previously indicated, the *formula* was usually selected from the list of *formulae* included in the *edictum perpetuum*. If no appropriate *formula* for the plaintiff's action was located in the edict, the praetor could adapt a *formula* designed to cover cases of a similar nature (*actio utilis, actio fictitia*), or compose a *formula* for a new action (*actio in factum*).[31] The *formula* was then presented to the plaintiff (*iudicium dare*) who notified its contents to the defendant in the presence of the praetor. The *in iure* phase of the proceedings was completed by the announcement of the *formula* and its acceptance by the defendant (*iudicium accipere*).[32] This stage of the proceedings that finalized all the elements of the dispute was termed *litis contestatio*. An important consequence of the *litis contestatio* was that the judge could take into consideration the parties' claims as formulated at the time of the *litis contestatio*. Subsequent events did not affect the nature of the case or the basis engaged by the judge to deal with it.[33] Moreover, after the *litis contestatio* the plaintiff was precluded from instituting legal proceedings against the defendant by using the same action in respect of the same facts or cause of action.[34] The *litis contestatio* also entailed the substitution of the plaintiff's claim by a claim for pecuniary compensation, as the condemnation of the defendant under the formulary system always resulted in a monetary payment to the plaintiff.[35]

The procedure apud iudicem *or* in iudicio

In this phase of the procedure, the judge (*iudex unus, iudex privatus*), or a panel of judges tried the case with a view to forming a verdict either accepting or rejecting

71

the plaintiff's claim as expressed in the *formula* issued by the praetor.[36] The parties were normally represented by competent advocates (*oratores*) who initially addressed the court by broadly outlining the merits of their case.[37] Before the commencement of the trial, the judge swore a solemn oath that he would exercise his functions lawfully and impartially. The necessary evidence was then presented and the parties or their representatives delivered arguments, which prompted the judge to issue a judgment.[38]

The parties' claims and the presentation of the evidence during the trial were limited to the issues as enumerated in the *formula*. The arguments were primarily concerned with facts: the plaintiff sought to prove the facts that supported his claim; the defendant either denied the factual basis of his opponent's claim, or accepted it but asserted that there were good reasons for recognizing an exception. Arguments might also focus on the interpretation of the law or the *formula* relating to the plaintiff's action. A party could argue, for example, that the law governing the issue should be accorded a broader meaning than the one usually adopted, or that the purpose of the law was different from that assumed by his adversary. Both oral and documentary evidence could be adduced, although the judge had a wide discretion in determining the manner of presentation and permissibility of evidence.[39] In the absence of direct evidence, the court occasionally relied on presumptions (*praesumptiones*) when the existence of certain facts could be logically inferred from other established facts.[40] However, these presumptions were defeasible as they could be refuted by further evidence. Although there was no settled rule pertaining to the onus of proof (*onus probandi*), it was generally recognized that the respective parties must prove their allegations.

After all the evidence was presented and the arguments delivered, the judge pronounced his verdict (*sententia*), usually in the presence of the parties or their representatives.[41] Prior to determining a case, a judge had to acquire the necessary legal knowledge of his own accord. If necessary, he could consult a council (*consilium*) of experts, but did not have to adopt their opinions. When a decision was not attained because the facts or the legal positions were vague or ambiguous, the judge could swear that 'the case is not clear to him' (*rem sibi non liquere*). This entailed the nomination of another judge or the deferral of the decision until more evidence was obtained.[42] In deciding a case, the judge was bound by the wording of the *formula* that formed the basis of the relevant lawsuit. If the plaintiff had claimed that the defendant owed him something, the judge's verdict had to read either *condemno* ('I condemn'), or *absolvo* ('I absolve') if the claim proved unfounded.[43] When the judge decided on a divisory action (*actio communi dividundo*), the verdict had to read *adiudico* ('I award').[44] A plaintiff would lose the case if he had elaborated in the *intentio* (i.e. the part of the *formula* containing his claim) a request for more than he was entitled to (*plus petere*).[45] If he had asked for less (*minus petere*), he was only entitled to what he had requested. In the latter case, the plaintiff could sue again for the remainder of the debt. However, the relevant action could not be granted by the same praetor as it could be blocked by an *exceptio litis dividuae*.[46]

The judge's decision generated an obligation for the unsuccessful party to execute it (*iudicatum facere oportere*).[47] A decision that adjudged an object to one party or, in a divisory action, to several people (*adiudicatio*) actually created new ownership rights on the adjudged property or share. It should also be noted that certain decisions entailed the condemned party enduring a diminution of his esteem or reputation in the eyes of the Roman society (*infamia*), accompanied by the loss of certain civil rights (such as the right of holding certain offices and the right of bringing a civil or criminal action in a court of law). This occurred when the person condemned had committed an act involving personal turpitude, such as theft (*furtum*) or wilful fraud (*dolus malus*).[48]

The judge's decision was final. During the Principate era, a right of appeal (*appellatio*) against judicial decisions moulded by the *per formulam* procedure was finally recognized and was directed to the emperor or one of his officials. The purpose of an appeal was either the reversal of a decision or its modification.[49] The validity of a decision could be challenged by the unsuccessful party but a rejected challenge obliged him to pay double the amount specified in the original judgment (*revocatio in duplum*).[50]

Execution

If the plaintiff's claim was accepted, the defendant had to comply with the condemnatory judgment. He could comply voluntarily or, if resistant, be compelled to do so by means of a new action, known as *actio iudicati*. The plaintiff instituted the *actio iudicati* against the condemned defendant (*iudicatus*) on the expiry of a thirty-day period after his condemnation by the judge (in the *in iudicio* phase) or his acknowledgment of the debt before the praetor (during the *in iure* phase). The *actio iudicati* was instituted in the same way as any other action: it was raised before the praetor (*in iure*) and a new *formula* was composed with a view to investigating the merits of the case. Before the case was referred to a judge for trial, the defendant had to provide security that the debt would be paid if he lost the case (*satisdatio iudicatum solvi*).[51] If the judge discerned that the previous condemnatory judgment had been justified, the defendant was condemned to pay twice the amount specified in the original judgment.

If the defendant was condemned at a trial for an *actio iudicati*, or he admitted his debt before the trial ended, execution of the judge's decision followed as a matter of course. Execution could be directed either against the condemned defendant personally or against his property. In the former case, the execution was conducted in the same manner as in the *legis actio* procedure: the praetor issued an order (*decretum*) that authorized the plaintiff to seize and imprison the defendant (*duci iubere*).[52] This form of execution was governed by the provisions of the Law of the Twelve Tables relating to the *manus iniectio iudicati*.[53] However, the provisions regulating a creditor's right to kill his debtor or sell him as a slave no longer applied. In normal circumstances, the condemned defendant worked off his debt under the supervision of the plaintiff. The execution directed at the defendant's person was gradually superseded by execution directed at his property engaging a praetorian decree known as *missio in possessionem*. After the lapse of a certain period (fifteen or thirty days, depending on the case), the condemned defendant was branded with *infamia*. This did not occur if he or another person acting on his behalf had meanwhile discharged the debt. Usually, the defendant's property was then sold by public auction (*venditio bonorum*) and the plaintiff obtained payment from the proceeds of such sale.[54] When more than one plaintiff existed and the proceeds were not sufficient to cover all the claims, a proportional division of such proceeds was effected among them.

Following the *venditio bonorum*, the debtor's property was consigned to the highest bidder (*bonorum emptor*). However, the latter did not acquire full ownership before the completion of the *usucapio* period.[55] The buyer of the property could be granted an *interdictum possessorium*[56] for obtaining possession of the property, as well as other actions for the payment to him of debts originally due to the insolvent debtor (*actio Rutiliana, actio Serviana*).[57] It should be observed that the insolvent debtor whose property was sold through a *venditio bonorum* was not always released from his obligations towards his creditors. A year after the *venditio bonorum* the creditors could initiate a new sale of any property the debtor had acquired in the interim, if their claims were not fully covered by the proceeds of the earlier sale.

As the *venditio bonorum* entailed grave consequences for the defendant, certain categories of persons were not subjected to this action. These included members of the senatorial class and persons construed by the law as incapable of regulating their own affairs (provided they had no guardian). If a person belonging to one of these categories became insolvent, his property was placed by the praetor's order under the control of an administrator (*curator distrahendorum bonorum gratia*).[58] The latter conducted the sale of the insolvent person's property by individual items (not as a whole) until sufficient money was obtained to satisfy the creditor's claim. This method of execution, termed *bonorum distractio*, did not result in *infamia* for the insolvent person. Finally, a *lex Iulia* introduced in the era of Augustus recognized that a person who became insolvent through no fault of his own could seek permission by the praetor or the provincial governor to surrender his entire property to the creditors (*cessio bonorum*). This tactic averted the consequences (especially the *infamia*) that an execution by a *venditio bonorum* entailed.[59] If the debtor's request was accepted, he was entitled to a *beneficium competentiae*. This special remedy granted the debtor an opportunity to pay his creditors only as far as his means permitted.[60] The property (or part thereof) surrendered was sold at a public auction and the proceeds were divided among the creditors.

Extraordinary praetorian remedies

An array of extraordinary legal remedies was developed from the praetor's activities in his capacity as a jurisdictional magistrate. These were classified under four headings: *stipulationes praetoriae, missiones in possessionem, restitutiones in integrum* and *interdicta*.

Stipulationes praetoriae

The praetor could impose a *stipulatio* (a verbal solemn promise) on one or both litigants in order to ascertain the normal progress of the trial and ensure certain behaviour from the parties by compelling them to assume the duty of performing or refraining from a specific action.[61] Moreover, such a compulsory *stipulatio* could be imposed on a person at the request (*postulatio*) of another to ascertain the latter's protection against certain eventualities.[62] Hence, the praetorian stipulations were categorized: *stipulationes iudiciales* were stipulations aimed at securing the parties' cooperation during a trial;[63] *stipulationes cautionales* entailed the promise of an action to a person if certain circumstances occurred;[64] and *stipulationes communes* were stipulations that related to both the above purposes.[65] If the promise embodied in the *stipulatio* was not fulfilled, an ordinary action lay against the contravening party. Moreover, non-compliance with the praetor's order or the absence of the party designated to assume the obligations imposed by the *stipulatio* could provoke a *missio in possessionem* in favour of his adversary.

Missiones in possessionem

A *missio in possessionem* was a coercive measure applied by the praetor by virtue of his *imperium*. Pursuant to this measure, a person obtained possession of another person's property in terms of the whole estate (*missio in bona*) or some particular object (*missio in rem*). The praetorian decrees concerning *missiones* were issued either to ascertain the normal progress of a trial, or to secure the debtor's property for the satisfaction of his creditors, or to induce the debtor to assume a special obligation through *stipulatio* for security purposes if he refused to do so voluntarily. The legal situation of the party favoured by the *missio* decree varied from real possession to simple custody of the relevant property (or part thereof).

Restitutiones in integrum

The *restitutio in integrum* was a legal remedy invoked when a person who had suffered unjust loss deriving from the strict application of the law requested the praetor to order a restoration of the previous legal position. It amounted to the setting aside of a legal act deemed otherwise lawful under the *ius civile*, on the basis that it would be unfair or inequitable to uphold the consequences of such legal act. This remedy was granted by a praetorian decree (*decretum*) after the praetor evaluated the circumstances that prompted the claimant's request (*causa cognita*). The best-known case that engaged this remedy pertained to the legal acts of minors[66] who had entered into transactions under conditions detrimental to their own interests. The circumstances where the praetor would grant a *restitutio in integrum* were enumerated in the *edictum perpetuum*.

Interdicta

The *interdicta* were the oldest and probably the most important legal remedies granted by the praetor.[67] An *interdictum* was a summary order issued by the praetor that prohibited a person from acting or persevering with an act, or demanded that he perform a certain act.[68] It was issued under certain circumstances in response to an application by a person who alleged that his right or rights were infringed, and was usually based on a *formula* embodied in the praetorian edict. A great medley of rights could be protected in this way, such as the right of an individual or the public to enjoy their property without interference, or any right or interest with a private or public nature that was worthy of protection.[69] Evidently, an essential reason for the existence of the interdict was that it provided a swift and convenient means for permanently or temporarily resolving a legal dispute. However, one should note that an *interdictum* was effective only when the person against whom it was issued agreed to comply with the relevant order. If he failed to comply, the claimant could resort to the normal court procedure in order to verify or defend his right.

Three main categories of interdicts existed: the *interdicta exhibitoria, interdicta restitutoria* and *interdicta prohibitoria*.[70] An *interdictum exhibitorium* ordered a person to produce (*exhibeas*) a person (e.g. a child or a slave) or an object (e.g. a testament) he possessed, but did not impose the duty to deliver the person or object to the claimant. The *interdicta restitutoria* were concerned with the restoration (*restitutas*) of objects to their former condition, or the restoration of possession to a person who had been deprived of it. An *interdictum prohibitorium* operated to prohibit a person from a specific act, such as from hindering the claimant's exercise of a property right. For instance, if the value of a house would be likely to be substantially diminished by some act of the person in possession of that house, a person claiming a property right over the house could request the issue of an *interdictum prohibitorium* forbidding such an act.[71]

Criminal justice

We observed in Chapter 3 that, during the early Republic, the prosecution and punishment of crimes against the state (*crimina publica*) fell within the jurisdiction of the magistrates and the *comitia*. On the other hand, retaliation for offences against private persons and their property (*delicta privata*) was left to the injured person. The authority of the magistrates to adjudicate criminal acts (*cognitio*) emanated from their right of supreme coercion (*coercitio maior*) attached to their *imperium*. Originally, acts of magisterial *coercitio* were not preceded by a formal procedure and the punishments imposed were determined by the magistrates at their discretion. However, a rule established in an early period declared that citizens could appeal to the centuriate assembly against capital sentences imposed by magistrates (*provocatio ad populum, ius provocationis*). When a citizen could appeal to the *comitia* against a sentence imposed by a magistrate, the original sentence was always appealed against and eventually it became a mere preliminary to the real trial before the *comitia*.[72] The magistrates still attended to minor infractions by engaging police measures, such as attachment of property, monetary fines and even corporal punishment. However, by the middle of the second century BC all offences of a serious nature fell within the jurisdiction of the *comitia centuriata* and the *comitia tributa*. Cases involving offences against the liberty and property of private citizens were never submitted to the assemblies. Before Sulla's era, redress of such wrongdoings was sought in private proceedings and the state's role was confined to prescribing the rules for averting excessive retaliation towards the offender.

Adjudication of public crimes by the people may have been efficacious in the context of a small city-state composed of conservative farmers and middle-class citizens. However, as socio-economic and political conditions became more complex, especially in the period following Rome's wars of expansion, comitial trials proved increasingly inadequate to deal with the complicated issues that criminal prosecutions frequently invoked. Quite apart from the fact that trials by the people were cumbersome and time-consuming, the escalating number of cases made adjudication of public crimes by the assemblies very difficult.[73] Inevitably, popular criminal justice eventually had to be replaced by a new and more functional court system. The gradual evolution commenced in the early second century BC with the creation, by decision of the people or the senate, of special *ad hoc* tribunals (*quaestiones extraordinariae*) for the investigation of certain offences of a political nature. These embraced offences such as abuse of power or dereliction of duty by magistrates and provincial officials, and conspiracies against public order and the existence of the state.[74] An early illustration of a special *quaestio* was the commission established by the senate in 186 BC to investigate and punish the crimes committed by members of the Bacchanalian societies.[75] A tribunal of this kind consisted invariably of a magistrate *cum imperio* (i.e. a consul or a praetor) surrounded by a body of assessors (*consilium*) selected by the magistrate or the senate.[76] The court's decision was determined by the majority of the assessors and no appeal against it was allowed as the court was regarded as representing the people.

In the transformed socio-political conditions of the later Republic, the *quaestiones extraordinariae* provided a more efficient means of dealing with public crimes than the *iudicia populi* whose role in the administration of justice gradually diminished. However, it was only with the introduction of standing courts of justice (*quaestiones perpetuae*) that a stricter regulation of criminal procedure was finally realized.

The development of a standing court system

A turning-point in the history of Roman criminal law was the creation of standing juror courts (*quaestiones perpetuae*) authorized to adjudicate crimes of a specific nature. The first of these courts was instituted to address the abuse of power and corruption of senatorial magistrates charged with the provincial administration. In 149 BC the tribune L. Calpurnius Piso initiated the *lex Calpurnia repetundarum*, a plebiscite that established a standing tribunal (*quaestio de repetundis* or *repetundarum*) chaired by the *praetor peregrinus* that tried cases involving extortion (*crimen repetundarum*) – an offence frequently committed by provincial magistrates against the people of their provinces.[77] The proceedings in this court bore a strong resemblance in form to a civil action,[78] and a defeated defendant was obliged to return the illicit gain to those affected.[79] No appeal from this court to the *comitia* was allowed, nor could its decisions be suspended by tribunician veto.

The establishment of the *quaestio repetundarum* later inspired the creation of several other standing courts by special statutory enactments *ex post facto* for individual crimes. In most cases this embraced crimes committed by high-ranking magistrates or army officers during performance of their duties,[80] such as high treason (*crimen maiestatis*), electoral corruption (*ambitus*) and embezzlement of public money (*peculatus*).[81] Under Sulla's government, the standing court system was extended further and the entire machinery of the *quaestiones perpetuae* was overhauled to place the administration of criminal justice on a more firm and consistent basis. The *quaestio repetundarum* was reorganized by the *lex Cornelia de repetundis*, and the *quaestio de maiestate* instituted by Saturninus in *c.* 103 BC was recognized as the principal court for high treason by the *lex Cornelia de maiestate* of 81 BC.[82] The court dealing with electoral corruption (*de ambitu*) was also retained, while Sulla's own *lex Cornelia de ambitu* introduced heavier penalties for this crime.[83] With regard to homicide, a court for hearing cases of poisoning (*quaestio de veneficis*) was apparently established before the time of Sulla.[84] A court attending to cases of assassination (*quaestio de sicariis*) had been created as early as 142 BC, but it appears to have operated only as a *quaestio extraordinaria*. Both forms of homicide were encompassed by Sulla's *lex Cornelia de sicariis et veneficis* of 81 BC, which also stipulated the punishment of those who attempted to procure the unlawful conviction of a person under this enactment.[85] One of the permanent courts established by Sulla tackled certain forms of injury (*iniuria*) caused by acts of violence, such as beating (*pulsare*), striking (*verberare*) and the forcible invasion of another person's house (*domum introire*).[86] Sulla also introduced a *quaestio de falsis* that functioned as a court dealing with cases involving the forgery of official documents, wills and the counterfeiting of money.[87] After Sulla's era more *quaestiones perpetuae* were implemented such as the *quaestio de vi* for crimes of violence,[88] the *quaestio de plagiariis* for kidnapping, treating a free man as a slave and inciting a slave to leave his master,[89] the *quaestio de sodaliciis* for electoral conspiracy[90] and the *quaestio de adulteriis* for adultery and the seduction of unmarried women.[91] Generally, the permanent courts were governed by rules similar to those governing the extraordinary courts and, like the latter, were regarded as operating under the authority of the people.[92] It is germane to mention that the supreme jurisdiction of the *comitia* remained unaffected, in principle, by the establishment of the standing court system. In practice, the old comitial procedure was seldom engaged when trial by a *quaestio perpetua* was available. The exception to this pattern was when special circumstances existed, such as where an important political issue was at stake. As the system of the *quaestiones perpetuae* approached completion, the role of the assemblies in the administration of criminal justice ceased.

According to the statute of 149 BC that established the *quaestio repetundarum*, the members of this court were recruited exclusively from among the senators. As provincial magistrates invariably belonged to the senatorial nobility, the above rule could engender some favour for the provincial magistrate charged with extortion. A magistrate who was retired from office and charged with extortion had the benefit of a trial by his peers and his chances of acquittal were thus greatly increased. As new permanent courts were brought into existence, this would naturally hold good in their case also. As a result of the senate's understandable reluctance to punish members of its own class, the new court system became a convenient instrument of self-protection for the senatorial oligarchy. It is thus unsurprising that the organization of the jury courts surfaced as one of the most highly contested issues in the later Republic.

In 123/122 BC the younger Gracchus, seeking to implement his basic policy aim of curbing the senate's powers, procured the passing of a statute (*lex Acilia*) whereby the right of sitting as members of the *quaestiones perpetuae* was transferred from the senators to the equestrians. At first, eradicating the senatorial monopoly on the administration of criminal justice appeared to be a move in the right direction. It meant that if members of the senatorial nobility controlling the provincial adminis-tration were accused of abuse of power, they would face a tribunal composed of *equites*. But in reality the transfer of control over the court system to the *equites* did not diminish the deleterious influence of factional politics on the administration of justice. It simply allowed a class whose political role was once largely neglected to participate in what was originally regarded as an 'in-house' affair. Naturally, the senatorial nobility refused to acquiesce in this situation. Thus, the issue of member-ship within the standing courts persisted as a prominent apple of discord and the subject matter of various legislative measures throughout the last century of the Republic. Sulla's short-lived reform restored the senate's control of the court system, which was expected in view of his general policy trends. After this event, the *lex Aurelia* of 70 BC established a more equitable balance in the composition of the juror lists. This law provided that each *quaestio perpetua* was to consist of one-third senators, one-third *equites* and one-third *tribuni aerarii* (the latter are commonly understood to have been *equites* but with a lesser property qualification). In the last decades of the Republic, when the internecine strife between the senatorial factions peaked, it may appear that the equestrians had the upper hand in the standing courts.[93]

As stated earlier, each *quaestio perpetua* was competent to deal only with a partic-ular category of offence. The nature of this category was defined in the statutory enactment establishing the *quaestio*, as amended possibly by subsequent legislation. A court of this type embodied a considerable number of non-official members and was chaired by a president referred to as *quaesitor*. According to the system finally adopted, the president was normally a praetor. However, any other magistrate or even a private citizen (usually an ex-magistrate) invested with magisterial powers could be appointed president.[94] The members of the court were not the president's nominees but were chosen in accordance with the provisions of the statute establishing the particular *quaestio*. Generally, a large body of qualified citizens was summoned and a complicated process involving challenges on both sides reduced this body to the prescribed number.

The form of the proceedings in the permanent courts was essentially accusatorial, as opposed to inquisitorial. This meant that no action could be initiated unless a citizen laid a formal accusation (*accusatio*) against another and thereby undertook to prosecute at the trial.[95] The sole function of the court was to hear and assess the evidence and arguments presented by the prosecution and the defence respectively, and thereafter to convict or acquit. The president publicly announced the verdict, which was thus nominally his verdict. Nevertheless, he was bound to decide the case in accordance with the opinion of the majority of the members as ascertained by a ballot. Hence, it was the members who constituted the actual adjudicators. Note that no sentence was pronounced as the penalty for the particular offence was stipulated by the statute that established the *quaestio*, and liability to this penalty ensued automatically from the conviction. A person found guilty by a *quaestio perpetua* could not appeal to the people against the court's decision.

The first step in a criminal prosecution was the *postulatio*, which constituted an application by a citizen to the magistrate directing a particular *quaestio* for permission to instigate charges.[96] This was an essential preliminary requirement, as the applicant might be precluded by law from laying charges against any person, or against the particular person he intended to prosecute.[97] After permission to prosecute was granted, the accuser stated the name of the accused and the offence committed (*nominis et criminis delatio*) in a formal and written manner while the accused was present.[98] The document containing the accusation (*inscriptio*) was then signed by the accuser and by all those supporting his claim (*subscriptores*). Moreover, the accuser had to swear an oath that he did not issue a false accusation out of malice (*calumnia*) or in collusion with the accused (*praevaricatio*).[99] After the magistrate had formally accepted the indictment (*nominis receptio*), the accused became technically a defendant (*reus*) and the trial date was set. The accuser was granted sufficient time to prepare his case (*inquisitio*) – in most cases, ten days appears as the minimum period but in certain cases (especially when evidence had to be gathered from overseas) a longer period might be allowed. The accuser might also request the summoning of witnesses (a maximum of forty-eight) by the magistrate, although the latter was free to summon as many as he thought fit (*testimonium denuntiare*).[100] The next step in the process was the selection of the members of the court designated to try the case.[101] These were chosen by lot (*iudicium sortitio*) from the annual list of jurors (*album iudicum*) prepared by the praetor at the beginning of each year.[102] After the required number of jurors was selected in this way (fifty and seventy-five were typical), both the accuser and the defendant had an opportunity to disallow a specified number of jurors (*iudicum reiectio*).[103] The presiding magistrate then replaced the disqualified jurors by drawing more names from the *album iudicum* (*iudicum subsortitio*).[104]

During the trial, the accuser and the defendant dominated the scene, with their advocates and witnesses engaged in cross-examinations that were often rancorous.[105]

The jurors listened in silence, while the presiding magistrate was mainly responsible for the orderly progress of the proceedings.[106] Both oral and documentary evidence was admissible.[107] Witnesses (*testes*) testified under oath and were examined by their own side and cross-examined by the other.[108] After all the evidence was presented and the closing speeches delivered, the magistrate convened the jury (*mittere iudices in consilium*) and placed the question of the defendant's guilt or innocence to the vote. In early times the vote was open, but the enactment of the *lex Cassia* in 137 BC entailed the use of a secret ballot (*per tabellas*) to determine the court's decision. Each juror was given a small tablet marked on one side 'A' (*absolvo*) and on the other 'C' (*condemno*). He then erased one or the other and cast the tablet into an urn (*sitella*). Jurors also had the third choice of 'NL' (*not liquet*: not proven) if they were unable to reach a decision.[109] The verdict was determined by the majority of the votes: if there was a majority of 'C's the accused was pronounced guilty by the presiding magistrate; if the 'A's predominated or if there was an equal number of votes, he was pronounced not guilty. If the majority of the jurors voted '*non liquet*' the presiding magistrate announced the necessity for a more thorough investigation into the case and fixed a day for a new hearing (*ampliatio*).[110]

As previously stated, the penalties imposed by the standing courts were specified in the statutes that instituted these courts, and liability to these penalties routinely followed upon conviction. There existed two kinds of penalties: capital and monetary.[111] In theory, most crimes of a serious nature were capital but it was practically unknown to inflict the death penalty (*poena mortis*) on a Roman citizen deriving from a condemnation on a criminal charge in normal circumstances. The reason is that persons tried by these tribunals enjoyed a statutory right of fleeing into exile before the court pronounced its final sentence.[112] When, as invariably happened, a condemned person invoked this right, a resolution passed by the vote of the people declared his legal status as an exile and interdicted him accordingly from using water and fire (*aquae et ignis interdictio*).[113] The normal effect of this interdiction rendered the culprit liable to summary execution if discovered on Roman territory, which after the Social War (91–88 BC) covered the whole of Italy.[114] Hence, condemnation by a standing court on a capital charge virtually amounted to a sentence of banishment. It is feasible that some late republican statutes expressly substituted interdiction from fire and water with death as the penalty for certain crimes.

The modern observer can hardly fail to form an unfavourable appraisal of the Roman administration of criminal justice. A survey of civil law and procedure would fare better as this field displayed logical categorization from an early stage and generally produced adequate results. Roman criminal justice appears as haphazard, capricious, opportunistic and remote from the contemporary standards of equal protection of the laws. Proceedings in the standing courts were cumbersome and trials could be protracted as cases were often heard more than once. Although a jury of less than a hundred members could grasp complicated evidence and assess the parties' credibility better than a crowd of thousands, jurors were often as susceptible to corruption and bribery as the people in the turbulent *iudicia populi*. A less unfavourable appraisal of the Roman criminal justice system is formed if one contemplates the immense pressures of a rapidly expanding empire. Further, the adverse circumstances of a largely haphazard evolution engendered many new concepts and categories of criminal wrongdoing (such as crimes against public order and the security of the state, various types of fraud, corruption and abuse of office) that furnished the framework for the subsequent development of the criminal law.

7

THE PRINCIPATE:
THE HISTORICAL, SOCIAL AND
CONSTITUTIONAL BACKGROUND

The reforms of Augustus

Octavian became sole master of the empire after his victory at Actium and the conquest of Egypt. As the Roman world remained in a state of confusion, he had to restore order and establish some form of government to guarantee permanent security. During the turbulent years after Caesar's assassination, Octavian developed from an adroit politician into a political leader of the highest order. He saw that a return to the old republican system was out of the question as that system could no longer meet the organizational needs of the empire, nor guarantee the political stability required for the efficient administration and defence of the state. At the same time, he realized that an attempt to establish an absolute monarchy would offend republican sensitivities and might lead to further unrest. The Roman conception of the state was so entwined with the republican regime and its ruling class that political stability was virtually impossible without upholding the republican traditions. Based on this realistic appraisal of the situation, Octavian engaged in masterful manipulations to transform the Roman system of government into a system that was republican in form and semblance, but monarchical so far as actual executive power was concerned. He succeeded where Caesar had failed by concealing his essentially monarchic position, and appealing to respected precedents and traditional constitutional norms to make it appear that he was 'restoring' the Republic. Few of his informed contemporaries were fooled, and few cared. After so many years of anarchy and civil war, the Roman world was ready to accept stability under an enlightened ruler who professed to respect the political, social and economic sensibilities of the classes that mattered.[1]

Octavian-Augustus gradually established and maintained his autocracy in a lengthy process; the legitimization of his position on a long-term basis in 27 BC was merely one stage. In seeking to eliminate the danger of factional strife, the main cause of the Republic's ills, he gradually neutralized the bewildering medley of family alliances and pressure groups that made up the senatorial oligarchy; became the chief political patron of the state; and made all Romans his clients in one way or another. He achieved this without destroying the traditional institutions of the republican state. The assemblies and the senate still met to carry out their traditional functions, and the prerogatives of the senators and equestrians were maintained. Augustus ostentatiously contented himself with a few decisive elements of authority such as the proconsular power (*imperium proconsulare*) over the frontier provinces, which gave him the supreme command over the greatest part of the army,[2] the consular power (*imperium consulare*) for the city precincts of Rome (from 19 BC onward) and the expanded powers of the tribunate (*tribunicia potestas*) whereby he could effectively control legislation. On various occasions, he was given the powers of a censor, which secured for him a voice in the composition of the senate. Moreover, as holder of the position of *pontifex maximus* (after 12 BC), he exercised general supervision over the religious affairs of the state. But, more important than all these powers and titles bestowed on Augustus was the personal authority (*auctoritas*) he enjoyed, which warranted his superiority over all other organs of the state.[3] Augustus, unlike Caesar, refrained from assuming dictatorial powers and professed to be no more than *princeps*, a term simply meaning 'the first citizen of the state'. He boasted that he had not taken a single magistracy in conflict with ancestral custom and that the official powers he possessed were not greater than those of his colleagues in the office concerned. The truth, however, is that as the powers of the *princeps* were not subject to the limitations traditionally imposed on magisterial authority, initiative passed from the senatorial oligarchy to one man and the whole system functioned under the potentially autocratic though benevolent control of an emperor.[4]

Perhaps Augustus' most revolutionary reform was extending the base of the socio-political elite to include the equestrian classes of Italy, which began to play a prominent role in social and political life. Augustus secured the support of the equestrians by allowing them a greater degree of participation in the government of the state. He used equestrian civil servants to counteract senatorial disloyalty, especially in the financial administration and sensitive military posts, and patronized their advancement to the senate. The equestrian class was then open to rejuvenation from below, as successful elements of the lower classes could now achieve equestrian rank. Thus, society was more mobile and dynamic than during the Republic, as talented or ambitious men advanced in imperial service. Moreover, Augustus reorganized the Roman army as a professional standing force and, at the same time, reduced the number of legions. He realized that an excessively large army drained the state's human and natural resources, and was unnecessary and potentially dangerous once the civil wars ended. He used this new army, a remarkably efficient fighting machine, as the instrument of a distinctly imperialistic foreign policy for much of his reign. At the end, however, he set himself the task of creating permanent defensive frontiers behind which Roman civilization could develop peacefully. Augustus attempted to change the moral tone of Roman society that had strayed far from traditional Roman values. Thus, he promoted old religious cults and sought to transform upper-class morals by legislation. Large families were encouraged, childlessness became a disability for aspiring office-holders and adultery was made a criminal offence. Ultimately, however, changing the moral fabric of society from above proved to be an impossible task.

The new system instituted by Augustus, however successful it proved to be over the next two centuries, was marred by a basic weakness. This derived from the contradiction between Augustus' constitutional position as a Roman magistrate, whose tenure derived from the senate and the people, and his *de facto* status as emperor whose maintenance of power ultimately depended on army support. The stability of the empire depended normally on continuity of imperial person and policy, and yet the very skill Augustus used to disguise his power under republican forms increased the difficulty of transmitting that power to a successor. Aware that he could not legally nominate a successor, Augustus sought to resolve the problem by elevating to positions of power certain persons from within his own family whom he regarded as suitable candidates for the imperial office. When he died in AD 14, the sole survivor of this group of contemplated successors was his adopted stepson, Tiberius; the senate and the people had no hesitation in proclaiming Tiberius as emperor. Although the 'adoptive emperorship' provided an answer to the new crisis of the system, succession remained a perennial concern and no solution was ever devised to the problem of deposing an emperor without recourse to violence. It is no wonder that the empire was ruled by a succession of short dynasties, whose reign was punctuated, at least in the first century AD, by frequent plots, intrigues and assassinations.

Organs of the imperial administration

As noted earlier, in the system founded by Augustus the powers of the emperor were those held by the higher magistrates of the Republic, but these powers were now combined and concentrated in one person. In the course of time these powers were gradually extended, although their legal basis remained largely unchanged.[5] The *princeps*, in the end, became the governing statesman and ruler with such enormous resources at his disposal that he could personally take on the tasks of the state. But the new political system was not identical with the rule of a single person, but with that of the imperial household (*domus principis*) – the family and dynasty of the *princeps*, his relatives, advisers and stewards.

In order to manage the wide-ranging responsibilities of his office, the emperor required assistants answerable directly to him. The early emperors relied heavily on members of their own household, especially freedmen, to fill government posts, although certain important positions were reserved for senators and members of the equestrian class.[6] The new imperial officials differed from the magistrates of the Republic in some important respects: they were chosen by the emperor himself, without the involvement of the senate or popular assemblies, and reported directly to him; they were appointed for an indefinite period of time, although the emperor could dismiss them at any time at his pleasure, and were paid for their work according to their rank; they were not granted *imperium* or *potestas* (their only powers were those delegated by the emperor, who could approve, reverse or modify their decisions as he thought fit), and the principle of collegiality did not apply to them.

The most important imperial officials were the praetorian prefect (*praefectus praetorio*) and the city prefect (*praefectus urbi*). From the time of Augustus, the praetorian prefect was commander of the special military units, which served as the emperor's personal bodyguard (*praetoriani, cohors praetoria*). The office evolved into one of the most powerful in the state and its holders, who were drawn from the equestrian class, became the chief advisers of the emperors in military and civil matters.[7] Their military command extended over all the troops stationed in Italy and, from the third century onwards, they assumed important administrative and judicial functions. Their jurisdiction extended all over Italy (with the exception of an area including Rome and a hundred mile zone around the city) and the provinces.[8] Among the holders of the office of the *praefectus praetorio* were some leading jurists of the imperial period, such as Papinianus, Paulus and Ulpianus. The city prefect was originally the representative of the emperor in Rome when the emperor was absent. During the early Principate, the office was transformed into a permanent one and the city prefect was made responsible for maintaining public order in Rome with the Roman police (the urban cohorts) at his disposal. Moreover, after the abolition of the old standing courts under Emperor Septimius Severus (AD 193–211), he was granted broad jurisdictional powers in Rome and the surrounding area up to a distance of a hundred miles from the city.[9] Other important officials of this period were the prefect of the grain supply (*praefectus annonae*), appointed for an indefinite period to oversee the supply of grain and other provisions to the market in Rome and to regulate prices,[10] and the prefect of the watch (*praefectus vigilum*), the head of Rome's fire brigades (*cohortes vigilum*), whose duties included policing the city by night and dealing with fires and any other natural emergencies that might arise.[11] Another category of officials with a varying extent of power was that of the procurators (*procuratores*).[12] Procurators acted as agents of the emperor in fulfilling a number of tasks within the civil administration, especially in the provinces, such as the collection of taxes, the management of state revenues and the supervision of public buildings and factories. The most common duty for a procurator was to serve as governor of a minor province or territory.[13]

When dealing with important administrative and legal matters the emperors, beginning with Augustus, often consulted a body of advisers (*consilium principis*) composed of trusted friends (*amici Caesaris*), state officials and experts. Under Hadrian (AD 117–38), the *consilium principis* became a permanent organ comprising the highest officers of the state, and its members (*consiliarii*) received regular remuneration for their services. Eminent jurists who held senior positions in the imperial administration (such as Julianus, Papinianus and Ulpianus) often participated in the *consilium*, and played a major role in the development of imperial legislation and the dispensation of justice. By the middle of the third century AD, the *consilium* was the most important element of the imperial administration as it assumed most of the functions and responsibilities of the senate.[14]

In the early years of the Principate, the imperial civil service lacked structure, and Augustus and his immediate successors conducted the administration as part of their private business, relying on private secretaries from their own households, especially freedmen. An important change introduced during the reign of Claudius (AD 41–54) was the transformation of those secretaryships into powerful ministries with names indicating the different tasks assigned to them. The department *a rationibus* dealt with matters relating to public finance, the *a libellis* responded to petitions from private citizens, the *ab epistulis* handled the emperor's official correspondence, the *a cognitionibus* investigated judicial disputes referred to the emperor and the *a memoria* performed the secretarial work on all decisions, letters, appointments and orders issued by the emperor. These departments were manned at a lower level by slaves (*servi Caesaris*) and at a higher level by freedmen. However, the role of freedmen in the imperial service was restricted in later years. Domitian (AD 81–96) and Trajan (AD 98–117) appointed equestrian secretaries and, from the time of Hadrian (AD 117–38), the heads of the various departments were selected exclusively from the equestrian class. Equestrians also played an increasingly important part in the management of the imperial treasury (*fiscus*), which was the repository for the flow of taxes levied in the imperial provinces and from which the emperor paid the salaries of state officials and soldiers.[15]

The senate, the magistrates and the assemblies

As noted before, in the new system of government inaugurated by Augustus there was no break with the past. The powers he was invested with were conferred upon him in forms compatible with republican precedents, and the Republic itself still functioned. The assemblies and senate still met, the regular magistrates were elected each year, and the senate continued, as in the past, to be recruited from ex-magistrates. Augustus was successful because he was able to establish a stable regime, a disguised kind of monarchy cleverly hidden behind a constitutional, republican façade. But the new political system was heavily encumbered by its contradictions between façade and reality. However successful Augustus' programme proved to be, neither he nor his successors resolved the contradictions inherent in the elective theory supporting the new regime and its dynastic practice. In the course of time, the absolutism inherent in the imperial system became progressively more pronounced and, inevitably, the relics of the republican state (senatorial independence of action and the sovereignty of a people legislating and electing magistrates in popular assembly) withered away.

The senate

After the establishment of the Principate, politically and socially the most important group of the governing class within the state was still the Roman senate. Aware of its influence and usefulness as an instrument through which he could legitimize his regime, Augustus exalted the senate and augmented its powers.[16] The senate retained control over the public treasury (*aerarium*), governed the senatorial provinces through proconsuls and, for a time at least, retained the privilege of minting coinage. In later years, the prestige of the senate was enhanced further by its employment as a court of justice, dealing with cases involving offences committed by senators and state officials. Its resolutions (*senatus consulta*) also gained added importance, finally acquiring the full force of law, as the senate gradually became a legislative body replacing the popular assemblies. Officially, the senate had become a full partner in the government. Theoretically, it was even more: the ultimate source of the emperors' power, as their *imperium* and legitimacy on accession was derived from the senate's approval of their nominations.[17] Hence, a dichotomy emerged as a great distinguishing feature of the Principate: the growth of two closely interrelated, yet theoretically independent, authorities. Yet, in reality, although the senate retained a great deal of its prestige and rights as a political forum, it was substantially under the control of the emperor who regulated its composition, dominated its proceedings and prescribed its tasks. Elections of magistrates always corresponded with the wishes of the emperor; legislative proposals brought before the senate by the emperor or his representatives were accepted without much debate; the conduct of foreign policy was in the hands of the emperor, who also controlled all the politically important provinces; and the management of public finances was gradually assumed by the emperor following the establishment of the imperial treasury (*fiscus*). Thus, in the end, the division of government between the emperor and the senate was more apparent than real; although the emperors owed all their powers to the senate, once these powers were given the senate became virtually impotent and unable to retract them, even if it had desired to do so. During the later part of the Principate, the senate endured further debilitation with the increased centralization of the imperial administration, the broadening of the role of the *consilium principis* and the transfer of jurisdiction in many areas to the praetorian and city prefects. Although by the third century AD the senate had lost most of its competence, it remained influential because of tradition and the social standing of the senatorial class (membership of that body was still regarded by many as the high point of a political career).

The magistrates

After the establishment of the Principate, the old republican magistrates were still elected each year and men in public life passed, as before, through the regular *cursus honorum* (quaestor, aedile or tribune, praetor, consul). Occasionally, the emperors forged their power by relying on some of the most important magistracies, such as the consulship and the tribunate. In fact, however, the authority of the magistrates was now considerably limited. The consuls no longer directed the political life of the state, nor did they hold military command as these functions were transferred to the emperor. Their role was confined to summoning and presiding over the senate and the assembly, and supervising the administration of justice in certain criminal and civil cases.[18] Nevertheless, the consulship remained until the closing years of the Empire, an important status symbol and a gateway to the highest offices in the imperial administration.[19] The praetors retained the civil and criminal jurisdiction they had held during the Republic.[20] However, their role in the administration of justice gradually decreased in importance following the expansion of the emperor's judicial functions, and the establishment of new civil and criminal courts under the jurisdiction of imperial officials.[21] The tribunes continued to exist down to the fourth century AD, but their authority was considerably diminished by the decline of the popular assemblies and their complete dependence on the will of the emperor.[22] In the early years of the Principate, Augustus and his successors occasionally took over the duties of censor, especially those pertaining to the supervision of public morals (*cura morum*) and the selection of senators (*lectio senatus*). From the time of Domitian (AD 81–96) it became customary for the emperors to assume censorial powers for life and, as a result, the censorship ceased to exist as an independent office. The prefects of the watch and grain supply acquired an extension of their functions that deprived the aediles of most of their earlier responsibilities; the role of these magistrates was now confined to the supervision of markets and games, and the enforcement of sanitary regulations in the city.[23] From the time of Nero, the supervision of the old state treasury (*aerarium*) that had been the chief task of the quaestors was now entrusted to two prefects of praetorian rank appointed by the emperor as its directors.[24]

The assemblies

During the early years of the Principate, the *comitia centuriata* and the *comitia tributa* continued to function as legislative and elective bodies.[25] Despite the limitations placed by the regime on freedom, which were real though not apparent, there was keen competition in the assemblies for magisterial posts and legislative proposals were submitted to them in accordance with ancient forms.[26] However, from the beginning of the new order, the political role of the assemblies was destined to wither away, yielding to the necessities of a society transformed from a city-state into an empire in which leadership had shifted from short-term magistracies to the supremacy of a single ruler. Thus, as early as the time of Tiberius, the election of magistrates was transferred from the centuriate assembly to the senate[27] and by the end of the first century AD popular legislation was superseded by the decrees of the emperor and the resolutions of the senate.[28] As a result, the assemblies lost their significance as independent political bodies, although they continued in existence in an honorary or ceremonial capacity until the end of the third century AD.

The empire in the first and second centuries AD

During the period AD 14–68, Rome was ruled by the emperors of the Julio-Claudian house who were Augustus' descendants by blood or adoption. These included Tiberius (AD 14–37), Caligula (AD 37–41), Claudius (AD 41–54) and Nero (AD 54–68). After a chaotic civil war (AD 68–69) during which the emperorship passed to three persons in succession, Vespasian (AD 69–79) established the Flavian dynasty, which lasted through the reigns of his sons Titus (AD 79–81) and

Domitian (AD 81–96). The assassination of Domitian in AD 96 left no heir of the Flavian house to claim the emperor's seat and the senate chose a new emperor from among its ranks, Nerva (AD 96–98). In order to secure the allegiance of the army and to resolve the succession problem, Nerva adopted Trajan, a successful general from Spain, as his son and joint ruler. Trajan became emperor in AD 98. The system of 'adoptive emperorship', as employed by Nerva, was applied successfully well into the second century AD. It enabled a series of capable rulers, known as the Antonines, to accede to the imperial throne. These included Trajan (AD 98–117), Hadrian (AD 117–38), Antoninus Pius (AD 138–61) and Marcus Aurelius (AD 161–80). The age of the Antonines was a period of political tranquility, during which the emperors and the senate worked together in relative harmony.[29]

During the first two centuries of the Principate, Rome consolidated its position as the dominant power in the Mediterranean world. Furthermore, Roman civilization reached its highest level of achievement under the prevailing peace and security within the empire's boundaries. Externally, the empire expanded until it included all the countries within the natural boundaries outlined by Augustus: Thrace, the Rhine regions, Britain, Armenia and Mauretania. The administration of the new frontier provinces (where the bulk of the Roman army was stationed) was organized by the emperors themselves, while the administration of the existing provinces remained with the senate.[30] At the same time, measures were introduced with the aim of improving the situation of the provincials: the process of bringing to justice provincial magistrates accused of extortion was simplified, provincial taxation was reorganized and a permanent civil service was formed to conduct the census and oversee the collection of taxes;[31] the development of new urban centres was encouraged;[32] new roads were built providing excellent means of communication throughout the empire; and banditry and piracy were suppressed. Moreover, from the early years of the Principate, Roman citizenship began to spread in the provinces, and the provincial elite was gradually absorbed into the equestrian and senatorial classes. As a result, the political and cultural differences between Italy and the provinces gradually decreased, and the concept of empire was strengthened.[33] The period of the Principate is marked by the progressive Romanization of the provinces, especially those of the West.

These developments were the background to an economic expansion in the Mediterranean world unparalleled before modern times. The imperial government generally adopted a laissez-faire attitude towards agriculture, industry and commerce, except for the production and distribution of a few basic or strategic commodities (especially the grain supply for the city of Rome). Doctrinaire economic programmes in the modern sense were virtually unknown, and the economy depended primarily on the maintenance of peace and security for its continued development. The bulk of Rome's wealth always derived from agriculture and stock-raising. Next to agriculture in importance were industry and commerce. International trade was facilitated by the expansion of the Roman road network, the security of transport, the establishment of a currency system for a whole empire and the opening of new markets in Italy and the provinces. In the second century AD, regular commercial contacts were established with lands as distant as India, China, Arabia, central and southern Africa, and the Scandinavian regions. Of far more importance was the trade conducted within the empire itself, between different provinces and cities. Grain and other agricultural products constituted the bulk of the trade, but manufactured articles played an increasing part, as did the necessary raw materials for every kind of industry. In the West, Italy was the chief centre of industry, supplying manufactured goods (such as pottery, metal and glass articles, and clothes) to markets from Britain to the Danube regions. In the East, many cities, such as Alexandria, Ephesus, Corinth and Antioch, became thriving industrial and commercial centres.[34] An outstanding social by-product of Mediterranean prosperity was the emergence of a numerically small but significant middle class in most of Rome's provincial cities and towns, which was composed largely of landowners, merchants, bankers and private contractors. This class furnished the members of the municipal councils (*decuriones*) who, after their election, became citizens of Rome. The councillors gave willingly and lavishly of their time and money, not only to govern their cities but also to embellish them with the material amenities of civilized life.

The first signs of an economic downturn appeared as early as the beginning of the second century AD, and this was due to several factors. The empire never created wealth in depth for a vast body of consumers, and the great majority of the population, whether peasants or city dwellers, lived at subsistence level. Trade and commerce benefited only a small minority; technology failed to develop, in part because of the inhibiting effects of cheap or slave labour; and industrial mass production was the exception rather than the rule. The Italian economy, based on the export of agricultural products (such as wine and olive oil) and manufactured goods to the provinces, declined when its overseas markets disappeared as the provinces increased their own agriculture and trade. Agricultural production flourished only as Rome's exploitable territory expanded and stagnated when the empire ceased to grow. Economic decline was precipitated further by the expansion of large-scale land ownership and the gradual disappearance of the small independent farmers, in both Italy and the provinces. As fewer countries were now conquered, the supply of slaves dwindled and slave labour became expensive. Consequently, large landowners began to lease parts of their estates to tenants.[35] Many small farmers were unable or unwilling to run the risks which small-scale farming involved, and thus gladly surrendered their lands and become tenants. Agricultural production declined as a result of the expanding tenant system and the change from systematic farming to the more primitive methods practised by the tenants. In turn, this decrease led to the gradual deterioration of living conditions in the cities, whose populations depended for their sustenance on the produce of the land. However, these were latent rather than actual problems in a relatively flourishing age, and the extent and effects of the empire's economic ills were not visible until the third century AD.

The social classes

During the Principate, the social classification of the Romans into the senatorial, equestrian and lower classes remained untouched. Augustus never pursued the aim of overturning or levelling existing social stratifications; he preferred to maintain, remodel and, above all, make them work in the context of the new political system that he introduced. Besides the traditional classes, the municipal aristocracy in Italy and the provinces formed an increasingly important, although remarkably heterogeneous, middle class. This system of social classification determined both the political and economic order, and the constitutional relationships of political power within the Roman state.

At the centre of the system – the Roman-Italian core of the *imperium Romanum* – the progressive social and economic differentiation in the late republican era led to an increasingly clear demarcation of the orders making up the upper class: the senatorial aristocracy and the equestrians. Office-holding and the possession of a considerable fortune remained the two basic prerequisites for admission to the senate,[36] and membership of the senatorial order continued to be *de facto* hereditary.[37] As political advancement was now a function of imperial patronage, the emperor ultimately decided who should receive such a privilege. The composition of the senate body underwent fundamental changes as more 'outsiders' or 'new men' (*homines novi*) were selected as members of the senatorial order, such as prominent equestrians from Italy and the provinces. Thus, by the third century AD the senatorial élite no longer had any connection with the old aristocratic families of the republican and Augustan periods. The realignment of the senatorial order was accelerated by the extinction of many older senatorial families from Rome and Italy, partly because of imperial persecution, and late marriages and few children in the senatorial families.[38]

As detailed earlier, during the last century of the Republic the equestrians established themselves as Rome's capitalist nobility whose income was derived mainly from business, industry, commerce and the financial management of state resources. Through their engagement in these activities they acquired considerable wealth and organizational skills and, from the early years of the Principate, they played an important part in the imperial administrative machinery. In time, the equestrian order was integrated into the empire's political structure and a hierarchy developed within this class determined by a person's rank in the imperial administration.[39] Equestrians who held top positions in the administration or the army, together with the leading senators, constituted the dominant political and military groups in the empire – a kind of aristocracy of office. In fact, there was hardly any difference between the senatorial and equestrian elites with respect to their functions, rank and privileges. Although the careers of equestrians may have been varied in the state administration and the army, this group of equestrians on empire service was only a fraction of the whole order. The great majority of equestrians, consisting of medium-to-large landowners and successful businessmen, were not involved in the government of the state. Thus, the crucial distinction in the social and political hierarchy within the empire was not simply the division between senators and equestrians, but the distinction between the particular echelons within these two leading orders. The equestrian class was always open to rejuvenation from below, as members of the lower classes who attained a measure of social success through public or army service could eventually achieve equestrian rank. At the same time, the equestrian class constituted the most important source of ongoing recruitment for the replenishment of the senatorial order as emperors regularly chose new senators from among the most eminent equestrians, including many of those from the provinces.[40]

A notable feature of the early imperial period was the rapid growth of urban life in the provinces and the emergence of an especially important social group, the order of the city councillors (*decuriones, ordo decurionum*) – the municipal aristocracy – whose wealth, like that of the imperial senatorial order, was derived almost exclusively from land.[41] The social quality of this group varied considerably from city to city according to the size, importance and economic conditions of the community concerned.[42] In addition to their normal duties pertaining to local government, city management and the administration of justice, the *decuriones* were expected to make regular contributions to all kinds of local causes, such as public games and festivals, and the building and maintenance of schools, temples, baths, libraries and such like. Thus, municipal offices, being unsalaried, were a heavy drain on the resources of their holders. In return, a *decurio* received various privileges and honorific titles from the community and could anticipate admission into the *ordo equester* or even into the *ordo senatorius*. Since the *decuriones* were recruited from the wealthy families, membership of the *ordo decurionum* gradually became hereditary in practice. By the third century AD, as economic and political conditions deteriorated everywhere, membership in municipal councils became obligatory for those with enough property, and the *decuriones* were responsible to the state for revenues due from municipal territories. As a result, the once valued civic *honores* increasingly evolved into essentially compulsory offices and very few people wished to shoulder the financial burdens which membership of the *ordo decurionum* entailed.[43]

Having completed our survey of the empire's upper classes, we come now to the amorphous category of lower class citizens, both urban and rural. As noted before, despite the official obeisance to the *populus Romanus* by the Augustan regime on an ideological level, the community of Rome's free citizens was subjected to a process of systematic elimination from politics. With the gradual decline of the popular assemblies, the citizenry ceased to play any part in the government of the empire. The prestige of participating in politics was supplanted by the assumption of a vested right to be fed and entertained at public expense, and this right was not taken away by the emperors. Popular apathy became more pronounced as the Romano-Italian element in the population was diluted more and more. A large proportion of the *plebs* now consisted of ex-slaves who acquired Roman citizenship following their manumission by their owners.[44] Although the ex-slaves were often superficially Romanized with a veneer of Roman culture, they were not representative of the Roman spirit as they had little sense of continuity with Rome's past. In general, the lower strata in Rome and the major urban centres of the empire (*plebs urbana*) enjoyed a better social position than the masses of the rural population (*plebs rustica*). In the cities there were better prospects for employment, greater opportunities to change occupations and more scope for a public life than in the countryside. Nevertheless, the life of most members of the *plebs urbana* was hard and living conditions were often wretched. The greater part of the free population of Rome eked out a meagre livelihood in craftwork, service trades or small shop-keeping, but hard work and ability by no means guaranteed economic and social success. Moreover, the number of people in the cities who could not earn a living continued to rise and increasingly more poverty-stricken citizens placed themselves under the protection of wealthy men, thereby becoming their clients.[45] Because the urban proletariat posed a potential threat to political stability, food and money were regularly distributed and impressive public spectacles were organized at public expense; this placed a heavy drain on the state's resources.[46] By far the largest class in society was that of the small farmers and peasants. The demands placed on the farming class became heavier on account of the urbanization process fostered by the imperial government. Since the people who actually worked on the farms were regarded as socially inferior to the city-dwellers, on whose lands many worked as tenants, the result was a widening of the rift between city and country. In the course of the second century AD, the city element became progressively more dependent on the labour of the rural workers, and these, in turn, became ever more oppressed.[47]

During the Principate period, the social distinction between the upper and lower classes found a clear expression in the legal notions of *honestior* and *humilior*. The *honestiores* ('honourable') were comprised of the privileged members of the governing class (senators, equestrians, civil servants, soldiers and members of the provincial town councils), while those belonging to the lower classes of society were collectively referred to as *humiliores* ('humble') or *tenuiores*. The *humiliores* had a distinctly inferior standing in the eyes of the law and were subject to heavy and degrading punishments (such as forced labour in the state mines, flogging and torture, condemnation to gladiatorial games and beast-hunts, and execution by crucifixion). By contrast, the *honestiores* were exempted from punishments of a shameful nature, and the pronouncements of death and other severe penalties against reputable citizens were very rarely enforced.[48]

The army

Soon after he gained control of the state, Augustus proceeded to reorganize the military establishment. In view of the strategic situation and the available economic resources, he decided to place the security of the state in the hands of a professional standing army, thus continuing the development pioneered by Marius around 100 BC. His decision seemed inevitable because a levy of civilian soldiers inducted for short periods of service could not provide the effective trained force that the situation demanded. Furthermore, as a result of the system developed for the empire's defence, the army was transformed from a field force into garrison troops stationed along the frontiers; the largest concentrations were on the Danube and the Rhine in the North, and the Euphrates in the East. At strategic points behind these frontiers, large fortified camps were established to serve as operation bases, and military roads were constructed to facilitate the rapid movement of troops. Although the emperor retained the right of ordering a conscription, voluntary enlistment supplied most of the recruits, and the officers came, as in the past, from the senatorial aristocracy and the equestrians.[49] As during the later Republic, the legionaries were drawn from Roman citizens living in Italy or the provinces, or from provincials who now received Roman citizenship on entering the service. Besides the regular units of citizens, a significant segment of the army consisted of auxiliaries: troops recruited from the non-Roman population of the provinces.[50]

Throughout the Principate period the emperor, as commander-in-chief of the army, was solely responsible for all matters relating to the organization and maintenance of the armed forces. He appointed the legates who commanded the legions stationed in the imperial provinces and the officers in charge of the auxiliary troops, determined the distribution of troops in the provinces and their tasks, and made arrangements for the payment of army officers and soldiers. The Roman army always had a peculiar sense of personal loyalty to the emperor and his family, being willing to accept even inept emperors if they continued in a dynastic succession. However, when a dynasty failed, as at the death of Nero and Domitian, there was always a danger that the armies would seek to elevate their own commanders to the imperial throne and thereby provoke civil war. As the ideological underpinnings of the system began to crumble in the late Principate period, the army assumed an increasingly important role in selecting and occasionally replacing emperors based on its own interests. This development is clearly seen in the period that followed the death of Alexander Severus (AD 235) when different armies each proclaimed as emperor the general who led them to victory over foreign foes or other mutinous troops, often forcing him to march on Rome in expectation of receiving increases in pay and largess.[51]

The expansion of the Roman citizenship

Roman citizenship was the status whereby a person was entitled to all the rights of the Roman civil law, such as the rights of voting and holding public office. At the same time, the community imposed on the citizen various obligations, such as military service and the payment of taxes. In general, a person was a Roman citizen if their parents had been citizens joined in legal marriage, or if their father had been a Roman citizen and their mother a member of a community to which Rome had granted the so-called 'right of marriage'. The citizenship was also granted to children born to a Roman woman and a slave or unknown father, and to slaves manumitted according to the proper legal form. Finally, additions to the citizen body might be made through the extension of the Roman citizenship to foreigners. During the Republic, the citizenship was initially granted to individuals[52] and whole communities (such as municipalities or veterans' colonies) in only special instances and after the Social War (91–87 BC) it was granted *en masse* to all Italian allies. In

Spain, Gaul, Africa and the Asiatic territories, Roman settlers as well as meritorious natives, who obtained the distinction of citizenship, played an increasingly important part in the process of Romanization of the provinces and, at the same time, safeguarded Rome's interests overseas.[53] By the end of the Republic and in the early Principate, a Roman or Romanized ruling class had arisen in the provinces, which constituted the backbone of Roman civilization. Augustus put a brake on the expansion of citizenship by designing a population policy that sought to preserve the Roman and Italian stock as the core of the empire. This entailed less frequent granting of individual naturalizations to foreigners while attempting to stem the flood of emancipated slaves. However, the realities of a coalescing empire forced his successors to adopt standards that were more elastic. Once Rome, Italy and the provinces had entered the stage of mutual assimilation, the citizenship was granted with increasing frequency to individuals or whole communities, often following the concession of the *ius Latii* (the intermediate legal status between citizen and foreigner given to members of Latin colonies). At the end, rather than being a conscious method for furthering Romanization, the extension of the citizenship to the provincials was its unavoidable result. Furthermore, in much the same way as Roman civilization had been transformed during the Principate into Romanism, Romanism itself became infused by foreign, especially Hellenistic, elements by way of cross-fertilization.

It may seem, therefore, merely the logical culmination of a process in the making for centuries that Emperor Caracalla issued an edict, the celebrated *constitutio Antoniniana* (AD 212), by which he bestowed Roman citizenship upon all the free inhabitants of the empire who were members of organized communities.[54] According to the historian Dio Cassius, one main reason for the introduction of this measure was the emperor's desire to increase the numbers of those who had to pay inheritance tax (*vicesima hereditatum*)[55] and the tax levied on the emancipation of slaves (*vicesima libertatis* or *vicessima manumissionum*)[56] – taxes which only Roman citizens were required to pay.[57] It has been suggested, moreover, that the enactment of this law may have been motivated by Caracalla's desire to mitigate public reaction to the assassination, ordered by him, of his brother Geta and the influential jurist and *praefectus praetorio*, Papinianus. Regardless of the emperor's motives, the *constitutio Antoniniana* is regarded as a milestone in the evolution of the Roman state. It signified the final transformation of the traditional *civitas* into empire citizenship[58] and led to the extension of Roman law to the whole empire. In the course of time, the interaction between the universalized Roman law, local law and custom led to the emergence of a complex legal system combining Roman and local, especially Greek, elements.

Despite the significance of Caracalla's edict on the level of political theory, the practical effects of granting citizenship to the mass of provincials must not be overrated. The political benefits deriving from the edict could have accrued, if at all, only to a handful of provincials (members of the local aristocracies) who may have aspired to a position in the imperial administration. For these individuals the grant of citizenship, or what was virtually equality with indigenous Romans or Italians, was a privileged extra status they could gain, over and above their existing rights. Roman citizenship may possibly also have been advantageous to a small number of individuals engaged in commercial transactions with Rome or other provinces. But for the great majority of the provincial population, especially the members of the lower classes, the potential advantages of citizenship were negligible as neither their personal status nor their fortune was in fact improved. In respect of this reality, and the mounting problems facing the empire in the early third century AD, the extension of the citizenship appears as little more than an empty gesture imparted by a political system in the throes of crisis.[59]

The crisis of the third century and the end of the Principate

Emperor Marcus Aurelius was succeeded by his son Commodus, an incompetent ruler, whose assassination in AD 192 initiated a period of upheaval not unlike that which followed the death of Nero in AD 68. This revolution brought to power Septimius Severus (AD 193–211), founder of the Severan dynasty (AD 193–235). The Severans exceeded all other Roman dynasties in using military force as a basis for their rule and exalting the autocratic character of the imperial office. Among the main developments marking the Severan epoch were the complete militarization of the state and administrative apparatus; the elimination of the senate as a factor in government with the virtual abandonment of the principle of diarchy (the double rule of the emperor and the senate);[60] an escalation of state intervention and repression; a systematic effort to strengthen the empire's frontier defences (partly through the military mobilization of population groups not yet properly Romanized); the extension of the Roman citizenship to practically all the free inhabitants of the empire (by the *constitutio Antoniniana*); and the decline of Italy to the level of a province. Yet neither Septimius Severus nor his successors achieved a lasting consolidation, nor could they arrest developments both within and outside the empire that led to fifty years of chaos following the death of Alexander Severus in AD 235. This catastrophic period marked the end of the political system of the Principate and produced a radical transformation of the imperial government and society.

The crisis of the third century derived from the influence of complex, interconnected factors (economic, political and military), and the trends instigating it were operative even beneath the surface of the seemingly peaceful and prosperous second century. Among the chief causes of economic decline were the creation of a vast and ever-expanding administrative and military apparatus, which the dwindling resources of the empire could no longer support, and the perpetuation of a class structure that failed to give the producing classes rewards equal to the burdens imposed on them. The peasant class, which was ultimately a pivot in the empire's economy, could no longer bear the burden of taxation and support such numerous classes as the soldiers, urban proletariat, state officials and estate holders with their numerous retinues. Crushed by the demands placed upon it by the state, the urban middle class also fell into decay and once prosperous municipalities teetered on the verge of bankruptcy. Just as these symptoms of economic weakness appeared in the late second century AD, the empire was engulfed by a series of epidemics that considerably reduced its productive population, and by the first wave of barbarian invasions.

The Roman territory in the Rhine and Danube frontiers, Greece and Asia Minor endured a series of attacks by aggressive Germanic tribes (Goths, Vandals, Alans, Alamanni and Franks). Meanwhile, the Persians governed by the Sassanid dynasty founded an empire in the East and launched raids deep into the Roman provinces.[61] Rome responded by setting up a network of fortifications along the frontier zones, but stemming the barbarian tide proved to be an impossible task for two reasons. First, as a result of the military policy of Augustus and his successors, the army had become a frontier garrison force lacking the support of large mobile reserves. Frontier provinces were frequently bereft of protection when Roman legions had to be shifted to areas under threat, and thus defence was practically impossible when the empire was simultaneously invaded on several frontier sectors. Second, the various frontier armies were now comprised of the least Romanized elements of the frontier populations and these tended to deteriorate into local militia, often guided by their own special interests. The weakening of the central government engendered disorder and civil war, as different field armies proclaimed their generals as emperors and used their own strength to plunder the lands of the empire. In these circumstances, the imperial title was itself a very dubious achievement as the generals raised to the throne were confronted with one crisis after another and, whether they failed or by drastic measures succeeded, they were almost certain to provoke an attack or their own downfall by usurpation.[62] In the wake of the devastation caused by war and plunder, the civilian populations and the economies were severely damaged, law and order broke down, commerce and industry came to a standstill and once flourishing urban centres fell into decay.

The scant central authority tried to meet the mounting cost of government by imposing heavy taxes and requisitions on the inhabitants of depopulated and devastated provinces. As these measures proved inadequate, the government resorted to the constant devaluation of the currency and this provoked disastrous inflation. It also initiated a return to a 'natural' economy where business transactions were made in kind rather than in worthless coin. The government responded to these trends by intensifying, tightening and consolidating state controls. It also regimented the agricultural and commercial classes in order to compel them to produce, collect and distribute necessary revenue, and to perform any other services considered essential by the state. Among the worst affected were the members of the municipal councils, the decurions, who were rendered personally responsible to the state for the taxes and requisitions demanded from their cities. Thus, they were reduced from being organs of independent administration to executive instruments of central control. As a result of the financial and other burdens placed on the decurions, this once strong and confident social grouping was practically annihilated.[63] State intervention and the ruthless severity of its nature, the institutionalization of compulsory services and occupational constraints, and the destruction of social classes, like the municipal aristocracy and a large part of the urban middle class, greatly undermined the ideological basis of the Principate's political system and the very values and advantages that once characterized the *imperium Romanum*. The crisis of the third century was accompanied by deep psychological changes that led to a transformation of the cultural and religious life of the empire. The breakdown of law and order, the corruption of a governing class dominated entirely by motives of power and the continual insecurity of life and property all provoked a feeling that the world was growing old and some terrible catastrophe was impending. As neither the Roman state religion nor the dominant philosophies of the Principate were seen to be capable of providing a cure for the ills of life, people turned for consolation to other-worldly philosophies,[64] or to one of the many mystery religions spreading from the Near East, such as Mithraism. Of much greater significance was the steady spread of Christianity, in spite of the sporadic but ruthless persecution of Christians by the imperial government.

In the later part of the third century, under a succession of competent emperors – Decius (AD 249–51), Claudius Gothicus (AD 268–70), Aurelian (AD 270–75) and Probus (AD 276–82) – the crisis was finally checked, discipline in the army was restored, external foes were repelled and imperial unity was re-established. However, victory was achieved at great cost, and the Roman world that emerged from the upheaval of the third century was very different from that of the Republic and Principate periods. The civilization and forms of social, political, economic and cultural life that had been characteristic of the ancient Greco-Roman world for centuries, had received a mortal blow and the coming of the Middle Ages was at hand.

8

THE PRINCIPATE:
THE SOURCES OF LAW

Introduction

As we observed in Chapter 7, Augustus succeeded with his consummate statecraft in establishing a form of government capable of engendering internal political stabilization and consolidating the Roman *imperium*. In all his earlier acts, Augustus made a great show of restoring the old republican forms of government. One method for accomplishing this so-called 'restoration of the Republic' was acknowledging the authority of the senate and the people, thereby appealing to the prevailing republican instincts held by a large section of the Roman population. Over time, the senate and the people responded by granting him the extraordinary powers he deemed necessary to complete the political reconstruction. In the end, all these powers were consolidated into a form where the individual elements could scarcely be distinguished. Thus, Augustus wielded a power greater than that normally accorded to any republican magistrate, and he virtually became the undisputed master of the state. His successors inherited his powers, but a long interval passed before the new system of government was so thoroughly institutionalized that the blatant exercise of imperial power was completely feasible. The *princeps*-emperor may be described as a magistrate with a super-*imperium*, outranking all other magistrates and liberated from the check of the tribune's veto by assuming the tribunician power himself. The existence of an *imperium* of this kind naturally had a tremendous influence on the development of the law. Initially, this influence manifested itself indirectly through the manipulation of the old republican institutions. Yet, as the last vestiges of the old regime gradually faded, the emperor became the only living source of law.

Contemporary writers designate the period from Augustus to the middle of the third century AD as the classical period of Roman law. During this period, legislative actions emanated from several sources. As under the Republic, laws existing technically as *leges* could only be passed by the citizens of Rome gathered in official assembly. Other legal sources developed in republican times included magisterial edicts, legal interpretations by jurists and practices sanctioned by custom. New sources of law were the resolutions of the senate (*senatus consulta*), and the various categories of imperial decrees (*constutitiones principum*).

The vested right of the assemblies to enact legislation was maintained as a regular function. Under Augustus and his successors, several important statutes were passed concerning marriage and divorce, the freeing of slaves and matters of legal procedure. However, these measures were all part of imperial policy and expressed the emperor's will. As the political functions of the assemblies declined rapidly under the new regime, popular legislation became obsolete and ceased to exist at the end of the first century AD.

As we have discerned, the magistrates of the Roman state originally possessed considerable freedom in exercising their *imperium*. On entering office, each magistrate customarily issued an edict informing citizens how he intended to administer the law. In time, these edicts were established by custom so that a new magistrate would adopt the edict of his predecessors and execute few, if any, changes. These general edicts, especially those issued by the praetor, engendered a new body of law known as magisterial or praetorian law (*ius honorarium, ius praetorium*). However, from the beginning of the imperial period the productive strength of the magisterial edict dwindled. Magisterial initiatives became increasingly rare with the gradual erosion of the magistrates' right to alter the edicts on their own authority. Finally, the codification of the *ius honorarium* during Emperor Hadrian's reign (AD 130) terminated the edict as a source of new law.

During the first three centuries of the Empire, the most productive element in Roman legal life was the work of the jurists. Roman jurisprudence originated with the priestly college of the *pontifices*. Since the second century BC, an increasing number of members from the Roman ruling class (*nobiles*) engaged in jurisprudence without being members of the *collegium pontificum* and they acquired a great part of the prestige held by the pontificate. The main activities of the jurists were the presentation of opinions on difficult points of law to magistrates, judges and litigating parties (*respondere*), the drafting of legal documents, such as contracts and wills (*cavere*) and the guiding of litigants on matters of legal procedure (*agere*). Besides these practical activities, the jurists were absorbed in two other tasks that notably contributed to the development of law: the writing of legal works (*scribere*) and the teaching of law (*docere*). Like the pontiffs, the jurists did not receive any remuneration for their services and only devoted some of their time to law as they were occupied with public life and the pursuit of high offices. However, in the last century of the Republic a group of jurists emerged who actually withdrew from politics to dedicate themselves to law. During the Principate the authority of the jurists was further enhanced. Seeking to initiate a certain indirect control over the jurists, Augustus granted a select group of specially qualified jurists the privilege of presenting legal opinions (*ius respondendi*) and delivering them with the emperor's authority (*ex auctoritate principis*). In the second century AD Emperor Hadrian introduced the rule that if a majority of jurists with the *ius respondendi* held the same opinion it was binding on the judge – in all other cases, a judge was free to choose between conflicting opinions. At that time, the most distinguished jurists were drawn into the imperial circle and exercised their chief functions as members of the emperor's administrative apparatus. By playing a direct role in governmental tasks and the central imperial administration of justice, the jurists contributed to the evolution of the new public law for the empire. However, their main interest was still principally focused on private law. Classical jurisprudence absorbed all the legal questions in this field that had arisen in the later republican period. These questions, enriched by the emergence of new issues, were categorized and often adequately answered for the first time. It should be noted that the classical jurists, like their predecessors of the republican period, were essentially practical men concerned with devising correct solutions to concrete questions rather than formulating general principles applicable to all times and all societies. The practical nature of their interests is reflected in their writings, as their major works evolved from legal practice and were composed primarily for legal practitioners. Throughout the Principate, legal development was promoted mainly by the jurists and their achievements essentially facilitated the full realization of the Romans' genius for law.

In republican times the senate exercised great influence on legislation, although it apparently did not have a formal right to directly enact legislation itself. For all practical purposes, its resolutions (*senatus consulta*) were treated as valid law and under normal circumstances could not be violated with impunity. Under the Principate, the *senatus consultum* became an officially acknowledged, and in fact the usually adopted, form of legislation. This situation derived from two factors: first, the senate increasingly embraced the task of guiding magistrates in issuing their edicts; second, by the end of the first century AD the senate had replaced the popular assemblies as the republican element of the constitution and the functions of the statute were assumed by the senatorial resolution. However, from the time of Augustus the senate's freedom of decision was already subject to the emperor's power. As a result, the senatorial resolutions became increasingly little more than mere declarations of the emperor's will.

The crucial factor that distinguishes the imperial era from the preceding age is the emperor's position and influence in the field of law. In the early Principate, the emperors indirectly achieved their legislative goals through controlled decrees of the senate and enactments of the people's assemblies. But as imperial power intensified at the expense of the old republican institutions, the emperors started to create new legal rules directly in a number of ways. Imperial legislation was designated the common name of imperial constitutions (*constitutiones principis*) and assumed diverse forms: administrative orders (*edicta*); precedent-creating judicial decisions of the emperor in individual cases (*decreta*); answers to questions of law submitted by officials or private citizens (*rescripta*); and instructions issued by the emperor to officials in his service (*mandata*).

During the first two centuries of the Principate, Roman law proliferated in the provinces as a consequence of the Roman citizenship policies and Romanization process. In the western provinces, where native legal traditions were generally weaker than those of the Hellenistic eastern provinces, Roman law spread more rapidly and with greater permanence. However, this law was not imposed on the subject peoples by force. On the contrary, the laws and customs of non-Roman communities generally operated intact except insofar as they might prove embarrassing to Roman rule. In a sense, Roman law evolved as the sole law of the Roman world when all the free inhabitants in the empire were granted Roman citizenship by the *constitutio Antoniniana* of Emperor Caracalla in AD 212 – but only in a sense. In reality, local systems of law did not disappear but remained applicable mainly in the form of custom. These systems adapted and influenced Roman law in diverse ways. Thus, the law operating in the provinces existed as a blend of Roman law and local practice. It varied in areas and was remote from the refinement and sophistication of the classical system. The process that has been labelled 'vulgarization' of Roman law emerged in this period and it was greatly advanced when the Principate age came to an end.

The decline of the comitial legislation

Augustus, intent on exercising his powers within the framework of the republican institutions, refrained from assuming the right to legislate alone. Instead, he abided by a tradition that accepted comitial enactment as the exclusive source of legislation. Thus, he used the assemblies to procure the enactment of the legislative measures that appealed to him. Some measures were passed directly on his motion and are hence called *leges Iuliae*.[1] Others were passed on the motion of consuls or praetors, though obviously he was their real promoter. In this way, important statutes were passed concerning legal procedure (*leges Iuliae iudiciorum publicorum et privatorum*);[2] marriage and divorce (*lex Iulia de maritandis ordinibus, lex Papia Poppaea*);[3] adultery (*lex Iulia de adulteriis coercendis*);[4] the repression of electoral corruption (*lex Iulia de ambitu*);[5] and the operation of the senate (*lex Iulia de senatu habendo*).[6] Other noteworthy legislative enactments of this period were the *lex Fufia Caninia* (2 BC) and the *lex Aelia Sentia* (AD 4) that introduced restrictions on testamentary manumission; and the *lex Claudia*, a law passed under Emperor Claudius, that abolished the guardianship of the nearest relatives (*tutela legitima*) over women.[7]

Almost since the emergence of the new order, comitial legislation was destined to wither away. It yielded to the necessities of a community transformed from a city-state into a world empire, and a political system where the leadership shifted from short-term magistracies to the supremacy of a single ruler. The substance of legislation had become too complicated to be entrusted to a metropolitan electorate renowned for volatility and generally ill-informed. Thus, after the reign of Claudius (AD 41–54) few legislative measures were passed through assemblies, and comitial legislation had entirely disappeared by the end of the first century AD.[8]

However, even as popular legislation was becoming obsolete the popular participation in public affairs was sustained as a constitutional fiction for the legalization and legitimation of the emperor's power. The republican idea of the sovereign people as the ultimate legitimation of political power was so strongly entrenched by tradition that a formal *lex*, as an act of popular endorsement, had to be passed to invest the *princeps*-emperor with supreme powers. Thus, the practice emerged whereby the senate passed a resolution on the accession of a new emperor that

103

recommended the conferment on him of the *tribunicia potestas* and those supplementary powers recognized as attributes of the imperial office. It also embraced the routine event where the people enacted the terms of this resolution in the form of a statute, commonly described by the old name *lex de imperio*.[9] Throughout the Principate, the legal basis of the emperor's position still derived from the grant of the republican proconsular and tribunician powers that Augustus originally acquired from the senate and the people. After comitial legislation in general had disappeared, this grant was regularly renewed by the senate, the successor of the assemblies' full legislative powers, on behalf of the *populus Romanus* upon the accession of the next holder of the imperial office.

The magisterial law

During the long period after the enactment of the Law of the Twelve Tables, an intricate legal system developed from the interaction between custom, enacted law and case law. It embodied different layers of legal norms that coexisted and were mutually influential. The Roman *ius civile* formed the earliest layer with its basis in statutory law and customary law as we have observed. From the middle of the third century BC, a second layer emerged: the *ius honorarium* or magisterial law created by the praetors and other magistrates charged with the administration of justice. This body of law originated from decided cases and its essence was common sense, expediency and fairness. During the later republican period, its practical importance surpassed customary and statutory law.

After the establishment of the Principate, Roman law still comprised the *ius civile* and the *ius honorarium*: the original core of the civil law and the law derived from the edicts of the jurisdictional magistrates (especially the praetors). However, since the inception of this period the productive strength of the magisterial edict started to weaken. As praetorian initiatives became increasingly rare, the *ius honorarium* gradually became fixed in form and nearly as crystallized and immutable as statutory law. The changes in the edicts forged by the magistrates largely pertained to measures introduced by other law-making agencies (for example, *senatus consulta*). Finally, pursuant to Emperor Hadrian's orders in the early second century AD, the permanent edict of the praetors and the aediles was recast, unified and updated by the jurist Lucius Salvius Iulianus (probably during the latter's praetorship). The codified edict was ratified by a *senatus consultum* in AD 130 and thereafter magistrates were bound to administer justice in individual cases exclusively on the basis of the reformulated edict.[10] Although edicts were still annually issued by magistrates, the latter had no control over their content. For all practical purposes, the *edictum perpetuum* thus evolved as established law; any further necessary changes had to be initiated by imperial enactment.

The codification of the edict marks the end of the *ius honorarium* as a distinct source of law. Thereafter, the imperial instruments of law-making attended to the further development of Roman law in a similar manner as in earlier times the edicts of the jurisdictional magistrates had refined and enlarged the original body of the civil law. However, the distinction between *ius civile* and *ius honorarium* persevered as long as the judicial system allied to these bodies of law still operated, and the Roman jurists could further develop these bodies by creative interpretation of the legal rules and institutions they embodied. Over time, new forms of dispensing justice superseded the traditional republican system of legal procedure as the socio-political environment changed. As a result, the distinction between the two bodies of law, having become one of form rather than substance, was obliterated. The fusion of *ius civile* and *ius honorarium* was also precipitated by the Roman jurists who, by developing both masses of law in common, gradually removed their boundaries. In the later imperial era the resultant combination of these two sources of law was designated *ius*, in contradistinction to the body of rules derived from imperial legislation known as *lex*.

Legislation by the senate

As we have observed, the senate in the republican era theoretically had no direct legislative powers. Its decrees (*senatus consulta*) were merely resolutions of advice to the magistrates and had no legal effect unless they were incorporated into a statute or a magisterial edict. However, in the later part of the republican period the senate exercised a very strong law-making influence through its ever-increasing involvement in the legislative process. Ordinarily, before legislative proposals were submitted to the people for approval the drafts were thoroughly discussed in the senate and any necessary amendments were executed in accordance with the views of the majority of senators. The final formulated draft would be incorporated in a *senatus consultum* advising the magistrate concerned to submit it to the people. Thus, the subsequent enactment of the proposed measure by the assembly virtually amounted to nothing more than a formal ratification by the people of the *senatus consultum*'s terms. Moreover, the senate increasingly assumed the task of guiding the praetors and other jurisdictional magistrates in the issuing of their edicts. In this way, the senate notably contributed to the creation of fresh *ius honorarium*: the law that derived its formal force from the *imperium* of a magistrate, as opposed to the *ius civile* that existed as the law extracting its formal force from statute or custom. The last years of the Republic featured the occasional event where a measure proposed by a magistrate that had the senate's sanction was not submitted to the people but immediately came into effect. A rationale is that the popular assemblies were now quite unrepresentative and demoralized, and thus could no longer serve as effective organs of government.

In the first decades of the Principate, the role of the senate in the law-making process was more pronounced as legislation by the assemblies faded. Although comitial and senatorial legislation apparently coexisted for a period, the senate progressively assumed the position of the state's regular legislative organ. In time, the *senatus consultum* rather than the *lex* became the chief means of legislation. Resembling the pattern followed under the Republic, the *senatus consulta* were couched in the form of instructions addressed to magistrates and were assigned the

105

name of the magistrate who proposed them rather than the reigning emperor. As elaborated in Chapter 7, in the early imperial period the senate still retained the tradition of existing as a privileged order but was actually composed of the emperor's nominees. From the start, the senate was virtually a tool of the emperor and had no free hand in the matter of legislation any more than it had in other matters. Indeed, most senatorial decrees were passed on the initiative of the emperor or at least with his acquiescence. The tribunician power was a characteristic element of the imperial office that could be wielded by the emperor to impede any act of the senate at any time. Therefore, we may surmise that during the Principate a *senatus consultum* was an ordinance that essentially engaged the authority of the emperor. Given this situation, it is easy to fathom that magistrates had to implement it precisely as if it were a statute, even though in terms of form the relevant instruction still committed its execution merely to their discretion. The fact that the *senatus consultum* was practically treated in much the same way as a statute rendered it a vehicle of legislation, although it appears unlikely that any specific constitutional action emerged to equate the resolutions of the senate with the *leges*.

In the first two centuries of the Principate, numerous *senatus consulta* were issued that effectuated important changes in the areas of both public and private law. An early senatorial decree of this period was the *senatus consultum Silanianum* of AD 10 that aspired to repress the frequent killing of masters by their slaves.[11] Other important senatorial resolutions of this period embraced: the *senatus consultum Vellaeanum* (AD 46) that forbade women from assuming liability for debts of others, including those of their husbands;[12] the *senatus consultum Libonianum* (AD 16) that imposed the penalties of the *lex Cornelia de falsis* for the forging of testaments;[13] the *senatus consultum Trebellianum* (c. AD 56) and the *senatus consultum Pegasianum* (AD 73) that concerned the acceptance of inheritances subject to *fideicommissa*;[14] the *senatus consultum Iuventianum* (AD 129) that addressed matters such as claims of the Roman public treasury (*aerarium populi Romani*) against private individuals for the recovery of vacant inheritances;[15] the *senatus consultum Macedonianum* (second half of the first century AD) that prohibited loans to sons who remained subject to *patria potestas*;[16] and the *senatus consultum Tertullianum*, passed in the time of Hadrian, that granted mothers the legal right of succession to their children's inheritance.[17]

In the course of time, as the senate degenerated into a servile instrument of the emperor, its authority as an autonomous organ of legislation diminished and its resolutions increasingly became little more than mere declarations of the emperor's will. Since the era of Emperor Claudius, senatorial resolutions were usually drafted by imperial officials and the relevant proposal was recited in the senate by either the emperor or, more often, an official acting in his name (*oratio principis*). The senators were then invited to express their views and a vote was conducted. However, the emperor's influence on the senate entailed the latter never failing to agree with the main premises of the proposal.[18] As the movement towards absolute monarchy advanced, the terms of the emperor's proposal were increasingly adopted as a matter of course by the senate without even the pretence of a discussion. By the end of the second century AD, this practice had become so routine that it was customary to label a *senatus consultum* as an *oratio* of the emperor on whose initiative the *senatus consultum* was passed.[19] The result was that, in the same way as legislation by the senate had superseded comitial legislation, imperial legislation gradually replaced senatorial legislation, which eventually vanished in the third century AD.

Imperial law-making

Augustus exhibited deference to the old republican institutions he claimed to have restored by consistently refusing to accept direct law-making powers that could supplant those of the established organs of legislation. So long as the principles of the Augustan constitution retained their vitality, the emperor achieved his legislative goals indirectly by regularly using the popular assemblies and then the senate. However, the emperor not only controlled legislation but, since the start of the Principate period, had diverse methods for creating new legal norms directly without appearing to legislate. The emperor's law-making authority was initially based on his magisterial powers, especially the *imperium proconsulare maius*, and his tribunician *potestas*. As the imperial power increased over time at the expense of the old republican institutions, the enactments of the emperors (*constitutiones principum*) were recognized as possessing full statutory force (*legis vigorem*) and functioning as a direct source of law alongside the *leges* and the *senatus consulta*.

The second century jurist Gaius enumerated imperial constitutions along with other sources of law and declared: 'A constitution of a *princeps* is what the emperor has authorized by decree, edict or letter. Nor is it ever doubted that this has the force of law, since the emperor himself receives his *imperium* by a law.'[20] In other words, the law that conferred *imperium* on the *princeps*-emperor (*lex de imperio*) transferred to him the authority to legislate in the name of the Roman people. When this quoted passage is considered in light of the actual legal situation in Gaius' era, it implies nothing less than whatever the emperor decreed as the law possessed the validity of a formal statute (*lex*), i.e. a statute like those which in the republican period were formally enacted by a popular assembly authorized by the senate. The foundation of the imperial legislative authority is not discovered in legal rationales but in political reality: the emperor's power evolved so that his assumption of a direct legislative role could not be challenged. Indeed, the growth of imperial legislative authority was seemingly gradual. The imperial office in the late Principate period operated as the ultimate source of all administrative, legislative and judicial activity. It did not resemble the same office as that established by Augustus. It displayed a far more autocratic nature and assumed many characteristics of a monarchy.

Four types of imperial constitutions are commonly recognized: *edicta, rescripta, mandata* and *decreta*.

Edicta

As elaborated previously, under the republican constitution the higher magistrates of the Roman state had the power to issue edicts or general proclamations that enumerated their orders or the policies they intended to observe in matters falling within their respective spheres of competency (*ius edicendi*). As holder of the magisterial *imperium*, the *princeps*-emperor also possessed this power. But as the emperor outranked all other magistrates in authority and his sphere of competence was virtually unlimited, his edicts were much broader in scope than those of the regular magistrates. These edicts addressed the entire business of the state and operated during and even after the reign of the emperor who issued them, unless they were repealed expressly or implicitly.[21] The scope of imperial edicts encompassed such divergent matters as private law, criminal law and procedure, the constitution of the courts, the organization and administration of the provinces, and the bestowal of the Roman citizenship.[22] The category of imperial edicts incorporated, for example, the *constitutio Antoniniana* (AD 212), whereby Emperor Caracalla granted the Roman citizenship to all the free inhabitants of the empire.[23]

Rescripta

The term *rescriptum* denoted the emperor's answer to a petition or inquiry. Such petitions and answers might relate to all sorts of matters, but the present context focuses on those that invoked and resolved questions of law. A distinction was delineated between two types of imperial rescripts: *epistulae* and *subscriptiones*. The former were embodied in a separate document and were addressed to state officials in Rome or in the Provinces.[24] The latter were responses to petitions from private citizens written on the margin or at the end of the application itself.[25] Rescripts were particularly important for the development of the private law in the second century AD, when it became customary for judges and private citizens to petition the emperors for decisions on difficult questions of law. Initially, the imperial opinion was deemed to have only an advisory character but it eventually acquired the same force as a general rule. When an imperial rescript settled a point of law invoked by the facts stated in a petition, any judge acting under the emperor's authority would naturally accept the latter's determination as binding if the statement of facts was validated as accurate.[26] Furthermore, the emperor's ruling on a point of law contained in a rescript was treated in practice as a binding statement of law for all future cases. In this way, a new body of legal rules developed that had assumed voluminous proportions by the end of the second century AD.[27] Jurists of this period formed private collections of imperial rescripts, large parts of which come down to us through the codification of Justinian and other post-classical compilations of law.

Mandata

The *mandata* were the emperor's administrative instructions to officials in his service that pertained to the conduct and execution of their official duties. As evidenced by the fragments preserved in later compilations of law, the most important *mandata* were addressed to provincial governors and concerned provincial administration (especially its financial side), while others dealt with private and criminal law and the administration of justice.[28] As originally a mandate was strictly personal, it continued in force only as long as both the emperor who issued it and the official subject to the mandate remained in office. When the emperor died or the official was replaced, the mandate had to be renewed. Gradually, the successive renewals established a body of standing instructions (*corpus mandatorum*) that acquired general validity not only for state officials but also with respect to the contacts of private citizens with the administrative authorities.[29] As officials were virtually bound to implement all the received instructions from the emperor and citizens could invoke these instructions in their favour, the imperial *mandata* operated in practice as a distinct source of law.[30]

Decreta

While the foregoing types of imperial law-making basically had a non-judicial character, the *decreta* were judicial decrees of decisions issued by the emperor in his capacity as a judicial organ. Under normal circumstances, the *princeps*-emperor rarely interfered with the course of ordinary judicial proceedings. Yet, from the start, an extraordinary jurisdiction was bestowed on the emperor and those to whom he delegated his powers (for example, the provincial governors, the *praefectus urbi* and the *praefectus vigilum*). This jurisdiction enabled the emperor to tackle any kind of case, whether as a judge in the first instance or on appeal.[31] Over time, the extraordinary jurisdiction of the emperor and his delegates assumed greater significance until it ultimately superseded the jurisdiction of the regular magistrates and courts.[32]

Cases referred to the emperor's tribunal were determined in accordance with the existing law. As the highest authority in the state, the emperor allowed himself considerable freedom in interpreting the applicable legal norms. He could even venture to defy some hitherto accepted legal rule if he felt that it failed to provide an equitable decision. Theoretically, the emperor's decision on the point at issue was only binding in the particular case but it was treated as an authentic statement of the law and binding for all future cases. In this way, the emperor in his judicial capacity contributed to the development of fresh legal principles and rules, and a doctrine of judicial precedent evolved. It should be noted in this context that as the emperor lacked expertise in legal issues, an important point of law invoked in a case before the emperor's tribunal would usually be debated at a meeting of the *consilium principis*. From the second century AD, this council embodied the most eminent jurists and thus the relevant decision represented the best legal opinion of the day.[33]

Imperial law-making, like the magisterial law-making of the later Republic, formed an important source of free and equitable rules that unravelled the rigidity of the Roman legal system, thereby adjusting it to the socio-economic conditions of a highly complex and pluralistic society. A notable element was the contribution of imperial legislation to the development of certain branches of law such as fiduciary law[34] and the law of succession. As noted, a multiplicity of imperial law-making functions existed in correlation to the emperor's diverse administrative and judicial activities. Considering this reality, the imperial norms did not form a homogenous body of law until the later imperial period, when attempts were made to introduce order into the mass of imperial laws claiming validity in the empire.

The jurisprudence of the Empire

In a socio-political system so deeply committed to law as an essential prerequisite of order, Roman jurisprudence was bound to sustain the important role it had played during the Republic. The work of the jurists attained great heights of achievement by the end of the republican era and formed the most productive element of Roman legal life during the Principate, as evidenced by the volume and quality of the juridical literature of this period.

Since the republican era, the jurists' authority in legal matters originated from their highly specialized knowledge, technical expertise and, primarily, the esteem in which the general populace held them. The social prestige of the republican jurists derived from their membership in the ruling senatorial class (*nobilitas*), which facilitated economic independence and the exercise of functions without remuneration. In an extremely conservative society, such as that of the Romans, the public actions of private citizens and state officials required the support of religious, political or legal authority. Thus, in legal matters, private parties and public authorities (including the jurisdictional magistrates) depended on advice (*consilium*) from the 'oracles of the law' – the jurists. Like their republican predecessors, the jurists of the Empire, when formulating their responses, were guided by their knowledge of legal decisions and juristic opinions of the past. From this knowledge they would generalize and then apply the generalization to the particular case. Although the jurists invariably dealt with concrete cases rather than the law in the abstract, they directly contributed to the development of the law, especially private law and the law of civil procedure, through their advisory activities.

In the Principate age, new fields of activity were exposed to the jurists. The administrative and judicial authorities encountered new demands generated by the shift from politics to administration, the expansion of the Roman citizenship in the provinces and the proliferation of legal transactions prompted by the growth of trade and commerce. These new demands could not be met without the active assistance of learned jurists. It is, therefore, unsurprising that not only did the jurists' advisory role grow in importance, but the jurists of the Principate started to engage directly in governmental tasks and the central imperial administration of justice. The emperors employed jurists to assist them in executing the multiplying tasks of the imperial administration from as early as Augustus' era with increasing regularity in the later Principate period. Many leading jurists served in important administrative posts, from various magisterial positions right up to the prefecture of the praetorian guard. Moreover, distinguished jurists were among the members of the emperor's *consilium* that evolved under Hadrian to resemble a supreme council of the state. In this way, the Roman jurist was gradually transformed from a member of the ruling class in an aristocratic republic into a servant of the imperial government. The Principate period featured the novel emergence of a legal profession in public service, as distinguished from the military profession that had been the prevailing organizational pattern in the earlier stages of Roman history.

The ius publice respondendi

A change in the nature of the jurists' role occurred in the early years of the Principate period, when Augustus allegedly issued an ordinance that granted specially qualified jurists the right to present opinions and deliver them by the emperor's authority (*ius publice respondendi ex auctoritate principis*) – a custom that prevailed until the time of Hadrian.[35] A great difference of opinion exists among modern scholars as to the significance and practical effects of Augustus' move.[36] According to some authors, only the patented jurists had the right to present opinions to magistrates or litigants on questions of law – opinions that were then binding for the judge. However, the majority of authors believe that the *ius respondendi* meant that some professional lawyers received from the emperor the right to speak in the latter's name, and that the imperial imprimatur conferred more prestige and weight to the opinions of the patented jurists.[37] It did not mean that jurists without this imperial licence were prohibited from offering advice, nor did it mean that judges were obliged to accept the opinions of the jurists with the *ius respondendi*. In practice, however, it was very difficult for a judge to ignore the advice of a jurist whose *responsa* were reinforced by the authority of the emperor. Moreover, opinions vary on the question as to who actually received the imperial licence. According to some authors, the *ius respondendi* was conferred only on a few jurists by Augustus and his successor, Tiberius. Most scholars accept, however, that this right was granted to various jurists until as late as the reign of Hadrian. Initially, only jurists belonging to the senatorial class were granted the *ius respondendi* but since Tiberius' era this privilege was also accorded to jurists from the equestrian class.[38]

This momentous privilege placed the recipients into a class quite apart from the other jurists.[39] In time, the authority of this relatively small group of privileged jurists was so great that no court of law could disregard their opinions. This entailed the opinions of the recognized jurists acquiring the force of law. It was confirmed by a *rescriptum* of Emperor Hadrian, declaring that the opinions of the jurists possessing the *ius respondendi*, if unanimous, had the same force as a statute. If there was no unanimity among the jurists, the judge was free to adopt any opinion he thought fit.[40] The emperor devised this rescript to establish clearly and definitely that if a uniform agreement existed between the authorized jurists, their unanimous opinion must be followed as binding. However, Hadrian concurrently abandoned the practice of granting the *ius respondendi* to individual jurists. Thereafter, opinions were presented in the form of imperial rescripts prepared, with supervision from distinguished jurists, by the two imperial chanceries: the *scrinium ab epistulis*, which attended to the correspondence with state officials and persons of high social status; and the *scrinium a libellis*, which dealt with petitions from private citizens.

However, the role of the private jurist inevitably dwindled once the imperial court in the second century AD and thereafter became an essential part of the legal system of the Principate. As long as private jurists were members of a senate that retained some authority, their *responsa* carried sufficient weight and played a part in the administration of justice alongside the emperor's rescripts. However, the jurists' *responsa* ceased to be regarded as authoritative when the senate lost all its power and authority in the third century AD to the emperor and his bureaucracy, and the senators no longer had any influence in the *consilium principis*. This entailed the erosion of independent jurisprudence not controlled by or enlisted to serve the imperial government. In its earlier phases the political system of the Principate was supported by the jurists' creative work, but during its later development the very existence of a legally trained imperial bureaucracy undermined and finally annihilated jurisprudence. In the third century AD, as imperial government increasingly assumed the characteristics of an absolute monarchy, the *responsa prudentium* ceased to function as a living source of law, having been superseded by the emperors' rescripts on legal and judicial matters. The jurists' opinions survived mainly through the imperial rescripts until the Dominate period when classical jurisprudence regained its importance for the evolution of Roman law.

The work of the jurists

Like their predecessors of the republican period, the jurists of the Principate were occupied by diverse activities relating to the practice of law. They presented opinions on questions of law to private citizens, state officials and judges (*respondere*); drafted legal documents, such as contracts and wills (*cavere*);[41] helped litigants on points of procedure, interpreting laws and formulas in their pleas and occasionally arguing cases as advocates themselves (*agere*).[42] Moreover, the jurists were engaged in the systematic exposition and teaching of law. In performing this task, they composed opinions when their students raised questions for discussion based on hypothetical cases. These opinions were almost equal in terms of influence to those formulated for questions arising from actual cases and indirectly helped to develop Roman law in new directions.

From a historical perspective, probably the most important of the jurists' activities was creating legal works. As noted earlier, during the late republican period the first collections of *responsa* from individual jurists were published and, as systematic teaching in law expanded, this practice became widespread in the Principate era.[43] The great majority of juristic works had a casuistic and practical nature: they were developed from legal practice and written primarily for legal practitioners. Only their expository works, such as elementary textbooks and manuals, exhibited the jurists' adoption of a more theoretical approach to law. Depending on their subject-matter and structure, the literary works of the classical jurists can be classified as follows.

(i) *Responsa, quaestiones, disputationes, epistulae* – collections of opinions or replies delivered by jurists with the *ius respondendi*. These types of works were written for practitioners and usually embodied two parts: the first part contained juristic opinions arranged according to the rubrics of the praetorian edict (*ad edictum*), while the second part linked the opinions with the *leges, senatus consulta* and *constitutiones principum* that they addressed. The responses in these collections were set forth in a casuistic form and dealt with an immense number of problems, sometimes in connection with the opinions of other jurists. The adaptation of the original *responsa* for publication occasionally necessitated the further elaboration of the adopted views, especially when the opinions of other jurists were challenged.[44] Some works in this category, especially the *quaestiones* and the *disputationes*, explored the real or fictitious cases discussed by the jurists in their capacity as law teachers. The juristic works known as *epistulae* contained legal opinions delivered in writing by jurists to judicial magistrates, judges, private citizens or other jurists. The *responsa*, the *quaestiones*, the *disputationes* and the *epistulae* (collectively designated 'problematic literature') are among the most instructive juristic works that reveal the acumen of the authors' legal thinking and the strength of their criticism towards divergent opinions.

(ii) *Regulae, definitiones, sententiae* – short statements of the law that originally related to specific cases, but were later reformulated in the form of legal principles with a more general nature. Couched in easily recalled terms, these works were 'rules of thumb' manuals intended for use by legal practitioners and probably also students.[45]

(iii) General works on the *ius civile* – some of these works were known as *libri ad Sabinum* or *ex Sabino* as they were modelled on the systematic treatise on the *ius civile* (*Libri III iuris civilis*) written by Massurius Sabinus, a famous jurist of the early first century AD and head of the school of the Sabinians.[46] Others drew upon the earlier work of the jurist Q. Mucius Scaevola, who lived in the first century BC. Essentially, these works were based on the jurists' interpretation of the provisions of the Law of the Twelve Tables together with the later development of the institutions of the civil law.

(iv) Commentaries on the *ius praetorium* (or *ius honorarium*), referred to as *libri ad edictum*[47] – these works examined the edicts of the magistrates and offered commentaries pertaining to those aspects of the *ius civile* they were intended to supplement or correct.

(v) *Digesta* – comprehensive treatises on the law dealing with both the *ius civile* and the *ius honorarium*.

(vi) *Institutiones* or *enchiridia* – introductory or expository textbooks written primarily for students at the beginning of their formal legal education. An illustration of this type of work is the Institutes of Gaius that dates from around AD 160.

The jurists also wrote treatises on individual *leges* or *senatus consulta*, handbooks describing the functions of various imperial officials and commentaries on the works of earlier jurists. Among the juristic literature of the classical period, the Institutes of Gaius is the only work that survives in its original form. The remaining literature is discoverable chiefly in the citations that appear in the Digest of Justinian and other later compilations of law.[48]

The major jurists

The group of jurists responsible for the development of Roman legal thinking in the Principate period was always small at any particular time. Nevertheless, over the course of nearly three centuries their total attained a considerable scale. Today we are aware of many jurists from fragments of their works incorporated in post-classical compilations of law and from references located in various historical sources. Important sources of our knowledge on the lives of the classical jurists are Pomponius' *Enchiridium*, embodied in the Digest of Justinian and containing a survey of jurisprudence until the time of Hadrian, various literary works by authors such as Tacitus, Aulus Gellius, Pliny the Younger and Cassius Dio and a number of inscriptions. At this point, it is important to identify the most important jurists and the period of their activity. The examination may be divided into three time periods: the early period (27 BC to *c.* 80 AD), the high classical period (*c.* 80 AD to *c.* 180 AD) and the late period (*c.* 180 AD to *c.* 235 AD).

The jurists of the early Principate period hailed from urban Roman families or from the Italian municipal aristocracy, and so they possessed a thoroughly Roman background. According to Pomponius, the jurists of this period divided themselves into two schools (*sectae*) that formed around two political rivals: Marcus Antistius Labeo and Gaius Ateius Capito.[49] A staunch supporter of the Republic and opponent of the Augustan regime, Labeo held the office of praetor. However, according to Pomponius, he refused the position of consul offered by Augustus.[50] He composed numerous highly influential works, including an extensive commentary on the Law of the Twelve Tables, commentaries on the edicts of the *praetor urbanus* and the *praetor peregrinus* and several collections of *responsa* and *epistulae*. At the time of his death, his written works amounted to 400 volumes.[51] Capito was purportedly a supporter of Augustus, by whom he was elevated to the position of consul.[52] He produced relatively few works, which included a collection of *quaestiones* relating to matters of public law, a book *de officio senatorio*, collections of *epistulae* and a number of books on the *ius pontificum*. Although it is difficult to assess precisely the exact contributions of either jurist to legal doctrine, Labeo was apparently the bolder and more vigorous thinker while Capito was probably the more ingenious.

The school of jurisprudence established by Labeo was named after the jurist Proculus, and so was designated the school of the Proculians (*Proculiani*). The supporters of the school led by Capito were referred to either as Sabinians (*Sabiniani*) in deference to Massurius Sabinus, or Cassians (*Cassiani*) deriving from C. Cassius Longinus. These two schools divided between them most of the leading jurists in the first century and a half of the Empire.[53] However, the meaning of the term 'sectae' used by Pomponius is not clear as very little is known about the organization and functions of the two schools. It appears that these schools were not places of instruction in law, although it is very probable that young lawyers were mainly educated within the framework of the 'school' community. These schools were essentially in the nature of aristocratic clubs or unions with their own techniques and courses of training, and each centred around a succession of distinguished jurists. In this respect, they resembled the Greek philosophical schools that had existed since the republican era as organized quasi corporations whose direction and management were transferred by one master to his successor. Information reveals that the two schools differed on a great array of individual questions of law. However, the surviving examples do not display the alleged conservatism of the Sabinians or the reformatory spirit attributed to the Proculians. In contrast to the Greek philosophical schools, there were apparently no deep-rooted theoretical differences that separated the two schools.[54] This induces the conclusion that the schools differed only with respect to the techniques they adopted for dealing with concrete questions of law rather than in their general attitudes or principles. As a modern commentator observes, the doctrines of each school must have derived from the accumulated opinions of their successive heads on different questions of law, perpetuated by tradition and adopted on account of conservatism and a sense of loyalty.[55] The Sabinian and Proculian schools seem to have disappeared by the end of the second century AD, as no evidence indicates that the leading jurists of the third century were members of either school.[56]

Massurius Sabinus, whose name is attached to the earlier school of Capito, occupies an exceptional position among the jurists. Although he was not a member of the senate nor admitted to the equestrian class until later in life, Tiberius granted him the *ius publice respondendi* in recognition of his outstanding ability as a lawyer.[57] His chief work was a comprehensive treatise on the *ius civile* in three books that exercised a strong influence on Roman legal thought and was subjected to extensive commentary by later jurists in works known as '*ad Sabinum*'.[58] Other works attributed to Sabinus included a commentary on the edict of the *praetor urbanus*; a collection of *responsa*; a monograph on theft (*de furtis*); and a commentary on the *lex Iulia de iudiciis privatis*.[59]

C. Cassius Longinus descended from a prominent plebeian family and lived in the times of Claudius, Nero and Vespasian. He was a student of Sabinus, whom he later succeeded as head of the Sabinian school.[60] He attained the urban praetorship and the consulship (AD 30), and served as governor of Asia and Syria several times between the years AD 40 and 49. Mercifulness did not appear as one of his virtues, as his name is associated with the persecution of slaves during the reign of Nero.[61] However, his reputation for legal knowledge was unparalleled and his works were highly regarded by his contemporaries. His chief work, an extensive treatise on the *ius civile*, is known to us mainly from references and fragments integrated in the writings of later jurists.

The jurists of the high and late classical periods were mainly natives of the provinces and descendants of Roman and Italian families who had settled outside Italy. Nevertheless, their legal work was thoroughly Roman in character and reflected very little foreign influence. A marked feature of the second and third centuries AD was the increasingly close connection between the jurists and the imperial administration. The leading jurists were gradually associated with the imperial government, at first as advisers and later as holders of high administrative offices.

Among the first jurists of the high classical period was Iavolenus Priscus, who was born about AD 60 and still alive during Hadrian's age. He headed the Sabinian (or Cassian) school and was a member of the *consilium principis* during the reign of Trajan. He also held the position of consul in AD 86 and served as governor of Germany, Syria and Africa. His main works encompassed a collection of *epistulae* in fourteen books, commentaries on the works of earlier jurists (*libri ex Cassio, ex Plautio*) and a collection of texts from Labeo's posthumous work *posteriores*.[62] Fragments of these works were included in the Digest of Justinian.

Publius Iuventius Celsus (*filius*) lived in the early second century AD and was leader of the Proculian school, like his father P. Iuventius Celsus the Elder. He also had a distinguished career in politics: he held the praetorship and the consulship, was a member of the *consilium principis* under Hadrian and served as governor of Thrace. Portions of his main work *Digesta*, which comprised thirty-nine books, are included in the Digest of Justinian. He also published collections of *epistulae, quaestiones* and commentaries.[63]

Salvius Iulianus, born in Hadrumentum in the province of Africa, was the last known head of the Sabinian (or Cassian) school and probably the most important jurist of the second century AD.[64] In addition to his manifold activities as a jurist, he had a brilliant political career during the reigns of Hadrian, Antoninus Pius and Marcus Aurelius. The diverse offices he occupied were those of tribune, praetor, consul, pontifex and governor of Germany, Spain and Africa. He was also a member of the now permanent *consilium principis*. The most important works he composed were the consolidation of the praetorian edict (*c.* AD 130) and his *Digesta*, a collection of *responsa* in ninety books. The *Digesta* exercised a potent influence on the legal thinking of the imperial period, as exhibited by the numerous references to this work by later jurists and the mass of fragments embodied in the Digest of Justinian.

Two more jurists of this period deserve mention with a focus on their activities as writers and teachers rather than their innovative contribution to Roman legal thinking: Sextus Pomponius and Gaius.

Pomponius lived in the time of Hadrian and Antoninus Pius and was a man of great knowledge and an enormously prolific writer. Yet, his work is characterized by clarity rather than by originality or depth. He appears to have acquired notoriety as an antiquarian rather than as a lawyer, even though some of his doctrinal writings are mentioned by later jurists and numerous fragments were included in the Digest of Justinian. No evidence indicates that he ever held public office and it is unknown whether he was granted the *ius publice respondendi* as no *responsa* of his are mentioned. His works included three treatises on the *ius civile* written in the form of commentaries on earlier juristic writings (*ad Quintum Mucium, ad Plautium, ad Sabinum*), an extensive commentary on the praetorian edict (discoverable in citations by later jurists), two comprehensive collections of casuistic material (*epistulae* and *variae lectiones*) and a series of monographs on various subjects (*stipulationes, fideicommissa, senatusconsulta* and such like). Pomponius' best-known work is the *Enchiridium* that embodies a short outline of Roman legal and constitutional history spanning the period from the kings through to his own day. The relevant fragment has been preserved in its entirety in Justinian's Digest, under the title '*de origine iuris*' ('on the origin of law') and, despite its gaps, constitutes a chief source of information on the historical development of Roman law.[65]

Although Gaius is one of the most renowned jurists of the Principate period, there is scant information on his life except for the material emerging from his writings.[66] Internal evidence suggests that he lived during the reigns of Hadrian (AD 117–38), Antoninus Pius (AD 138–61) and Marcus Aurelius (AD 161–80), and that he was a Roman citizen.[67] His style of writing and his knowledge of Eastern laws and customs have been construed to suggest that he was a teacher of law in a province within the eastern half of the empire, probably Asia. However, presently no convincing evidence exists to support this hypothesis. Since he refers to the leaders of the Sabinian school as 'our teachers', it is very likely that he studied law in Rome, and was thoroughly familiar with Roman law as practised and taught by the leading lawyers of the capital. In contrast to his contemporary, Pomponius, who was held in great respect and frequently cited by classical writers, Gaius is not mentioned by any of them. This suggests that he was not accepted as a member of the select group of jurists who possessed the *ius respondendi*. He was probably one of the many lesser jurists outside this select group, rescued from oblivion by the later recognition of his elementary treatise (the Institutes) as a major document of classical Roman law.[68]

Gaius published commentaries on the Law of the Twelve Tables, the provincial edict (*edictum provinciale*) and the edict of the *praetor urbanus*, monographs on various legal institutions (*fideicommissa*, manumissions) and collections of opinions. Various fragments of these works have been preserved in the Digest of Justinian. His most renowned work is his Institutes (*Institutiones*), an introductory textbook for students written about AD 161. Until the 1816 discovery of the Institutes text in Verona,[69] only fragments of the juristic literature from this period survived through later compilations of law such as the Digest of Justinian. Although the manuscript unearthed at Verona dates from the fifth or early sixth century AD (more than three centuries after Gaius' time), it is now generally perceived as a faithful reproduction of Gaius' original work.[70]

Since the Institutes was originally designed as an elementary textbook for beginners, its primary value lies in the information it imparts on the state of classical law and jurisprudence. The work as a whole is a simplified presentation of the institutions and rules of Roman law intended for contemporary readers who had access to primary legal sources. Thus, the treatment of the material is sometimes sketchy and there are passages that the modern reader may find abstruse rather than informative. On the other hand, the book is relatively systematic. In the text, the whole body of law is divided into three parts: the law of persons (*ius quod ad personas pertinet*), the law of property and obligations (*ius quod ad res pertinet*) and the law of actions (*ius quod ad actiones pertinet*).[71] The law of persons (Book 1) is a facet of the law that deals with the legal status of persons and their capacity to possess rights and assume obligations. This area encompasses matters relating to liberty and slavery (*status libertatis*), citizenship (*status civitatis*), family (*status familiae*), marriage and guardianship. The law of persons displays a remarkable feature in retaining the absolute character of the *patria potestas*, the power of the *pater familias* over his family members.[72] The head of the family was still supreme master of his household, but some methods were devised for enabling the sons to attain their freedom (e.g. *emancipatio*),[73] or to hold property to a limited extent. The law of property (Books 2 and 3) contains the rules governing immoveable and moveable property (including servitudes), testate and intestate succession, and obligations arising from contract and delict. In the classical law of property, there still survived the ancient division of property into *res mancipi* and *res nec mancipi*.[74] However, in Gaius' work we detect a principle of classification that is far more advanced: he articulates a distinction between corporeal and incorporeal property,[75] and also conveys a distinction between possession and ownership that is conceived as the quality of absolute dominion.[76] With respect to the law of obligations, Gaius draws attention to another important principle of classification: 'every obligation arises either from contract or from delict',[77] i.e. from voluntary undertakings (*obligationes ex contractu*) or as a result of the commission of a wrongful act (*obligationes ex delicto*). Gaius also supplies the principal classification of contracts, namely the fourfold division of contracts into real (*contractus re*), verbal (*contractus verbis*), literal (*contractus litteris*) and consensual (*contractus consensu*).[78] Finally, the fourth book elaborates the law of actions and is primarily devoted to a history of the *legis actio* procedure and a description of the formulary system. In this book, Gaius draws a distinction between personal actions (*actiones in personam*) and real actions (*actiones in rem*). The former actions were designed to enforce a personal right arising from an obligation and the attendant liability between two or more persons, while the latter were concerned with the enforcement of a real right over specific property.[79]

The importance of Gaius' Institutes is twofold. In the first place, it is the only juristic work from the Principate era that we have inherited nearly in its original length and form. Therefore, the work is an important source of classical Roman law. Second, the relative simplicity and lucidity of Gaius' style made the Institutes ideal for the ordinary lawyer and the student; thus, it was heavily relied on in later Roman law. Gaius' textbook was used as a model by the compilers of Justinian's Institutes, which played an important part in the reception of Roman law since the High Middle Ages.[80]

Gaius' work stands midway in the stream of classical Roman legal science. He was followed by a triad of truly great jurists who all lived and worked in the early third century AD: Aemilius Papinianus, Iulius Paulus and Domitius Ulpianus. During that time, the connection between the urban Roman jurists and the imperial government was more pronounced, and leading jurists attained the very highest administrative offices of the state.

Generally regarded as the greatest of the late classical jurists, Papinianus was a lifelong friend of Emperor Septimius Severus (AD 193–211).[81] In AD 203, the emperor elevated him to the position of prefect of the praetorian guard (*praefectus praetorio*) – the emperor's chief of staff, principal adviser and executive officer in civil and military matters.[82] Emperor Caracalla ordered the murder of Papinianus in AD 212 because, it was rumoured, he had refused to devise a justification for Caracalla's murder of his own brother and co-regent Geta. Papinianus did not compose general treatises and his works were mainly collections of opinions and discussions of special topics. These works included thirty-seven books of *quaestiones* and nineteen books of *responsa* that also contained references to opinions of other jurists and to judicial decisions adopted by the emperor and the prefects. He also composed a collection of *definitiones* (in two books) and a monograph on adultery. In keenness, breadth of reasoning and clarity of presentation his works were unsurpassed, and his authority settled the law for centuries on many controversial issues.[83] Numerous fragments of Papinianus' works were preserved in the Digest of Justinian and other post-classical compilations of law.

Iulius Paulus, a contemporary of Papinianus, was a member of the *consilium principis* during the reigns of Septimius Severus and Caracalla and held the office of *praefectus praetorio* under Alexander Severus. He was an enormously prolific writer and presented great commentaries on earlier legal works. Although modern scholars are at variance over the merits of his work, he clearly had an extremely independent, doctrinaire and critical spirit – his opinions and critical remarks on the opinions of earlier jurists evince the subtlety and sharpness of his thinking. His best-known work is a comprehensive commentary on the praetorian edict in eighty books (*ad edictum*). Among his writings are also a treatise on the *ius civile* in sixteen books (*ad Sabinum*), commentaries on various *leges*, *senatus consulta* and the works of other jurists (Iulianus, Scaevola, Papinianus), two collections of *decreta* and numerous monographs on various subjects in public and private law. An extensive collection of extracts from Paulus' works, known as *Pauli sententiae*, was widely used during the later imperial period.[84] Excerpts of this work are located in assorted post-classical compilations of law, such as the Digest of Justinian,[85] the Vatican Fragments, the *Consultatio*, the *Collatio* and the *lex Romana Visigothorum*.

Younger than both Papinianus and Paulus, Domitius Ulpianus was born in the city of Tyre in Phoenicia about AD 170.[86] He held several posts in the imperial administration, including head of the chancery *a libellis*, *praefectus annonae*, *praefectus urbi* and, from AD 222, *praefectus praetorio*. Although he enjoyed the favour of Emperor Alexander Severus, whose chief adviser he was, his attempt to keep too tight a rein on the praetorian guard led to his downfall: in AD 228 the praetorians mutinied and Ulpianus was murdered in the palace, without the emperor being able to protect him or punish those responsible.

Ulpianus is probably the most industrious of all the Roman jurists. His contribution to juristic literature includes fifty-one books on the *ius civile* (*ad Sabinum libri LI*), eighty-three books on the edict (*ad edictum libri LXXXIII*), two books of *responsa*, a legal manual for beginners in two books (*institutiones*), collections of *regulae* and *definitions* and numerous monographs on individual statutes, various state offices and matters of legal procedure. A thorough assessment of Ulpianus' ability as a jurist is difficult as only fragments of his many works exist. Yet, modern scholars regard him as one of the most learned and elegant writers on the law, if not the most brilliantly original. The extent of his influence can be judged by the fact that almost half of Justinian's Digest (about 42 per cent) is comprised of fragments extracted from Ulpianus' writings.[87]

After the age of the Severan emperors, classical Roman jurisprudence lost its vitality and rapidly approached its end. One chief reason for this event was the empire's general decline in the third century AD, especially the collapse of the political system of the Principate and the accompanying swift move towards absolutism. The last classical jurists are considered to be Herennius Modestinus, a student of Ulpianus,[88] and Aelius Marcianus (first half of the third century). Among Modestinus' main works are an extensive collection of *responsa* in nineteen books, a work on *differentiae* (controversial questions) in nine books, a collection of *regulae* (rules of law) and a treatise (written in Greek) on the exceptions from guardianship (*de excusationibus*). Marcianus' most renowned work is the *Institutiones*, an elementary treatise on law in sixteen books which the compilers of Justinian's Digest used extensively. He also wrote a collection of *regulae* and several commentaries and monographs that mainly addressed criminal procedure.

Defining features of classical Roman jurisprudence

As already noted, a most notable feature of Roman jurisprudence is its strictly legal and predominantly casuistic nature. In the Principate era the need arose to systematize the casuistic method engaged by the early lawyers. The jurists of this period responded to that need. Thus, the new 'systematic' legal science was a more sophisticated version of the old casuistic method used by the republican jurists. The Roman method was conditioned by the need to produce normative solutions for problems of decision-making. It was simply a methodical way of treating cases. Yet a clear improvement occurred as now the similarities and differences between cases were studied in a systematic manner. The starting-point of a systematic statement of law was often a settled case that was then compared with other real or fictitious cases.[89] Other elements contributing to the process were norms (e.g. statutes and juristic *regulae*) as well as various standards used in the normative discourse (e.g. *bona fides*). Often the function of such elements was mainly explanatory, pedagogical or informative rather than persuasive (especially in juridical treatises). The jurists simply sought to illustrate the relevant norm or principle through cases demonstrating its actual operation, usually without immersion in theoretical argument.[90] Norm-rationality and authority-based arguments furnish sufficient grounds for legitimizing the activity of professional lawyers and for justifying their decisions or decision-propositions whenever there is a state of evaluative identification between the holders of the norm-giving power and the legal profession. This applied to Roman legal science. As we ascertained earlier, its protagonists were originally members of the ruling senatorial aristocracy (*honorationes*), but during the imperial period the lawyers relied increasingly on the power of the emperor whom they were compelled to serve. In this respect, the *ius respondendi ex auctoritate principis* granted to lawyers during this period may be construed to mean not simply the right of presenting answers in matters of law with the authority of the emperor, but rather the right of presenting authoritative answers in matters of law based on the social power of the emperor.

The jurists of the Empire, like their republican predecessors, were men who dedicated themselves exclusively or essentially to the interpretation of the extant source material: the old *ius civile* and *ius honorarium* of Rome. They sought to preserve this law, while also developing it by devising new ways to apply its doctrines and institutions in a satisfactory manner. However, they did not consider that their tasks should encompass an analysis of the law from ethical, historical or other more general viewpoints. Nor were these jurists interested in the laws and customs of other nations, save insofar as these could be incorporated into the conceptual framework of their own legal system. The mass of doctrine embodied in the juridical literature is in no sense an application of a general philosophical, ethical or legal theory. On the contrary, it is the rationalization of concrete applications or a case law where cases are related, reconciled, categorized and systematized. The jurists sustained a conservative attitude and demonstrated an almost total lack of interest in legal concepts and norms originating externally or divergent from the Roman legal system as they understood it. For a long time these factors isolated Roman law from foreign influences and were therefore largely responsible for its clarity and systematical coherence.

The conservatism of the jurists is also reflected in their social and ethical attitudes. Reared in traditional Roman ideals and the doctrines of Stoic philosophy, they essentially held the common humane and enlightened views of the ruling classes within the empire. Their tasks and habits of reasoning were influenced by ethical standards such as *humanitas* (respect for human dignity), *pietas* (dutifulness, noblemindedness, respect for ancestral traditions) and respect for authority. But little evidence exists to imply that they consciously and systematically engaged ethical and philosophical precepts in their treatment of the law. Nevertheless, as men who received the general intellectual training of their time, they strove to anchor their decisions and decision-propositions on broader general principles. A remarkable quality of the jurists was their ability to look beyond the accidental elements of the individual case, the *species facti*, and to define the relevant legal problem as a *quaestio iuris* that must be answered in light of certain general principles. This tendency towards abstraction and simplification is natural and inevitable if the law is to consist in anything more than a collection of particular rules; but it carries with it the danger that a rule, once formulated, tends to dominate legal life rather than adapt to it. The legal genius of the Roman jurists was exhibited in their ability not only to construct abstract propositions by analysing legal problems, but also to render their abstractions sufficiently flexible for future synthesis into new principles when subsequent experience showed that change was desirable.[91]

The jurists were aware of the problems arising from the fact that the tenor and the intended meaning of a legal text did not always coincide. They also realized the significance of the linguistic context as a tool for facilitating a more thorough comprehension of texts than if they were examined in isolation. When engaged in the work of interpretation, they usually proceeded from a consideration of the letter (*verba*) of the relevant law (statute, edict, imperial constitution, senatorial resolution) and then continued with an inquiry into the intention or 'spirit' of the law (*sententia*). Depending on whether a legal rule had been expressed in broad or narrow terms, they sought to make more concrete through a restrictive construction or expand through an extensive construction the scope of the relevant provision.[92] In tackling problems relating to silence of or ambiguity in the law they often relied on the methods of comparison and analogy, and utilized such general concepts as *benignitas*, *clementia*, *caritas*, *utilitas* and *humanitas*.[93] Of particular importance for the jurists was the concept of *aequitas* that was engaged to correct or expand the existing body of law so it could meet the demands of social and commercial life. The significance the jurists assigned to *aequitas* is reflected in the definition of *ius* attributed to the jurist Celsus the Younger as 'the art of doing equity' or, in other words, a technical device for obtaining that which a good man's conscience will endorse ('*ius est ars boni et aequi*').[94] In determining what constituted equity in the circumstances of the case at hand, the jurisdictional magistrate or *iudex* was now aided by the rapidly expanding mass of precedents that were collected, discussed and annotated in juridical literature. To ignore these precedents would have been a psychological impossibility even for radical thinkers (and radical thinkers did not normally obtain *imperium* nor did they easily obtain the *ius respondendi*). The test of the *bonum et aequum* in this era was still the *ius gentium*, the norms governing civilized society as the Romans construed it. But the Roman *ius gentium* was now declared binding because it was also natural law (*ius naturale*), based on natural reason.[95] However, the assumed connection between *ius gentium* and *ius naturale* is far from clear as no generally accepted definition of natural law is revealed in juridical literature. Further, the meaning of the term appears to vary depending on the perspective adopted for its contemplation.[96]

The 'law of nature' was a familiar concept to many philosophical systems of antiquity but was given a more concrete form by the Stoic school of philosophy. This school held sway from the lifetime of its founder Zeno (336–264 BC) through to around the fourth century AD. Stoicism was thus a prevailing philosophy during the greater part of the Roman Republic and Empire. The Stoics had neither a completely consistent nor a fixed and unchanging doctrine, but key ideas detected in their works may be declared to constitute the basis of their philosophy. Their starting-point is the idea that the world is an organic whole, an intimate combination of form and matter and an order of interdependent tendencies, governed by a divine, rational principle (*Nous, Logos*) and moving towards a pre-determined end (*telos*).[97] The word 'nature' (*physis*) is used to refer to this cosmic order and to the structures of its component parts. All entities, including man as an integral part of nature, participate in divine reason that reveals itself in all things and causes all things to cohere into an animated unity. From this perspective, the Stoics argued that virtue cannot be attained simply through compliance with the laws of the state but through obedience to the natural law of divine reason as it discloses itself in human reason. Natural law, as founded in the natural order of things, is universally valid, immutable and has the force of law *per se*, i.e. independently of human positivization.[98] If all men, irrespective of race, nationality, social standing and such like, share in the divine reason in the same way, then in principle all are equal and together form one grand universal community governed by the natural moral law. This notion of a universal community, a *cosmopolis*, in which in principle all men are equal and equally capable of achieving the perfect moral life lies at the heart of the Stoic philosophy.[99]

In the transformed cultural and political world of the late Roman Republic and early Empire, the ideas of the Stoic philosophy exercised considerable influence in Rome – an influence reflected in the writings of Cicero,[100] Seneca and the Emperor Marcus Aurelius. Cicero (106–43 BC) endorses the Stoic view that the world is governed by a universal soul, a divine reason, whose dictates constitute an Eternal law (*lex aeterna*). This Eternal law coincides with the law of nature (*ius naturale*), which, as pertaining to man's communal life, furnishes the principles of right and wrong guiding human action. As a reflection of right reason (*recta ratio*), the law of nature is everlasting, immutable and universal. It does not encounter any limitations by people, place or time, and transcends the laws of any particular state or political community.[101] Compliance with its rules is a prerequisite for attaining justice (*iustitia*), as the essence of law (*ius*) in its broadest sense.[102] According to Cicero, the first task of justice is to prevent men from causing harm to others, and the second is to induce men to use common property for common interests and private property for themselves.[103] Justice requires all individuals to act in the interests of the human race, grant each his due and refrain from interfering with that which belongs to another or to the community as a whole.[104] Natural law also enjoins kindness (*beneficentia*) that is also occasionally termed benevolence (*benignitas*) or liberality (*liberalitas*). In general, the law derived from nature (*ius naturale/ lex naturae*) may be described as unwritten law (*lex non scripta*), as opposed to the written law (*lex scripta*) that constitutes the basis of the positive law of a state (*ius civile*).[105] The application of the *ius civile* is limited to the inhabitants of a particular state, while in contrast the *ius naturale* is applicable to all humankind, although it must be recalled that the *ius civile* itself is, at least to some extent, derived from nature. Closer to the *ius naturale* is the 'law of nations' (*ius gentium*), which assumes an intermediate position between the *ius civile* and the *ius naturale*. Cicero declares that where the *ius civile* of various political communities coincides, such law is simultaneously *ius gentium*. In this respect, all *ius gentium* is in fact *ius civile* but not *vice versa*.[106] It is germane to note another aspect of Cicero's thinking that reflects the general tenor of Stoic philosophy: unlike Plato and Aristotle, he advances the concept of 'community' beyond that of the city-state (*polis*). In fact, Cicero speaks of a 'hierarchy' of communities. Starting with the smallest group that exists as the domestic community (*domus*), he progresses to the next level occupied by the state (*civitas*) and then the human world community (*societas hominum*). Finally, he addresses the highest level: the universal community encompassing both gods and men (*civitas communis deorum atque hominum*), which is permeated by the World Soul and governed by the Eternal law. According to him, the perfect state is attainable through a mixed form of political constitution where the elements of Aristotle's three forms of government (monarchy, aristocracy, republic) balance and temper each other.[107] However, the ideal state must be established on natural law and serve the common interest.

Cicero's and the Stoics' philosophical views on the ideal law or the ultimate nature of justice apparently had no profound effect on the way the Roman jurists executed their traditional tasks. Although the jurists, as members of the educated higher classes, were familiar with current philosophical theories, they displayed little interest in linking philosophical speculation with everyday legal disputes and practices. There were also apathetic towards questioning the validity of positive law on the grounds that it conflicted with a higher law.[108] Even when the notions of nature and natural reason surface in the jurists' writings, they are often construed as common ornamentals, or possessing a meaning that is contextually variable with little connection to the philosophical idea of natural law. Although the concept of *natura* was vague, it provided an important device for the articulation and systematization of the law. However, the jurists defined its content without reference to divine reason, or to God's plan for the universe. Rather, they engaged references to the qualities of worldly things, states of affairs and modes of thought and action that were commonly accepted as reflecting the realities of everyday life.[109] In other words, the jurists did not juxtapose the law governing social relations in everyday life to a code of ideal natural law functioning as a master model. They developed the content of *natura* in close connection with the practical aspects of legal life and always in response to concrete needs and problems emerging from actual cases. From their viewpoint, discovering the appropriate legal rule or devising an acceptable solution to a legal problem presupposed a reasonable familiarity with both the nature of things on the ground and the ordinary expectations that social and legal relations entailed. Thus, the Roman lawyers alluded to the nature of an obligation (*natura obligationis*), the nature of a contract (*natura contractus*) and such like. A notable factor was the term *natura hominum* or *natura humana* that denoted the physical and mental qualities, and the psychological characteristics and attitudes common to all humans. In this respect, the postulates of nature did not emanate from metaphysical speculation, but from the findings of common sense and the need for order in human relations.[110] In the eyes of the Roman lawyers, certain methods of acquiring ownership were 'natural' or derived from natural law as they appeared to follow inevitably from the facts of life. This encompassed methods such as delivery of possession (*traditio*)[111] and occupation (*occupatio*), i.e. the acquisition of the actual control of a *res nullius* (an object belonging to no one).[112] Of course, such methods of acquisition were regarded as universal and therefore as facets of the *ius gentium*: the law actually observed by all humankind.

The fact that the Roman jurists regarded natural law, in the manner described above, as juridically valid is implied by their identification of *ius naturale* with *ius gentium*. This prevailed even though the former term referred to the supposed origin of a rule or institution and the latter to its universal application. If natural law is interpreted as law that ought to be observed, the identification of *ius naturale* and *ius gentium* is untenable as certain institutions of the law of nations clearly conflicted with natural law precepts. Thus, while according to natural law all people were born free, slavery was widely recognized in antiquity as an institution of the law of nations.[113] In view of this detail, the most one can say from a moral perspective is that the universal recognition of an institution as part of the law of nations could be regarded as constituting *prima facie* evidence that such an institution or principle originates from natural reason.[114] The Roman lawyers, however, never drew a clear distinction between positive law and law as it ought to be, nor did they adopt the philosophical conception of natural law as a higher law capable of nullifying positive law. One cannot locate in juridical literature an assertion that natural law is superior to positive law, in the sense that, in a case of conflict the former should overrule the latter. The jurists were not social reformers and their conception of natural law does not embrace anything resembling a revolutionary principle to support those rights that are termed in the modern era as 'inalienable human rights'. Thus, no matter how such institutions as slavery or the division of property appeared contrary to natural law they were still perceived as perfectly justified and legal. Today, attempts at regulating the complex problems of human coexistence by law engender decisions whose evaluative justification is very often far from self-evident. Although it is important to fathom whether a solution to a legal problem is justified on the strength of an authority, norm or precedent (or a combination of these), equally important is the question as to whether we are prepared to explore the social impact of the various decision alternatives. If the authority of institutions, their conceptual characteristics and the decision-propositions that they support are accepted without an evaluative justification of their social impact, we follow the path of the Roman jurists; we have adopted their institutional way of thinking, which focused on the nature of institutions rather than on the need to justify them by considering their broader social implications.

Ius naturale significantly contributed to Roman legal thought, but as a professional construction for lawyers it had little relevance to moral philosophy. It was not viewed as a complete and ready-made system of rules but as a means of interpretation. It existed linked with the *ius gentium* to enable the Roman jurists to test the equity of the rules they applied. When the result of this test was deemed inequitable, it justified them in deliberately departing from the rules. In this way, *ius naturale* played a decisive part in the process of adapting positive law to changing socio-economic conditions and shaping the legal system of an international empire.[115]

9

THE PRINCIPATE:
THE ADMINISTRATION OF
JUSTICE

Introduction

In the first few centuries of the Principate, the practice of distributing functions among different sets of authorities also prevailed in the administration of justice. Certain areas of civil and criminal jurisdiction remained with the traditional republican magistrates, while others were transferred to imperial authorities. As the republican element of the constitution withered over time, the latter surpassed and finally replaced the former. In the same period, the senate assumed an original jurisdiction of its own in cases involving certain crimes of a political nature. Whenever the imperial branch took over judicial functions the procedure adopted differed considerably from the traditional formulary procedure. The trial consisted of only one stage and judgment was delivered by a state official with an extensive discretion in applying both the procedural and substantive norms. As a result, litigation could proceed in a simpler and more convenient fashion while the juridical and administrative activities of the state were mainly captured by a central authority. In addition, a hierarchy of courts emerged and a relatively elaborate system of appeals developed from the lower to higher tribunals. The new form of procedure, known as *cognitio extraordinaria* or *cognitio extra ordinem*, did not play such an important a role in the development of Roman private law as the formulary procedure. Nevertheless, it engendered several notable principles that coincide in several respects with modern principles of civil procedure (especially in civil law jurisdictions).

Civil procedure

The formulary procedure

As we have observed, during the late Republic the formulary procedure gradually replaced the earlier *legis actio* procedure. By the end of this era, the formulary procedure had evolved as the main form of civil procedure in Rome – a development that acquired statutory sanction by Augustus' judicial reform legislation of 17–16 BC (*leges Iuliae iudiciorum publicorum et privatorum*).[1] In the altered conditions of the late Republic, the formulary procedure permitted the jurisdictional magistrates to introduce novel rights and remedies to accommodate the new socio-economic relations of an increasingly sophisticated society. For a great span of time after the establishment of the Principate the normal jurisdiction of the republican magistrates was fully maintained and the *per formulam* procedure remained the customary method for initiating legal action in disputes relating to private law. As explicated previously, the relevant procedure was divided into two phases. In the first place (*in iure*), the praetor determined the admissibility of the plaintiff's claim, i.e. whether the plaintiff should be granted an action at law. If the praetor was satisfied that the plaintiff had an arguable case, the appropriate *formula* was composed that nominated the judge (*iudex*) to try the case, stated the matter in dispute and prescribed the consequences of the judge's decision. The trial occurred in the second phase (*apud iudicem*) where the judge listened to the parties' pleadings, assessed the evidence and rendered a verdict in accordance with the *formula* agreed in the *in iure* phase.

The only element that changed in the formulary system during the Principate period was the function of the praetorian edict. As noted, in the closing years of the Republic the productive strength of the praetorian edict as a source of law faded and praetorian initiatives became increasingly rare. This trend prevailed during the Principate age and as the praetor's ability to develop new legal remedies diminished, the changes to the edict were based on measures introduced by other law-making agencies, such as statutes and senatorial resolutions. The creation of law administratively by the praetor finally ended during the reign of Emperor Hadrian when the content of the edict was permanently fixed following its codification by the jurist Julian. Thereafter, any requisite changes to the edict could only be introduced by imperial enactment. Although no longer an independent source of law, the praetorian edict perpetuated its contribution to the administration of private law well after the formulary system had fallen into abeyance in the third century AD.[2]

The cognitio extraordinaria

Since the early Principate age, the emperor or a state official acting on his behalf assumed, or was accorded, the right to decide certain cases when the positive law did not provide remedies. This right was effectuated by a procedure called *cognitio extraordinaria* or *cognitio extra ordinem*. The *cognitio* procedure could be employed not only in cases involving private disputes, but also in criminal cases and disputes between private citizens and state organs. The new procedure probably originated from the early practice that allowed jurisdictional magistrates to directly deal with certain cases either on the application of a party or on their own initiative. The magistrates tackled these cases by using their administrative authority to cut through the formalities observed in regular court proceedings. The procedure was widely adopted in the provinces during the later republican period, especially in criminal cases. It was also engaged in cases involving private disputes between foreigners and cases relating to disputes between Romans when not enough Roman citizens were available to serve as judges. Such cases were addressed by the provincial governor either directly or through a delegate (*iudex pedaneus*), without observing the rules governing the ordinary procedure. From the time of Augustus, the *cognitio extraordinaria* was the only form of procedure used in the imperial provinces where the administration of justice was directed by imperial officials who acted as representatives of the emperor (*legati Augusti pro praetore*). By the early second century AD, it had become the regular form of procedure in the senatorial provinces. In Rome and Italy the *cognitio extraordinaria* was employed from the beginning of the Principate, although not on a regular basis. In the course of time, the new procedure gradually superseded the formulary procedure. By the end of the third century AD, it was the ordinary form of procedure throughout the whole empire.[3]

The establishment of the *cognitio* procedure as the main form of legal procedure was partly due to its great simplicity and flexibility. It also partly derived from the fact that, in accordance with imperial ideas, it facilitated the centralization of state authority. The *cognitio extraordinaria* was a device – as had been the formulary technique in the past – facilitating the judicial care of legal situations when the existing positive law did not offer appropriate solutions. At the same time, it became the vehicle for the subsequent evolution of the imperial jurisdiction that competed with and, if necessary, replaced the jurisdiction of the ordinary (republican) jurisdictional magistrates. As the imperial system developed, the state increasingly intervened in the sphere of law. This entailed the situation where legal disputes were no longer based on an agreement between the parties to present such a dispute before a judge, but on the power of the authorities to place a dispute before its officials, attain a resolution and execute the decision. A petition by one of the parties usually initiated the state intervention, but the emperor could also set it in motion by a procedure called *evocatio* that transferred the case to his extraordinary jurisdiction. Thus, cases of special importance could be withdrawn from their regular forum for determination by the *princeps*-emperor sitting, as a rule, in consultation with his legal experts. The emperor could also delegate his jurisdiction to subordinates designated in accordance with the subject matter of the particular case. In Rome and Italy the magistrates concerned were the special praetors, such as the *praetor de liberalibus causis*,[4] the *praetor tutelarius*[5] and the *praetor fideicommissarius*[6] and various imperial officials, such as the *praefectus praetorio*, the *praefectus urbi*, the *praefectus annonae*, the *praefectus vigilum* and the *procuratores fisci*.[7] As noted, in the provinces the administration of justice was in the hands of the governors (*praesides*). Often these officials exercised their judicial functions through delegates (*iudices dati* or *pedanei*). These delegates were usually lower state officials appointed by their superiors. This contrasts with the *iudices* appointed by the praetor under the formulary system, who were private citizens chosen by the parties.[8] The practice of appeal from the lower to the higher instance and finally to the emperor ultimately emanated from this technique of delegating judicial functions from the *princeps*-emperor to his high-ranking officials and the latter's authority to sub-delegate the case to their subordinates. The rulings of the emperor as judge in the first instance or in the case of an appeal (*decreta*) were theoretically only binding in the particular case. In the course of time, they came to be regarded as authentic statements of law and binding in subsequent similar cases. Thus, a new body of substantive legal rules evolved from the operation of the new imperial branch of the administration of justice. This new body acquired equal rank with the two traditional legal systems: the *ius civile* based on the Law of the Twelve Tables and the subsequent comitial legislation; and the *ius honorarium* derived from the edicts of the republican magistrates.

The most significant feature of the *cognitio* procedure was the abolishment of the two phases *in iure* and *apud iudicem* and the occurrence of the entire procedure before only one official. The summons, accompanied by the plaintiff's statement of claim (*libellus conventionis*), was issued by the plaintiff to the defendant with the judge's support (*denuntiatio ex auctoritate*), or by the judge on the plaintiff's request.[9] This scheduled a date for the court appearance that was not less than twenty days later.[10] On the appointed day, the parties or their advocates appeared in court and presented their cases and the facts on which they relied.[11] Evidence might be oral or written, although generally the former was regarded as having relatively little value. After all the evidence was considered and the arguments of the parties heard, the trial culminated in a judgment (*sententia*) from the magistrate-judge. This verdict was recited publicly and in the presence of the parties concerned.[12] Unlike the formulary system where the judgment of the *iudex* was deemed final, the judgment in the *cognitio extraordinaria* could be appealed against. An appeal could ensue from a *iudex pedaneus* to the official who named him, from a lower to a higher magistrate, or in important matters, from a magistrate to the emperor. If the defendant was condemned without further recourse, he was granted a period (at least four months) to ensure compliance with the judgment. If the defendant failed to observe the judgment, the plaintiff could request the authorities to initiate steps for executing the judgment. The execution of a judgment could target the debtor's property and thus the relevant property would be officially attached and sold by auction. Alternatively, the execution could be directed against the defendant's person and this entailed the debtor's confinement in a public prison.[13]

The administration of criminal law

At the end of the republican period, the jurisdiction of the assemblies in capital crimes had entirely disappeared. The ordinary mode of criminal trial for serious offences featured a prosecution before a standing court (*quaestio perpetua*) at Rome. Less serious offences were dealt with in a summary fashion by lower-grade magistrates, the *tresviri capitales*. Shortly after the establishment of the Principate, the tasks of the *tresviri capitales* were assumed by imperial officials (*vigiles*) acting under the supervision of the *praefectus vigilum*.[14] On the other hand, the standing jury-courts remained in operation for quite a long time after they were reorganized by the *lex Iulia iudiciorum publicorum* of Augustus (17 BC). This enactment drastically revised the composition of the jury-courts in the spirit of broadening the socio-economic basis of public participation and prescribed the rules of procedure governing the conduct of trials. A general list of jurors was established comprising four categories based on status and property qualifications: senatorials, equestrians, the *tribuni aerarii* (closely akin to the equestrians, but possessing a slighter property qualification) and, finally, a new class formed by the owners of property worth two hundred thousand sesterces (*duocentenarii*) who would be summoned in cases of minor importance. Moreover, the minimum age for jury service was lowered from thirty to twenty-five, so that there were always sufficient citizens to serve as jurors. In 18 BC, Augustus completed the system of *quaestiones perpetuae* by creating two new tribunals of this kind: the *quaestio de adulteriis*[15] and the *quaestio de annona*. The jurisdiction of the first court encompassed cases of adultery (*adulterium*), extra-marital relationships involving women of a high social standing, and procurement.[16] The second court dealt with accusations against merchants who endeavoured to raise the market prices of foodstuffs, or who engaged in unfair practices relating to the supply or transportation of food.[17]

Trial by jury-courts was not readily amenable to official control and thus contrary to the spirit of the new imperial regime. Apart from this fact, the system of the *quaestiones perpetuae* had several deficiencies that were not adequately addressed by the Augustan legislation and subsequent senatorial resolutions. First, each *quaestio* was constituted in a specific manner according to the statute that originally established it (or possibly according to some subsequent statute), and could only tackle a particular offence category as specified in such statute. Hence, frequently a wrongful act that merited punishment as a crime was not punished as it did not precisely fulfil the definitional requirements of any of those offence categories for which *quaestiones* had been instituted. Second, the statutory enactment establishing a *quaestio* (or possibly a subsequent statute) prescribed the punishment for the specific category of offence in question, and this punishment automatically attached on conviction. Thus, the tribunal had no power to either increase or mitigate such punishment to address the circumstances of the individual case. In general, the penalties imposed for offences captured by the jurisdiction of the jury-courts were often regarded as too mild and therefore disproportionate to the gravity of the offences committed. In addition, proceedings in the jury-courts were expensive, laborious and even protracted as the cases were often heard more than once. Thus, since the early years of the Principate the work of the jury-courts was supplemented by the new extraordinary jurisdiction of the emperor and those officials to whom he delegated his judicial powers. At the same time, the *princeps*-emperor sanctioned the senate's assumption of an extraordinary criminal jurisdiction. In a sense, the senate may be construed to have replaced the popular assemblies' jurisdiction and this body was resorted to mainly in cases involving offences with a political nature or any case where the accused was a senator. In principle, these two jurisdictions were concurrent but reality exposes the more extensive nature of the emperor's jurisdiction from the start. As more offences fell within the sphere of the new tribunals' jurisdiction over time, the *quaestiones perpetuae* faded into the background and finally disappeared in the early years of the third century AD.[18]

The jurisdiction of the senate

The criminal jurisdiction of the senate originated in the early years of the Principate period when the senate evolved as a court of law on a par with the *iudicia publica*.[19] Initially, it dealt with cases connected with *laesio maiestatis*, conduct that affected the honour of the emperor and the people of Rome. It also addressed cases involving abuse of power perpetrated by provincial governors. In the time of Tiberius (AD 14–37), the senate's jurisdiction was enlarged to encompass not only crimes against the security of the state (such as treason) but also a wide range of serious crimes (including adultery, murder and forgery) committed by members of the *ordo senatorius*. In this way, the senate by the end of the first century AD had developed into a *forum privilegiatum* with exclusive jurisdiction over the crimes of senators.

Trials before the senate were conducted in accordance with a procedure that blended the old rules of senatorial debate with those of the public courts. A prosecution was launched by an application to a consul for leave to initiate an accusation (*postulatio*), followed by the accuser's formal announcement of the charge (*nominis delatio*). The magistrate to whom the application was submitted then formally registered the name of the accused (*nominis receptio*) and the trial date was established. On the appointed day, the senate was convoked and the trial commenced under the presidency of a consul. After the arguments of the parties were presented and the evidence heard, individual members submitted their motions and presented opinions. The verdict was attained by a majority vote without the involvement of the presiding magistrate. The emperor frequently participated in the judicial sessions of the senate and, as *princeps senatus*, cast the first vote that presumably carried decisive weight. The sentence became valid in law upon the final announcement of the verdict and its insertion in the official record as a senatorial resolution. No appeal to the people was available against a death sentence imposed by the verdict. Since the late second century AD, the jurisdiction of the senate was curtailed both substantially and procedurally. By the middle of the third century AD, the senators were no longer involved in the administration of criminal justice.

Imperial jurisdiction

Since the era of Augustus, the operation of the emperor's domestic tribunal started to resemble a public criminal court. In time, the emperor assumed jurisdiction not only over matters affecting him personally, such as conspiracies, but also over common-law crimes. He possessed the power to withdraw at his discretion any criminal case from the ordinary judicial authorities. In the early years of the Principate, this seems to have occurred on rare occasions. Despite any endeavours of an individual *princeps* to avoid determining cases directly as a judge, he was inevitably drawn into this activity by the appeals against court decisions and the increasing number of citizens' petitions for justice. Moreover, juristically inclined emperors like Claudius always sought to extend the imperial court's radius of competence by introducing cases to this court and determining them in the final instance.[20] However, a long time passed before the jurisdiction of the jury-courts and the senate was superseded by the imperial *cognitio*, especially in cases involving capital charges.

In the exercise of his criminal jurisdiction, the *princeps* emperor was not bound by the general rules governing ordinary criminal law proceedings and had complete freedom in the composition of his council of advisers (*consilium*). He also had a free hand in the definition of offences, the choice of penalty, the mode of punishment and the degree of its severity. As the decisions of the imperial court gradually acquired the status and force of laws, criminal law evolved from its static form to broaden in scope and complexity. However, criminal law was never the subject of scientific study to the same extent as Roman civil law. As a result, the administration of criminal justice was pervaded by an element of arbitrariness that easily rendered it an instrument of oppression.[21]

In Italy, the highest criminal jurisdiction under the emperor was assigned to the city prefect (*praefectus urbi*) and the praetorian prefect (*praefectus praetorio*). By the late second century AD, the former had jurisdiction over all crimes committed in Rome and in a zone within a radius of one hundred miles from the city;[22] offences committed outside that delineated area fell within the jurisdiction of the latter. These two high-ranking imperial officials had the unrestricted power to inflict any recognized form of punishment, capital or otherwise, on any offender. They could try any case in the first instance, but they also dealt with appeals against sentences of lower magistrates (central or local) endowed with an inferior criminal jurisdiction. In principle, a judgment of the *praefectus urbi* or the *praefectus praetorio* could be appealed against before the emperor. Of course, the latter could refuse to entertain such an appeal and deem the judgment in question as final. By the Severan period (late second century AD), the magistrate responsible for the maintenance of security in the capital (*praefectus vigilum*) had acquired jurisdiction in criminal matters such as arson, burglary, robbery and theft, although he probably referred particularly grave cases to the city prefect.[23] A specialized jurisdiction over offences connected with the food supply of Rome was assigned to the *praefectus annonae*.[24] Moreover, some criminal jurisdiction was assigned by decree of the senate or imperial constitution to the consuls and praetors who tried cases *extra ordinem* assisted by a body of assessors (*consilium*).

As regards the senatorial provinces, the governor was the highest criminal (as well as civil) judge in the province. He could attend to cases either in the first instance or on appeal from lower courts. With respect to non-Roman citizens (*peregrini*), his power to inflict punishment was unfettered and no appeal against his sentences was allowed. However, his authority was fairly limited in cases involving Roman citizens: he was not entitled to pronounce the death sentence on citizens unless the latter were first granted the opportunity to have their case judged in Rome. In the imperial provinces, criminal justice was administered by imperial officials acting as representatives of the emperor (*legati Augusti*). From as early as the first century AD, the emperors started to grant those *legati* who commanded troops in their province the power to execute soldiers (Roman citizens). The latter did not possess the right to present their case before a court in Rome. In the course of time, the mass of Roman citizens living in the provinces greatly increased and it was practically impossible to send all those charged with capital offences to Rome for trial. As a result, this power (*ius gladii*) was granted to all provincial governors and was made applicable to civilians as well. However, whether or not a governor was also entitled to execute a death sentence without first applying for and receiving special authority from the emperor to do so seems for a long period to have depended on the precise terms of the particular grant. After the *constitutio Antoniniana* of AD 212 extended the Roman citizenship to all the free inhabitants of the empire, all provincial governors could wield their own authority to order the death of Roman citizens. This action was averted if a condemned person successfully appealed against the sentence. Indeed, whenever a provincial governor had duly pronounced a capital or non-capital sentence on a Roman citizen it was always theoretically possible for the latter to appeal to the emperor despite the great practical difficulties that this could entail.[25] If provincial appeals were allowed, they were usually delegated by the emperor to either the *praefectus urbi* or the *praefectus praetorio* whose decision in most cases was regarded as final.

In trials before extraordinary criminal tribunals the adopted procedure differed from that engaged under the system of the *quaestiones perpetuae* in some important respects. As we have discerned, proceedings in the latter system were set in motion by a private citizen (not a state organ) who assumed the role of the accuser by filing a charge against the alleged offender with the magistrate presiding over the competent jury-court. The *cognitio extraordinaria*, on the other hand, had a predominantly inquisitorial character. A criminal prosecution was initiated by a state organ (such as a police official or other public official) acting on information provided by the injured party or a private informer, so no formal accusation by a citizen was necessary. The magistrate in charge of the proceedings had a more active part in the trial than the president of a jury-court. The former could resort to inquisitorial methods at any time if the supposed interests of justice so demanded. Moreover, in contrast to the system of the *quaestiones perpetuae* where the guilt or innocence of the accused was determined by a panel of jurors, both the verdict and the sentence were now determined by the magistrate at his discretion. As there were no fixed penalties, the magistrate was in principle free to impose any penalty he deemed appropriate by considering the nature of the offence, the particular circumstances and the offender's personal and social position. Over time, a body of norms developed from imperial enactments, juristic opinions and the practice of the courts. These norms more definitely fixed the scope of offences and matters relating to criminal liability and punishment.[26] Some norms were concerned with procedural matters while others pertained to the requirements of criminal responsibility, such as conduct, intent and defences.[27]

As previously noted, during the later Republic capital punishment practically ceased to be inflicted on Roman citizens except in times of civil unrest or strife. In cases falling within the jurisdiction of the standing jury-courts, the accused ostensibly enjoyed a statutory right of fleeing into exile within a short period after he was found guilty of a capital crime. On availing himself of that right, he was then denied fire and water by a vote of the people (*aqua et ignis interdictio*). Such an outcome essentially amounted to a sentence of banishment from Roman territory, which after the Social War (91–88 BC) meant banishment from Italy.

After the establishment of the Principate, the foregoing position remained practically unchanged in the case of condemnation on a capital charge by a *quaestio perpetua*. On the other hand, when a Roman citizen was declared guilty of a capital crime by an extraordinary tribunal this often entailed death. In the third century AD, the standing jury-courts virtually vanished and proceedings before extraordinary tribunals became universal. This period also featured the extension of the Roman citizenship to all the free inhabitants within the empire. As a result of these events, the capital punishment of Roman citizens became widespread.

This text previously made reference to the distinction between the *honestiores* and the *humiliores*[28] and the fact that the former occupied a privileged position in the eyes of the criminal law.[29] In relation to capital punishment (*poena capitis*), the force of this distinction is exhibited by the fact that offenders belonging to the *honestiores* were, as a general rule, decapitated or conferred some other form of relatively painless and honourable death[30] while offenders attached to the *humiliores* were usually subjected to cruel and degrading modes of execution, such as crucifixion, impalement, exposure to wild beasts and burning at the stake.[31] A similar distinction between the *honestiores* and the *humiliores* applied in connection with the non-capital punishments.[32] The most common forms of punishment imposed upon members of the *honestiores* class were deportation (*deportatio*) usually to an island or oasis, and expulsion (*relegatio*) entailing the offender's exclusion from residence in a specified territory (normally Italy and one's own province). The former punishment had a more serious nature and it was accompanied by the loss of citizenship and property, though not of personal freedom.[33] The punishment of expulsion was a mild form of exile involving simple internment in an island without further consequences.[34] Other forms of punishment often inflicted on members of the upper classes included expulsion from the *ordo* to which the offender belonged, exclusion from holding civic office[35] and prohibition from pleading in the courts of law.[36]

The next focus is the non-capital punishments commonly imposed on offenders attached to the class of *humiliores*. These punishments embraced penal servitude in or around the mines,[37] confinement accompanied by some form of hard labour for the public benefit,[38] flogging, flagellation and branding.[39] Condemnation to confinement for life with hard labour in the mines (*ad metalla*) was eventually held to involve loss of liberty. On the other hand, condemnation of a Roman citizen to confinement accompanied by some lesser form of hard labour for the public benefit (*in opus publicum*) was ultimately deemed to entail the loss of citizenship but not personal freedom.[40]

10

THE DOMINATE:
THE HISTORICAL, SOCIAL AND
CONSTITUTIONAL BACKGROUND

Introduction

The work of the so-called 'soldier emperors' in the late third century AD saved the Roman world from utter collapse. It also paved the way for the systematic changes of structure initiated by Diocletian (AD 285–305) and completed by Constantine the Great (AD 312–37). Diocletian and Constantine realized the temper of the times and, like their predecessor Augustus, integrated the elements developed in the chaotic era into a system that had the permanence of a constitutional form. The pressure of military, fiscal and administrative demands provoked the creation of a system that may be construed as imparting a permanent form to a state of emergency. They established an intricate network of state intervention and supervision of individuals and social groups, an expansion of bureaucracy and police control, an organization of small administrative and legal units commanded by new intermediate authorities and a hitherto unknown degree of state planning and managerial intervention in every sphere of life. However, their measures were not promulgated and implemented throughout the empire at one precise moment. Rather, this process occurred in a largely fragmentary fashion during the five and a half decades that separated the accession of Diocletian and the death of Constantine. The transformation of the Roman state and society that transpired under these emperors inaugurated the last phase of Roman history, known as the 'Dominate' (*dominatus*), and ushered in the medieval world as well.

The reforms of Diocletian

As elaborated in the previous chapter, the Roman Empire experienced difficulties in the third century AD that derived mainly from deficiencies in the empire's political, social and economic institutions. These innate shortcomings, rather than the power of external foes, weakened and threatened to destroy the state in the half-century preceding Diocletian's rise to power. A serious defect in the system was the lack of a regularized imperial succession. In the late second and third centuries AD, the oft-repeated phrase 'succession by revolution' accurately portrayed the established pattern in the accession to the imperial throne. Dynastic sentiment failed to entrench in the system and the emasculated senate was habitually powerless, so that the army became the ultimate arbiter in the appointment and removal of emperors. The empire's administrative problems were exacerbated by the political instability engendered by the ruler's degradation to the status of an army instrument and the accompanying perversion of the military function. This undermined the empire's ability to defend its borders and further aggravated the economic malaises that beset the Roman world throughout the third century AD. The character of the new regime established by Diocletian and consolidated by Constantine is reflected in the solutions they devised for these problems.

The empire was so plagued by internal problems and external threats that it could no longer be governed efficiently by a single ruler engaging the prevailing administrative means. Diocletian devised a system whereby imperial rule was divided but the principle of imperial unity remained intact. In AD 285 he appointed Maximian, one of his most capable generals, as Caesar and co-ruler. In AD 286 Maximian was promoted to Augustus and acquired dominion over the West, while Diocletian assumed rulership of the East. In AD 293 each Augustus appointed a Caesar as his assistant and successor; the four ruled jointly and each controlled one-quarter of the empire.[1] The necessity for distributing the administrative and military duties generated a graduated, quadripartite, collective imperial summit that was still essentially dominated by Diocletian. At the same time, the rank and authority of the rulers were not limited to their own regions: all four were recognized throughout the empire.[2] This so-called tetrarchic system was designed to facilitate the administration of the empire and also to discourage any attempts at usurpation by establishing a stable succession mechanism. As an institutional device, it proved successful during the reign of Diocletian by presenting the empire with a more efficient government and defence mechanism against foreign foes.

The establishment of the tetrarchy was pertinent to another problem: the exaltation and stabilization of the imperial office within the realm. Diocletian and his successors sought to bolster their authority by imbuing the imperial ideology with a new form and content. The emperor was elevated to the position of an absolute monarch and invested with the dignity and grandeur of the oriental god-kings. Secluded in his palace and set apart by a framework of complicated ceremonial and court etiquette, the monarch demanded divine veneration from his courtiers, officials and community. The practice originated from an old tradition evident in Augustus' era when the *princeps*-emperor was granted divine status in the Eastern provinces, while in Rome and the West, a dead emperor was declared divine by an act of the senate. Even if a divine element was recognized as the basis for the *auctoritas* of the *princeps* in this earlier period, the emperor was only transformed into a divine, absolute monarch in the later years of the third century AD.[3] Diocletian's arrangements institutionalized the transformation. The new stylized emperorship of the late antiquity was predominantly based on religion. Diocletian and his successors portrayed themselves as members of a hierarchy encompassing gods and emperors, and sought to mobilize the imperial cult to reinforce empire solidarity.[4] In later years, the recognition of Christianity as the state religion compelled an adaptation of the imperial cult to the demands of a stringent

136

monotheism. The emperor was installed by the grace of God and his empire existed as a reflection of the heavenly kingdom; both were deemed divinely inspired and protected, and everything remotely connected with the imperial personage partook of imperial sanctity.

From an administrative and military perspective, Diocletian's measures were designed to facilitate internal control and effective defence against foreign attacks. But the chief threat to imperial power was internal rather than external, and this problem was granted priority. Thus, the greatly expanded bureaucratic apparatus was centralized in the imperial consistory composed of the highest court officials. A complicated system of administrative checks and balances was instituted to avert the accumulation of power by potential rivals. Diocletian's reorganization of the provincial administration was particularly impressive and durable. As the power of any given official was directly related to the size and wealth of the area he governed, the provinces were reduced in size and their number doubled. Thereafter, the central function of the governor was general public administration and the administration of justice.[5] In all the provinces with standing troops, the governor relinquished command to a military officer called *dux*. Thus, civil authority within a province was separated from military authority in such a manner that effectively foiled any prospect of rebellion from ambitious provincial officials. Diocletian facilitated the central government's control of the provincial administration by creating new administrative districts superior to the provinces, the dioceses, while neighbouring dioceses were incorporated into larger units called prefectures.

The problem of defence against external enemies dictated a radical reform of the army in terms of organization, armament and military tactics. Diocletian considerably increased the size of the army to a total strength of around half a million soldiers. A new and powerful mobile reserve force (*comitatus*) was established to support the troops stationed along the frontiers (*limitanei*) and protect the provinces against barbarian incursions. In the capital, new forces were attached to the crack imperial troops who accompanied the emperor. In principle, Roman subjects were obligated to perform military service yet, in practice, the imperial government encountered an acute shortage of Romans available for army duty. Like their immediate predecessors, Diocletian and his successors depended increasingly on the enlistment of barbarians in auxiliary units. Within the army the principle of separation of powers, which sought to protect the emperor from insubordination, was operative, and superior command of cavalry and infantry was divided. These reforms suppressed the threats of revolution and barbarian invasion and, to a degree, the provinces revived with the return of peace.

The administrative and military reforms of the late third and early fourth centuries AD greatly inflated state expenditure. This increased financial outlay encumbered the strained economy. For state survival, economic life had to be converted to harmonize with harsh reality and this was the precise aspiration of the Tetrarchs. They developed the old levies in kind (*annona*) that had originally provided the state's armies with their physical necessities. These levies were reinstated to redress the inadequacy of the taxes collected in cash by the government and to protect the state against inflation. The *annona*, formerly an extraordinary tax, was henceforth applied to the rural population on an annual basis.[6] The new system of taxation liberated the government from the vicissitudes of monetary debasement and price fluctuations, for it now mainly paid its officials and troops in agrarian products and other commodities. At the same time, this enabled the formulation of an orderly budget based on the agricultural produce of the empire, and it constrained the extraordinary requisitions that were such a burden during the third century AD. Besides the *annona*, various monetary taxes were imposed in accordance with fairly specified criteria,[7] and the system of compulsory public labour and extraordinary contributions, introduced during the later Principate period, was regularized and further developed.[8]

In contrast to the reorganization of the tax system, the Tetrarchs' endeavour to reform the currency did not attain success. The only measure that endured was the change in coin production. This involved the abolition of the old local and provincial issues and the establishment of a decentralized but strictly supervised system of large imperial mints. However, the public distrust of the monetary system was merely increased by the assignment of new face values to the coins, whose purchasing power further declined as inflation escalated at an appalling rate.[9] The Tetrarchs' responded with the famous Edict of Prices (*edictum de pretiis*) in AD 301, which was a systematic attempt at price regulation by the state and thus also a form of state planning in the economic sector.[10] This law proved largely ineffectual, however, due to the lack of an adequate enforcement mechanism and a parallel regulation of supply.

Many other economic initiatives exhibited the regime's liking for state control.[11] These included the construction of state factories for the production of food, textiles and military supplies, and the increased interference of the state in the internal and external commerce of the empire. The state control over the empire's productive resources expanded until, by the middle of the fourth century AD, nearly all forms of socio-economic activity important to the state were regulated by the government. Ultimately, the economic policies of Diocletian and his successors failed to restore balance in the economy. The price regulation and currency reform failed to stimulate production and curb inflation; tax collection remained unsatisfactory owing to the prevailing corruption; trade and industry waned as the state, once the main customer, became a large producer itself. The peasantry, originally the foundation of the empire's economic system, was overburdened by taxation. This compelled many farmers to abandon their lands or become tenants of senatorial landlords. Encumbered by the imposed fiscal burdens, the urban middle class deteriorated and the cities declined – a decline precipitated by the loss of their former market function owing to the movement towards self-sufficiency of the great senatorial estates. In general, economic conditions throughout the empire steadily deteriorated, especially during the latter part of the fourth century AD. However, it is a mistake to regard the Dominate as a period of uninterrupted and universal economic decline, for there were important differences in the levels of prosperity maintained in different parts of the empire. As the West plummeted into primitive conditions, the state-controlled economy in the Greek-speaking eastern provinces achieved some success and private enterprise flourished in spheres that disinterested the state. In many eastern cities, such as Constantinople, Alexandria and Antioch, manufactured goods were produced on a large scale, and Egyptian agriculture displayed signs of recovery. At the same time, trade resumed or increased within and between provinces, and commerce with Persia, India and the Far East progressed. At the end of the fourth century AD, the empire's political division into a western and an eastern part reflected the new economic reality that determined their respective destinies during the closing years of the Dominate era and the ensuing centuries.

The empire of Constantine the Great

Diocletian and Maximian had ruled the empire for more than twenty years when, in AD 305, the former initiated their abdication. The two Caesars, Constantius Chlorus and Galerius, became the new Augusti, and each named a Caesar as his aid and heir. But this arrangement did not last very long. Shortly after Constantius' death in AD 306, the system of the tetrarchy disintegrated into hopeless confusion and this provoked new civil wars between the claimants to the throne. In AD 312 Constantine, the son of Constantius, defeated his chief opponent Maxentius and thereby became the sole emperor of the West. In the following year, Licinius acquired emperorship of the East. But in AD 323 war erupted between the two Augusti. In AD 324 Licinius was finally defeated and Constantine became ruler of the entire empire. Constantine completed the work of Diocletian, infusing the empire's organization with the basic characteristics it retained until the fall of the Western empire and its transition to the Byzantine Empire in the East.

During Constantine's reign the transformation of the imperial government into an absolute monarchy was completed. At the summit of the *imperium*, Diocletian's *collegium* of the Augusti and Caesars was replaced by a sole ruler of the empire accompanied by a new dynasty. The aggrandisement of the emperor's position was further exaggerated by the ideological extension of the emperor's ruling power over the entire world, the elevation of his victorious attributes to a universal level and, above all, the sanctification of the ruler's position by Christianity. The imperial tradition permanently adopted *proskynesis*, or *adoratio*, the eastern ceremony of genuflection addressed to divinity, and purple robes, jewelled diadems, richly adorned belts, sceptres and other ceremonial regalia derived from oriental kings and priests.

The administrative and military policies of Constantine so closely resembled those of Diocletian that it is not always possible to identify which emperor was responsible for a particular institution. Diocletian's system of dioceses and provinces was only slightly modified; the separation between the stationary frontier troops and the mobile field army was maintained, while the number of Germans and other non-Romans in the army expanded; the regimentation of large sections of the population into rigidly defined hereditary castes according to occupation, function and office was further recognized; and Diocletian's financial, taxation and monetary policies were mainly retained.[12] In general, the policies of Constantine and Diocletian may be described as conservative as they merely represented the culmination of existing tendencies.

The policies of the two emperors contrasted most sharply in the field of religion as Diocletian remained a pagan while Constantine embraced Christianity and rendered it the favoured religion of the state. Christianity was an oriental mystery cult with a message and organization that enticed many followers from among all classes of Roman society. During the first two centuries of the Principate, Christians were largely tolerated even though their religious practices were regarded as immoral and subversive by many Romans, especially the governing classes. The pagans construed Christianity as highly suspect because its adherents, as strict monotheists, refused to worship the empire's gods and participate in the imperial cult that guaranteed the unity of the empire. However, the actual persecution of Christians was sporadic rather than general and accidental rather than organized. Even though from the late first century AD the confession of Christianity constituted a capital offence, there were no systematic attempts to eradicate the new religion. However, the relative peace between the Roman state and the Christian church was violently disrupted by the crisis of the third century when the emperors formed a strategy to save the state by reviving and embracing old religious practices. Their attempts to revive observance of the pagan religion and public acts of loyalty deepened the gulf between the state and Christianity. The occasional persecutions of Christians that characterized the earlier period were supplanted by a more organized effort to expunge the Christian faith. The systematic persecution of Christians was instigated during the reign of Decius (AD 250–51) and under Valerian (AD 257–59), but this ended in failure as Christian resistance solidified and assumed greater militancy. After the fall of Valerian in the war against the Persians, the persecution of Christians ceased. This entailed the return of confiscated Church property, and many Christians entered the imperial civil service. The last great persecution of the Christians occurred during the reign of Diocletian, and was probably inspired by his Caesar, Galerius, who was a determined opponent of the Church. Convinced that Christianity posed a serious threat to the religious and political unity of the Roman state, the Emperor and Galerius issued four edicts between AD 303 and 304 dictating the destruction of Christian churches and liturgical books, the imprisonment of the clergy and the infliction of the death penalty on all Christians refusing to present offerings to the Roman gods. Despite all the hardship inflicted on the Christians, the wave of persecution did not achieve its goal. Failing to secure the solid support of the pagan population, the government was unable to enforce the relevant laws efficiently, and gradually the persecutions eased or ceased. In AD 311 Galerius, the Augustus of the East, acknowledged the failure of the official policy by issuing an edict granting the Christians the rights to worship their God and rebuild their churches on the condition that they refrained from acts offending public order. After a decade of persecution, Galerius' edict engendered a dramatic reversal of the Roman state's attitude towards Christianity, recognizing it as *religio licita* and preparing the ground for further development.

But the status of Christianity became definite only when Constantine removed his political rivals and thereby acquired the sole rulership of the empire. He attributed his victory over Maxentius (AD 312) to the intervention of the Christian God. Shortly after this accomplishment in AD 313, Constantine and Licinius met in Milan and agreed to adopt a policy of complete toleration that granted Christians unrestricted freedom and ordered the return of confiscated Church properties.[13] This development marked the beginning of the ultimate triumph of Christianity. Although Constantine was only baptized a Christian shortly before his death, he became a lavish patron of the Church, which he supported with generous gifts and privileges.[14] Leading Christians of his day, pleased with the new turn of events, did not object to the pagan practices the emperor preserved.[15]

Convinced that the integrity and survival of the empire depended on the unity of the Church, Constantine endeavoured to use his imperial power and prestige to resolve the emerging disputes within the Church. To obtain the clergy's judgment on disputed matters and determine the correct or orthodox position in dogma and discipline, he adopted the Christian practice of convening synods or councils and assumed the responsibility for enforcing their decisions.[16] He perceived that as divine will had selected him to rule the empire, his duty to God was to thwart the spread of false dogma and strife within the Church. His incessant interventions had enduring effect not only in the Donatist controversy,[17] but also in the dogmatic conflicts associated with the names of Arius and Athanasius. Of particular importance was the ecumenical council which he summoned in AD 325 at the city of Nicaea in Asia Minor to settle the Arian controversy.[18] All bishops of the empire were invited to attend this council presided over by Constantine, who directed the deliberations and forced his preferred theological solutions upon the bishops. The Council of Nicaea and others that followed in the fourth century AD confirmed the position of the emperor as head of the Christian Church ('caesaro-papism'). After the council of Nicaea, the Church appeared as a unified society embracing all Christian congregations of the empire, and Church and state were increasingly intertwined. At the same time, the political organization of the Roman state existing after the reforms of Diocletian and Constantine furnished the Church with a model on which to fashion its own system of administration.[19]

It remains controversial whether Constantine's attitude towards Christianity derived from a genuine religious conviction or political calculation. Regardless of the emperor's motives, it is doubtful whether Christianity would have triumphed as the empire's dominant religion without an imperial patron, such as Constantine, to enhance its popularity and influence. At the same time, Constantine's personal decisions in matters of faith, his opinion of Christianity not only as a religion but also as a facet of social politics, and more specifically, his view of the Church and its role, unquestionably assumed world historical significance.[20]

Another revolutionary change initiated by Constantine was the foundation of a new imperial capital on the old site of Byzantium in the East. In the course of time, this developed as the largest urban concentration in medieval Europe and a great centre of civilization. The choice of Byzantium as the location for the new city is indicative of the fact that the empire's vital political and economic centre had shifted to the East.[21] The decision also probably emanated from Constantine's desire to disengage from the pagan past and centre the empire on a new Christian foundation. The new city, called Constantine's city or Constantinople, was strategically located midway between the important Danubian and eastern frontiers on the crossroads between Europe and Asia Minor, and possessed a better commercial situation than Rome. This location not only provided Constantinople with immense economic vitality, but also rendered it an effective political and administrative centre. In time, Constantinople was regarded as a second Rome.[22] Like the old capital, it was excluded from the standard provincial and diocesan organization; it had its own senate, modelled on that of Rome; its inhabitants received the privilege of free distributions of grain; and the city's highest official was promoted to the rank of the Roman *praefectus urbi* in AD 359. Moreover, the city was adorned with magnificent churches, palaces and public buildings. Constantine's dedication of the new imperial capital in AD 330 marked the end of half a century of momentous reforms. Those reforms, with their roots in the disorder of the third century AD, institutionalized the transitional trends in late Roman society and paved the way for the ensuing Middle Ages.

The emperor and his officials

The fourth century AD featured the completion of the Principate's transformation into an absolute monarchy with an oriental form. Under the new system, the sovereignty of the Roman people was transferred to the emperor, whose right to rule was based on the divine will revealed in his selection by a human agency.[23] Surrounded by his privy council of high court officials, the emperor was an omnipotent divine monarch (*dominus et deus*)[24] and the sole authority in all spheres of government, administrative, military, legislative and judicial. He appointed and dismissed the public officials, who were now considered servants of the throne rather than as serving the state as an abstract entity. He directed foreign policy, determined matters of war and peace, and regulated economic policy. The emperor, ruler by divine grace, was also the sole author of laws and their final interpreter. His unchallengeable legislative supremacy conformed to the nature of an absolute monarchy whose omnipotence precluded constitutional or any other limitations on the emperor's law-making power. The emperor was also the supreme judge and all other judges were deemed his representatives. Moreover, after the adoption of Christianity as the state religion, the emperor occupied a quasi-ecclesiastical position vis-à-vis the official Church. He exercised control over Church matters and was responsible for formulating and implementing religious policy.[25] By definition and on principle, the emperor was virtually omnipotent. Yet, established norms guided his exercise of administrative, legislative and judicial functions and powers. Although he was entitled to change these norms as he saw fit, he was bound to observe them to transform his decisions into practical results. The emperor was held to exist above the laws, in the sense that he could not be held responsible for his legislative and administrative acts; however, he was bound to respect the laws and abide by his own edicts as his authority rested on obedience to them.

When embarking on the various tasks of government, the emperor depended on a machinery of official and non-official confidants who proffered him advice and cooperation to facilitate his formulation of policy decisions. He also relied on an apparatus of execution that translated his decisions into the realities of the political process. Shaped under Diocletian and extended during Constantine's reign, the administrative apparatus of the Dominate was an elaborate outgrowth of the bureaucracy developed during the Principate period.

The most important group of imperial functionaries in Constantine's era were the *comites*. These trusted commissioners of the emperor were dispatched on special duty to control particular regions or appointed to execute policy decisions. These high state officials and others constituted the *sacrum consistorium*,[26] the supreme privy council of the emperor in legislative, judicial and administrative matters.[27] Besides its advisory functions, the *consistorium* at times operated as an imperial court of justice and addressed appeals from the decisions of lower courts.

Different branches of the administration were directed by ministers and many of these officials had subordinates in the dioceses and the provinces. The highest minister was the *magister officiorum*, whose function as head of the central adminis-tration merged with that of the prefect of the praetorian guard.[28] He exercised general superintendence over the secretarial bureaus of the palace (*scrinia*), the imperial intelligence service (*agentes in rebus, curiosi*), the imperial bodyguard (*scholae palatinae*) and the public post system. Moreover, as master of the cere-monies he exercised control over all the emperor's personal attendants and regulated imperial audiences. The second most powerful official at court was the *quaestor sacri palatii*, the imperial minister of justice. Usually selected from among those with considerable legal training, this minister acted as the emperor's adviser on legal matters. He played an important part in the preparation of legislative enactments and legal decisions issued by the emperor. From the fourth century AD, he presided over the imperial council (*sacrum consistorium*), when the latter assembled in the absence of the emperor. The financial administration of the state was directed by an official bearing the title of *comes sacrarum largitionum*. He managed the state trea-sury (*fiscus*), supervised the collection and disbursement of taxes paid in money, and controlled the operation of mines, mints and state factories. Moreover, he had juris-diction over matters relating to taxation (his decisions were final and not subject to appeal before the emperor). The financial sphere also concerned the *comes rerum privatarum* (or *comes rei privatae*). This official was entrusted with the administra-tion of the emperor's private property and the management of imperial lands (*res privata principis*). Each of these four ministers was aided by an office staff (*officium*), whose members (*officiales*) were mainly freedmen. In addition to these civil officers, there existed corresponding military officers who commanded the palace guards and the elements of the field army attached to the emperor (*palatini*).

Resembling the practice in the Principate, various administrative tasks were assigned to separate departments or cabinets (*sacra scrinia*) that were each managed by a *magister*. The *scrinium epistularum* responded to letters sent to the emperor by government officials; the *scrinium libellorum* handled various petitions (*libelli*) addressed to the emperor by magistrates and private citizens; the *scrinium dispositionum* dealt with the emperor's private matters, including the organization of his personal correspondence; and the *scrinium memoriae*, first introduced in the time of Hadrian, was responsible for drafting official documents, such as those containing decisions and orders issued by the emperor. The *scrinia* operated under the general superintendence of the head of the imperial offices (*magister officiorum*).

Besides the officials resident at the central imperial court, an important branch of the administrative apparatus consisted of officials engaged in provincial rather than central government, and these operated at a distance from the court. The latter formed a separate administrative hierarchy whose structure was linked with the territorial division of the empire into prefectures, dioceses and provinces. Near the end of the fourth century AD, there were four prefectures (Gaul, Italy, Illyricum and the Orient) divided into twelve dioceses and over a hundred provinces. Each prefecture was ruled by a praetorian prefect (*praefectus praetorio*), the highest-ranking civil official of the provincial administration.[29] The praetorian prefect embraced a wide ambit of responsibilities, such as the employment of officials within the prefecture, the collection of taxes, the minting of coin, the recruitment and quartering of troops and the provisioning of the army. Moreover, as supreme judge in his territory, he heard appeals instituted in accordance with legal procedures and had the power to decide whether a case before him should be referred to the emperor. No evidence implies that the praetorian prefect was unable to issue edicts that possessed the force of law; yet, his main function was the administration of the law rather than its creation (which was an imperial prerogative).

Subordinate to the prefects were the chiefs of dioceses, called vicars (*vicarii*), and the provincial governors. All officials, irrespective of their rank, were competent throughout the sphere of civil administration.[30] The vicars formed an intermediate tier of administration between the praetorian prefects and the governors of the provinces they controlled. These officials were required to perform an array of administrative tasks that broadly resembled those undertaken by the praetorian prefects, and also served as judges for appeals submitted against sentences passed by a provincial governor. The governors of the diverse provinces were divided into three categories depending on their rank. The highest category embodied the *proconsules* who ruled the provinces of Africa, Asia and Achaia. Secondary in terms of authority, were the *correctores* and the *praesides*. A provincial governor was assigned a diversity of administrative tasks, including the collection of taxes, the supervision of public works and services and the implementation of orders from the central government. He also had charge of the administration of justice within his province and heard appeals from the decisions of lower courts, and ensured the peaceful outcome of legal proceedings.[31] In accomplishing his duties, a provincial governor was supported by a sizeable staff (*cohortales*, *domestici*, *consiliarii*, *cancellarii*).

It should be noted that the system of provincial administration was more complicated and less stable than the above description may suggest, and it was not adopted consistently. In practice, the subordination of vicars to prefects was only superficial as they could directly report to the emperor who also addressed the appeals from their judgments. Besides exercising direct control over the governors of certain provinces, namely Asia and Africa, the emperor often directly intervened in the affairs of provinces, thereby bypassing the praetorian prefects and the vicars. During the fifth century AD the office of vicar dwindled in importance and several dioceses were governed directly by praetorian prefects. In the same period, the provincial government system was increasingly affected by the intensified threat of Germanic invasion and the empire's struggle to confront this.

The cities of Rome and Constantinople were exempt from diocesan government and each was administered by a city prefect (*praefectus urbi*). As the emperor's chief officer within the city, the prefect was entrusted with an extensive range of responsibilities, such as the maintenance of order in the city; the supervision of public games and festivals; the repair of public buildings; the operation of the imperial postal system; military recruitment; tax collection; the publication of imperial laws; and the transmission of senatorial resolutions to the emperor. Moreover, he had responsibility for the regular provisioning of the city, having under his command the *praefectus annonae*. Finally, a chief function of the city prefect resided in the sphere of law enforcement. His court contended with appeals from judgments of the *praefectus annonae* and other officials of civil jurisdiction, and he was the exclusive judge in cases involving persons of senatorial rank. The only apparent limitations on his power were his lack of direct responsibility for military matters, and the fact that he was still ultimately subject to the emperor to whom he submitted unresolved problems.

The intricate administrative machinery ensured a measure of order and regularity for revenue collection and judicial proceedings; but it was cumbersome, expensive and often inefficient. Despite the tight controls that theoretically existed, the system was rife with corruption as office-holders sought career advancement and self-enrichment at the expense of civilians. The increased burden imposed on taxpayers by the enlarged civil and military establishments was thus aggravated by the officials' extortion practices. The central government's efforts to secure honest and efficient administration were nullified by the bureaucracy,[32] and an almost impassable barrier evolved between the emperor and his subjects.[33]

The senate and the old magistrature

Since the third century AD, the Roman senate was bereft of all power but was still in existence during the Dominate. Under Diocletian's reign it embraced about six hundred members, but in Constantine's era it expanded considerably with the enrolment of equestrian magistrates and provincial officials. In the middle of the fourth century (*c.* AD 340), Emperor Constantius II founded a new senate at Constantinople. He recruited members from Roman senators residing in the East and from holders of administrative posts in Constantinople and the eastern provinces.[34] By the close of the fourth century AD, the senates of Rome and Constantinople had each swelled to around two thousand members, and both bodies continued to grow at an increasing pace.[35] In practice, however, only fifty senators had to attend to form a quorum for resolutions; this indicates how slight the political competence of that body had become.

The senates functioned mainly as municipal councils[36] and performed certain ceremonial tasks, such as the inauguration of a new emperor. Occasionally, the senate was requested to offer its advice to the emperor on current affairs; it conferred with imperial officials on matters concerning the senatorial class and presented legislative proposals that were then submitted to the emperor by the city prefect. However, it no longer operated as a court of justice with jurisdiction over its own members; trials involving senators now proceeded before the city prefect or a provincial governor.[37] Although the senate as a body was divested of all authority, admission was still greatly sought after. Senators were highly respected in society and they were granted many privileges, such as exemption from taxes and other financial burdens in the municipalities where their estates were situated. Moreover, they enjoyed certain privileges in lawsuits and, as a rule, shameful forms of punishment or torture were not employed against them. However, in return for these privileges they incurred certain obligations: they were liable for a landed property tax (*collatio glebalis* or *follis senatoria*) and habitual special contributions to the state (*aurum oblaticium*), and had to fund public games and festivals in Rome and Constantinople.

The old republican magistrates who still prevailed were the consuls, praetors and quaestors, but they were divested of all their former powers. Two consuls were nominated annually, one at Rome and the other at Constantinople, until AD 541 when Emperor Justinian abolished the consulship. The consuls imparted their names to the year, but their duties were limited to organizing public games and festivals. Nevertheless, the consulship was still regarded as a high honour and was frequently held by the emperor himself. The praetors and quaestors were appointed by the emperor from the ranks of the senators on recommendation of the city prefects, and their functions were broadly similar to those of the consuls.[38]

The social structure of the late Empire

The social and economic development of the Roman world in the late imperial era is directly linked with the profound changes that emerged during the crisis of the third century AD. Clear indications of the altered structure and direction of the late Roman society embrace: the expansion of the senatorial aristocracy at the expense of the old equestrian order and its virtual monopoly of the great state offices; the power consolidation of the senatorial land barons and the growing inability of the central government to control them; the decline of slavery and the extension of the colonate system over large areas; the further weakening of the cities' governing classes (*decuriones*, *curiales*) owing to the incessant excessive demands imposed by the government; the institutionalization of rigidly defined and closely regulated hereditary castes, each with a definite rank in society; the polarization between the impoverished masses and the concentrated wealth and power of privileged dignitaries and the increasing alienation of large sections of the population from the Roman state; and the growing proportion of non-Roman elements in the Roman military, among both the soldiers and the officers (including those of the highest rank).

Purely from an objective basis there is a case for construing the late imperial society as still consisting of three main social classes (if the *curiales* are regarded as a middle class). However, this traditional division was no longer decisive. An essential factor was the polarization between the privileged elite of state functionaries and senatorial landlords on the one hand, and the impoverished masses of the population on the other. A real dichotomy appeared in imperial society, based on the division of subjects into two classes: the *honestiores* (or *potentiores*) and the *humiliores* (or *tenuiores*).

During the Principate era the upper classes consisted of senators, equestrians and the decurions of the cities (generally called *curiales* during the late Empire). They displayed more or less graduated distinctions with respect to origin, function, wealth and prestige. However, in the course of the third and fourth centuries AD, the structure of the upper classes underwent a considerable transformation. The senatorial aristocracy of the late Empire had only vague and tenuous genealogical links with the senatorial order of the Republic and the Principate. It no longer mainly encompassed a few families of ex-magistrates and large estate-owners and their next-of-kin, as in the past. It was now a broad and highly heterogeneous social class whose members originated from all parts of the empire. This class embodied high state officials and ex-officials and their descendants, members of the imperial household, retired high-ranking army officers, prominent members of the provincial administration and other persons of distinction (including many foreigners). The only common features between these groups with senatorial rank were the basic privileges and obligations of their members.[39] The divisions within the senatorial class were further accentuated after the establishment of a second senate in Constantinople (AD 357), which admitted many Roman citizens from the eastern part of the empire. Whereas the Roman senate comprised many representatives of the ancient Roman nobility, the Constantinopolitan senate was predominated by 'new men' – social climbers, often from humble origins, who only attained a senatorial position after a long career in the imperial administration or the army. Moreover, in the Roman senate the great landed proprietors still formed the most important economic group, while many eastern senators had risen from craftsmen and tradesmen of Constantinople. Generally, the western senators also held more conservative attitudes than those of the East, as manifested by their general opposition to Christianity and adherence to traditional pagan practices. Besides the distinction between eastern and western senators, there were further subdivisions within the senatorial order. These were prominent in the West where different senatorial factions were formed by groups of senators who shared common interests and places of residence.[40]

An important consequence of the structural changes in the fourth century AD was the demise of the old equestrian order, the foundation of the empire's administrative system in the Principate period. During the early years of the Dominate, the position of the equestrians was temporarily strengthened as a result of the administrative reforms of Diocletian, who used equestrians instead of senators in many government posts. However, this tendency was reversed when Constantine enrolled highly placed equestrians into the senatorial order and transformed the higher equestrian offices into senatorial offices. As a result, the leading groups of the equestrian class were gradually absorbed into the senatorial order, while the rest were allotted the same status as low-ranking public officials. Although the equestrian order was not formally abolished, the dynamism and prestige of the former *equites* was a thing of the past.

The members of the municipal aristocracy (*curiales*)[41] were still positioned among the privileged upper classes. A distinction was drawn between a smaller group of the wealthiest and most influential city councillors (*principales*), and the general ruck of *curiales*. The members of both groups had identical rights and obligations, and enjoyed the same legal privileges as those existing during the late Principate. Yet the public offices held by the *curiales* were still no more than burdens imposed upon them by the state. As their economic situation worsened, they encountered greater difficulties in fulfilling their obligations. The *curiales'* basic functions embraced the responsibility for the grain supply, public order, and the construction and maintenance of public buildings in their city. They were also required to finance public games and festivals and collect all the taxes in their community, being personally liable for the total amount to the state.[42] Eligible citizens sought to escape these burdens by every means, which prompted the government to render the service on municipal councils compulsory[43] and hereditary,[44] and restrict the municipal councillors' freedom of movement. The *curiales* were prohibited from either leaving their town (even when they wished to visit the emperor on civic business) or disposing their estates without the permission of the provincial governor.[45] Many *curiales* faced financial ruin and hostility from fellow townsmen, who deemed them mere tax collectors for the state. Therefore, they endeavoured to circumvent their responsibilities by fleeing their towns. Many joined the army or, in connivance with corrupt officials, acquired privileged status without compliance with regulations. The imperial government introduced several measures to curtail the legal and illegal defections from the curial order, but these had scant success.[46] As the wealthier, more mobile *curiales* escaped their burdens in the cities, they encumbered the dwindling number of remaining poorer colleagues with increased fiscal responsibilities. The late fourth century AD featured the depletion of the urban middle class that supplied the members of the town councils and the entire class faced extinction, especially in the more backward western provinces.

Whereas the upper classes of the late Empire were composed of various groups with diverse positions in society, the lower classes assumed a more uniform shape.

Their rights and standard of living were equalized by the widespread impoverishment and deprivation among the urban and rural sections of the population, and by their increasing social, political and economic dependence. This process of levelling is noticeable in the development of the law. On the one hand, the legal position of slaves was improved by an array of imperial laws that rendered them equal to the free individuals in many respects. But, on the other hand, the free masses of the population were reduced almost to the level of slaves by the restrictions and compulsory demands imposed by the state. Despite the sharp contrast between the privileged social groups (*honestiores* or *potentiores* or *potentes*) and the impoverished masses (*humiliores* or *tenuiores* or *plebei*), the lower class retained its distinctions. As before, it comprised free craft workers, traders, the lower status personnel in the administration of the community, small farmers who owned some land, free land workers, the tenants (*coloni*) now attached to the estates that had employed them and a relatively small proportion of freedmen and slaves that varied in number from region to region. The class was augmented by new groups: displaced persons and fugitives deprived of their means of subsistence by foreign invasions, state persecution or compulsion; war prisoners assigned to great landlords as labourers; monks and hermits; and, finally, foreigners who settled as allies in imperial lands.

During the late Empire the traditional distinction between the *plebs urbana* and the *plebs rustica* was maintained. However, the social gap between the two groups was not as marked as it had been during the Principate. The members of urban *plebs* enjoyed certain advantages in comparison to the rural population: they were exempted from the poll tax (*capitatio*); in Rome, Constantinople and other large cities of the empire, they occasionally received free distributions of grain and were entertained at the state's expense. Yet, the general economic situation of the *plebs urbana* did not surpass that of *plebs rustica*. The most important factors that socially and economically levelled the urban lower classes were the cities' economic decline, owing to the abiding deterioration of city production and city trade, and the increasing fiscal burdens imposed upon the city population by the state. As the government was forced to intervene to ensure the supply of essential commodities and services, the urban trades and professions were enveloped by strict state control. Throughout the empire all businessmen, tradesmen and craftsmen were organized into associations, now called *corpora*, which operated under the supervision of state officials.[47] Like the *curiales*, the members of these associations (*corporati*) were required to devote much time, energy and resources to serving the state or their municipalities. To secure the fulfilment of state requirements, the government made membership in the *corpora* compulsory and hereditary. Measures were also introduced to thwart any attempt by the *corporati* to evade their obligations by changing their occupation, enrolling in the army or becoming tenants of senatorial landlords.[48] Initially, only persons engaged in the trades vital to the state, such as mariners (*navicularii*) and bakers (*pistores*), were bound to their occupations. As the state wrestled with greater difficulties in the production and transportation of essential commodities, direct state control was extended to other professions, and members of the compulsory corporations experienced more severe oppression.

The peasantry (*plebs rustica*) formed the great majority of the population and was economically the most important class. Like the urban *plebs*, it was composed of several groups: besides the agricultural workers that constituted the largest group, there were also craftsmen, miners, casual and seasonal labourers, and even some independent farmers with their own smallholdings. Most of the workforce on the large estates consisted of tenant farmers (*coloni*) tied to the soil. The declining number of slaves working on the estates now formed an insignificant part of the agricultural labour force, except in some parts of the western Mediterranean such as Sicily and Spain. Despite the peaceful phase in the fourth century AD, the living conditions of the diverse groups within the rural population were uniformly bad and the poverty in the countryside was as prolific as that in the cities. The peasants paid a disproportionate share of imperial taxes and were subject to oppression by government agents and senatorial landlords. The desperation engendered by the growing demands of the state and corrupt officials prompted many farmers to place themselves as clients under the protection of powerful land barons or influential officials or to abandon their land and live as brigands.[49] As the farmers' abandonment of the land threatened state revenues in kind, the government intervened and institutionalized the system of serfdom (*colonatus*). Like the *curiales* and the *corporati*, the tenant farmers (*coloni*) were now prohibited from entering public service or another occupation, and their status became permanent and hereditary.[50] They were bound to their employer's estates and transferred with the land from one owner to another. However, as free citizens, they were not absolutely under the power of the owner and could not be disposed of detached from the land.[51] Although some imperial edicts were issued during this period that defined the rights and duties of the *coloni*, the condition of the *coloni* evolved to resemble servitude – a halfway status between free men and slaves.[52] As economic conditions worsened, social development within the *plebs rustica* orientated towards a general levelling out. The patent social divisions within this class that existed in the early Principate separating, for example, an independent peasant from an agricultural slave, were erased and social dependency assumed an increasingly uniform pattern among all groups of the rural population.

The small landowners and the tenant farmers faced hardship in extracting a livelihood from their lands, particularly in view of heavy taxation and the extortionate methods of its collection. On the other hand, the great senatorial landlords maintained and even improved their standard of living through profiting from their substantial estates and capital, their monopoly of the civil offices, and privileged legal status. The immunities of the senatorial order and the growing wealth and influence of its members imparted an almost manorial character to the great landed proprietors who developed more political and economic independence. As the central government diminished in authority, the great land barons assumed police powers and jurisdiction on their estates, formed private armies to deflect barbarian attacks, collected taxes on behalf of the state and even occasionally imposed taxes and other exactions on the districts they controlled. Their great power compelled individuals and whole village communities, anxious to avoid the burdens imposed by the municipal and imperial authorities, to seek their protection as clients and tenants – a relation referred to as *patronicium*. Like the early Roman *patronatus*, the *patronicium* embraced a recognition of mutual obligations (usually regular payments in kind or money by the weaker party in return for protection against the authorities). However, in the late Empire this institution was directed unambiguously against the state. All government attempts to suppress the practice by law ended in failure. The legal recognition of the *patronicium* in AD 415 entailed the acceptance and sanctioning of the removal of not only large estates and their personnel, but also entire populations of large districts from the sphere of government control.

The proliferation of the *patronicium* strengthened the position of the landed aristocracy, which gradually became a state within the state. At the same time, this further undermined the government's ability to obtain the resources required to maintain the machinery of power. The only course of action for the government was to increase the burden of taxation in the territories and cities under its direct control, which fuelled the discontent and hatred felt by the masses of the underprivileged. Despite the plight of the lower classes and the recurrent social uprisings that erupted in the city and the countryside, late antiquity did not see a general class conflict between the oppressed masses and the Roman state and its governing class. A social revolution was fundamentally impossible as the resistance to force and oppression was never supported by a revolutionary ideology for the transformation of society. The collapse of the Roman system of government in the West and the passage from the ancient to the medieval social system did not emanate from revolution. It originated from a complex process of disintegration precipitated by the increasing alienation of society from the state and the consequent inability of the central government to resist the decentralizing tendencies of the great landlords and the pressure of barbarian invasions. The transformation of the Roman state into a machinery of power supported by relatively small groups, and the consequent absolutization of state demands, provoked the refusal of large sections of the population to identify themselves with the state. Through the violent oppression of the largest groups in society, the totalitarian state of late antiquity increasingly disconnected itself from its roots in the Roman social system. Thus, the rule of the emperor and his machinery of power, exalted to unprecedented heights by an artificial enhancement of the system's brilliant façade of display, finally became an end in itself: a pure burden that only oppressed society with its coercive measures and impositions. With mounting indifference to the state's fate and few individuals prepared to sustain the regime, the forces of dissolution acquired momentum and the demise of the political system of the late Empire appeared unavoidable.

The final years of the Roman Empire

After Constantine's death in AD 337, imperial unity was sustained for a period under his successors, Constantius II (AD 337–61)[53] and Julian (AD 361–63). But in AD 364 Valentinian I recommended the division of the empire's administration and granted the rule of the eastern half to his brother Valens. At this time, the tide of Germanic invasions escalated under pressures from the east and this posed a serious threat to the territorial integrity of the empire. While, in the West, Valentinian (like Constantine, Constantius and Julian) successfully defended his territory against the renewed attempts of Germanic tribes to advance over the river Rhine into Gaul, in the East Valens was compelled to admit the Germanic Visigoths into the area south of the river Danube (AD 376). This tribe was forced to seek refuge in the empire under pressure by the Huns, a fierce nomadic people whose advance from Asia into the area north of the Back Sea prompted great migrations among the Germanic peoples of eastern and central Europe. The influx of thousands of Goths into the empire caused chaos as the imperial authorities were not equipped to manage the provisioning and policing of the newcomers. The Visigoths soon revolted and defeated Valens in AD 378, who was killed at the battle of Adrianople. Although the Visigoths did not exploit their victory and were repelled before launching an attack on Constantinople, the destruction of the entire eastern Roman army at Adrianople demonstrated that the security of imperial territory was no longer guaranteed.

The accession of Theodosius I in AD 379 introduced an energetic soldier-emperor to the throne who, though not successful in thwarting the Visigothic menace, provided the tottering empire with an essential respite period. After an inconclusive war, Theodosius formally permitted the Visigoths to settle as allies on the right bank of the river Danube in AD 382. However, the tribe was not integrated with the Roman population, as customary in similar past cases, but were treated as a separate people living within the empire's frontiers. Danger existed in the novel admission of a large barbarian nation that would remain unassimilated and the massive barbarian recruitment into the Roman army encouraged by Theodosius; the consequences became evident in the ensuing years. Under Theodosius, the East relished a period of relative peace, while the West struggled in turmoil and confusion. Two successive revolts of the Roman legions in Britain and Gaul led to the deaths of Gratian, the Augustus of the West (AD 383) and his successor Valentinian II (AD 392). In AD 394 Theodosius instigated an offensive and defeated the rebellious officers in the West, thereby becoming sole ruler of the empire. Once more, the empire was united, but Theodosius only briefly survived his triumph – he died early in AD 395.

As a staunch supporter of Christianity, Theodosius engaged drastic measures to eliminate both paganism and Christian heresies by asserting the emperor's right to exercise authority in Church matters.[54] However, during his reign the difficulties that assailed the empire – economic decline, depopulation, corruption and the increasing power of the great landlords – did not diminish but intensified. Some of his policies, especially that of enlisting Goths and other Germanic elements in his armies, eventually proved detrimental to the state's interests.

The collapse of the Roman state in the West

Theodosius was the last emperor to rule over the Roman Empire in its entire extent. After his death the empire was divided anew between his two sons: Arcadius (AD 395–408) governed Constantinople and the East, and Honorius (AD 395–423), though only eleven years old, was the nominal ruler of the West. Although a fiction of imperial unity was preserved, the two parts of the empire greatly diverged in both the legislative and administration spheres. By the end of the fourth century AD the defence of the Western empire crumbled and successive invasions by the Goths, Alans, Suevi, Vandals, Franks and other Germanic tribes degraded imperial authority to a shadow of its former self. The political power of the central government faded as the German element within the Roman army acquired more dominance, both qualitatively and quantitatively. The western emperors depended entirely on the support of Germanic war bands and warlords who, as 'king-makers', actually ruled the state. Rome and the Roman West repeatedly endeavoured to enlist Constantinople's support. However, the eastern empire was preoccupied with its own problems and could only offer temporary and limited assistance. From AD 406 the imperial government at Milan or Ravenna was powerless to curtail the permanent, large-scale settlement of Germanic tribes in its territories. Moreover, the government could not avert the ultimate indignity, the sack of the empire's ancient capital, Rome, in AD 410 and again in 455. In the late fifth century the Italian peninsula, largely isolated by the establishment of the Visigoths in the north-west and the Vandals in the south, was an easy target for another Germanic people, the Ostrogoths. Shortly after the German general Odovacar deposed the last emperor of the West, Romulus Augustulus (AD 476),[55] the eastern emperor Zeno (AD 474–91) commissioned the Ostrogothic leader Theodoric to conquer Italy for the empire. In AD 488 Theodoric, supported by his entire nation, invaded Italy and five years of fighting culminated in the ousting of Odovacar and control of the peninsula. After this triumph, he established the Ostrogothic kingdom and ruled as actual king of the Romans and Goths in Italy, although he appeared to acknowledge a vague dependence on the emperor at Constantinople. The establishment of the Burgundians and Franks in Gaul and the Saxons in England entailed the complete dismemberment of the Western Roman Empire, and a new host of Germanic kingdoms surfaced within the former Roman provinces in the West.[56]

As the Roman Empire in the West disintegrated, the civilization and forms of social life characteristic of the ancient Greco-Roman world were gradually dissolved. The ancient Greek ideal of urban life that the Romans introduced throughout the Mediterranean basin declined. Many cities disappeared altogether, giving way to forms of habitation constructed around fortified manors and small village communities. Although some great urban centres in Italy and Gaul still exhibited signs of commercial activity, trade and industry decayed and economic life reverted to an agricultural and pastoral type, geared to maintaining local self-sufficiency. As centralized authority disintegrated everywhere, the political conditions shifted towards the decentralized localism associated with the feudal system. During the same period, the general culture in the West displayed a sharp downward trend emanating from the chaos caused by the Germanic invasions and the decline of the cities. However, vestiges of the ancient Greco-Roman civilization prevailed throughout this era and, over time, their fusion with both the crude culture of the Germanic peoples and the learning of Christianity produced a new synthesis which furnished the basis for the cultural revival of the eleventh and subsequent centuries.

The survival and transformation of the empire in the East

While the Roman Empire in the West succumbed to the control of Germanic warlords, the eastern empire survived the crisis with its institutions and frontiers largely intact. The emperors at Constantinople successfully guarded their territory in Asia Minor against the restored power of Persia and resisted the infiltration of the Germanic barbarians and the decentralizing influence of the great landlords and generalissimos. The empire in the East survived as its socio-economic circumstances were more favourable: it did not feature a complete divorce of society from the state as had occurred in the West; a close relationship existed between the emperor and the landowning senatorial aristocracy; the Church played a greater role in state affairs and supported the state energetically; the eastern provinces had a relatively healthy economy and urban life remained robust. Above all, the eastern empire's defensive capabilities and military potential were far better than those of the western empire.[57] Nevertheless, the eastern empire was clearly on the defensive, being constantly threatened by barbarian invasions and plagued by internal conflicts.

In AD 527 a vigorous new ruler, Justinian, ascended the throne at Constantinople. Imbued with the Roman imperial tradition, Justinian directed all his energies to fulfilling his essential ambition: the restoration of the Roman Empire to its earlier grandeur. To this end he inaugurated a programme that focused on three goals: the re-establishment of imperial rule throughout the Mediterranean basin; the restoration of unity in the Church through the enforcement of religious orthodoxy; and the systematic restatement and consolidation of the law.

Despite the utter collapse of the Roman power in the West, certain conditions were favourable to a reconquest. The indigenous population regarded the Goths and Vandals as Arian heretics, whereas the emperor of Constantinople represented the religious establishment. Moreover, the complex system of alliances that Theodoric forged with the Vandal and Visigothic kingdoms had collapsed after his death (AD 526), diplomatically isolating the Ostrogoths and Vandals. After concluding a peace agreement with the Persian Empire in the East, Justinian mounted an expedition under general Belisarius against the Vandal kingdom of North Africa in AD 533. Within a year the Vandals were defeated and Africa was restored to its former position as a province of the empire. The invasion of Sicily in AD 535 marked the initiation of the reconquest of Italy. After a bitter struggle that endured for more than two decades, the Ostrogothic kingdom was overthrown and Rome, the empire's ancient capital, was recaptured. In AD 554, Justinian's ambitions directed him to the far western Mediterranean, where southern Spain was wrested

from the Visigoths and adjoined to the empire. By exploiting the diplomatic isolation of his opponents in the West and assuming a defensive stance in the East,
Justinian succeeded in converting the Mediterranean once more into an imperial
lake. However, the reconquest of Africa, Italy and Spain entailed mixed blessings for
their inhabitants; their initial acceptance of imperial rule was soon tempered by
misgivings prompted by the obligations placed upon the population by the imperial
authorities.

Within the empire, Justinian introduced a series of administrative reforms
designed to protect his subjects against the rapacity of government officials and
soldiers, and to curb the oppression of the rural population by powerful land
barons. Moreover, he adopted measures devised to revitalize commerce and
industry, and embarked on an extensive architectural and artistic programme,
furnishing the empire with churches, public buildings and fortifications.[58] However,
he encountered impediments when endeavouring to restore religious orthodoxy
within the Church, whose unity was threatened by various schisms.[59] Despite his
interests in improving the administration, his intentions were rarely realized as the
officials he relied on were frequently corrupt, even though they were efficient at
collecting the taxes requisite for attaining his goals.

Among Justinian's grandiose projects, the most successful and most historically
significant was his compilation and systematization of Roman law. Although in the
later imperial period local custom and law prevailed, the legal relations of society
were formally based on the enormous legal repository created from centuries of
imperial edicts and legal opinions of famous jurists. All this information, including
material inconsistent with current legal practice or obsolete, was scattered in the
central and provincial administration archives, and the libraries of law schools and
jurists. Under these conditions, legal practitioners and state officials had a
perplexing task of discovering the precise state of current law. Justinian succeeded,
with the assistance of his minister of justice, Tribonianus, in assembling the vast
literature on Roman law, combining the simplification and codification of the law
with legal reform and the transformation of legal education. Despite its limitations,
his codification is one of the greatest monuments of legal activity the world has ever
known. It furnished the basis for the further evolution of law in the Byzantine East,
and supplied later Western Europe with the common ground on which the civil law
systems of the Continent were built.

The centralizing forces manifest in Justinian's political, legal and religious
programme ultimately failed to overcome the centrifugal tendencies within the
empire. His reconquest of the West proved ephemeral, and exhausted the empire
both economically and militarily, which contributed further to the weakness
emanating from sectarian and cultural diversity. Shortly after Justinian's death
(AD 568), renewed attacks by Germanic tribes reduced imperial authority in the
West to a few strong points. Spain fell to the Visigoths and another Germanic tribe,
the Lombards, invaded Italy from the North conquering most of the peninsula. At
the same time, Persian armies advanced through the eastern provinces and the Slavs
and Avars permeated the Balkans. In AD 627 Heraclius, a capable emperor,

succeeded in stemming the Persian incursions and halting the Slavic assaults. From around AD 630, the Moslem conquests ensued with the Arabs capturing Egypt, Syria and part of Asia Minor. But as the imperial boundaries receded, retrenchment produced a comparative strengthening of the state and the eastern empire acquired the homogeneity that the policies of Justinian had failed to effectuate. During this period the transformation of the eastern Roman Empire into the medieval Byzantine Empire was completed.

The Byzantine Empire originated from the crises of the later Roman period, which transmuted the world of antiquity. The elements of continuity between the worlds of Byzantium and antiquity are as clear and undeniable as the differences. During this momentous transformation, the empire lost its Latin and pagan character and assumed a Greek–Christian form. However, Byzantium, like the Roman Empire, remained a polyglot, multinational and polysectarian state during the greater part of its existence. Moreover, this transformation further accentuated the religious differences between East and West, which gradually induced the separation of the Greek Orthodox and Roman Catholic Churches. At the same time, the Byzantine Empire inherited its organization from the Roman Empire. Roman law remained in force as a living system with its incorporation in Byzantine law and the concept of *imperium Romanum*, now existing as *imperium Christianum*, furnished the basis for all Byzantine political theory. The empire prevailed for almost a thousand years until 1453 when Constantinople, the imperial capital, was conquered by the Ottoman Turks.

11

THE DOMINATE:
THE SOURCES OF LAW

Introduction

As we have observed, in the fourth century AD the imperial system of government completed its transformation into an undisguised autocracy that received its definite form under Emperors Diocletian and Constantine the Great. The entire sovereignty of the Roman people was deemed to be transferred to the emperor, who existed as the sole authority in all spheres of government: legislative, administrative, judicial and military. On principle, the emperor as an absolute monarch was omnipotent and his activities in ruling the state were not subject to any constitutional constraints. However, the emperor actually exercised his governmental functions and powers with guidance from established substantive and procedural norms. Although he might change these norms at his discretion, he was bound to observe them to ensure that his decisions produced the intended practical results. In the final analysis, it may be declared that the observance of these norms constituted a kind of intra-organ control over an authoritarian regime.

Under the Dominate, the emperor emerged as the sole source of laws and also their final interpreter. Although the old *leges* and *senatus consulta* remained valid, the 'pluriformity' that characterized legislative activity during the Principate and the Republic ceased to exist. The unchallengeable legislative supremacy of the emperor conformed to the essence of the new system of government, whose absolutist nature barred constitutional or any other legal limitations.[1] The imperial enactments (*constitutiones*) with their diverse appellations of *edicta, rescripta, decreta* or *mandata* were now collectively designated *leges* – this signified legal norms with the highest validity. These enactments furnished the basis for the formation of a new body of law (*ius novum*), in contrast to the old law (*ius vetus*) as traditionally interpreted by the jurists during the Principate era. This new body of law differed markedly from the law of the classical period with respect to both substance and form. The prevailing social and economic conditions, and the enhanced importance of the imperial civil service induced the requirement for new regulations. The existing legal system was unprepared for these essentials, and thus the great majority of imperial constitutions pertained to public law and fiscal policy matters. Furthermore, most of the new imperial law was not strictly Roman in character but exhibited the influence of foreign (especially Greek) institutions. Since the era of

Constantine the Great, this law was also moulded by ideas derived from Christian ethics. Generally, the legislation of the Dominate displays elements of so-called 'vulgar law': statutes are composed in an inflated, grandiose style while their provisions have an ill-arranged, vague and unrefined form; and these are often deficient in affording an exhaustive and unambiguous determination of the relevant issues. At every turn, one can detect an absence of the scientific preparation that is a necessary prerequisite for all sound legislation. While the quality of the imperial laws declined, their quantity rapidly increased as often conflicting enactments were produced in great profusion, resulting in a chaotic mass that had little practical use. Since the late third century AD, the government endeavoured to instil some order into the mass of laws claiming validity in the empire. In AD 438, Emperor Theodosius issued an official code of imperial law, but the attempts to create order out of chaos only attained a fair measure of success with the reign of Justinian (AD 527–65).[2]

As previously noted, during the Principate era the elected judicial magistrates and the jury-courts in criminal matters were gradually replaced by officials appointed by and acting as delegates of the *princeps*-emperor. The idea of *ius* as something which a magistrate would assist a Roman citizen to obtain remained a dominant one; however, after the formulary procedure was entirely superseded by the *cognitio extraordinaria* the manner whereby the magisterial *imperium* was initiated had completely changed. Under the Dominate the administration of justice, like all other state activities, became thoroughly bureaucratized. Imperial officials practically assumed all traditional judicial functions, adjudicating in the name of the emperor as his representatives. The pattern of decentralization governing the administration of the empire also presented itself as the natural frame for the judicial organization, concurrently reducing the caseload of the emperor's court. Besides the regular courts, special courts were established to deal with particular matters and categories of persons. Moreover, from the time of Constantine the Great, a significant part of private law (especially family law) was increasingly encompassed by the jurisdiction of Church organs. Moreover, for the first time in Roman history an elaborate system of appeals was developed that corresponded closely to the empire's administrative structure.

As we have discerned, the work of the jurists during the first two centuries of the Principate was the most creative element in Roman legal life. However, in the third century AD jurisprudence entered a period of rapid decline and the *responsa prudentium* soon ceased to be a living source of law. Under the Dominate, jurisprudence was no longer the driving force it had been in the past and the works of the classical age were treated as a body of finally settled doctrine. The demise of classical jurisprudence derived from a combination of factors: the cultural decay precipitated by the catastrophes of the third century AD; the increasing absolutism of the emperor, who sought to install himself as the sole source of legal developments; and the growing influence of Christian thinking that had an ethical orientation with little use for the subtleties of the secular jurisprudential techniques. Other changes within the Roman legal system also accelerated the decline of jurisprudence, such as the final consolidation of the praetorian edict, the obliteration of the distinction between *ius civile* and *ius honorarium*[3] and the gradual abandonment of the Roman tradition of distilling legal norms from the body of individual cases in favour of a system where decisions in individual cases were controlled by previously formulated general rules. However, it cannot be asserted that the decline of classical jurisprudence was tantamount to a collapse of legal culture in general. Lawyers were still essential in the imperial court, the various government departments, and those agencies in Rome and in the provinces that governed the administration of justice. In the late third and early fourth centuries AD, many state officials in Rome were men steeped in the classical tradition and they sought to defend this tradition against the inroads of eastern and vulgar legal influences.[4] However, it is clear that in the late imperial era the social position of the lawyers and the character of their work had radically changed. The new lawyers no longer worked as individuals who, as members of the senatorial aristocracy, experts in law and representatives of a great and living tradition, presented opinions on legal problems and recorded them in writing. These lawyers were mere state officials, anonymous members of a vast bureaucratic organization, who simply prepared the resolutions for issue in the name of the emperor. In the fifth century AD, legal scholarship experienced a period of growth centred around the law schools of the East. However, unlike the classical jurists, the law teachers of this period did not deliver any new opinions on questions of law, nor did they develop a truly scientific jurisprudence. Their primary concern was rendering the works of the classical age more accessible by new publications, summaries, anthologies and commentaries. Despite their lack of originality, these jurists introduced a new insight into the operation of Roman law and preserved the bulk of the material which the classical jurists had left to posterity.

Another remarkable phenomenon of the later imperial period was the so-called 'vulgarization' of Roman law. The disappearance of the division between *civis* and *peregrinus* after the enactment of the *constitutio Antoniniana* in the early third century AD entailed the fading of the old distinction between *ius civile* and *ius gentium*: in theory every free man in the empire was now a citizen governed by the same, universal, Roman law. However, local systems of law prevailed in the form of custom that was now recognized as an authentic source of law on an equal footing with imperial legislation. Roman law and these systems mutually infiltrated each other with the former losing many of its earlier, 'purely Roman', characteristics. The law that actually applied in the provinces was a mixture of this 'debased' Roman law and local practice, varying from area to area but lacking the subtlety and sophistication of the classical system. In the West, the 'vulgarization' of Roman law attained its peak in the fifth century AD and it provided the historically important link between classical law and the legal systems of the Germanic successors to the Roman Empire.

The end of this period of Roman legal history is marked by a work that emerged as the final statement of Roman law: the codification of Emperor Justinian. As the ancient world dissolved, Justinian successfully assembled, in an enduring form that could be passed on to the future, the written heritage of Roman law spanning

159

hundreds of years of legal development. Originally issued in the years AD 533–34, the Justinianic codification comprised three parts: the Institutes (*Institutiones*), an introductory textbook on Roman law intended for student use; the Code (*Codex*), an extensive collection of imperial constitutions; and the Digest (*Digesta*), containing a large number of excerpts from the works of the classical Roman jurists. To these three books were subsequently added the new statutes issued by Justinian and his successors (*Novellae leges*). Justinian's codification both completed the development of Roman law and became the principal medium whereby Roman law was transmitted to the modern world.

Imperial legislation

In the Dominate period the emperor was endowed with the full power to create law, nevertheless the exercise of this power had to be regulated to ensure that all law-making acts were genuine manifestations of the emperor's will. Among the four types of imperial constitution that had developed during the Principate (edicts, rescripts, decrees and mandates), the edicts (*edicta imperatorum*) or *leges generales* were the most important as they embodied legal norms of general application.[5] An edict was usually issued in the form of a letter addressed to a high official (generally a praetorian praefect), who had a duty to publicize its contents; it could also be addressed to the people or some section thereof (e.g. to the inhabitants of a particular city), or to the senate (either of Rome or of Constantinople, depending on the circumstances).[6] When an edict was addressed to the senate, no *senatus consultum* was passed to confer formal validity on the emperor's wishes, which now existed as law *per se*. Simply, the terms of the statute were recited in the senate, recorded and retained in the archives of that body. The drafts of legislative enactments were prepared by the minister of justice (*quaestor sacri palatii*) with the assistance of legal experts and discussed in the imperial council (*sacrum consistorium*). After the division of the empire into two parts, legislative measures were almost invariably issued in the name of both *Augusti*, even when they emanated from only one of them,[7] although, obviously these measures had no effect within the realm of the other *Augustus* without the latter's consent. In fact, it often transpired that an enactment issued by the emperor of the East was adopted by the emperor of the West, but the reverse ostensibly did not occur.

As the emperor acquired the full power of creating law directly by engaging the *leges generales*, indirect law-making by means of *rescripta*, *decreta* and *mandata* essentially lost its earlier importance. The *rescripta* (now also designated *leges speciales*), i.e. responses of the emperor to legal questions invoked by actual cases and submitted to him by private citizens or state officials, remained an important source of law until the reign of Diocletian,[8] but thereafter their use fell largely into disrepute. The incompetence and corruption that took hold among government officials apparently enabled many petitioners to obtain rescripts that upheld totally unsound legal views, and problems were exacerbated by the real danger of forged rescripts. Several complicated and often inconsistent enactments were issued during this period to curtail the abuses connected with the employment of rescripts, but these attained little success. In AD 315, Constantine ordained that a rescript was invalid if it deviated from a *lex generalis*.[9] Moreover, a law issued by Arcadius in AD 398 stipulated that a rescript was only binding in the individual case that it concerned.[10] Pursuant to this enactment, rescripts were no longer regarded as generally valid and thus their role as a source of new law apparently ended. However, Emperors Theodosius II and Valentinian III in AD 426 sought once more to make imperial rescripts an indirect law-making force by decreeing that, as it constituted a declaration of a general principle in an individual case, a rescript could be considered generally binding.[11] This view seems to have prevailed during the time of Justinian's reign in the sixth century AD.

The mandates (*mandata*) were originally directions of the emperor to provincial governors and other state officials. These essentially fell into disuse during the Dominate as they were incorporated into the edicts or *leges generales*.[12] As regards the emperor's decisions in his capacity as a judge in the first instance or on appeal (*decreta*), these gradually disappeared as an indirect source of law. This derived from the increasing practice of the emperors to delegate judicial functions to their officials. During the later imperial period, few records allude to the use of judicial decisions as precedents in subsequent cases. Justinian affirmed that the emperor's rulings on points of law as a judge were, in principle, universally binding, yet he expressly forbade the use of judicial decisions as precedents. This essentially meant that judges had to decide cases in accordance with abstract general rules of law and not merely in accordance with the decisions of other judges (except the emperor) in previous cases (*legibus, non exemplis, iudicandum est*).[13]

In the later imperial period two new kinds of imperial constitution emerged, namely the *sanctio pragmatica* and the *adnotatio*. A *sanctio pragmatica* generally consisted of a reply by the emperor to a petition, but it apparently ranked as a more formal manifestation of the emperor's will than an ordinary rescript and practically had the same effect as a *lex generalis*. Accordingly, it was commonly used in replying to petitions that requested the settlement of matters of general public interest or the issuing of decisions with a scope of application that extended well beyond the interests of the parties involved. A *sanctio pragmatica* might be employed, for example, to effect administrative reform, regulate the operation of government bodies or corporations or confer important privileges on certain groups.[14] The term *adnotatio* was probably used to denote a decision of the emperor in response to a petition or any other communication directly addressed to him and written in the margin of the petition.[15]

Finally, a form of subordinate legislation that originated from the late Principate period was embodied in the edicts of the praetorian prefects (*edicta praefectorum praetorio*).[16] The provisions of such edicts mainly addressed administrative matters and were binding within the prefecture of their author, provided that they did not conflict with the general law of the empire.

The jurists' law

As noted, during the Dominate era imperial legislation became the principal source of law and the sole means for modifying the current body of law. The old law, created and developed by the former agencies of legislation, remained valid. However, it was customary to cite this law not by reference to the original texts (e.g. *leges, senatus consulta, edicta magistratuum*), but by reference to the classical jurists' commentaries on them. Moreover, the past emphasis on the development of new law through interpretation of extant legal materials evaporated. The focus now attached to the study and elucidation of the jurists' writings from the Principate era. As jurisprudence ceased to exist as a living source of law when it was annihilated at its source by the absolutism of the imperial system, literary production in the legal field sank to the level of merely compiling, editing and abridging earlier juristic works. The latter were now treated as a body of finally settled doctrine that could be applied in a case at any time. This body of law was designated *ius* in contradistinction to the body of law derived from the enactments of the emperors, known as *lex*.

However, serious problems beset the application of *ius* – problems that were intensified by the general passivity of the judges in an age of absolutism, who shied away from seeking original solutions and preferred to rely essentially on established authority. But the sheer vastness of the juridical literature by the classical jurists made it virtually impossible for the average lawyer to familiarize himself with the material. Furthermore, the classical works contained an extensive range of opinions that often reflected incompatible or contradictory viewpoints. Judges, who were expected to base their decisions on established authority, often faced the problem of choosing between two or more conflicting sources that, in principle, were deemed equally authoritative. The problem was exacerbated by the fact that, at a time when legal texts circulated only in manuscript copies, many works attributed to classical jurists were actually not written by them. This situation generated a great deal of confusion as to the state of the law and also opened the door to abuse, as advocates often sought to deceive judges by producing captious quotations from allegedly classical texts. This prompted the urgent need to discover a way to identify those works that formed part of the authoritative juridical literature and the appropriate solution to adopt if the classical authorities displayed conflicting opinions. The government's response was a series of legislative enactments prescribing the juristic works that should be relied on by the courts and fixing the degree of authority accorded to different sources.

In AD 321, Emperor Constantine endeavoured to address some problems caused by the controversies of the classical jurists. He issued a constitution forbidding the quotation of the critical comments (*notae*) by Paulus and Ulpianus on the *responsa* of Papinianus, thus rendering the latter jurist supreme.[17] This was soon followed by another enactment whereby Constantine confirmed the authority of Paulus' other works (especially the *sententiae*, a collection of pronouncements and rules).[18] Both the above laws are connected with the well-established practice in this period of reading in court opinions of classical jurists pertinent to the legal question under consideration. Judges were expected to adopt the solution supported by the unanimous opinion of the authorities, or, in case of disagreement, to forge their own decision. As very little continuity or consistency existed between judges, even this limited discretion of the judges proved problematic. Thus, in AD 426, Theodosius II (Eastern emperor, AD 408–50) and Valentinian III (Western emperor, AD 423–55) aspired to regulate the use of classical authorities in court through an enactment later designated the 'Law of Citations'.[19] In this statute, the emperors stipulated that, thereafter, the writings of the classical jurists Papinianus, Ulpianus, Paulus, Modestinus and Gaius should be regarded as legally binding. If the authorities adduced on a particular issue disagreed, the judge should adopt the view of the majority; in the case of a tie, priority should be accorded to the opinion that had the support of Papinianus. If the opinions adduced were equal in number on each side and no relevant utterance of Papinianus could be detected, the judge was directed to exercise his own judgment in selecting the best proposed solution. The views of earlier jurists might also be considered if these were quoted by the five principal jurists and the authenticity of the quotations was confirmed by reference to the original sources (through a comparison of manuscripts). In other words, if one of the five jurists quoted and endorsed the opinion of a jurist external to this group, then the former was deemed to have espoused this opinion. The Law of Citations achieved a measure of uniformity and predictability in the administration of justice. It provided a partial solution to the problem generated by the unwieldy mass of juridical literature and by the lack of adequate resourcing in terms of both skilled judicial professionals and legal materials. However, the mechanical treatment of the legal authorities it adopted clearly indicates the low level to which jurisprudence had sunk. It also bears witness to the degree to which judges had lost the freedom and even the ability to engage in creative thinking and form independent judgments.

The law schools

In the later republican age, when jurisprudence emerged as a science, legal education was entirely in private hands. Novices were inducted into the law by prominent jurists, whose everyday activities (presenting *responsa*, assisting parties in legal proceedings and such like) they were permitted to observe. Under the Principate, the private character of legal instruction was relatively more systematized but remained largely unchanged.[20] However, towards the end of this period a system of public legal instruction emerged to principally train those who wished to embark on a career in the imperial civil service. The first law school was probably established in Rome during the late second century AD and followed by a second such school in Beirut during the early third century AD.[21] As the administrative demands of the empire escalated, especially during and after Diocletian's and Constantine's reorganization of the government, new law schools were established in places such as Alexandria, Caesaria, Athens and Constantinople[22] in the East, and Carthage and Augustodunum in the West. At the same time measures were introduced to promote systematic legal instruction.[23] Over time, the professional lawyers educated in the law schools (*causidici, advocati*) replaced the earlier orators (*oratores*), whose training in law was usually only elementary. An edict of Emperor Leo I, issued in AD 460, ordained that postulants for the bar of the Eastern praetorian prefecture had to produce certificates of proficiency from the law professors who instructed them. This requirement was soon extended to the inferior bars, including those of the provinces.[24]

Besides training people for functions in the civil service, the law schools cultivated a scholarly approach to law with a focus on the study and elucidation of the juristic works from the classical period that had evolved into a unitary and peculiar body of law (*ius*). The extent to which the ideal of a full education in classical law was realized naturally varied in different periods and places. In the early years of the Dominate period (late third and early fourth centuries AD), a substantial scholarly interest in law apparently existed in the West, with most of this interest probably revolving around the law school in Rome. Since Constantine's era, and especially after Constantinople became the seat of government, the empire's intellectual centre and thereby the centre of legal culture gradually shifted to the East.[25] In the fifth century AD the study of the classical authorities, particularly at the law schools of Beirut and Constantinople, engendered a new type of theoretical jurisprudence (as opposed to the largely practical and casuistic jurisprudence familiar to the classical and earlier periods). The jurists of this period preserved and rendered the works of the classical jurists accessible to practitioners through the production of new copies, anthologies and abridgments. They were also concerned with adapting the classical materials to the demands and conditions of their own times.[26] Through these activities, they laid the foundation for the subsequent codification of Roman law by Emperor Justinian.

In the law schools the teaching was conducted by professional law-teachers (*antecessores*),[27] and the courses offered were components of a fixed curriculum that focused entirely on the study of classical juristic works and imperial constitutions. First, the Institutes of Gaius were discussed and then followed the study of the classical jurists' opinions *ad ius civile* and *ad edictum* embodied in collections, with special attention to the works of Papinianus and Paulus. In the final year, the focus converged on the study of current law and this involved an examination of imperial constitutions going back to the middle of the second century AD. In the East, legal instruction was delivered in the Greek language but knowledge of Latin was necessary for reading the classical texts. The method of instruction was similar to that used in the schools of rhetoric: a classical work was discussed and clarified in stages and, when possible, compared or contrasted with other relevant works. In this way, general legal principles were formulated and applied to resolve specific problems of law arising from actual or hypothetical cases. At the end of their studies, which spanned a maximum of five years, students were awarded a certificate that entitled them to serve as advocates in the courts or to join the imperial civil service.

The East-Roman law professors were admiringly termed the 'teachers of the universe', and the most celebrated and influential encompassed Cyrillus, Patricius, Eudoxius, Leontius, Amblichus and Demosthenes. It is established that these men composed a diversity of works: commentaries on imperial constitutions and texts of classical jurists, summaries (*indices*), annotations and collections of rules on particular legal questions. As noted earlier, these works were concerned not so much with developing new legal ideas but with helping novices and practitioners to acquire a sound knowledge and understanding of the material imparted by the classical Roman jurists. Despite its lack of originality and its tendency towards simplification, post-classical legal science did succeed in resurrecting genuine familiarity with the entire classical inheritance and facilitating its adaptation to the conditions of the times. Their new insight into the essence of the classical law enabled court lawyers trained at law school to enhance the technique of imperial legislation and successfully tackle the task of legal codification. The improvement of legal technique is manifested by the fact that the imperial laws of the late fifth and sixth centuries were superior in clarity and style to those of the early post-classical period. Essentially, the work of the late imperial jurists preserved the spirit of classical jurisprudence and facilitated its entry into the codification of Justinian and thereby into modern law.

Late imperial juridical literature

As elaborated previously, in the later imperial age the problems surrounding the application of *ius* were magnified by the fact that the manuscripts containing the works of the classical jurists were few and scarce. Thus, these materials were not easily accessible to legal practitioners, especially those working in the provinces. Moreover, as a result of the general decline of legal culture, especially in the West, lawyers encountered increasing difficulties with handling and comprehending the language of the classical texts. Connected to these problems was the appearance of legal works that mainly embodied compilations of assorted extracts from the works of the classical jurists, intended primarily for use by students and legal practitioners. The authors of these works (whose names remain largely unknown) selected parts from the original texts that would appear interesting to contemporary readers, while other parts were reproduced in a summary form or altogether omitted if they were deemed useless or superfluous. Occasionally passages were replaced with those composed by the authors or entirely new passages were added to render the material more intelligible or adapt the classical texts to transformed conditions. From the viewpoint of a modern scholar, this tampering distorted rather than improved the texts. However, it must be acknowledged that from the perspective of these early lawyers the classical works were largely outdated and in need of 'modernization'. Irrespective of its form, the juridical literature of the later imperial period patently reveals one aspect: the extent to which legal thinking remained under the spell of classical jurisprudence. The legal science that existed at that time was concerned exclusively with the classical jurists, whose works were regarded with an almost religious awe by legal practitioners and judges.

Probably the most important post-classical compilation of juristic literature is the so-called 'Vatican Fragments' (*Fragmenta Vaticana*) discovered in 1821 within the Vatican library. This work was presumably devised as a handbook for practitioners and it contains extracts from the writings of the jurists Papinianus, Paulus and Ulpianus who lived in the late second and early third centuries. It also includes imperial constitutions (*rescripta*) dating from the period AD 205–372, which were reproduced from the Gregorian and Hermogenian Codes.[28] The texts are arranged in titles according to the subject-matter or area,[29] with each title preceded by a note indicating the name of the jurist from whose work the materials were extracted or, if the text is a rescript, the name of the emperor who issued it. This collection, although incomplete, has immense value for the study of Roman law as it embodies materials that are not located in other sources or that were transmitted to us only in a greatly abbreviated form.[30]

Another work, dating from the early fourth century AD, is known under the title of *Collatio Legum Mosaicarum et Romanarum* or *Comparison between Mosaic and Roman Laws* (sometimes abbreviated to *Collatio*).[31] Ostensibly, the purpose of this work was to compare some selected Roman norms with related norms of Mosaic law to show that basic principles of Roman law corresponded with or possibly derived from Mosaic law. Like the Vatican Fragments, it is subdivided into titles, each of which starts with a quotation from the first five books of the Old Testament (especially the maxims of Moses) followed by extracts from the works of the jurists Paulus, Ulpianus, Papinianus, Modestinus and Gaius, and imperial constitutions from the Gregorian and Hermogenian Codes. The author of this work remains unknown, although the attempted comparison of Roman and Mosaic law evinces that he was probably of Jewish origin.[32]

Two other collections originating from the same period must also be mentioned: the *Sententiae* of Paulus (*Pauli sententiarum ad filium libri quinque*) and the *Epitome* of Ulpianus. The former mainly consists of brief pronouncements and rules attributed to the third century jurist Paulus. It covers an extensive range of topics relating to both private and criminal law, and appears to have been used as a handbook by legal practitioners. As no evidence indicates that Paulus composed a book called *Sententiae*, this work is now generally assumed to be a brief presentation of Roman law extracted from the writings of Paulus (and possibly other classical authorities) by an unknown author from the latter part of the third century AD. The *Pauli Sententiae* seems to have been very popular throughout the late Empire, as it is cited frequently in compilations of law and imperial constitutions of this period.[33] Although the work has not survived in its original form, it has been reconstructed on the basis of excerpts retrieved from the Digest of Justinian, the *Lex Romana Visigothorum* and other post-classical sources.[34] Scholars postulate that the *Ulpiani Epitome* is an abridgment of Ulpianus' work *liber singularis regularum* (Rules of Law in one Book).[35] It was composed in the late third or early fourth century AD and, like the *Pauli Sententiae*, was probably intended for use by practitioners. This work was conveyed to the modern world in a fragmentary form through a manuscript dating from the tenth or eleventh century.[36]

A subsequent work that probably originated from the late fifth century AD is the *Consultatio veteris cuiusdam iuris consulti* (Consultation with an Ancient Jurisconsult), normally abbreviated to *Consultatio*. This work was presumably designed for instructional purposes and it consists of several legal questions accompanied by answers based on Paulus' *Sententiae* and post-classical compilations of imperial law.[37] It is mainly concerned with the operation of various pacts, especially in the area of family law. The *Consultatio* was first edited by Cujas (*Jacobus Cujacius*)[38] in 1577, but the manuscript relied on did not survive.

Two important works from the East have survived: the Syrio-Roman book of law and the *Scholia Sinaitica*. The former was composed in Greek by an unknown author and published in the late fifth century AD, probably in Constantinople. Apparently, it was used as a textbook for students in the law school of Beirut. In the past, scholars believed that the author of this work drew upon both Roman and Greek sources. However, the current view is that the law contained in the Syrio-Roman book is mainly of Roman origin.[39] The *Scholia Sinaitica* acquired its name because the relevant manuscript was discovered at the monastery of St Catherine of Sinai (in 1880) and it most likely dates from the late fifth century AD. The fragments are part of a commentary in Greek on the work of Ulpianus *libri ad Sabinum*, probably composed at the law school of Beirut and used for educational purposes. The work presents us with a clear view of the teaching methods at the law schools in the East, and thoroughly illustrates the post-classical commentators' approach to the classical texts.[40]

Trends in post-classical law

As noted in the introduction, the legislation of the Dominate period reflects the influence of non-Roman elements on official Roman law (especially vulgar law). The enactment of Caracalla's *constitutio Antoniniana* (AD 212) extended Roman citizenship to all the free inhabitants of the empire, and thereafter Roman law was theoretically the common law of the realm. As a result, the old distinction between *ius civile* and *ius gentium* withered away. However, in reality the imposition of a uniform legal system did not entail forcing Roman law pure and simple upon the peoples of the empire, who continued to live by the law they were used to. In the eastern Mediterranean, in particular, the common Greek culture and language had produced a distinct body of law, whose origins are located in the Greek city-states as well as the Hellenistic monarchies of Syria and Egypt. This body of law operated alongside Roman law and was enforced by officials on equal terms with the latter law. It did not merely sustain itself in a half-submerged condition, but it contributed distinct elements to the Roman system through a process of cross-fertilization. This process had been operative for centuries but accelerated after the intellectual centre of the empire shifted from Rome to Constantinople in the fourth century AD. This entailed the 'Orientalization' or 'Hellenization' of Roman law, and the 'Romanization' of Greek-Hellenistic and other local bodies of law. Similar processes featured in the Western provinces of the empire, and also in Italy and Rome itself. This precipitated a phenomenon that is generally labelled the 'vulgarization' of Roman law.

The term 'vulgar' law refers to the legal views and practices of lay people – a body of 'popular' or 'folkish' law untouched by the artifices of the legal experts. This genuine customary law was initially regarded as supplementary and unofficial. Finally, in the fifth century AD it attained recognition as an authentic source of legal norms on a par with imperial legislation.[41] The increasing ascendancy of customary or 'vulgar' law – that is, legal solutions adopted by practitioners at a local or regional level – may partly be attributed to the fact that imperial legislative enactments reached local magistrates and courts, if at all, with great delay and in a piecemeal fashion due to the uncertainty of communications. Moreover, at a time when printed books did not exist, local courts and practitioners had no access to the bulk of the classical legal sources. The enhanced role of custom as a source of law was also reinforced by the fact that, while the emperor and his bureaucracy created all law, they were often unfamiliar with the prevailing conditions in the provinces. Thus, many imperial enactments were at variance with local practices and conceptions of justice. Setting aside long-established local customs was not easy and thus the actual implementation of imperial legislation in the provinces sometimes proved an impossible task.[42] But vulgar law did not pertain only to customary law. An important source of vulgar law was also the imperial enactments, which were often influenced by foreign legal ideas and practices. Another factor emerged after the recognition of Christianity in the fourth century AD, when Christian ethics started to exercise considerable influence on certain branches of Roman law, such as family and criminal law.

The body of law that evolved from the interaction between Roman and foreign elements was markedly inferior to the classical system in terms of logic and abstract refinement. Yet, it was closer to the prevailing conditions of life and thus had some practical advantages. Non-Roman influences are detected at many points of the legal system. For example, the importance of the written document (a heritage of the Hellenistic tradition) as a prerequisite for a binding agreement was now generally recognized. At the same time, freedom of contract was promoted by the abandonment of the cumbrous formalism that existed previously. Under the influence of Greek-Hellenistic law, which adopted a narrower conception of paternal authority than Roman law, Emperor Constantine introduced restrictions to the traditional Roman institution of *patria potestas* by conceding that persons *in potestate* could have proprietary rights in certain circumstances. Thus, it was recognized that a child was entitled to the property a mother bequeathed to them, even if the child remained under the *potestas* of their father.[43] The influence of certain Greek customs is also reflected in Justinian's decision to replace the complicated *adoptio* procedure of the *ius civile*[44] with a simpler procedure that merely required the father, child and intending adoptor to appear before an official and have the *adoptio* inserted in the court roll.[45] A feature alien to old Roman law that was adopted from the customs of the near East was the *donatio propter nuptias*: a donation by the husband to the wife before the marriage to provide for the wife's domestic needs and to ensure that she had an estate should the marriage be dissolved by divorce or by the husband's death. In the course of time, the tendency developed to regard the *donatio propter nuptias* as existing in the interests of the children rather than the wife. The influence of Christian principles concerning the sanctity of marriage is exhibited in legislative enactments of Constantine and some of his successors that sought to curtail, by imposing severe penalties, the freedom of spouses to declare a divorce without proper justification.[46] The prevalence of Christian ethical principles during the fourth century AD entailed disrepute for the institution of concubinage (*concubinatus*), a permanent union between a man and a woman not legally married. Concubinage was discouraged through the introduction of various restrictions on the rights of children born out of such a union (*liberi naturales*). To avert such restrictions, the parents, or in some cases the children, resorted to some form of legitimation, such as legitimation by the subsequent marriage between the parents of such children.[47] In the field of criminal law, the influence of Christian ethics is displayed in the abolition of certain cruel forms of punishment such as crucifixion and gladiatorial combat. This influence is also evident in the introduction of new criminal offences pertaining to the suppression of heretical cults and practices. The list of pertinent illustrations could easily be enlarged.

12

THE DOMINATE:
THE ADMINISTRATION OF
JUSTICE

The court system

In the bureaucratic state of the late Roman Empire, imperial officials exercised practically all traditional powers and functions relating to the administration of justice. Most officials had little or no legal training, and therefore were often assisted by legal assessors (*adsessores*) who had received legal education and had usually belonged to the legal profession.[1] Moreover, it was quite common for senior officials to perform their judicial functions through delegates (*iudices dati* or *pedanei*); the latter were usually low-ranking officers and their decisions could be appealed against before the officials who appointed them. In general, the system of appeals corresponded directly to the hierarchical structure that was observed with regard to the administrative tasks performed by the various state officials.

At the lowest level of jurisdiction were the municipal courts (*curiales*), which possessed an extremely small sphere of competence. In the field of criminal law their powers were restricted to punishing minor offences and, in the case of other offences, to conducting the preliminaries of the trial that would normally proceed before the provincial governor. In civil matters, these courts could only tackle cases where the amount of money at stake was trivial, unless their jurisdiction was extended by agreement between the relevant parties. In civil and criminal cases, the provincial governors functioned as the regular (i.e. normally competent) judges of the first instance (*iudices ordinarii*) and, in addition, dealt with appeals against sentences passed by municipal courts.[2] According to the circumstances, appeals against the governor's decisions were managed by the *praefectus praetorio* of the prefecture or by the *vicarius* of the diocese that encompassed the province in question.[3] A further appeal from a *vicarius* to the emperor was feasible, but a judgment passed by a *praefectus praetorio* could not be contested on appeal as the latter was deemed the personal representative of the emperor.[4] Under exceptional circumstances, the *praefecti praetorio* and the *vicarii* could hear cases as judges in the first instance such as when a litigant suspected that a powerful adversary would intimidate the provincial governor. As regards Rome and Constantinople, the *praefectus urbi* was the highest judge within the city and the surrounding territory enveloped by his authority, and he heard appeals from ordinary judges officiating within these bounds. In theory, the emperor could exercise jurisdiction in all kinds of civil or criminal cases as a judge of first instance and on appeal. However, in practice he rarely tried cases in person as the nature of the imperial office during this period did not permit close contact between him and his subjects (cases submitted to him were usually managed by the *praefectus praetorio* or another state official authorized to act in the emperor's stead).

The system of courts outlined above dealt with the ordinary array of cases, whether of a civil or criminal nature. In addition to the ordinary courts, there existed many special courts that addressed particular types of cases (usually administrative) or cases involving individuals from a particular group or class. Most of these courts had their roots in the established principle that a magistrate had administrative jurisdiction over matters connected with his departmental tasks and a disciplinary jurisdiction over his subordinates. In the fourth century AD, the sphere of competence of the special courts tended to expand at the expense of the regular courts and this provoked frequent clashes of jurisdiction. The category of special courts encompassed, for example, the court of the *rationalis* (the official who represented the public treasury in a diocese) that handled disputes relating to taxation and other fiscal matters. A decision issued by the court of the *rationalis* could be appealed against before the *comes sacrarum largitionum*, the minister in charge of state finances. Cases regarding disputes over crown property could be tackled by provincial governors or be referred to the *comes rei privatae* (or *comes rerum privatarum*), the official responsible for the administration and management of the emperor's private property. The special jurisdiction of the *praefecti annonae* captured matters such as claims to bread rations in Rome and Constantinople, disputes over membership in the bakers' guilds and claims of merchants for loss of corn by shipwreck. The *praefectus urbi* dealt with cases involving violations of public order and breaches of building regulations. Illustrations of special jurisdictions that applied to certain categories or classes of persons included the disciplinary jurisdictions of military commanders and heads of government departments over soldiers and members of the bureaucracy respectively.[5] Members of the senatorial order fell within the exclusive jurisdiction of the *praefectus urbi* if they were domiciled at Rome or Constantinople, or within the jurisdiction of their provincial governor.[6] In such cases, the decisions of provincial governors were subject to review by the emperor or the urban or praetorian prefects. Members of the clergy also enjoyed certain jurisdictional privileges in the sphere of civil law, although in criminal cases they remained subject to the jurisdiction of the secular courts. In the middle of the fourth century AD, Emperor Constantius decreed that bishops accused of criminal offences could be tried before a council of bishops with an appeal to the imperial appellate courts.[7] However, this privilege seems to have been revoked in later years.[8]

Judicial protection of the lower classes

As noted previously, the society of the late Empire was a non-egalitarian and rigidly stratified society where the mass of the common people (*humiliores*) were exposed to the arbitrariness of an all-powerful and deeply corrupt administrative apparatus that favoured the upper classes. Yet members of the lower classes were not entirely bereft of protection against the abuses of an arrogant officialdom. The *defensor civitatis* or *plebis* was one of the institutions established by the state for the redress of grievances suffered by the poor and lowly. The office first appeared in the diocese of the Oriens during the early fourth century AD and by the end of that century it had been extended throughout the whole empire.[9] The *defensores* were probably chosen initially by the citizens from among persons with a high social status (*honorati*) deemed sufficiently qualified to contest their peers' excesses, and this selection then awaited confirmation by the praetorian prefect or the emperor. These individuals were entrusted with the special duty of protecting the common people in a municipality against acts of extortion and oppression committed by the bureaucracy and the mighty landowners (*potentiores*, *possessores*). This authority enabled them, for example, to prevent torture in criminal proceedings, veto the arrest of a person suspected of a crime and intercede against unfair fiscal exactions and enforced military service. Moreover, they were endowed with a minor jurisdiction in civil and criminal matters that was subject to an appeal to the provincial governor, and could arrest and transfer to the governor those accused of serious crimes.[10] For a phase, the *defensor* and his court were apparently successful in providing cheap and swift justice to members of the lower classes. However, in the long term the institution failed to achieve its goal of alleviating the conditions of the poor and the underprivileged. Probably the greatest difficulty was to locate, in this degenerate age, strong and upright men willing to undertake the burdens of the office and capable of resisting the pressures of the powerful. Hence, different methods for appointing holders of the said office were engaged now and then. Ultimately, the *defensor civitatis* became simply another extraordinary magistrate and an instrument of the bureaucracy and the land-owning elite whose abuses he was originally destined to curb.

As the institution of the *defensor civitatis* proved short-lived, oppressed people increasingly sought protection from the Christian Bishops whose influence in the administration of secular justice tended to intensify. From the perspective of the civilian population, the operation of the administration became increasingly oppressive and Christianity assuaged this situation. The faith embodied an egalitarian ideology that viewed all humans as equal before God and it exercised a mitigating influence in several fields on the conditions of the oppressed classes and groups. For example, bishops had no direct criminal jurisdiction but could frequently defend refugees who sought sanctuary in churches, or intervene in favour of the accused or the convicted in criminal trials. Moreover, these bishops as religious heads of their towns were more effective than the *defensores* in protecting impoverished citizens against the unfair demands of imperial officials. As regards the administration of justice, Christians generally adhered to the exhortation of Apostle Paul not to submit their disputes to the secular courts[11] and thus they would normally present their private law disputes before local bishops. This practice occurred even before the recognition of Christianity as the official state religion. Constantine the Great formally recognized this kind of jurisdiction (*episcopalis audientia*) and proclaimed that the decisions of Church authorities were legally binding.[12] The power of bishops to decide a civil case was later restricted to cases submitted to them by agreement of both parties concerned.[13] Although a sentence passed by the *episcopalis audientia* could not be appealed against, this form of procedure became very popular as it was simpler, more expeditious and less costly than that of the regular courts.[14] One may declare in conclusion that, during a period featuring the worst lawlessness thus far in Roman history, the influence of the Church constituted an important element of civil stability and protective justice.

The civil procedure

In the fourth century AD, an edict of Emperors Constantius and Constans (AD 342) officially abolished the old *per formulam* procedure that had been wholly superseded by the *cognitio extraordinaria* in the later years of the Principate era.[15] The establishment of the *cognitio extraordinaria* was closely connected with the development of an extensive bureaucratic organization in the late imperial period, which required greater immediate control by officials. The state displayed an increasing tendency to intervene in the legal sphere and consequently the resolution of legal disputes was no longer based on an agreement between the parties to present a dispute before a judge. Such resolutions were now contingent on the power of the administrative apparatus to place a dispute before its officials, attain a determination and execute the decision. The *cognitio* procedure did not exert such a great influence on the development of Roman private law as with the case of the formulary procedure. Yet this procedure enabled litigation to proceed in a simpler and more convenient fashion, and it was ideally suited for the type of state created by Diocletian and his successors.[16] On the other hand, the pace of justice was slow because the courts were always overstretched and judicial magistrates normally had to devote much time to other administrative duties. Moreover, the cost of litigation was often beyond the means of ordinary people. The costs embraced advocates' fees, bribes to officials and, in the case of appeals, long trips to distant cities. In addition, court fees (*sportulae*) were high and inclined to increase despite the government's periodic attempts to curb them.

The first step in a civil action was a declaration by the plaintiff or his representative to a jurisdictional magistrate outlining the factual and legal basis of his case against his adversary, and requesting the start of a trial (*postulatio simplex*).[17] After a preliminary assessment of the plaintiff's case, the magistrate served on the defendant a summons accompanied by the plaintiff's statement. This form of summons was termed *litis denuntiatio* and was deemed to be issued by the plaintiff to the defendant with the assistance of the magistrate and under official authorization (*denuntiatio ex auctoritate*). The *litis denuntiatio* mandated the appearance of the defendant before the judge within four months to contest the plaintiff's claim. If the defendant failed to appear following three monthly summons (*trina denuntiatione*), the magistrate could prosecute him for insubordination (*contumacia*) or order that he be brought before him by force.[18] By the time of Justinian's reign, the *litis denuntiatio* was superseded by a new method of summoning the defendant: the plaintiff had to submit a statement of claim (*libellus conventionis*)[19] to the relevant judicial magistrate that presented the facts supporting his case and requested the magistrate to summon the defendant. Thereupon the defendant was notified of the plaintiff's claim and granted ten days (twenty days in Justinian's period) to respond in writing (*libellus contradictionis* or *responsionis*)[20] and provide security that he would be present on the day of the trial.[21] If the plaintiff or the defendant did not appear on the day of the trial (*contumacia, eremodicium*), a judgment could be delivered by default.[22] However, the matter could be re-instituted and the issues retried later.

On the day of trial, the parties and their legal representatives swore oaths of good faith[23] and proceeded to present the vital facts, and the pro and contra arguments in a brief form.[24] As under the formulary system, the defendant could raise a defence (*exceptio* or *praescriptio*) to counter the plaintiff's claim, for example on the grounds of fraud (*exceptio doli*). Pleas pertaining to jurisdiction or a party's capacity to participate in the process could be treated as preliminary pleas, and interlocutory decisions on procedural and other matters were also possible. The term *litis contestatio* referred to the moment when the parties concluded their pleadings.[25] However, the parties were relatively free to modify their claims and defences during the course of the trial.

In the next phase of the proceedings, evidence was presented and arguments delivered. Evidence might be oral or written, but the former was deemed to possess relatively little value.[26] The court summoned witnesses, who were often required to provide surety for their appearance. The presiding judge interrogated these witnesses and their answers were recorded. Generally, the evidence of a single witness did not carry any weight, while the credibility of the presented evidence was contingent on the social status of the witness.[27] In normal circumstances, hearsay evidence was not permissible and declarations issued under oath were now quite general.[28] The acknowledgement of the plaintiff's claim by the defendant before the judge (*confessio*) carried special weight as a means of evidence, but did not necessarily entail the termination of the proceedings.[29] In general, the presiding magistrate had considerable freedom in assessing the evidence within the limits set by the statutory rules governing the trial process and by the instructions of his superiors. In this regard, the introduction of defeasible and indefeasible presumptions (*praesumptiones*) played an important role.[30]

The trial culminated in the magistrate's judgment (*sententia*), embodied in writing and announced publicly in the presence of all the relevant parties at a formal sitting of the court.[31] In contrast to the formulary procedure, the judge in the *cognitio* procedure was free to sentence the defeated party to an atonement other than the payment of damages (*condemnatio pecuniaria*) – for example, he could order the defendant to hand over a specific object. Moreover, Justinian stipulated that if the defendant was absolved the judge could condemn the plaintiff to render the verified reparation that he owed in the context of the same transaction.[32] After the publication of the court's decision, the plaintiff was precluded from instigating another action against the defendant for the same object.[33] The defendant could raise an *exceptio rei iudicatae* against such an action – a defence based on the claim that the same matter had definitely been resolved in a previous trial.

As noted earlier, a decision of a judge could be appealed against (*appellatio*) to a higher tribunal and then a superior tribunal until it reached the court of the praetorian prefect. An appeal to the emperor was only feasible in matters of importance and, in most cases, an appeal could not progress beyond two instances.[34] Moreover, during Justinian's reign appeals against interlocutory judgments were, in normal circumstances, no longer permitted. The relevant party had to issue notice of appeal (*libellus appellationis*) within two or three days[35] (or within ten days, in Justinian's time)[36] of the judge's decision, and the appeal proceeded with little delay. The appellate court could confirm the decision, whereupon the appellant incurred penalties to the lower court and the other party. Alternatively, this court could quash or modify the decision but did not remit it for resentencing to the lower court.[37]

Execution under the *cognitio* procedure was simpler than under the formulary system. If the defendant was condemned, he had to comply with the judgment within a minimum period of two months (or four months, under Justinian) after the announcement of the decision or when the decision was rendered final on appeal.[38] If he failed to comply, the plaintiff could notify the authorities with a request for execution of the decision. Where specific performance was ordered, such as the return of a particular object to the plaintiff, the court could employ its officers to effectuate it or to enforce compliance with the order.[39] Where the condemnation was pecuniary, execution could proceed against the debtor's person or property. In the former case, the debtor would be confined in a public prison. The law forbade an execution against the person that entailed confinement in private prisons,[40] but this was frequently ignored (especially in the Eastern provinces) as revealed by the contemporary literature; the imperial legislation was powerless to change this practice. When execution was levied against the debtor's property, court officers seized the relevant property to retain it as a pledge (*pignus in iudicati causa captum*). If the debtor did not comply with the court's decision within two months, this property was sold for the benefit of the creditor.[41] If several creditors existed, the entire property of the insolvent debtor could be sold in a piecemeal fashion (*distractio bonorum*) at an auction organized by the administrator of the debtor's estate (*curator bonorum*).[42]

Resolving private disputes through arbitration

As an extra-judicial method for dealing with private controversies, arbitration (*arbitrium*) was based on a formal agreement (*compromissum*) between the relevant parties to submit their dispute to an arbitrator (*arbiter*) for resolution. The parties selected the arbitrator whose scope of authority was prescribed in the *compromissum*.[43] However, the decision of the arbitrator (*pronuntiatio arbitri*) was not binding unless the parties had assumed the obligation of abiding by the decision by means of reciprocal stipulations backed by penalties.[44] In Justinian's era the arbitrator's decision was binding if both parties had signed it, or if neither party expressed disapproval to the arbitrator or the other party within ten days from the announcement of the decision.[45]

Criminal law and procedure

In the late Empire, the scope of existing offence categories was extended and several new offences were introduced by imperial legislation to tackle new forms of wrong-doing induced by societal changes. For example, the crime of extortion (*crimen repetundarum*) was defined in a broader manner to encompass all kinds of infractions perpetrated by state officials in the course of their administrative or judicial tasks.[46] The ambit of crimes such as treason (*crimen maiestatis*) and corruption (*ambitus*) was likewise expanded,[47] and more severe penalties were instituted for the offence of misappropriation of state property (*peculatus*).[48] Diverse offences were subsumed under the crime of sacrilege (*sacrilegium*) and these involved neglect or violation of imperial orders or enactments.[49] The concept of violence (*vis*) was also extended to cover acts of violence and various kinds of abuses committed by private individuals and state officials.[50] After the recognition of Christianity as the official religion of the empire, acts of opposition to the established religious doctrine were punished as crimes. This embraced acts such as adherence to sectarian beliefs or to a dissident religious sect, the propagation of heretical doctrines and refusal to observe religious holidays.[51] Moreover, an assortment of disadvantages was imposed on rene-gades, pagans and Jews.[52]

Overall, criminal legislation in the later imperial age was fragmentary and often inconsistent with little attention devoted to the subjective requirements of criminal liability such as *dolus* or *mens rea*.[53] The removal of all limitations on the emperor's power entailed the non-existence of safeguards in practice against the arbitrary exercise of power (except perhaps through the Church). It also meant that there were no restrictions on the punishments that could be inflicted with the emperor's authority. The statement of the jurist Hermogenianus that interpretation should be used to mitigate rather than aggravate the penalties of the laws,[54] and the notion that it is better to let the guilty go unpunished than to condemn the innocent,[55] mentioned in the Digest of Justinian, meant very little in the later imperial period. In this savage and degenerate age, only the wealthy and powerful individuals who could corrupt or intimidate state officials and judges were relatively safe from arbitrary punishments.

The criminal justice process

After the disappearance of the standing jury courts (*quaestiones perpetuae*) in the third century AD, the *cognitio extraordinaria* emerged as the regular procedure for criminal trials. Nevertheless, many rules of the old statutes that instituted the *quaes-tiones perpetuae* and clarified particular offence categories were still deemed relatively authoritative.

In most cases, criminal proceedings were set in motion by a public prosecution conducted by a judicial magistrate.[56] Proceedings by *accusatio*,[57] where the prosecution was conducted by any competent member of the public, were still feasible.[58] However, these proceedings were now rare due to the high risks they entailed for the accuser (if the prosecution was unsuccessful the accuser faced the same punishment that the accused would have suffered, if convicted).[59] Proceedings by *cognitio* were instigated in one of three ways: (i) following a report by a minor official (e.g. a municipal officer) charged with security duties; (ii) following a denunciation by the injured party or a private informer; and (iii) at the initiative of a judicial magistrate. In the first case, the official who lodged an incriminating report had to appear in court to present the case against the accused. To some extent, his role corresponded to that of a private accuser in the *accusatio* proceedings. Like a private accuser, an official who laid a charge was liable to punishment if the trial did not entail the conviction of the accused. However, unlike a private accuser, he was only liable if he had initiated a false accusation knowingly and maliciously. In the second case, a private citizen informally denounced another to a judicial magistrate. The latter was obliged to act on such denunciation and to officially institute and conduct criminal proceedings against the suspect.[60] The denouncer did not play a formal role during the trial, and could not be prosecuted if the charge was unsubstantiated.[61] In the third case, an official vested with judicial functions initiated the collection of incriminating information and launched criminal charges against those detected as offenders by his agents.

In the *cognitio* proceedings, the judge, at his discretion, determined the date of the trial.[62] Once the trial date was established, the judge had a duty to summon the accused (this could be done either by personal notice or by edictal citation) and arraign all the witnesses required to testify in the case. In the majority of cases (especially those involving offences of a serious nature), the alleged offender would be detained in a state prison[63] and could languish there for months waiting for the commencement of his trial.[64] At the hearing, the officer who reported the crime to the judicial magistrate was required to appear before the court and elaborate the matter, in a similar manner as an accuser addressed the court at the beginning of an accusatorial hearing. The remainder of the hearing also essentially corresponded to the equivalent stages of an *accusatio* trial, although the inquisitorial element was more pronounced than in the latter. On the other hand, when the prosecution was galvanized by information supplied by private denunciators or reports submitted by agents of the judicial magistrate, the hearing would essentially have comprised a purely inquisitorial interrogation of the accused and an examination of the available evidence. However, the judge had the discretion to select the manner of these details. The judge was only constrained by the rules relating to the collection and submission of evidence.[65] It was recognized that a suspect could only be sentenced if the court was convinced of his culpability; if uncertainty predominated, the suspect was granted the benefit of doubt and absolved with a release from all restraints. A suspect's confession was deemed to constitute conclusive proof of guilt, and judges were not allowed to pass a death sentence unless the suspect had confessed or the witnesses were unanimous in identifying him as the wrongdoer. In these circumstances, judges were tempted to use torture in a limitless manner to extract concordant evidence or, best of all, a confession during interrogation[66] when the accused or the witnesses belonged to the lower classes (*humiliores*).[67]

After weighing the presented evidence, the judge announced his verdict that either declared the accused guilty or absolved of the crime. If the accused was convicted, the judge proceeded to determine the punishment to be imposed and the trial procedure ended with the passing of the sentence.[68] The law stipulated the penalties that a judge could impose. Once the judge determined that the accused's conduct conformed with the description of the relevant crime, he was obliged to impose the prescribed punishment regardless of any mitigating or aggravating circumstances.

As regards the available forms of punishment, the position was not ostensibly different from that in the later years of the Principate. However, the penalties now imposed were generally harsher than those in earlier times. The most severe punishment in Roman criminal law was the death penalty (*poena mortis, poena capitis*).[69] As a rule, condemned criminals were executed in public immediately after the passing of the sentence if no appeal was lodged.[70] This usually occurred in the locality where the crime had been committed. There were four general forms of execution that the sentencing judge could impose. The most lenient of these forms was decapitation by the sword (*decollatio, capitis amputatio*). The remaining three forms of execution were the aggravated ones: garotting (*ad furcam, patibulum damnatio*), death at the stake (*vivi crematio*) and execution at the public games.[71] Other severe forms of punishment included forced labour in the mines (*ad metalla*),[72] gladiatorial combat (*ad ludum*),[73] forced labour in the public works (*opus publicum*) for life[74] and deportation (*deportatio*).[75] The less severe, non-capital punishments embraced banishment without loss of citizenship (*relegatio*),[76] forced labour in the public works for a fixed term, confiscation of property,[77] corporal punishment[78] and fines (*multae*). Incarceration was not recognized as a regular form of punishment; as in earlier times, the sole function of a prison was to secure temporarily those persons awaiting trial, or convicted criminals anticipating the execution of a severe sentence.[79] A judge had to contemplate certain factors when selecting the form of prescribed sentence to impose (e.g. the death penalty or another capital punishment) or determining the appropriate penalty in exceptional cases where his discretion governed the sentence. The essential factors encompassed whether the convicted person had a free or servile status and, in the former case, the offender's social class. Generally, a servile status and inferior social status operated as aggravating factors.[80] On the other hand, persons with a higher rank (*honestiores*) enjoyed certain penal privileges: they were not sentenced to death by garrotting or at a public game, nor condemned to the mines or subjected to flagellation or forced labour in the public works. Aggravating factors embraced transgression in office, the high incidence of the crime at issue in a particular area and recidivism. Whereas the facts that the offender was youthful, a minor participant in the crime and a slave who committed the offence on the order of his master all served as mitigating factors.

13

THE DOMINATE:
THE CODIFICATION OF ROMAN
LAW

The first codifications

In the later imperial era, a great problem that confronted the administration of justice was the vast and diffuse nature of the legal materials that constituted the fabric of law. The Roman imperial government was always inefficient in collecting and harmonizing the enactments of emperors, the opinions of the jurists and the other legal sources recognized by the courts. The relevant records embodied material that was inconsistent with current legal practice or outdated. Further, they existed as a disordered mass scattered in archives of the central and provincial administration, as well as in the libraries of law schools and jurists. Under these conditions, it was difficult to ascertain the current state of the law. Even the central administrators and judicial magistrates had only a very imperfect knowledge of the law and precedents that were engaged as the basis of their decisions. The legal history of the late Empire is marked by the successive efforts of the imperial government to remedy this situation. The high-handed methods adopted to achieve legal certainty are characteristic of both the autocratic form of government and the totally dependent attitude and unquestioning subservience to authority that prevailed among the judges and jurists in this period.

Under the Principate, imperial edicts (*edicta*) were posted in the principal towns of the empire and remained on display for a short period (probably a month). In all likelihood, the decrees (*decreta*) were not officially published but could be ascertained from the record of the case issued to the successful litigant. The rescripts (*rescripta*) were also recited in court and preserved in the court record, while the mandates (*mandata*) were communicated to and retained by the officials to whom they were issued. The enactments of the emperors were thus accessible to lawyers and the general public when they were issued, but no permanent central record of imperial legislation was retained. On the other hand, private lawyers from as early as the second century AD started to compile collections of imperial constitutions. For example, we know of a collection of thirteen rescripts of Septimius Severus published in AD 200, and a collection of decrees produced by the jurist Paulus in the closing years of the Principate.[1]

During the reign of Diocletian, the lack of any official collection of imperial constitutions was partly remedied by the publication of two private or 'semi-official' collections of law: the *Codex Gregorianus* and the *Codex Hermogenianus*. The former collection, published towards the end of the third century AD (probably in AD 291) by one Gregorius, contained imperial constitutions (mostly rescripts) from Hadrian (AD 117–30) up to and including Diocletian. These materials were arranged by subject matter in books and titles according to the traditional scheme observed by the classical jurists in their *Digesta*, and chronologically within each title. Around the same time (probably in AD 295), Hermogenianus[2] published a supplementary collection of constitutions that were issued during the reign of Diocletian. His book was simply subdivided into titles, while the constitutions it contained were arranged in chronological order. The Hermogenian Code was re-edited several times and new constitutions were added; but both this code and the preceding Gregorian Code remained as unofficial collections. On the other hand, some evidence indicates that the production of these codes was approved or authorized by Diocletian's government. This is corroborated by the fact that their authors enjoyed regular access to the archives of the imperial chancery, which suggests that they held senior positions in the imperial administration and performed their work under official supervision. The extraordinary authority that the Gregorian and Hermogenian Codes acquired after their publication is a more significant fact that distinguishes them from all private collections of legislation. The courts recognized these codes as authoritative and exhaustive records of all imperial legislation existing up to the date of their publication. Moreover, the codes were included among the principal texts of legal education and served as models for the first official law code produced in the fifth century AD on the orders of Emperor Theodosius II. As neither of the above-mentioned codes survived, information on their content is based on extracts incorporated in subsequent compilations of law such as the *Fragmenta Vaticana*, the *Collatio* and, especially, the Code of Justinian.[3]

The Theodosian Code

A considerable degree of uncertainty still prevailed in legal practice as to which constitutions and opinions were authoritative, despite the existence of the Gregorian and Hermogenian Codes and various collections of juristic material. As noted previously, in AD 321–22 Emperor Constantine enacted a number of statutes designed to provide guidance to judicial authorities on the use of the classical litera-ture. Nearly a century later (AD 426), the so-called 'Law of Citations' issued by Theodosius II and Valentinian III aspired to establish a veritable hierarchy for the opinions of celebrated jurists. On that basis, it installed a body of juristic opinion alongside the existing collections of imperial constitutions.[4] However, this law apparently proved insufficient or otherwise was possibly devised merely as a provi-sional measure. This prompted the same emperors in AD 429 to appoint a commission of distinguished lawyers and officials to rectify the situation. First, they had to compile a collection of all the imperial constitutions produced since the time of Constantine that were still in force. The next task was to combine this new collection with the Gregorian and Hermogenian Codes and classical juristic texts to create a code that would constitute a harmonious and comprehensive statement of the law. However, the execution of this project seems to have encountered insurmountable difficulties. Finally, in AD 435 a second commission was appointed to assemble all the extant constitutions issued since the reign of Constantine into a single compendium. The principal rationale for this new project appears to have been the government's desire to enable the legal practice to access the imperial legislation, which existed in a disorganized state.[5] The commission completed their assignment within a period of three years. The new collection was published in AD 438 under the name *Codex Theodosianus* and acquired the force of law first in the East and, shortly afterwards, in the West.[6] It was declared that the new code would be valid 'in all cases and in all courts and shall leave no place for any new constitution that is outside itself, except those constitutions which will be promulgated after the publication of this code'.[7] The Theodosian Code was essentially an extension and continuation of the Gregorian and Hermogenian Codes that were used as its models and still engaged by the courts. Moreover, the new code did not affect the application of the Law of Citations that prescribed the weight of authority accorded to the works of classical jurists.

The Theodosian Code embodied over 3,000 constitutions from the time of Constantine (*c.* AD 312) to AD 438. The material was arranged in sixteen books, each of which was divided into titles relating to specific topics. The germane parts of all the constitutions addressing a particular subject were inserted under the appropriate title in chronological order. While the code also comprised constitutions that were already abrogated by the time of compilation, it was easy to apply the rule of statutory construction whereby earlier legislation was repealed by later, inconsistent legislation, thus rendering it a simple matter to determine which constitutions represented valid law. The first five books focus on private law; books 6–8 address matters of constitutional and administrative law; criminal law is the subject of book 9; books 10–11 contain the law relating to public revenue; books 12–14 stipulate the rules governing municipalities and corporations; book 15 includes provisions pertaining to public works and games; and book 16 elaborates provisions on ecclesiastical matters. As the above description evinces, the majority of the constitutions embodied in the code are concerned with matters of public law.

The Theodosian Code has been transmitted virtually in its entirety with only some minor lacunae. Modern reconstructions are based partly on later collections, particularly the *Lex Romana Visigothorum* and the Code of Justinian, and partly on two manuscripts, one dating from the fifth century AD and the other from the sixth century AD.[8]

The Germanic codes of Roman law

We have observed that the early fifth century AD featured the gradual detachment of Western Europe from the control of imperial officials and its surrender to the power of various Germanic kings. The latter did not attempt to impose their own laws and customs on the Romans residing in their territories, nor did they adopt Roman law for their own subjects. Thus, as the Roman Empire in the West disintegrated, the once universal system of Roman law was replaced by a plurality of legal systems. The Roman part of the population continued to be governed by Roman law (*leges romanae*), while the newly settled Germanic peoples observed their own laws and customs (*leges barbarorum*). This entailed a revival of the ancient principle of the 'personality of the laws' that had fallen into abeyance after the enactment of the *constitutio Antoniniana* (AD 212): within every community, some groups would claim as their right the application of one of several existing bodies of legal rules. For the Romans in these Western communities, the old forms, legal rules and statutes were still in force. The magistrates were now responsible to Germanic chiefs though they still administered legal justice in a familiar manner. However, the courts in this period encountered serious difficulties with the administration of justice, which derived from the uncertainty regarding the content and authority of imperial and juristic law, and the general decline of legal culture in the West. To rectify this problem, some German kings considered it necessary to order the compilation of legal codes containing the personal Roman law that applied to their Roman subjects. The most important codes were the *Lex Romana Visigothorum*, the *Lex Romana Burgundionum* and the *Edictum Theoderici*. Although much of the law embodied in these collections is a crude reflection of the classical system, they possess great importance for legal historians: besides depicting the state of the law and society at the dawn of the Middle Ages, they preserved several Roman legal texts that cannot be located in any of the extant Roman sources.

In AD 506, the King of the Visigoths Alaric II promulgated the *Lex Romana Visigothorum* – hence, it is also known as the Breviary of Alaric (*Breviarium Alarici*). It contains extracts from the Gregorian, Hermogenian and Theodosian Codes, a number of post-Theodosian constitutions, an abbreviated version of Gaius' Institutes (*Epitome Gai*), sections of the *Sententiae* by Paulus and a short *responsum* of Papinianus as a conclusion. Some of the texts are accompanied by interpretations (in the form of paraphrases or explanatory notes) aimed at facilitating their understanding and application.[9] As the code was devised to replace all other sources of law, it was proclaimed that imperial constitutions and juristic opinions not included in it had no binding force in the courts of law.[10] The *Lex Romana Visigothorum* remained in force in Spain until the seventh century;[11] in Southern France, its application prevailed (even though no longer as an official code) until the twelfth century.[12]

The *Lex Romana Burgundionum* was composed during the reign of King Gundobad of the Burgundians and was promulgated by his son Sigismund in AD 517 for use by the Roman inhabitants of his kingdom. It is based on the Gregorian, Hermogenian and Theodosian Codes, a shortened version of the Institutes of Gaius and the *Sententiae* of Paulus. Unlike the Visigothic Code mentioned above, it does not contain any extracts from the original Roman sources. Instead, the materials are incorporated into a set of newly formulated rules that are systematically arranged and distributed over forty-seven titles.[13] The *Lex Romana Burgundionum* never possessed the importance or the popularity of the Visigothic Code, and apparently became obsolete soon after the Burgundian kingdom was conquered by the Franks in the middle of the sixth century AD.[14]

In the late fifth century AD, King Theodoric II (AD 453–66), ruler of the Visigothic kingdom of Southern France, enacted the *Edictum Theoderici* that was applicable to both Romans and Visigoths.[15] It has one hundred and fifty-four titles and contains materials distilled from the *Sententiae* of Paulus, the Gregorian, Hermogenian and Theodosian Codes and post-Theodosian legislation.[16]

The codification of Justinian

As we have already observed, Justinian's desire to achieve unity in law prompted his far-reaching legislative programme that was designed to transform the legal world of his realm. The imperial government had already endeavoured in the fifth century AD to create some order in the mass of laws claiming validity in the empire. However, the Theodosian Code as the first official codification of the law was, from the outset, incomplete as it ignored the important part of Roman law based on the writings of the classical jurists. Furthermore, many new imperial constitutions were issued after the enactment of that code and several constitutions that it embodied became obsolete. On the other hand, the Law of Citations (AD 426) may have provided a partial solution to the problem caused by the unwieldy mass of classical legal literature. It enhanced the chances for uniformity and predictability in judicial decision-making. Yet from the viewpoint of scientific arrangement and thoroughness, it was obviously inadequate. This situation urgently dictated the formulation of a comprehensive and authoritative statement on the entire Roman law that had legally binding force, clarified the changes induced by the post-Theodosian legislation and removed the uncertainty surrounding the content and authority of juristic works. One of Justinian's first tasks after his ascension was the production of such a statement that would replace all former statements of law in juridical literature and legislation. At the same time, he resolved to improve the quality of legal instruction by introducing an educational system based on dependable legal sources that would present the law clearly, thoroughly and systematically. A key figure in this undertaking was Justinian's legal adviser, Tribonianus, a man of exceptional talents who successively occupied the most illustrious offices in the imperial administration.[17] Significant contributions also emanated from Theophilus, professor (*antecessor*) at the law school of Constantinople, and Dorotheus and Anatolius, who taught at the law school of Beirut. As noted previously, their new insight into the operation of the classical law enabled the jurists from these two schools to enhance the standards of legal scholarship and supply the methods that made the projected legal reform possible.

The first Code

On 13 February AD 528, Justinian, by means of the *Constitutio Haec*, entrusted a ten-member commission chaired by the *quaestor sacri palatii* with the task of consolidating all the valid imperial constitutions into a single code. The commission consisted of seven senior state officials that embraced Tribonianus, who was then *magister officiorum*, two distinguished advocates and Theophilus, a professor at the law school of Constantinople. The commissioners were instructed to draft a collection of imperial enactments by drawing on the Gregorian, Hermogenian and Theodosian Codes, and on the constitutions issued between AD 438 and 529. They were empowered to delete outdated or superfluous elements from the texts, eliminate contradictions and repetitions, and effect any necessary amendments to update the material. The constitutions were to be arranged systematically according to the subject matter and listed in chronological order under appropriate titles. The new collection was published on 7 April AD 529 under the name *Codex Iustinianus* and came into force on 16 April AD 529 (by virtue of the *Constitutio Summa*). It replaced all earlier codes, and any omitted imperial enactments could not be quoted in the courts of law (with a few exceptions). As imperial constitutions were copiously issued after AD 529, this first code was soon outdated and replaced in AD 534 by a revised edition. The only surviving material from Justinian's original code (designated *Codex vetus*, the old Code) is an index discovered on a fragment of papyrus in Egypt during the early nineteenth century.[18]

The Digest or Pandects

After the completion of the first Code, Justinian directed his attention to the goal of systematizing the part of the law based on the works by the classical jurists (*ius*). During their work on the Code, the compilers encountered many questions on points of law that had invoked different opinions from the classical authorities and these could not be settled under the Law of Citations. A condensation and simplification of the entire juridical literature was urgently required and, as a preparatory step, Justinian arranged the publication of a collection of fifty constitutions (the so-called *quinquaginta decisiones*) on 17 November AD 530. In this collection, he endeavoured to provide solutions to controversies that had arisen among the classical jurists and to abrogate obsolete legal concepts and institutions.[19]

After the Fifty Decisions, Justinian issued the *Constitutio Deo Auctore* on 15 December AD 530 whereby he instructed Tribonianus (then minister of justice) to institute a commission of sixteen members. The objective was to collect, review and present in an abridged form the entire mass of Roman law contained in the writings of the classical jurists. Tribonianus selected one senior imperial official, Constantinus; two professors from the law school of Constantinople, Theophilus and Cratinus; two professors from the law school of Beirut, Dorotheus and Anatolius; and eleven distinguished advocates. The commissioners were to scrutinize and assemble extracts from the works of the old jurists who were conferred the *ius respondendi* by the emperor, and those juristic works that were recognized or relied on by later authorities.[20] Next, the selected materials had to be harmonized and systematized within the limits of a single comprehensive work that comprised fifty books subdivided into titles.[21] Like the compilers of the first Code, the commissioners were granted wide discretionary powers: they were free to determine which juristic writings to incorporate, remove superfluous or obsolete institutions, resolve contradictions and shorten or alter the texts to adapt them to contemporary requirements. The collection was to exist as a correct statement of the law at the time of its publication and the only authority in the future for jurisprudential works (and the embodied imperial laws).

It was anticipated that the work would require at least ten years to complete, yet the commission worked with amazing speed and produced the collection in only three years. The work, known as *Digesta* or *Pandectae*,[22] was confirmed on 16 December AD 533 by the *Constitutio Tanta* (in Latin) or *Dedoken* (in Greek) and came into operation on 30 December AD 533. From that date, only the juristic texts embodied in this work were legally binding; references to the original works were declared superfluous and the publication of commentaries on the Digest was prohibited.[23] As Justinian states in the introductory constitution, nearly 2,000 books containing 3,000,000 lines were digested and reduced to 150,000 lines while 'many things and of highest importance' were altered in the process.[24] The work integrated the writings of thirty-nine jurists that spanned a period from about 100 BC to AD 300.[25] However, some four-fifths of the work consisted of extracts from the writings by the five great jurists from the late Principate period (Ulpianus, Paulus, Papinianus, Gaius and Modestinus),[26] while the remaining thirty-four jurists contributed only one-fifth of the entire collection. This disparity may be explained by the fact that the works of the five classical jurists mentioned above were the most recent and widely used, and therefore the best preserved.

As already noted, the Digest consists of fifty books and each is sub-divided into titles (*tituli*),[27] fragments (called *leges*) and, where necessary, sections or paragraphs, the first of which is called the *principium* (or *proemium*). In accordance with Justinian's instructions, the titles were placed, as far as possible, in the same order as in the *Codex vetus* and the *edictum perpetuum*.[28] The beginning of each fragment enumerates the name of the jurist quoted, together with the title and section of the book from which the excerpt was taken. Four numbers are thus required to identify a citation in the Digest: book, title, fragment and section (or three, if the fragment is short, or if a reference alludes to the first paragraph).[29]

An enduring question that has puzzled Romanist scholars is how the compilers of the Digest successfully completed an enormous work within such a remarkably short time. Friedrich Bluhme, a German legal historian, presented an answer to this question in the early nineteenth century and his theory (known as 'Massen-theorie') is still accepted by most scholars today.[30] Bluhme asserts that the structure of the texts within the various titles suggests that the extracted juristic writings were divided into three sections or parts ('masses'), and that each section was the subject of the work of a separate sub-committee. Bluhme refers to the first section as the 'Sabinian mass' and this consisted mainly of extracts from the commentaries of Ulpianus, Paulus and Pomponius on the *ius civile*. Its arrangement conformed with the system devised originally by the classical jurist Masurius Sabinus in his work *Libri tres iuris civilis*. The second section, known as the 'edictal mass', concentrated on the commentaries of Ulpianus and Paulus on the *edictum perpetuum* (*ad edictum*) and other closely related texts. The third section displayed a far more casuistic nature than the other two and contained juristic opinions (*quaestiones, responsa, epistulae*) of Paulus, Ulpianus and Papinianus and other jurists. Bluhme designated this part the 'Papinian mass' because of the special weight assigned to the *responsa* of Papinianus. Bluhme also distinguished a fourth, smaller section that he referred to as the 'post-Papinian' or 'appendix mass' and this embodied materials from the works of less famous writers. After the different sub-committees completed their work on each group of juristic texts, their members convened to assemble, arrange and consolidate the selected fragments into a coherent whole.[31]

When Justinian ordered the preparation of the Digest, he was concerned with preserving the substance of the classical juristic law and producing a body of law that would fulfil the needs of his own time. However, accomplishing both these objectives was an impossible enterprise. In reviewing and arranging the juridical literature, the commissioners discovered that many problems had been highly controversial among the past legal experts and remained so for centuries. Moreover, many rules and institutions were palpably antiquated and no longer functional or were incompatible with contemporary legislation or with altered conceptions of equity (particularly in view of the fact that meanwhile Christian ethics had become prevalent). Such obsolete material had to be either eliminated or adapted to contemporary requirements. The changes (additions, suppressions, substitutions) to the classical texts initiated by the commissioners are known since the sixteenth century as interpolations (*interpolationes* or '*emblemata Triboniani*'). These alterations did not always attain their purpose and unavoidably obscured the meaning of the original works, and misrepresented the intentions of their authors.[32] As a result, much of the law contained in the Digest was neither the authentic law of the classical period nor an accurate statement of the law in Justinian's own day. Rather, it existed as a layered amalgam that ignored many of the post-classical changes.[33] The problem was further exacerbated by Justinian ordering a ban on any commentary addressing his codification.

As early as the sixteenth century, a perception of Roman law as a historical phenomenon evolved from the influence of the Humanist movement. Thereafter, scholars have endeavoured to detect the interpolations in the codification of Justinian to uncover the true character of classical law. The problem attracted a great deal of attention, particularly in the late nineteenth and early twentieth centuries when many scholars in Germany and Italy elaborated techniques (based largely on a linguistic analysis of the texts) for the identification of the interpolations. However, the search for the interpolations ultimately acquired a cult-like fervour that entailed great exaggeration over the nature and extent of the alterations introduced by Justinian's compilers. Nowadays, scholars recognize that not all contradictions and inconsistencies in the Digest are attributable to the codifying commission. Undoubtedly, the works relied upon originated from the classical era. However, when these materials reached the commission they had already been altered (either consciously or unconsciously) by earlier copyists and editors. In general, a text is likely to be deemed interpolated if it deviates from another version of the same text that has come been transmitted to us via an earlier reliable source, such as the Vatican Fragments or the Institutes of Gaius. Moreover, texts dealing with legal concepts or institutions that are confirmed as obsolete in Justinian's time are presumably interpolated because the compilers had to adapt them to contemporary requirements. In any other case, a hypothesis of interpolation must be treated with great caution.[34]

The Digest was preserved for posterity in various manuscript copies that mainly derive from the eleventh century and later – the period that featured the revival of Roman law in Western Europe. The oldest manuscript dates from the sixth century (*c.* AD 550) and was probably one of the approximately eighty copies produced in Constantinople for use by various government departments. A note on this manuscript indicates that it was in Italy in the tenth century and it is known to have been kept in Pisa since the middle of the twelfth century (hence its alternative name *Littera Pisana*). In 1406, Pisa was captured by the Florentines and the document was transferred to Florence where it has since been stored (bearing the name of *Littera Florentina* or *Codex Florentinus*). The medieval manuscripts are almost all copies of the *Codex Florentinus*.[35] Parts of the Digest have also been conveyed to us in the Greek language through the *Basilica*, a Byzantine law code issued in the tenth century by Emperor Leo the Wise.[36]

The Institutes

As already noted, an important goal of Justinian's programme was to enhance the quality of legal education that had been largely haphazard, unsystematic and based on fragmentary sources. In connection with this goal, the Digest as an authoritative and comprehensive statement of juristic law had a central role in legal practice and was also designed to serve as the basis for higher instruction in the law schools. However, Justinian realized before the work was even completed that it was too extensive and complex for students to use (especially for those in the first year of their studies). Moreover, the Institutes of Gaius that had served for centuries as an introductory textbook was now outdated in several respects. It was requisite to produce a textbook that would present beginners with a good foundation in the basic principles of contemporary law before progressing to the more detailed and weightier aspects of the legal system. In response to this need, Justinian ordered in AD 533 the preparation of a new official legal manual for use in the empire's law schools. The task was entrusted to a three-member commission consisting of Tribonian and two of the four professors engaged in the preparation of the Digest (Theophilus from Constantinople and Dorotheus from Beirut). The commissioners were instructed to produce a book that reflected the law of their own time, omitting any obsolete matter and incorporating any necessary references to the earlier law. The completed work was confirmed on 21 November AD 533 under the name *Institutiones* or *Elementa* (by virtue of the *Constitutio Imperatoriam maiestatem*) and came into force as an imperial statute, together with the Digest, on 30 December AD 533 (by way of the *Constitutio Tanta* or *Dedoken*).[37]

The compilers of Justinian's Institutes relied heavily on the Institutes of Gaius (about two-thirds of the entire work consists of materials gleaned from the latter text). They also used the *res cottidianae* ('everyday matters'), a rudimentary work attributed to Gaius; elementary works by jurists such as Ulpianus, Paulus, Marcianus and Florentinus; imperial constitutions (including many of Justinian's own enactments); and any accessible parts of the Digest.

Justinian's Institutes retained Gaius' division of the subject mater into three parts, i.e. the law relating to persons, the law relating to property and the law relating to actions. It also replicated his division of the work into four books.[38] Otherwise than in Gaius' Institutes, each book is subdivided into titles and the titles into paragraphs.[39] Unlike the Digest's presentation of material as a collection of extracts, the compilers of the Institutes adopted a narrative style. They sacrificed citations and attributions, but produced a blended, continuous essay under each title to increase its comprehension. On the other hand, the method of composition does not appear considerably different from that engaged by the compilers of the Digest. The provenance of the individual passages is discoverable, although creating the impression of a continuous text would have involved a different management of the extracts than that required in the preparation of the Digest. The presentation of the Institutes is couched in the form of a dogmatic, mechanical lecture. The work has much less colour and character than that of Gaius – features that may well be attributed to the largely derivative nature of the work.

Numerous manuscript copies of the Institutes were produced in Justinian's time, but none have survived.[40] We have inherited the work through various manuscripts that nearly all date from the tenth century or later. The *Codex Taurinensis* of the tenth century is the most famous of these manuscripts and it incorporates notes (*scholia*) that apparently originated from the time of Justinian. These manuscripts, combined with the text of Gaius' Institutes discovered in 1816, furnished the basis for most of the modern reconstructions of Justinian's Institutes.[41]

The second Code

As noted previously, the Code of AD 529 soon became antiquated, mainly due to the fresh legislation issued by Justinian subsequent to its enactment. Thus, at the beginning of AD 534 the preparation of a new edition was assigned to Tribonian, Dorotheus and three of the advocates who had participated in the compilation of the Digest. The commissioners were instructed to adapt the Code by inserting the new constitutions, including the 'Fifty Decisions' (*quinquaginta decisiones*) mentioned earlier. In this task, they eliminated obsolete or superfluous provisions, removed contradictions and repetitions, and filled in the gaps in the texts. It would appear that the commissioners worked with great speed as on 16 November AD 534 the *Constitutio Cordi* confirmed the refashioned Code under the name *Codex repetitae praelectionis* and it came into force on 29 December AD 534. It was declared the sole authority with respect to all imperial legislation that had been issued up to the date of its publication.[42]

The Code is divided into twelve books, each consisting of several titles dealing with specific legal topics. The titles present the relevant constitutions in chronological order; the headings of the constitutions list the names of the emperors who issued them and the persons to whom they were addressed; the constitutions are subdivided into paragraphs with the first labelled as the *principium*. The first book addresses jurisdictional and ecclesiastical matters; books two to eight elaborate private law; book nine pertains to criminal law; and books ten to twelve deal with administrative law issues. The oldest of the approximately 4,500 enactments contained in the Code dates from the era of Hadrian (early second century AD), while the majority (approximately 1,200 constitutions) originate from the reign of Diocletian (late third/early fourth century AD). The Code incorporates around 400 enactments produced by Justinian.[43]

Shortly after the Code came into force, several manuscript copies were produced that, despite Justinian's prohibition, embodied commentaries and abbreviations of contemporary jurists. The *Codex Veronensis* is the oldest manuscript copy that has been preserved and it probably derives from the sixth or seventh century AD. It is only fragmentary and has been supplemented by reference to other manuscripts. It appears that a complete manuscript copy was never used in the early Middle Ages. In certain manuscripts the Greek constitutions have been removed, while in others the last three of the Code's twelve books have been omitted. From the ninth century AD, the text of the Code was supplemented by reference to complete manuscripts that were apparently still extant. However, the last three books were not restored to their original position until the eleventh century when, together with Justinian's Institutes and the *Authenticum* (one version of Justinian's Novels), they were incorporated into a volume designated the *Volumen Parvum*. In the sixteenth century, the influence of the humanist movement prompted Cujas and Agustin to restore the Greek constitutions. Dionysius Gothofredus published the complete Code in his *Corpus Iuris Civilis* in 1583.[44]

The Novels

After the enactment of the *Codex repetitae praelectionis*, Justinian's legislative activity persevered unabated as political and social developments dictated changes in the law unforeseen by earlier legislation. As the new enactments were introduced after the Code, they acquired the name of *Novellae constitutiones* or *Novellae leges* (new laws) and this is the derivation of the modern name, 'Novels'. Before the end of Justinian's reign, over one hundred and fifty such enactments were issued with the great majority dating from the period prior to Tribonian's death in AD 546. Most of these enactments addressed matters of administrative and ecclesiastical law and certain areas of private law (particularly family law and the law of intestate succession).[45] In the *Constitutio Cordi* of 16 November AD 534, Justinian expressed his intention to compile an official collection of these later laws when a sufficient array had been issued – but he never executed this intention. Information on this material is gleaned from a few private and unofficial collections created during and after Justinian's reign, and assembled by later editors.

The oldest collection of Novels that we know of is the *Epitome Iuliani*, an abridged version of a collection of one hundred and twenty-four constitutions dating from the period AD 535–55. Julianus, a professor at the law school of Constantinople, compiled this collection during the reign of Justinian. It was probably intended for use in the recently recaptured Italy, as indicated by the fact that the Greek constitutions it contains were translated into Latin.[46]

Another work also written in Latin is the *Authenticum* (or *liber Authenticorum*), an anonymous collection of one hundred and thirty-four constitutions originating from the period AD 535–36. The exact date of its publication has not been ascertained – it may have been composed in the sixth century AD, but the oldest manuscript copies date from the eleventh century. Irnerius, a leading representative of the School of the Glossators (eleventh–thirteenth century), regarded it as an authentic, official collection of Novels ordered by Justinian for use in Italy (hence, its designation as *Authenticum*). The prevalent view today is that Irnerius was mistaken and that it was probably designed as a teaching aid for use in the law schools of the empire. The collection embodies the Latin Novels in their original text and the Greek ones in a faulty Latin translation.[47]

The most extensive collection of Novels is the so-called *Collectio Graeca*, consisting of one hundred and sixty-eight constitutions issued in Greek by Justinian and his successors, Justin II (AD 565–78) and Tiberius II (AD 578–82).[48] It was published after AD 575, probably during the reign of Tiberius II, and is accessible to us through two manuscripts originating from the thirteen and fourteen centuries.[49] Although the *Collectio Graeca* was predominantly used in the Byzantine East,[50] it was apparently unknown in the West until the fifteenth century. It was introduced into Western Europe by Byzantine scholars who fled to Italy shortly before and after the fall of Constantinople to the Ottoman Turks (1453) and was brought to light by the humanist scholars of the fifteenth and sixteenth centuries.[51]

The Corpus Iuris Civilis

Justinian's legislative work is mainly comprised of the Code (*Codex repetitae praelectionis*), the Digest, the Institutes and the Novels. All four compilations together constitute the material known as *Corpus Iuris Civilis*. The latter term did not originate in Justinian's time;[52] it was invented by Dionysius Godofredus (1549–1622), who produced, in 1583, the first scholarly edition of Justinian's codification that remained the standard edition until the nineteenth century.[53]

Conclusion

The outstanding feature of Justinian's reign was its focus on the idea of unity – unity in territory, religion and law. In this respect, the legal codes compiled under his authority should be viewed as interconnected parts of an organic whole. Recognizing the role of law as a tool of integration, Justinian aspired to produce a comprehensive, systematic and authoritative statement of the existing law based on the legal inheritance of the classical period. It was designed to replace all former statements of law in both legislation and jurisprudence. This goal is particularly evident in the Digest, the largest and definitely the most important part of his codification. The accomplished work fell short of this objective, and this is unsurprising owing to the magnitude of the task and the swift completion of the work. Perhaps a more important rationale for this shortcoming was the general intellectual climate of the age – an intellectual climate that was unfavourable to the kind of creative legal thinking that constitutes the hallmark of the classical age.

From the viewpoint of legal history, Justinian marks the end of the ancient world. Compared to the achievements of the classical period, his legislation may perhaps be regarded as the product of an era of decay. Yet Justinian did succeed in assembling and preserving most of the Roman legal heritage for posterity – an immense body of legal materials spanning hundreds of years of legal development. But his work was not a mere compendium of the Roman legal experience, nor a mere revision of existing law. The Code and the Novels contained a great deal of reformatory legislation that impressed almost every branch of the law. The influence of the Justinianic codification has been tremendous. In the Byzantine East, it prevailed as a basic document for the further evolution of law until the fall of the empire in the fifteenth century. In Western Europe, it remained forgotten for a long period but was rediscovered in the eleventh century. Initially treated as the object of academic study, it later experienced a far-reaching reception – a reintegration as valid law that led to its becoming the common foundation upon which the civil law systems of Continental Europe were built. As a historical source, Justinian's *Corpus* comprehensively depicts the way that Roman law and legal thinking evolved from the first century BC until the sixth century AD. It also reveals a great deal about the state of the law and society at the dawn of the Middle Ages.

EPILOGUE

The legislation of Justinian marks the end of the history of Roman law in antiquity; at the same time, it heralds the beginning of a phase occasionally labelled the 'second life' of Roman law, i.e. its history from the early Middle Ages to modern times. The destiny of Roman law after Justinian's era is beyond the scope of the present work. However, the post-Justinianic development is tremendously significant to the modern jurist, as far as Roman law forms an important part of the intellectual background of contemporary legal culture. A brief survey of the history of Roman law in both the East and West after Justinian's era will be useful in highlighting some of the factors that account for the preservation and later reception of Roman law in Continental Europe.

In the Eastern Empire of Byzantium, the legislation of Justinian remained in force and applied until the fall of Constantinople in 1453. As the most important parts of the codification were written in Latin, it was from the outset difficult to use in a Hellenized environment whose daily life was conducted in Greek. Thus, in the period after Justinian's death various works in the form of translations, summaries, paraphrases and commentaries on the existing law were produced in abundance. As in the post-classical era, the social conditions and intellectual climate of the Byzantine world required the simplification and popularization of the intricate legal heritage. This inspired the development of a whole new genre of legal literature that included several important legislative works and was designed to adapt the Roman law of Justinian to the prevailing conditions. The most important of these works encompassed: the *Ecloga Legum*, a collection of extracts from Justinian's law codes produced by Emperor Leo III the Isaurian and published in AD 740; the *Eisagoge* or *Epanagoge*, a formulation of law from a historical and practical perspective devised as an introduction to a new law code under Emperor Basil I (AD 867–86); the *Basilica* (*basilica nomima*), an extensive compilation of legal materials from Greek translations of Justinian's *Corpus* in sixty books that was enacted at the beginning of the tenth century by Emperor Leo VI the Wise;[1] the *Epitome Legum* composed in 913, a legal abridgment based on the legislation of Justinian and various post-Justinianic works; the *Synopsis Basilicorum Maior*, a collection of excerpts from the above-mentioned *Basilica* that was published in the late tenth century; and the *Hexabiblos*, a comprehensive legal manual in six books compiled around 1345 by

Constantine Harmenopoulos (a judge in Thessalonica). Some of these works, such as the *Hexabiblos*, were habitually used throughout the Ottoman period and played an important part in the preservation of the Roman legal tradition in countries formerly within the orbit of the Byzantine civilization.[2]

As noted previously, the collapse of the Roman state in the West entailed the replacement of the once universal system of Roman law with a plurality of legal systems: the Germanic conquerors lived according to their own customs, while the Roman portion of the population remained governed by Roman law. When Justinian reincorporated Italy into the empire (AD 553), his legislation was introduced to this realm.[3] However, its validity was only sustained for a brief period as most of the Byzantine territories in Italy fell to the Lombards in AD 568. After that time, Justinian's legislation only applied in those parts of Italy that remained under Byzantine control. The rest of Italy displayed a similar pattern to Gaul and Spain as Roman law prevailed through the application of the personality of the laws principle. It also existed through the medium of the Church, whose laws were imbued with the principles and detailed rules of Roman law. In the course of time, as the fusion of the Roman and Germanic elements of the population progressed, the division of people according to their national origin tended to break down. The system of personal laws was gradually superseded by the conception of law as entwined with a particular territory: a common body of customary norms now governed all persons living within a certain territory. As a result, Roman law as a distinct system applicable within a certain section of the population fell into abeyance. The diversity of laws no longer persisted as an intermixture of personal laws, but as a variety of local customs. However, the customary law that applied in all the regions was a combination of elements from Roman law and Germanic customary law. Moreover, Roman law sustained its potent influence on the canon law of the Church. It also moulded the legislation of the Germanic rulers, who maintained the Roman system of provincial administration in view of its effectiveness. However, in comparison with ancient Roman law, the overall picture of early medieval law exhibits a progressive deterioration that is clearly reflected in the declining standards of legal education. In this respect, the carry-over of the Roman legal tradition from late antiquity to the early Middle Ages may be described at best as only a sign of survival and not a revival.

From the eleventh century, transformed political and economic conditions in the West (particularly in Italy), created a more favourable environment for cultural development. The new scholarly enthusiasm for the heritage of classical antiquity and the economic expansion generated by the growth of trade and the rise of towns entailed a renewed interest in Roman law. This interest was precipitated by the discovery at Pisa in 1077 of a manuscript copy of the Digest that dated from the time of Justinian. But the revival of Roman law was also the product of the existing political conditions: the authoritarian tenor of Justinian's *Corpus* was perceived as congenial for buttressing the claims to centralized power by emerging dynastic monarchies.

The centre of legal revival was the University of Bologna, the oldest in Western Europe. This university became the seat of the School of the Glossators, under the leadership of famous jurists such as Irnerius, Rogerius, Azo, Accursius and Odofredus. The jurists of Bologna set themselves the task of presenting a complete statement of Roman law through a painstaking analysis of Justinian's *Corpus*. The jurists' work of interpretation was closely aligned with their methods of teaching and it was executed by means of notes (*glossae*) that elucidated difficult terms or phrases in a text, and provided the necessary cross-references and reconciliations that rendered the text usable. The missing element in the Glossators' approach was the historical dimension; they attached little import to the facts that Justinian's codification was compiled more than five hundred years before their own time and was mainly composed of extracts deriving from an even earlier date. Instead, they perceived it as an authoritative statement of the law that was complete in itself, as demonstrated by their rational methods of interpretation. They devoted little attention to the fact that the law actually in force was very different from the system embodied in it. Nevertheless, the Glossators succeeded in reviving a genuine familiarity with Justinian's entire work; their new insight into the ancient texts galvanized the development of a true science of law that had a lasting influence on the legal thinking and practice of succeeding centuries.

By the end of the thirteen century, jurists had shifted attention from the purely dialectical analysis of Justinian's texts to the problems invoked by the application of the customary and statute law. They also explored the conflicts of law that emerged in the course of inter-city commerce. This development is associated with the emergence of a new breed of jurists in Italy, the so-called Commentators. Their primary interest was adapting the Roman law of Justinian to the new social and economic conditions of their own era. Bartolus de Saxoferrato and his pupil Baldus de Ubaldis were among the chief representatives of the School of the Commentators. The Commentators successfully rendered the Roman law of Justinian applicable to the environment of the city-states and small principalities in prosperous Italy. They also conferred a scientific basis to contemporary law, especially to those areas of the law that required the development of new principles for legal practice.

Over time, Roman law as expounded by the Glossators and the Commentators entered the legal life of Continental Europe through the activities of university-trained lawyers and jurists. It formed the basis of a common body of law, legal language and legal science – a development known as the 'Reception' of Roman law. This common law (*ius commune*) served as an important universalizing factor in Europe at a time when there were no centralized states or unified legal systems, but a multitude of overlapping and often competing jurisdictions of local, feudal, ecclesiastical, mercantile and royal authorities. It should be noted, however, that the process of reception was complex and characterized by a lack of uniformity. The reception of Roman law in different parts of Europe was affected by local conditions, and the actual degree of Roman law infiltration varied considerably from region to region. In parts of Southern Europe, such as Italy and Southern France, where Roman law was already part of the applicable customary law, the process of reception may be described as a resurgence, refinement and enlargement of Roman law. On the other hand, the process of reception in Germany and other Northern European regions was prolonged and, in its closing stages, much more sweeping. The common law of Europe that gradually emerged towards the close of the Middle Ages derived from a fusion between the Roman law of Justinian, as elaborated by medieval jurists, the (largely Romanized) canon law of the Church and Germanic law. The dominant element in this mixture was Roman law, although Roman law itself was considerably transformed under the influence of local custom, statutory and canon law.

In medieval and even later times, there was no clear connection between the state and the legal order. The federal constellations, a characteristic feature of feudalism, were not based on the idea of national interests; their role was only instrumental. In contrast, the interests of commerce and agriculture displayed more stability as they were relatively permanent structural elements of life. In relation to these elements, national frontiers were immediately relevant. In the sixteenth and subsequent centuries, the feudal nobility was defeated by a central power that also represented the interests of the expanding urban class and the lower gentry. As a result, the role of legislation gained prominence as a means of centripetal policy. Further, the idea of a national social consensus, or that the members of a nation had common interests, emerged as a basic assumption. During that period, the nascent idea of the nation-state and the increasing consolidation of centralized political administrations diversely affected the relationship between the received Roman law, Germanic customary law and canon law.

The rise of nationalism entailed an enhanced interest in the development of national law and this precipitated the move towards the codification of law. The demand to reduce the law to a code emanated from two interrelated factors: the necessities of establishing legal unity within the boundaries of a nation-state and developing a rational, systematized and comprehensive legal system adapted to the conditions of the times. The then dominant School of Natural Law with its ratio-nalist approach to institutional reform and emphasis on system-building provided the ideological basis of the codification movement, which engendered the great European codifications of the eighteenth and nineteenth centuries. When new civil codes were introduced in the various European states Roman law ceased to operate as a direct source of law. However, as the drafters of the codes drew heavily on the Romanized *ius commune*, Roman legal concepts and institutions were incorporated in different ways and to varying degrees into the legal systems of Continental Europe. Moreover, through the process of legal borrowing or transplanting, these legal elements permeated the legal systems of many countries around the world.

NOTES

1 THE MONARCHY AND EARLY REPUBLIC: THE HISTORICAL, SOCIAL AND CONSTITUTIONAL BACKGROUND

1 This is evidenced by the formation of religious associations or leagues between the various Latin communities, which precipitated their later political unification.

2 A person remained under the control of his *pater familias* until the latter died or his *patria potestas* was extinguished. Release from the *patria potestas* was usually effected through the formal method of *emancipatio*: a child was freed from paternal control and became master of his own affairs (*sui iuris*) following a process involving his fictitious sale by his *pater familias*. The *patria potestas* could also be terminated in several other ways, such as when the *pater familias* was deprived of his freedom or citizenship (*capitis deminutio*); when a daughter passed into the control of her husband following a formal marriage *cum manu*; and when a child was formally adopted by another or was assigned certain religious positions.

3 During the early Empire, the role of the *gens* as a social institution diminished in importance. This mainly derived from the social conditions of the times provoking a gradual weakening of the sense of unity that once prevailed among clan members.

4 The clients may originally have been foreigners who settled in the area of Rome after their tribes were subjugated by the Romans. As they did not enjoy any rights under Roman law, they placed themselves under the patronage of powerful Roman families, by offering their services and receiving protection in return. But the clientship was not an original Roman institution, as it was seemingly widespread throughout the Greek world and existed also among the Sabines, Etruscans and other Italian peoples. However, its role in Rome's social and political development was much more decisive than anywhere else in antiquity.

5 During the later republican period, large numbers of poor and underprivileged citizens (mostly members of the plebeian class), and even entire communities, sought to place themselves as clients under the protection of powerful Roman families or individuals in high office. In this form, clientship had a profound effect on Rome's socio-political life, especially during the closing years of the Republic.

6 Several theories have been advanced to explicate the origins of this division, but there is little definite information. According to a theory accepted by many modern scholars, the patricians descended from the early clan patriarchs (*patres*) who formed the senate (*senatus*), the powerful council of elders that nominated and presented advice to the kings. The families that provided the early *patres* assumed a noble status as a class distinct from the rest of the population. This view seems to be supported by the fact that the term '*patres*', which was originally confined only to senators, was later used as synonymous with the term '*patricii*' (members of the patrician class). But the distinction between patricians and plebeians may also be explained on an economic basis. With the progressive differentiation of wealth, that emerged well before the city of Rome was

196

established, those few families that controlled large tracts of land assumed a predominant position in society and formed the inner circle of Roman nobility from which the *patres* were chosen. On the origins of the Roman social classes see F. Ferenczy, *From the Patrician State to the Patricio-Plebeian State*, Amsterdam 1976, 15–16; J. C. Richard, *Les origines de la plèbe romaine. Essai sur la formation du dualisme patricio-plébéien*, Rome 1978; T. J. Cornell, *The Beginnings of Rome*, London 1995, 242 ff; R. E. Mitchell, *Patricians and Plebeians: The Origins of the Roman State*, Ithaca and London 1990.

7 It is believed that they acquired the right to vote in the assembly (*ius suffragii*) in the later years of the regal era (late sixth century BC), when they were included in the Roman *classes* following the constitutional reforms attributed to King Servius Tullius. The important right of appealing from the magistrates to the assembly against certain severe forms of punishment (*ius provocationis*) was probably first granted to them shortly after the establishment of the Republic in the late sixth century BC.

8 As stated in the Law of the Twelve Tables (*c.* 450 BC). It has been argued, however, that the rule forbidding intermarriages between patricians and plebeians was first introduced with the Law of the Twelve Tables by the patricians in order to preclude wealthy plebeians from entering the senate. This prohibition was finally removed by the *lex Canuleia* in 445 BC. See A. Watson, *Rome of the XII Tables*, Princeton 1975, 20 ff.

9 According to writers of the Augustan era (first century BC – first century AD), no real distinction existed between plebeians and clients during this period; the term *plebs* simply denoted Rome's subordinate class in general, while the term *clientes* referred to members of the same class in relation to the various noble houses under whose protection they had placed themselves. This description may be accurate in view of the social conditions in the later Republic, when a great portion of the client population was incorporated into the *plebs*, but circumstances were different in earlier ages. The nature of the patron–client relationship, as traditionally understood, would never have permitted the clients to rise, either collectively or individually, against their patrons in the way the plebeians did; nor would it be possible for a patrician to treat another patrician's client as ruthlessly and tyrannically as the plebeians were so often treated during the archaic era, for a client enjoyed the protection of the *gens* to which his patron belonged.

10 One theory declares that initially only moveables, such as domestic animals, farm implements and such like, could be privately owned, whereas immovables were subject to collective ownership by the members of the Roman *gentes*. See G. Diòsdi, *Ownerhip in Ancient and Preclassical Roman Law*, Budapest 1970, 19 ff.

11 An ingot of bronze was called *stipes* or *stips* (hence the word *stipendium*: pay); the term *libripens* was used to describe the person who weighed the bronze on a pair of scales (*libra*). This ancient practice provided the form in which certain legal transactions of Roman law were expressed (for example, the transference of certain kinds of property by *mancipatio*).

12 The first four of these kings (Romulus, Numa Pompilius, Tullius Hostilius and Ancus Marcius) are believed to have Latin or Sabine origins, while the last three (Tarquinius Priscus, Servius Tullius and Tarquinius Superbus) were Etruscans. There is meager information on the character and development of the Roman state during the Monarchy. It seems probable that the political unification under one king of the various settlements in the area of Rome was completed in the seventh century BC.

13 The Roman kings were often attributed magic powers but did not profess to have divine descent, nor claim any special connection with the gods other than through the taking of the auspices.

14 The king rarely interfered in private disputes and any necessary intervention featured only his mere pronouncement of the general norm that had to be observed. He then relegated the determination of the case to the regular judges or specially appointed arbiters.

15 Roman tradition declares that Rome's first king, Romulus, established a council of clan elders that comprised one hundred members. In later years, the number of senators was

increased to two hundred and, at the end of the Monarchy, it had reached three hundred members.

16 According to Roman tradition, the curiate assembly was instituted by King Romulus shortly after the founding of the city.

17 For military and political purposes, the entire citizen body (*populus Romanus Quirites* or *populus Romanus Quiritium*) was divided into three tribes (*tribus*): the *Ramnes*, *Tities* and *Luceres*. Each tribe was headed by a tribal commander (*tribunus*). The tribes were subdivided further into smaller groups known as *curiae* (wards or brotherhoods of men), each consisting of several clans (*gentes*). There were thirty *curiae* in all, ten in each tribe. Membership in these groups was probably hereditary. Each *curia* was distinguished by a different name and had its own place of assembly (also called *curia*) where its members held their religious ceremonies (*sacra*), settled disputes over the legitimacy of a person's membership in their group and witnessed the formalities relating to adoptions and testaments. The *curiae* originated from the prehistoric organization of the Italian tribes into groups of clans, probably bound together by blood ties and united for common defence. Besides kinship, territorial proximity between different clans must also have played a part in the formation of these groups.

18 Rome's new army was based on a heavily armed and well-disciplined infantry (*hoplites*), whose members fought in a regular line of battle according to the principles of the Greek *phalanx*.

19 Following Rome's military reorganization in the late sixth century BC, the state increasingly relied upon the plebeian class for its military strength. During the military campaigns of the early republican period, many plebeians gained a share of the *ager publicus* – the new lands acquired by Rome in the course of the wars. The number of wealthy plebeians continued to increase with the expansion of Roman territory and this entailed the strengthening of the position of the plebeian class in Roman political life.

20 Moreover, the *leges Liciniae Sextiae* aspired to improve the position of the poor and address the problem of debt that generated the condition of servitude experienced by large numbers of plebeians.

21 As F. Adcock remarks, 'the social equalization of patrician and plebeian notables was translated into a sharing of political power . . . A nobility, conferred on members of leading families by holding office, made aristocracy secure by broadening its basis.' *Roman Political Ideas and Practice*, University of Michigan Press 1975, 28. And see T. J. Cornell, *The Beginnings of Rome*, London 1995, 340–44; G. Alföldy, *The Social History of Rome*, London 1985, 31 ff.

22 The unification of Italy did not entail the formation of a single state. Rather, Italy was a conglomeration of many communities and individual city-states under Roman control. Communities in alliance with Rome (*civitates foederatae, socii Italici*) retained their autonomy. Despite the fact that they were regarded by the Romans as foreigners (*peregrini*), the inhabitants of these communities enjoyed certain rights under Roman law, such as *commercium* (the right to trade with Romans on equal terms and to use the forms of contract available to Roman citizens) and *conubium* (the right to enter into a valid Roman marriage). Every allied community was bound to Rome by a special treaty (*foedus*) that stipulated the rules governing its relations with Rome. Although these treaties differed from one case to another, they all obliged the allied communities to aid Rome militarily and to surrender control over foreign relations. Many formerly independent communities that, as a result of Roman territorial expansion, had been incorporated into the Roman state were allowed to retain some local autonomy and to govern themselves in accordance with their former constitutions. These communities were referred to as *municipia* and their inhabitants as *municipes*. The category of *municipia sine suffragio* (municipalities whose members did not have the right of suffrage) embraced those communities of Roman citizens whose inhabitants had all the obligations but only the private rights of the Roman citizenship. On the other hand, citizens belonging to

municipia cum suffragio enjoyed all the private and public rights of the Roman citizenship, including the right to vote in the Roman assemblies. The status of the *municipia sine suffragio* was a halfway stage in the process towards the complete amalgamation of formerly independent communities with Rome. This process was completed in the early first century BC, when all the communities in Italy became *municipia cum suffragio* and their inhabitants were granted full Roman citizenship. The municipal system was a distinctly Roman approach to solving the problem of local government in an enlarged city-state. It provided a means of incorporating previously independent communities into the Roman state without the dissolution of their community life or an abrupt break with their previous customs, traditions and culture. The term *coloniae* denoted the new settlements founded by Rome in the conquered lands of Italy and elsewhere. There were two types of colonies: Latin colonies (*coloniae Latinae*) established by Latin citizens (but in some cases Romans and citizens of allied states were also enrolled); and Roman colonies (*coloniae civium Romanorum*). The inhabitants of the former enjoyed *commercium* with Rome, but not *conubium* (unless this right was explicitly granted to them). Latin colonists (*Latini coloniarii*) could acquire full Roman citizenship if they became magistrates in their own towns (*per magistratum*), or if the citizenship was accorded to them by law. Each Latin colony had full rights of local self-government, with its own laws, magistrates and a constitution closely modelled on that of Rome. The Roman colonies were composed of Roman citizens as well as elements of the local population. Their laws were those of Rome and in their external relations they had to adopt the policies of their mother city. In the course of time, especially after the enactment of the *lex Iulia* (90 BC) and the *lex Plautia Papiria* (89 BC), the distinction between the Roman and Latin colonies vanished and the political differences between the Romans and the inhabitants of the allied communities disappeared. As a result, the various ethnic elements in Italy became a single nation and a uniform culture developed on the basis of common citizenship. On the organization of Italy and the expansion of the Roman citizenship see A. N. Sherwin-White, *Roman Citizenship*, 2nd edn, Oxford 1973; E. T. Salmon, *Roman Colonisation*, London 1969; P. A. Brunt, *Italian Manpower*, Oxford 1987; M. Humbert, *Municipium et civitas sine suffragio*, Paris 1978; C. Nicolet, *The World of the Citizen in Republican Rome*, London 1980.

23 This theory was proposed by the famous German historian Theodor Mommsen. See Mommsen, *Römisches Staatsrecht* I, Leipzig 1887, repr. Graz 1971. Consider also H. F. Jolowicz and B. Nicholas, *Historical Introduction to the Study of Roman Law*, 3rd edn, Cambridge 1972, 8.

24 W. Kunkel, *An Introduction to Roman Legal and Constitutional History*, 3rd edn, Oxford 1973, 14–15; F. Wieacker, *Römische Rechtsgeschichte* I, Munich 1988, 223–24. This approach draws support from the fact that the sources, when referring to the early years of the Republic, allude to different colleges of magistrates (*praetores, iudices, consules, decemviri legibus scribundis, tribuni militium consulari potestate*) that were entrusted with diverse political, judicial and military tasks.

25 During the Republic, when both consuls died or abdicated, the senate appointed an *interrex* for a five-day term to supervise the election of new consuls.

26 The lowest office in the order was the quaestorship; above this position in the scale was the aedileship, then the praetorship and then, highest of all, the consulship. The censorship and the dictatorship were not included in the *cursus honorum*. During the early Republic the order in which the offices were held does not appear to have received legislative recognition. The *lex Villia Annalis* probably embodied provisions setting out rules concerning the regular succession of the offices (*certus ordo magistratuum*).

27 The *imperium* was conferred on a magistrate by a special law of the curiate assembly (*lex curiata de imperio*).

28 *Ius dicere*: declaring the law. The jurisdiction of the higher magistrates embraced the resolution of disputes between citizens (*iurisdictio inter cives*) and the confirmation of

personal legal acts, such as adoptions, emancipations and such like (*iurisdictio voluntaria*). The lower magistrates (*magistratus minores*) had no *imperium* and limited *iurisdictio*.

29 However, during the early Republic this principle meant little, as a person could be re-elected to the same office for several years in succession. This practice was often adopted by the tribunes and did not cease until 342 BC when it was enacted that no one could lawfully be re-elected to the same office unless ten years had passed from the time he was first elected to office, and no one could occupy two magistracies in the same year. Furthermore, a law enacted probably in the first half of the second century BC stipulated that no one could hold the consulship twice. Notwithstanding these restrictions, the assembly and the senate reserved the right, when circumstances so demanded, to suspend the relevant rules or introduce exceptions to the law in favour of certain individuals.

30 With the exception of the dictatorship and, until 242 BC (when the office of the *praetor peregrinus* was created), the praetorship.

31 With the exception of the tribunes.

32 Moreover, a dictator appointed for a specific purpose could use his extensive powers in pursuance of that purpose only and might be lawfully resisted if he attempted to interfere in unrelated matters. And if he was entrusted with the conduct of ordinary constitutional proceedings, such as the annual elections of magistrates, he was obliged to act in accordance with the established constitutional norms.

33 The perpetual dictatorships of Sulla and Caesar in the last century of the Republic were established by special statutes and should be considered as departures from the traditional constitutional norms at a time when, as a result of factional strife and civil wars, the republican system of government verged on collapse. In this era the dictatorship, as originally understood, no longer existed.

34 Some scholars assert that, until the creation of the praetorship, the task of declaring the law and supervising civil litigation fell to the pontiffs. See A. Watson, *The Law of the Ancient Romans*, Dallas 1970, 24–25. However, the most widely accepted view is that this task was entrusted to the consuls until the office of praetor was established, See H. F. Jolowicz and B. Nicholas, *Historical Introduction to the Study of Roman Law*, 3rd edn, Cambridge 1972, 48. And see F. Wieacker, *Römische Rechtsgeschichte*, Munich 1988, 429–34.

35 Outside the city these were represented by lower jurisdictional magistrates referred to as *praefecti iuri dicundo*.

36 Eight more praetors were added by Caesar in the second half of the first century BC.

37 The part of a praetor's edict that he adopted from the edict of his predecessor in office was termed *edictum tralaticium*.

38 Like the consuls and the praetors, the censors were elected by the assembly of the centuries (*comitia centuriata*), which was summoned for that purpose by the consuls.

39 In performing this task they were bound by the *lex Ovinia* (*c.* 318–312 BC), which ordained that only the worthiest men of every class should be appointed as senators.

40 These derived mainly from taxes paid by Roman citizens and provincials, and the exploitation of lands, mines and other state assets. The public revenues were not collected by the state directly, but were let or leased to contractors – tax-farmers (*publicani*) and collectors of other public revenues – who undertook, at their own risk and expense, to levy the dues and pay a fixed sum annually to the Roman public treasury. The job of the censors was to establish the framework for these contracts, or leases, by stipulating the conditions under which these were granted, and to let them out to the highest bidder.

41 A person whose conduct was stigmatized by a censor was branded with ignomony or infamy (*ignominia, infamia*) and was thus deprived of certain political rights and privileges or fell from a position of honour.

42 Although the aediles belonged to the *magistratus minores*, they were entitled to use a curule chair (*sella curulis*), which had been a prerogative of the higher magistrates.

43 In the last century of the Republic, Sulla raised their number to twenty, and Julius Caesar to forty.

44 The so-called *quaestores provinciales* served in the Roman provinces overseas where they acted as assistants to the governors.

45 The term *ius agendi cum populo* denoted the right of a magistrate to summon an assembly of the people and submit proposals to it.

46 Moreover, the curiate assembly bestowed *imperium* on the dictator after his nomination by the consuls. The power of *imperium* was conferred on a magistrate by a special law of the curiate assembly, referred to as *lex curiata de imperio*.

47 When the curiate assembly was summoned to perform these functions, it was referred to as *comitia calata*. The people's role in these cases was confined to witnessing a formal procedure as mere observers.

48 These were referred to as *lictores curiati*.

49 As noted before, the centuriate assembly was originally the assembly of the Roman people in military array, but it subsequently evolved as a political assembly.

50 As the total number of centuries was a hundred and ninety-three, the votes of at least ninety-seven centuries were required to pass a proposal ($193 \div 2 + 1$ centuries).

51 Thus, the fact that Roman women were not directly engaged in the defence of the city explains, to some extent, why they did not have any political rights.

52 Laws (*leges*) were referred to as *leges consulares* or *leges praetoriae*, depending on the type of magistrate that had proposed them.

53 Before a proposal was submitted to the people, it was usually discussed in the senate, whose approval was often vital, and in informal gatherings of citizens (*contiones*). A *contio* could be summoned by a magistrate for the purpose of calling the citizens' attention to various matters of public interest. Only the presiding magistrate and those who had obtained his permission to speak could address the meeting.

54 According to the Law of the Twelve Tables, citizens charged with capital offences could only be tried before the assembly of the centuries.

55 Those who owned land were enrolled in the rural tribes or districts where their property was situated, while landless citizens, freedmen (*libertini*) and newly admitted citizens were included in the four urban tribes. As membership in a rural tribe implied wealth and the ownership of landed property, most of the citizens enrolled in these tribes enjoyed a relatively high social status. The social significance of the rural tribe is manifested by the fact that a citizen's transference from a rural to an urban tribe (*tribu moveri*) was regarded as a form of social downgrading. In the later Republic, membership in a tribe became largely hereditary and was no longer determined on the basis of a person's place of residence.

56 The citizens were assigned to the different tribes by the censors as they administered the census.

57 But, as noted, sentences involving death and other severe penalties, such as the loss of a citizen's freedom or political rights, could only be appealed against before the assembly of the centuries.

58 The creation of this assembly was an early success of the plebeians in the struggle of the orders.

59 By a series of legislative enactments culminating in the *lex Hortensia de plebiscitis* of 287 BC.

60 The jurisdiction of the plebeian assembly also captured appeals against decisions of the tribunes imposing fines and other minor penalties. It remains unclear, however, whether the relevant procedure was deemed to be connected with the original *provocatio ad populum*.

61 Hence its description as *concilium plebis tributum*.

62 Like the regular *comitia*, the *concilium plebis* was controlled by its wealthiest members. These were the representatives of the new patricio-plebeian nobility that emerged in the closing years of the conflict of the orders.

2 THE MONARCHY AND EARLY REPUBLIC: THE SOURCES OF LAW

1 There were two general classes of priests in Rome: those who exercised general supervision over all religious matters without attachment to one particular god; and those who were associated with the worshipping of particular gods. The first category embraced the *pontifices*, the *augures*, the *quindecemviri sacrorum* and the *epulones*.

2 Livy 1. 20; Dionysius 2. 73.

3 The law governing the activities of the pontiffs, created and regulated by the pontiffs themselves, was termed *ius pontificium*.

4 *Ius* was also distinguished from morals (*mos, mores*), the non-formally enforceable rules of conduct addressed to an individual's conscience.

5 For example, failure to fulfil a solemnly assumed (by *sponsio*) contractual obligation.

6 Thus, *ius* was defined by jurists of the imperial period as 'the art of good and equitable' (Celsus D. 1. 1. 1), and as that which is always 'just and fair' (Paulus D. 1. 1. 11). According to Ulpianus, *ius* requires 'living honestly, harming no one and giving each one his due' (D. 1. 1. 10. 1; see also *Inst.* 1. 1. 3). The connection between law and justice is also reflected in Ulpianus' definition of jurisprudence as 'the knowledge of things divine and human, and of what is just and unjust' (D. 1. 1. 10. 2; see also *Inst.* 1. 1. 1).

7 This meaning of *ius* is better conveyed in English by the word 'right' as a noun.

8 G. 1. 3. In the imperial period the term *leges* referred to laws originating from several sources, such as decrees of the senate and imperial constitutions. Sometimes the term *leges* was used to signify the entire body of positive law, irrespective of its sources.

9 In the later imperial era the term *ius* denoted the entire body of law based on the works of the leading jurists of the classical period. *Lex*, on the other hand, signified the law contained in the enactments of the emperors, which were the principal source of law in this period. On the concept of *ius* see A. A. Schiller, *Roman Law: Mechanisms of Development*, New York 1978, 224 ff; M. Kaser, *Römische Rechtsgeschichte*, Göttingen 1976, 59 ff; F. Wieacker, *Römische Rechtsgeschichte*, Munich 1988, 267 ff; A. Guarino, *Storia del diritto romano*, Naples 1996, 124 ff, 420 ff.

10 According to Gaius, 'the rules enacted by a given state for its own members are peculiar to itself and are called civil law' (G. 1. 1).

11 Hence, the description of the Roman *ius civile* as '*ius proprium Romanorum*'.

12 The primary rights of the citizens entailed a number of derivative rights or privileges. For example, the *ius intercessionis*, i.e. the right of the higher magistrates to veto official acts of other magistrates, was a secondary or derivative right with respect to the *ius honorum*. The words *facultas* and *potestas* were used to denote a specific right or power derived from a primary right.

13 For example, what was referred to as Latin law (*ius Latinum* or *ius Latii*) applied to certain groups who enjoyed some rights of the Roman citizenship. These groups included the inhabitants of communities in Latium, colonies founded by Romans and members of other Latin states (*coloniae Latinae*), as well as certain categories of freedmen.

14 But the term *peregrini* did not apply to all foreigners indiscriminately, but only to those who had some sort of relationship with Rome (for example, citizens of states in alliance with Rome). Those with no connection to Rome were usually referred to as *barbari* (or *hostes*, if they were at war with Rome).

15 D. 1. 2. 2. 2; 1. 2. 2. 36; and see Dionysius 3. 36.

16 See A. Watson, *Roman Law and Comparative Law*, Athens, Georgia 1991, 10; O. Tellegen-Couperus, *A Short History of Roman Law*, London 1990, repr. 1993, 19.

17 Livy 3. 31. 8. and 32. 6. 7.

18 Livy 3. 32–33; Dionysius 10. 55–57.

19 Dionysius 10. 58. 4.

20 See A. Watson, *Roman Law and Comparative Law*, Athens, Georgia 1991, 12.

21 The Law of the Twelve Tables does have some elements in common with Athenian law, but these are not of the kind that could suggest a direct influence. The relevant provisions

that, according to Cicero, were extracted from the laws of Solon, pertain mainly to the settling of disputes between neighbours, the right of forming associations (*collegia*) and restrictions on displays at funerals. Cicero, *De Leg.* 2. 23. 59; 2. 25. 64. For more detail see F. Wieacker, *Römische Rechtsgeschichte* I, Munich 1988, 300 ff. R. Westbrook, drawing attention to certain similarities between the Law of the Twelve Tables and the codes of eastern peoples, such as the Babylonian Code of Hammurabi (*c.* 1700 BC), proposes that the idea of recording the law was introduced to Italy by the Phoenicians from the East. 'The Nature and Origins of the Twelve Tables', *Zeitschrift der Savigny Stiftung für Rechtsgeschichte* 105, 1988, 74–121.

22 Pomponius reports that the Decemvirs, when performing the work of codification, consulted the advice of the Greek philosopher Hermodorus the Ephesian, then in exile at Rome. D. 1. 2. 2. 4.

23 Important sources of information on the Law of the Twelve Tables are the works by Cicero, Aulus Gellius, Macrobius, Livy, Plutarch and Dionysius of Halicarnassus. A commentary on the Twelve Tables was written by the jurist Gaius in the second century AD under the title *ad legem duodeci tabularum*, which has been partly preserved in the Digest of Justinian.

24 See R. Schöll's, *Leges duodecim tabularum reliquiae*, Leipzig 1868. Schöll's reconstruction is based on the work of H. Dirksen, *Übersicht der bisherigen Versuche zur Kritik und Herstellung des Textes der Zwölf-Tafel Fragmente*, Leipzig 1824. See also P. F. Girard and F. Senn, *Les lois des Romains*, septième édition par un groupe de romanistes, Naples 1977, 25–73; FIRA I, Florence 1940–43, repr. 1968–69, 23 ff; Bruns, *Fontes* I, Tubingen 1909, repr. Aalen 1969, 15 ff. For an English translation see E. H. Warmington, *Remains of Old Latin* III, Loeb Classical Library 1938, 424 ff; A. C. Johnson, P. R. Coleman-Norton and F. C. Bourne, *Ancient Roman Statutes*, Austin 1961, 9–13. And see M. Crawford (ed.), *Roman Statutes*, London 1996.

25 Table I prescribes the way a defendant could be summoned by the plaintiff to court and Table II stipulates the rules governing court procedure. Table III recognizes the right of a creditor to put an insolvent debtor to death or to sell him into slavery (following the condemnation of the debtor by a court of law). The power of the head of the family (*patria potestas*) over his family members is given legislative recognition under Table IV. This includes provisions confirming the customary right of a father to inflict corporeal punishment upon a son, to sell him into slavery or even to put him to death. Table V contains rules pertaining to matters of succession and guardianship. For example, it provides that if a person died intestate, or if his will was found to be invalid, his property should pass to his nearest agnates (*agnati, sui heredes*) or, in the absence of agnates, to the members of his clan (*gentiles*). According to another provision, if a man was unable to manage his own affairs, his person and property should be placed under the power of his agnates or, in default of these, his *gentiles*. Table VI includes provisions regulating the acquisition and transference of private property. It is stated, for example, that a person would acquire ownership upon two years of uninterrupted possession of landed property, or one year in the case of other property (this mode of acquiring property was termed *usucapio*). The transference of property by *mancipatio* (a formal transaction involving an imaginary sale and delivery) or *nexum* (a bilateral transaction accomplished like the *mancipatio*) is also recognized, together with an early form of contract known as *stipulatio*. The latter was a verbal contract based on a spoken question (*spondere?* – do you promise on your oath?) followed immediately by a spoken answer (*spondeo* – I promise on my oath). The contract was strictly interpreted on the basis of the pronounced words. Table VII deals with matters relating to disputes between neighbouring owners and contains provisions prescribing the distance between buildings, the width of roads, and the right of an owner to gather fruits that had fallen from his tree onto neighbouring property. Table VIII contains provisions concerning delicts and crimes, and prescribes the punishments which these entailed. It is established that a person who injured another was

exposed to retaliation (*lex talionis*), but the effects of this rule were mitigated by the fact that in many cases the injured party could only seek compensation for the injury suffered. Although the penalties provided were extremely harsh, the number of offences punishable by death was rather limited. Table IX includes provisions relating to public law. It renders it unconstitutional for a magistrate to propose a law imposing penalties or disabilities upon a particular person only, and declares that no one should be put to death except after a formal trial and sentence. It states, moreover, that only the assembly of the centuries could pass laws affecting the political rights of citizens and that no citizen should be condemned on a capital charge (i.e. a charge involving loss of life, freedom or citizenship) without the right of appeal to the assembly. Table X addresses sacral law and matters relating to the burial or cremation of the dead. Finally, Tables XI and XII embody general provisions, such as the prohibition of intermarriage between patricians and plebeians (Table XI) and rules relating to the liability of a slave's master for offences committed by the former (*noxae deditio*).

26 The historian Livy refers to the Law of the Twelve Tables as 'the source of all public and private law' (*fons omnis publici privatique iuris*). *Ab urbe condita*, 3. 34. 6.

27 Important statutes of this period in the field of public law encompass: the *lex Valeria Horatia* (449 BC), which recognized the inviolability of the plebeian tribunes; the *lex Canuleia* (445 BC), which removed the rule prohibiting intermarriages between patricians and plebeians; the *lex Aemilia* (434 BC), which limited the duration of the censorship to eighteen months; the *leges Liciniae Sextiae* (367 BC), which admitted plebeians to the office of consul and established the praetorship; the *lex Publilia Philonis* (339 BC), which removed the rule directing that the legislative enactments of the popular assemblies had to obtain senate approval after their passage; the *lex Ogulnia de auguribus* (*c.* 326 BC), which granted the plebeians access to the college of the pontiffs; and the *lex Hortensia de plebiscitis* (287 BC), which rendered the resolutions of the plebeian assembly binding on all citizens. Two favourite objects of the legislation from this period were land and debts. According to Livy, no less than fifteen proposals for agrarian reform were adanced by the tribunes of the plebeians from 481 to 385 BC but remained ineffective for lack of ratification by the senate. In the same period, however, a statute was passed that opened the Aventine Hill to settlement, and two of the *leges Liciniae Sextiae* mentioned above limited the extent of public land (*ager publicus*) that could be held by a single family and also lightened the burden of debts for the plebeians. Later in the fourth century BC many statutes were passed that established a limit on the interest rate charged on debts for borrowed money, such as the *lex Duilia Menenia* of 357 BC and the *lex Genucia* of 342 BC. Other statutes eased the debtors' burden with respect to the securities they could be requested to provide against the risk of non-payment, as well as pertaining to the sanctions they incurred for non-payment. Thus, the *lex Poetelia Papiria* of 326 BC forbade the private imprisonment of the debtor by the creditor, which entailed the former becoming a slave of the latter. Regarding private law statutes, the *lex Aquilia* (286 BC) set general rules of liability for damage caused to another person's property, and the *lex Atinia* (second century BC) excluded stolen property (*res furtivae*) from *usucapio* (the acquisition of ownership through possession of a thing for a prescribed period of time).

28 See G. 1. 3. It should be noted, however, that the sources provide contradictory information on when and how the *leges* and the *plebiscita* acquired the same status.

29 The same procedure was established for elections of magistrates by the *lex Maenia* passed probably in the early third century BC.

30 D. 1. 2. 2. 6 (Pomponius).

31 Modern scholars disagree over whether, before the establishment of the praetorship, the first phase of the proceedings occurred before a pontiff or a consul. In any event, there was no apparent conflict between the magistrate and pontiff as the magistrate was often a member of the pontifical college or closely associated with its members. See on this O. Tellegen-Couperous, *A Short History of Roman Law*, London and New York 1993, 22,

24, 159–60; F, Schulz, *History of Roman Legal Science*, Oxford 1946, 7; H. F. Jolowicz and B. Nicholas, *Historical Introduction to the Study of Roman Law*, 3rd edn, Cambridge 1972, 88–89; M. Kaser, *Das römische Zivilprozessrecht*, Munich 1966, 22.

32 The practice of applying to the pontiffs for some formula was apparently well established before the law that accorded the *legis actio* its name had established the necessity for such a formula.

33 However, usually after the third manumission the 'buyer' sold the son back to his father, who at once manumitted him. In this way, the father acquired the status of patron over his son and thus retained rights of succession with regard to him.

34 Another example of a rule developed through juristic interpretation is the rule relating to the guardianship of freed persons. According to Gaius: 'The same law of the Twelve Tables assigns the guardianship of freed men and freed women under puberty to the patrons and their children. This form of guardianship is called statutory, not because it was expressly stated in that body of law, but because it has been accepted by interpretation as if it had been introduced by the words of the statute. For, by reason that the statute ordered that the estates of freed men and freed women who died intestate should go to the patrons and their children, the early jurists deemed that the statute willed that tutories also should go to them, because it had provided that agnates who were heirs should also be tutors.' G. 1. 165.

35 The historical sources are far from reliable on this point, however.

36 D. 1. 2. 2. 6. 35 and 38 (Pomponius).

37 See Cicero, *Brut.* 20; D. 1. 2. 2. 7 and 38 (Pomponius).

3 THE MONARCHY AND EARLY REPUBLIC: THE ADMINISTRATION OF JUSTICE

1 The *aediles curules* and the *quaestores* also exercised jurisdiction in certain cases, but not nearly to the same extent as wielded by the praetor.

2 The parties could, in most cases, select a judge of their own choice from a list of citizens qualified to serve as judges in civil and criminal trials (*album iudicum*). During the Republic, the *album iudicum* was prepared every year by the praetorian office. At first, the *iudices* were probably chosen from among the senators.

3 Towards the end of the third century BC, two courts were established to deal with more intricate cases: the court of the *centumviri* and that of the *decemviri stlitibus iudicandis*, which were composed of a hundred and ten judges respectively.

4 A *legis actio* could be initiated only on certain days, called *dies fasti* (ant. *dies nefasti*). There were forty days in a year when legal disputes could be presented before the praetor.

5 As in the modern law of civil procedure, Roman law recognized the existence of two parties to litigation: the plaintiff (*actor* or *petitor*) and the defendant (*reus*). In proceedings concerning the division of common property (*actio communi dividundo, actio familiae erciscundae*), either party was at the same time plaintiff and defendant. Only free persons, who normally had to be Roman citizens, could act as parties to litigation (*litigantes, litigatores, adversarii*). Other than in certain exceptional cases, *filiifamilias* and *filiaefamilias* were also not permitted to participate in litigation. Boys under the age of fourteen and girls under the age of twelve (*impuberes*) could engage in litigation only with the approval of their guardian or tutor (*auctoritate tutoris*), while women were permitted to litigate only under certain circumstances. Children and insane persons were usually represented in court by their tutors or guardians (*tutores, curatores*). Under a *lex Hostilia* (an early statute of unknown date), a person who had been taken prisoner in war, or who was absent on an official mission, could be represented by another citizen in a trial involving an allegation of theft committed against the absent person's property (*actio furti*). During the late Republic, foreigners (*peregrini*) could also participate in litigation (disputes between foreigners and between foreigners and Roman citizens were assigned to

the *praetor peregrinus*, whose office was established in 242 BC), while entities, such as corporations and similar bodies of persons, could act through their agents. Generally, engaging in litigation on behalf of another person (*alieno nomine*) was banned during the period of the *legis actio* procedure. However, in later times, a party was allowed to conduct his case through a representative who, depending on the method of his appointment, was referred to as *cognitor* or *procurator*. The *cognitor* was nominated by the party he was to represent during the *in iure* phase of the proceedings in a formal manner and in the presence of the other party.

6 See Festus, '*contestari litem*', in Bruns, *Fontes* II, p. 5.

7 G. 4. 11.

8 G. 4. 12–29.

9 G. 4. 13.

10 An *actio in rem* was initiated to establish the plaintiff's claim to some corporeal object (*res*), as opposed to a claim of the defendant, or to compel the defendant to acknowledge some property right, e.g. a servitude (*servitus*) that the plaintiff claimed to possess. This action was founded on the claim that the plaintiff had a better right to something than anyone else in the world, and could be instituted against anyone who invaded or disputed such right. According to Gaius (G. 4. 5), the *actiones in rem* were also referred to as *vindicationes* (vindications). An *actio in personam*, on the other hand, was initiated by the plaintiff in order to compel the defendant to perform a contractual or delictual obligation. Such an action was based on a specific obligation and directed against a determinate person or his heirs. Among the personal actions, those aimed at compelling the defendant to render or perform something (*dare facere oportere*) were termed *condictiones* (G. 4. 5).

11 The Law of the Twelve Tables (T. 2. 1) provided that when the value of the object in dispute exceeded one thousand asses, the *sacramentum* was five hundred asses; in all other cases, it was fifty asses. As this was a large sum of money at the time of the Twelve Tables, it effectively limited rash or unwarranted litigation.

12 The forfeiture of the *sacramentum* was originally regarded as a form of sacrifice to the gods (*piaculum*) aimed at expiating the offence of perjury committed by the party whose assertion was proved false. See P. Noailles, *Du droit sacré au droit civil*, Paris 1949, 9–15, 72–87, 109–35.

13 In order to avoid later condemnation, a party could acknowledge his opponent's claim (*confessio in iure*), or remain silent, in which case he was regarded as having confessed.

14 Strictly speaking, it was the magistrate who assumed control over the disputed property and it then existed in the custody of a man endowed with *imperium*. The magistrate could then assign it to either party, and only by such assignment did it transfer into the possession of either claimant.

15 Very little is known of the way in which the *legis actio sacramento in personam* was conducted. Apparently, in this case a simple assertion was issued by the plaintiff, again supported by an oath and backed by a wager, to which the defendant replied by admitting or denying the claim. See Val. Probus 4. 1, in Girard, *Textes* I, 13.

16 The *stipulatio* consisted of an oral promise or undertaking in terms of which a person solemnly promised to make a specific performance to another person by means of responding in a particular, formal way to a particular question posed to him. The answer had to accord with the question perfectly; any difference or restriction rendered the contract void. This type of contract was used for any kind of obligation, from the payment of money to the most complicated performances.

17 There was scant information on this *legis actio* until the discovery of a certain fragment of the *Institutes* of Gaius in 1933.

18 G. 4. 18–20; *Inst.* 4. 6. 15; Festus, '*condictio*', in Bruns, *Fontes* II, p. 5.

19 A loan for consumption, established when one person transferred the ownership of certain funds or a quantity of replaceable objects to another person on the understanding

that an equal amount of money or objects of the same kind and quality would be
returned to the giver at some later point in time.

20 A verbal agreement where the object promised was precisely defined and fixed.

21 *Condicere*: 'to give notice'.

22 The office of the *iudex* was intermediate between the modern judge and juror, possessing
less power than the former and having more extensive functions than the latter.

23 The *iudex* was free to conduct the trial when and where he chose and could adjourn the
proceedings as necessary. According to a provision of the Law of the Twelve Tables (T. 2. 2),
a trial could be postponed if a party fell seriously ill (*morbus sonticus*), or if a party was
engaged in another trial involving a foreigner (*status dies cum hoste*). In later years, additional reasons for the postponement of a trial were introduced (Bruns, *Fontes* I, p. 131).

24 Evidence was presented only in relation to matters of fact. Both oral (*testes*) and documentary (*tabulae, epistulae, codices, rationes*) evidence was considered, but oral testimony
carried special weight. The Law of the Twelve Tables (T. 8. 22) provided that if a person
had observed a transaction *per aes et libram* and refused to appear as a witness, he was
declared infamous and incapable (*improbus*) of giving evidence or having evidence given
on his behalf (*intestabilis*). (*Per aes et libram* denoted a legal transaction involving the use
of copper and scales – e.g. *mancipatio, nexum* – and the performance of certain formal
acts in the presence of five Roman citizens acting as witnesses.) Before giving evidence,
witnesses had to take an oath.

25 In the later republican period, the Romans began to engage the use of *oratores* and *advocati* in litigation. The *advocati*, who were usually leading citizens, did not act in a
professional capacity. Their role was to assist the citizens unable to argue their case themselves either because they lacked the requisite skill or had a lower social status (e.g.
clientes).

26 With respect to the *legis actio per iudicis arbitrive postulationem*, the *legis actio per condictionem* and, probably, the *legis actio sacramento in personam*, the judge's verdict expressed
the condemnation (*condemnatio*) or exoneration (*absolutio*) of the defendant. Regarding
the *legis actio sacramento in rem*, on the other hand, the verdict simply identified the party
who should retain the property in dispute. In cases involving an *actio in personam*, the
party who lost the case (*iudicatus*) was subject to a *legis actio per manus iniectionem* – one
of the two *legis actiones* discussed below.

27 The relevant procedure and the particular accompanying *legis actio* were not created by
the Law of the Twelve Tables, but were apparently in existence before that law was
enacted (although they were probably modified by it). The name of the *legis actio* under
consideration seems to indicate what all procedures may have been originally, i.e. legal-
ized forms of self-help.

28 See G. 4. 21; *lex Urson*. 61. 1–2, in Bruns, *Fontes* I, p. 123. The *legis actio per manus
iniectione* could be relied on, however, only in those cases where no sureties (*praedes*) had
been rendered by the party who was defeated in the trial.

29 The *vindex* could either pay the judgment debt or defend the debtor by denying that the
manus iniectio was justified (G. 4. 21). If, however, in the subsequent trial the creditor's
claim was confirmed, the *vindex* could be condemned to pay double the amount owed by
the principal debtor who, after the intervention of the *vindex*, was probably released from
the debt.

30 XII Tables, T. 3. 5; Aul. Gell. 20. 1. 46–47 in Bruns, *Fontes* I, p. 21.

31 The Law of the Twelve Tables contained a provision (T. 3. 6), which, if literally interpreted, gave creditors permission to divide the body of a debtor into pieces with each
creditor seizing a piece proportionate to his claim. Although no evidence in the sources
reveals that an execution of this kind ever occured, there is no doubt that in the archaic
period the treatment of debtors by their creditors was extremely cruel. The position of
debtors seems to have improved with the enactment of several statutes in the fourth
century BC. Probably the most important statute was the *lex Poetelia Papiria* of *c.* 326 BC,

which abolished the extreme penalties of death or sale into slavery that had hitherto applied to defaulting debtors.

32 G. 4. 26–29.

33 The *pignoris capio*, like the *manus iniectio*, must originally have been regarded as a justified form of self-help and did not constitute a *legis actio* unless it entailed a suit where the creditor was plaintiff. As a remedy, it was allowed in cases of a public character involving claims relating to military service, religion or revenue. In the first case, the remedy was established by custom prior to the enactment of the Law of the Twelve Tables, in the second it was provided by the Twelve Tables (T. 12. 1) and in the third it was created by law subsequent to the Twelve Tables (G. 4. 28).

34 Unlike other forms of statute process, the *legis actio per pignoris capionem* could be applied even in the absence of the debtor and on days when jurisdictional activity was in abeyance (*dies nefasti*). See G. 4. 29.

35 After that time, the *legis actio* procedure was used only in certain exceptional cases. On the system of *legis actiones* see V. Arangio-Ruiz, *Cours de droit romain (les actions)*, Naples 1935, repr. 1980, 5–26; G. Pugliese, *Il processo civile romano, I, Le legis actiones*, Rome 1962; H. Lévy-Bruhl, *Recherches sur les actions de la loi*, Paris 1960; M. Kaser, *Das römische Zivilprozessrecht*, Munich 1996, 25 ff; *Römisches Privatrecht*, Munich 1989, 357 ff; C. A. Cannata, *Profilo istituzionale del processo privato romano I, Le legis actiones*, Turin 1980; B. Albanese, *Il processo privato romano delle 'legis actiones'*, Palermo 1987.

36 The crime of treason was committed when a Roman citizen acted in a way that rendered him an enemy of the Roman state. Its scope embraced acts such as assisting an enemy in time of war, inciting an enemy to attack the Roman state, delivering a Roman citizen to an enemy and inciting an internal rebellion. A less grievous crime with a similar nature consisted of acts tending to impair the power, dignity or honour of the Roman state (*crimen laesae maiestatis*). However, the dividing line between these two types of crime was not precisely delineated.

37 *Parricidium* is a word of uncertain derivation that in an early period appears to have acquired, through a process unknown to us, the significance of willful murder in general. It seems that, initially, *parricidium* was as a rule treated merely as a private delict presenting the deceased's kin with the right to execute vengeance on the offender. Indeed, avenging the killing of a kinsman was regarded as a religious duty. This notion was so deeply rooted, that long after murder was established as a crime against the state and subject to public prosecution, a kinsman was bound to initiate such a prosecution and, if he failed to do so, was not allowed to obtain any of the deceased person's inheritance.

38 However, with reference to the situation in primitive times, it is impossible to draw a clear distinction between secular and religious crimes. Treason, for example, may be regarded also as an offence against the gods protecting the community, and the execution of the offender as a sacrifice to them.

39 The category of *delicta privata* encompassed, for example, offences such as theft (*furtum*), bodily injury (*iniuria*), robbery (*rapina*), defamation of character and, since the enactment of the *lex Aquilia* in 286 BC, unlawful damage to another person's property (*damnum iniuria datum*). The *delicta privata* were regarded as existing within the field of private law.

40 A religious element is evident, for example, in the punishments imposed on the patron who wronged his client (XII T. 8. 21), on the witness who refused to testify at a trial (XII T. 8. 22) and on the person who depastured or cut down a neighbour's crop by stealth in the night (XII T. 8. 9).

41 The notion of *provocatio ad populum* first appears in the sources that elaborate the case of Horatius in connection with the crime of *perduellio*. See Livy 1. 26.

42 Scholars have expressed doubts as to whether the *duumviri perduellionis* and the *quaestores parricidii* originated from the time of the kings, and there is evidence suggesting that the right of appealing to the assembly was first granted by a *lex Valeria* after the establishment

of the Republic. See J. L. Strachan-Davidson, *Problems of Roman Criminal Law*, Oxford 1912, repr. Amsterdam 1969, 1, 126, 144, note 1; T. Mommsen, *Römisches Staatsrecht*, Leipzig 1887, repr. Graz 1971, 2, 523; *Römisches Strafrecht*, Leipzig 1899, repr. Graz 1955 and Darmstadt 1961, 155.

43 Religious offences, on the other hand, were dealt with by the pontiffs.

44 However, since the middle of the third century BC cases of *perduellio* were usually tackled by the *tribuni plebis* and the appointment of *duoviri perduellionis* became virtually obsolete.

45 The original title of the quaestors seems to have been *quaestores parricidii*, which indicates that their duties in the administration of criminal justice came first in order of time. As their financial duties assumed increasing prominence, they were designated as *quaestores parricidii et aerarii*, and finally as *quaestores* simply. This, at any rate, is a possible explanation for an obscure matter.

46 The term *poena capitalis* denoted not only the sentence of death, but also a penalty entailing the loss of liberty or citizenship.

47 Cicero, *De Re Publica* 2. 31; Livy 2. 8; 3. 55; 10. 9; Val. Max. 4. 1. 1; Dionysius 5. 19; D. 1. 2. 2. 16 (Pomponius). And see Th. Mommsen, *Römisches Staatsrecht*, 3rd ed., Leipzig 1887, repr. Graz 1952, 163–64; *Römisches Strafrecht*, Leipzig 1899, repr. Graz 1955 and Darmstadt 1961, 56–57; A. H. M. Jones, *The Criminal Courts of the Roman Republic and Principate*, Oxford 1972, 1–39.

48 The right of appeal was re-confirmed and extended by the *lex Valeria Horatia* of 449 BC, the *lex Valeria* of 300 BC and the *leges Porciae* (first half of the second century BC). The *lex Valeria* is declared to have extended this right to corporal punishment, while under the *leges Porciae* an appeal could be raised against capital sentences and sentences of scourging (*verberatio, castigatio*) pronounced on Roman citizens anywhere (originally, the right of appeal lay only against sentences pronounced within the city of Rome or a radius of one mile therefrom). By the latter legislation, the magistrate who refused the *provocatio* was probably rendered liable to a charge of treason. The question of whether the right of appeal was available to citizens serving as soldiers has been a source of difficulty to historians. Although in theory it appears that under one of the *leges Porciae* every citizen soldier had this right, in practice it is unlikely that a military commander would allow an appeal where the exigencies of military discipline called for an immediate execution of the sentence.

49 See B. Santalucia, *Diritto e processo penale nell' antica Roma*, Milan 1989, 31–89. Consider also J. L. Strachan-Davidson, *Problems of the Roman Criminal Law*, Oxford 1912, repr. Amsterdam 1969, 138–40.

50 As early as the middle of the fifth century BC, a series of legislative enactments (*lex Aternia Tarpeia, lex Menenia Sextia*) established the maximum limits for fines imposed by magistrates. See Aulus Gellius, *N. A.* 11. 1; Dionysius 10. 50; Cicero, *De Re Publica* 2. 35. As regards imprisonment, it should be noted that in republican times this was normally regarded as a means of preventing escape and not as a form of punishment.

51 The jurisdiction of the popular assemblies embraced only political crimes or offences that affected the interests of the state.

52 The magistrate might include more than one charge in the same accusation and could withdraw or amend the charge (or a charge) at any stage of the trial. Although he was not allowed to leave the penalty open, he could alter the punishment he initially proposed at a later stage of the proceedings.

53 During this period (three market days amounted to twenty-four days) the citizens would have ample opportunities to discuss with one another the case and the issues it involved.

54 The voting procedure was governed by the same rules as those applicable when the assembly had to decide on a legislative proposal.

55 If the assembly was prevented from meeting at all (e.g. because of a tribunician veto) or proceedings were halted before the voting was completed (e.g. because of the appearance of an ill omen), the accused was released, as if he had been found not guilty.

56 On the *iudicia populi* and the institution of the *provocatio ad populum* see A. H. M. Jones, *The Criminal Courts of the Roman Republic and Principate*, Oxford 1972, ch. 1; J. L. Strachan-Davidson, *Problems of the Roman Criminal Law*, Oxford 1912, repr. Amsterdam 1969, 127 ff; W. Kunkel, *Untersuchungen zur Entwicklung des römischen Kriminalverfahrens in vorsullanischer Zeit*, Munich 1962, 9 ff; J. Martin, 'Die Provokation in der klassischen und spaten Republik', (1970) *Hermes* 98, 72; R. A. Bauman, *Crime and Punishment in Ancient Rome*, London and New York 1996, ch. 2; 'The lex Valeria de provocatione of 300 BC', (1973) *Hist.* 22, 34–47; E. Staveley, 'Provocatio during the fifth and fourth centuries BC', (1954) *Hist.* 3, 413; B. Santalucia, *Diritto e processo penale nell' antica Roma*, Milan 1989, ch. 2; V. Giuffré, *La repressione criminale nell' esperienza romana*, Naples 1998, 24 ff.

4 THE LATE REPUBLIC: THE HISTORICAL, SOCIAL AND CONSTITUTIONAL BACKGROUND

1 The city-state of Carthage, situated on the northern coast of Africa near present-day Tunis, was originally a Phoenician colony in the ninth century BC. The Carthagenian empire extended over the northern coast of Africa from the Gulf of Syrtis westward beyond the Strait of Gibraltar, southern Spain, Sardinia and most of Sicily.

2 After a country was conquered a Roman magistrate, usually the one who accomplished the conquest, and a commission of senators (*legati*) were entrusted with the task of organizing it as a province. They arranged the terms of peace with the defeated local population, designated the boundaries of the new province and composed a constitution prescribing the form of governance for the province. Upon the return of the *legati* to Rome, these arrangements were presented to the assembly for approval as a legislative proposal (*rogatio legis*). The proposal, once it became law (*lex data, lex provinciae*), formed the constitutional charter regulating the organization and administration of the province. A province was governed by a Roman magistrate with *imperium*, usually a consul or a praetor. In the last century of the Republic, Sulla's *lex Cornelia de provinciis ordinandis* (81 BC) dictated that consuls and praetors, after their year in office expired, had to serve as governors of provinces as pro-magistrates (*proconsules* or *propraetores*) for one more year. Besides his military and administrative duties, the governor had supreme jurisdiction with respect to matters of both civil and criminal law. Each province comprised several communities (*civitates*) that enjoyed local self-government but had no political bond of unity. A distinction existed between three categories of communities: free and federate (*civitates liberae et foederatae*), free and non-tributary (*civitates liberae et immunes*) and tributary (*stipendiariae*). The first category embraced those communities (very few in number) that retained their independence. These were permanently bound with Rome by treaties of alliance. The second category captured a small number of communities to which Rome had granted, by virtue of the provincial charter and without the existence of a bilateral treaty, certain privileges, such as exemption from taxation (however, these privileges could be revoked by the senate at any time). The third group, which was by far the most numerous, furnished most of the taxes imposed upon the province. The task of collecting taxes in the provinces was assigned to private contractors (*publicani*) who formed companies referred to as *societates publicanorum*. Besides the ordinary taxes, such as the property tax (*tributum*), that they were required to pay on a regular basis, the provincials were often subjected to the arbitrary demands of local Roman officials. They were required, for example, to provide winter shelter for the troops, equip and maintain ships for war or transport and provide supplies for the governor's household. As these burdens were usually imposed at the discretion of the governor or local magistrates, they were often used as a means of intimidation and oppression. An attempt to check the abuses of power by provincial governors and magistrates was initiated in 149 BC with the passing of the *lex Calpurnia de repetundis*. Under this law, which

was confirmed by subsequent enactments, a regular court was instituted (*quaestio perpetua*) to deal with cases of extortion and other abuses committed by provincial magistrates.

3 The *ordo senatorius* embodied all the descendants of families that had been represented in the senate, whether or not members of the immediate family were senators at a given time. The position that a person occupied within the senatorial class depended largely on the rank of the state offices his family members had held.

4 In early times the Romans used, instead of coins, lumps or bars of copper (*aes*) that were not counted but weighed. These bars were called *stipes* or *stips*. The only Roman coin minted before the third century BC was a heavy copper coin called the *as*. In the third century BC, as economic activity increased, the Romans adopted coinage based on a silver standard that was common among the Hellenistic states of the East. The basic silver coin was the denarius that was subdivided into four brass sesterces and sixteen bronze asses. For a closer look at the early development of Roman coinage see C. H. V. Sutherland, *Roman Coins*, London 1974; R. A. G. Carson, *Coins of Greece and Rome*, 2nd edn, London 1970; H. Mattingly, *Roman Coins*, 2nd edn, London 1960; M. Crawford, *Coinage and Money under the Roman Republic*, London 1985.

5 Activities such as these were regarded as undignified and therefore unsuitable for members of the senatorial nobility.

6 The term *equites* originally referred to those citizens who were wealthy enough to be included in the eighteen centuries of knights (*centuriae equitum*), which constituted the cavalry of the Roman army. These citizens comprised the prestigious equestrian centuries of the centuriate assembly.

7 To minimize the financial and other risks associated with their work, most *publicani* were organized in companies known as *societates publicanorum*. Several companies competed to undertake a public work, and the one with the lowest tender was usually awarded the contract. These contracts were usually composed by the censors (hence their description as *leges censoriae*), who were also entrusted with the task of granting the relevant leases. The granting of a lease by the state occurred in the open and was decided by public auction. The company's chairman (*manceps*) carried out the bidding and provided guarantees to the state for the proper discharge of the terms and conditions of the contract.

8 On the Roman social classes during the Republic see M. Gelzer, *The Roman Nobility*, Oxford 1969; C. Nicolet, *L'ordre équestre à l'époque républicaine*, Paris 1966; H. Hill, *The Roman Middle Class in the Republican Period*, Oxford 1952; G. Alföldy, *The Social History of Rome*, London 1985, ch. 2 and 3.

9 According to the ancient law of nations (*ius gentium*), not only enemy soldiers seized in battle, but even entire populations of conquered territories were subject to enslavement.

10 The geographer Strabo of Amasia reports that on this island a maximum of ten thousand people could be sold as slaves on one day alone. Most of these slaves were victims of kidnapping by pirates or prisoners captured during wars between eastern states.

11 Educated slaves were often employed as instructors, clerks or physicians. On the estates, an educated slave could become estate manager, work supervisor or book-keeper.

12 A slave could be released from slavery (*manumissio*) in three ways: by a formal announcement by the master in public and before a higher magistrate (usually a praetor) that the slave was free (*vindicta*); after the enrolment of a slave as a Roman citizen by the censor, according to the master's request (*censu*); and under his master's will (*testamento*). Besides these legally recognized ways of manumission, there were other informal ways of liberating slaves, for example, when a master in the presence of his friends declared his slave to be free (*manumissio inter amicos*), or when he expressed such a wish in a letter (*manumissio per epistulam*), or even when he shared his table with his slave (*manumissio per mensam*).

13 The deep resentment felt by slaves against their Roman masters erupted in a series of large-scale slave revolts during the late second and early first centuries BC.

14 In relation to his former master, now termed *patronus*, a liberated slave was referred to as

libertus. The relationship between a *libertus* and his *patronus* was similar to that between a client and his patron.

15 A large part of Rome's urban proletariat was formed by liberated slaves.

16 For more detail on the position of the freedmen and slaves see S. Treggiari, *Roman Freedmen during the Late Republic*, Oxford 2000; W. L. Westerman, *The Slave Systems of Greek and Roman Antiquity*, Philadelphia 1955; M. I. Finley (ed.), *Slavery in Classical Antiquity*, Cambridge 1960; M. K. Hopkins, *Conquerors and Slaves*, Cambridge 1978; E. M. Staerman, *Die Blütezeit der Sklavenwirtschaft in der römischen Republik*, Wiesbaden 1969; A. Watson, *Roman Slave Law*, Baltimore 1987; K. Bradley, *Slavery and Society at Rome*, Cambridge 1994, repr. 1997; J. F. Gardner, *Being a Roman Citizen*, London and New York 1993, ch. 2; K. Christ, *Krise und Untergang der römischen Republik*, Darmstadt 1979, 82 ff; J. C. Dumont, *Servus. Rome et l'esclavage sous la République*, Rome 1987.

17 Important channels of Greek culture were the Greeks who entered Rome as ambassadors, teachers, physicians, merchants and artists, as well as the large numbers of educated Greek slaves who were employed in Roman households.

18 During this period a national literature emerged in Rome based on Greek standards.

19 The Stoic philosophy was introduced in Rome by the philosopher Panaetius of Rhodes (185–109 BC) who became a leading member of the circle of influential writers and philosophers gathered around Scipio Aemilianus (the so-called 'Scipionic circle'). The Stoic ideal of a world-state based on the brotherhood of men exercised a strong influence on Roman thought and provided one of the foundations that established the Empire's political philosophy.

20 Essentially, Gracchus' bill was a restatement, with some modifications, of an earlier law, the *lex Licinia Sextia* of 367 BC, that had fallen in abeyance.

21 Instead of submitting the bill first for discussion in the senate, as custom required, Tiberius proposed it directly to the assembly where it was bound to succeed. Moreover, the bill was passed only after Tiberius had successfully removed his fellow tribune, who was bribed by the opposition and blocked the bill by exercising his right of veto.

22 The senate, however, did not interfere with the work of the land commission entrusted with implementing Tiberius' law and many smallholdings were created and farmed, as shown by the census of 125 BC.

23 As the senatorial court mentioned above had refused to allow those declared guilty to appeal to the assembly, a law was passed that established the right of appeal from such judicial commissions and provided that only the people's assembly had the right to impose capital punishment on a Roman citizen.

24 One of these measures was the *lex Sempronia iudiciaria* of 122 BC, whereby the right of serving as jurors in criminal trials, which until then had belonged exclusively to senators, was transferred to the *equites*.

25 For closer scrutiny of the Gracchan period see A. Lintott, *Violence in Republican Rome*, Oxford 1968, ch. 12; D. Stockton, *The Gracchi*, Oxford 1979; H.C. Boren, *The Gracchi*, New York 1969; A. H. Bernstein, *Tiberius Sempronius Gracchus: Tradition and Apostasy*, Ithaca and London 1978; G. Alföldy, *The Social History of Rome*, London 1985, 73 ff; K. Christ, *Krise und Untergang der römischen Republik*, Darmstadt 1979, 117 ff.

26 As F. E. Adcock explains, 'A Roman group in politics was not a large body of men of all classes pursuing principles or far-reaching long-range policies (such as, for instance, nationalisation of means of production and exchange), a body of government to whom control of the government is a means to an end, the end being the carrying through of a consistent programme dictated by principles or theories. A Roman political group in the revolutionary age was normally a small group of nobles and their personal adherents pursuing interests of themselves or their leaders to advance careers, to enjoy power and profits, or to meet some immediate crisis by this or that means, sometimes beneficent but not always so'. *Roman Political Ideas and Practice*, 6th edn, Ann Arbor 1975, 61–62.

27 The tribunes' right of general veto was limited and they could not introduce legislation

into the assembly without the previous approval of the senate. Moreover, Sulla abolished trials before the popular assemblies and replaced them with trials by jury, giving the senate full control over the administration of justice.

28 This period is marked by the failed conspiracy of L. Sergius Catilina, a member of the aristocracy. With the support of elements from the *populares* he tried to seize control of the state. It is also marked by the political activities of the orator M. Tullius Cicero, a staunch supporter of the *optimates*, who advocated a united front of the propertied classes, both senatorial and equestrian, to stabilize the government on the occasion of the Catilinarian conspiracy.

29 The Parthian empire extended over a large area between the Persian gulf and the Caspian Sea, on Rome's eastern borders.

30 Soon after his defeat, Pompey was assassinated in Egypt where he had fled, but the war between the two camps continued until 45 BC, when the last remnants of the senatorial forces were destroyed in Spain.

31 After their defeat Antony and Cleopatra escaped to Egypt and, when the country fell to Octavian, they committed suicide in Alexandria.

32 On the crisis and fall of the Republic see in general S. Gruen, *The Last Generation of the Roman Republic*, Berkeley 1974; A. Lintott, *Violence in Republican Rome*, Oxford 1968; M. Beard and M. Crawford, *Rome in the Late Republic*, London 1985; P. Brunt, *The Fall of the Roman Republic*, Oxford 1988; R. Syme, *The Roman Revolution*, Oxford 1939; L. Taylor, *Party Politics in the Age of Caesar*, Berkeley 1949; G. Alföldy, *The Social History of Rome*, London 1985, ch. 4; K. Christ, *Krise und Untergang der römischen Republik*, Darmstadt 1979; E. Betti, *La crisi della Repubblica e la genesi del principato in Roma*, Rome 1982.

5 THE LATE REPUBLIC: THE SOURCES OF LAW

1 As noted earlier, this applied exclusively to Roman citizens according to the principle of the personality of the laws.

2 As he had no access to the *legis actio* procedure.

3 The office of the *praetor peregrinus* was created in *c.* 242 BC.

4 From an early period, the Romans realized that certain institutions of their own domestic law (for example, contracts of sale, service and loan) were also evident in foreign legal systems. These institutions that Roman law had in common with other legal systems were construed by the Romans as belonging to the law of nations (*ius gentium*) in a broad sense. However, this understanding of the *ius gentium* had little practical value for the Roman lawyer as the specific rules governing the operation of such generally recognized institutions differed considerably from one legal system to another.

5 Where *bona fides* was accepted as the basis of a legal obligation, the intention of the parties to the contract rather than the form observed was decisive for the generation of legal consequences. However, the recognition of the role of *bona fides* as a basis of liability did not entail abandonment of the *stipulatio* that existed as the principal formal contract of the *ius civile*. Instead, both consensual contracts and *stipulatio* existed for a long time alongside each other. Neither did this mean that consensual contracts were only relevant to transactions involving foreigners. Roman citizens, among themselves, increasingly used informal agreements as the role of ritual in concluding agreements decreased.

6 One might declare that the *ius gentium* was not entirely a technical name for a body of *iura*, but a means of justifying the introduction of new ones. The fact that an institution was discovered to exist in many nations was *prima facie* evidence that it was equitable and hence could be invoked in the praetor's court. However, disputes involving foreigners engaged legal institutions that did not all belong to the *ius gentium* when perceived as the law common to all nations. Certain institutions that citizens and foreigners could access were unique to the Roman system, such as the *stipulatio*.

7 According to the well-known statement of the jurist Papinianus. See D. 1. 1. 7. 1; *Inst.*1. 2. 7.

8 As stated by the jurist Paulus, 'custom is the best interpreter of statutes' (D. 1.3. 37).

9 Cicero, *De Inv.* 2. 22. 67; D. 1. 3. 32. 1 (Julianus); D. 1. 3. 35 (Hermogenianus).

10 At first, this announcement was probably issued before an *ad hoc* informal assembly of citizens (*contio*); in later times, the edicts were inscribed on wooden tablets that were exhibited in the Forum (the marketplace) so that citizens could easily inform themselves.

11 A temporary edict that was exceptionally issued on a specific occasion was called *edictum repentinum*.

12 The *formula* was the written document composed by the praetor that authorized the judge in a civil trial to condemn the defendant when certain facts were proved, or absolve him when the facts were unsubstantiated. See the section on the civil procedure in Chapter 6 below.

13 Such as claims arising from rent, purchase, lease, mandate and contracts for labour and the manufacturing of goods according to specification. Important innovations introduced by the praetor were intended to serve the banking and credit system, a more highly specialized system of production and maritime commerce.

14 By the end of the Republic the number of established *formulae* had become so great that, according to Cicero, there appeared to be a *formula* for every possible occasion. Moreover, Cicero reports that in his era those aspiring to careers as lawyers studied the *ius honorarium* alongside the Law of the Twelve Tables. Cicero, *Pro Rosc. com.* 8.

15 The concept of good faith (*bona fides*) probably had a Roman origin and initially appeared to be linked with the notion of *fas*, or divine law. However, a Greek influence cannot be ruled out. In the sphere of private law, *bona fides* was perceived in two ways: (i) from an objective point of view, *bona fides* was associated with the general expectation that persons should behave honestly and fairly in legal transactions; (ii) from a subjective point of view, *bona fides* pertained to a person's belief that his actions were just and lawful and did not violate another person's legitimate interest. Several general rules based on the concept of *bona fides* are included in the sources, e.g. '*bona fides* requires that what has been agreed upon must be done' (D. 19. 2. 21 (Iavolenus)), '*bona fides* demands equity in contracts' (D. 16. 3. 31. pr. (Tryphoninus)).

16 Aristotle defines equity (*epieikeia*) as a principle of justice designed to correct the positive law where the latter is defective owing to its universality (*Nic. Ethics*, 5. 10). As constituting a 'mean', or 'intermediate', i.e. a kind of compromise, the law must be expressed simply and in general terms. But while framing the law generally and simply, the lawmaker exposes it to deficiencies that produce injustice. A general rule is considered deficient and lacunary because it cannot precisely cover every potential case, as the human condition is imbued with complexities. Thus, a case may arise where one acted against the rule but no injustice was committed. To exclude such a case from the field of application of a broadly framed law, a new norm must be formulated to govern a determination of the case. The judge then has to allow equity to guide his discovery of the most appropriate solution, i.e. the one that best conforms to the justice that inspires the law. Furthermore, the law has a decisive form and can only evolve from sporadic attempts that are often too late. Once more, the judge assumes the task of correcting and completing the law. In contrast to positive law, which is only a rough or incomplete reflection of justice, equity is the precise reflection of justice. Therefore, the judge must constantly correct the errors or fill the gaps in the positive law by appealing to equity as a form of justice that extends beyond positive law.

17 Cicero's definition of the *ius civile* as 'the equity constituted for those who belong to the same state so that each may secure his own' (*Topica* 2. 9.), and the renowned aphorism of the jurist Celsius '*ius est ars boni et aequi*': 'the *ius* is the art of the good and just' (D. 1. 1. 1. pr.), are obviously inspired by the concept of equity as an abstract ideal of justice and as a touchstone of the norms of positive law. Linked with this perception of equity is the

distinction between *ius strictum* and *ius aequum*. The distinction was created on a philo-sophical-moral basis in order to differentiate the rigorous and inflexible rules of the operative law from the flexible norms inspired by the superior criteria of *aequitas*. In the early imperial epoch Roman jurisprudence, drawing upon the philosophical conception of *aequitas* as true justice, started to speak in some cases of superior equity, from which the jurisdictional magistrates drew inspiration and which, in turn, led to the develop-ment of *ius honorarium*. Thus, Roman jurisprudence laid the basis for the distinction between legal institutions conforming with or diverging from the principles of ideal justice. After the Christianization of the Roman Empire in the fourth century AD, the concept of *aequitas* was interpreted in light of Christian ethical principles. This new approach to the meaning of *aequitas* is reflected in the Justinianic codification, where *aequitas* is connected with values such as piety (*pietas*), affection (*caritas*), humanity (*humanitas*), kindness (*benignitas*) and clemency (*clementia*). This entailed the tendency of the notion of *ius aequum* to coincide with the Christian conception of *ius naturale*. In this respect, the abatement or derogation of laws in force was justified by reference to an *aequitas* construed as an expression of a law superior to the law in force because it was inspired by God – a law whose principal interpreter was deemed to be the emperor. Thus, for the first time, equity was perceived as a benign rectification of strict law rather than as an objective equation between conflicting interests.

18 The *bona fides* requirement that existed as the basis of the system of consensual contracts was virtually incorporated into the Roman *ius civile* by the *exceptio doli* and the *actio doli*.

19 The ownership of *res nec mancipi*, on the other hand, could be passed informally (e.g. by *traditio*). The origin of the distinction between *res mancipi* and *res nec mancipi* remains obscure, although it may be related to the fact that the *res mancipi* were extremely valu-able in the archaic period when agriculture formed the basis of Roman economic life. In later times, the formal methods for transferring ownership diminished in importance and, by Justinian's era, the distinction between *res mancipi* and *res nec mancipi* no longer existed.

20 Only Roman citizens or persons vested with the *ius commercii* could acquire ownership under the *ius civile* (*dominium ex iure Quiritium*).

21 G. 2. 41.

22 Introduced by Publicius, a *praetor urbanus*, probably in the first century BC. See G. 4. 36.

23 D. 21. 3. 3 (Hermogenianus).

24 Fictions were not an exclusively praetorian device used to adapt the legal system to changing socio-economic conditions. They were also embodied in statutes, such as, for example, the *lex Cornelia* (first century BC). According to this law, a citizen who died in captivity should be deemed to have died at the moment he was taken prisoner, i.e. as a free Roman citizen, so that his will made prior to captivity could be regarded as valid (*fictio legis Corneliae*).

25 The wife of a *pater familias* only fell under his authority when she had married him in a particular way. This form of marriage originated in the early archaic period and was known as *conventio in manum*. The power that the *pater familias* had over his wife in such cases was termed *manus* and was no different from *patria potestas*.

26 Hence the term *heredes sui et necessarii*.

27 The main categories of persons entitled to claim *bonorum possessio* were the *liberi*, i.e. the legitimate children of the testator, irrespective of whether they became *sui iuris* at his death or not (including emancipated children); the *legitimi*, i.e. those persons who could inherit under the *ius civile*; the *cognati*, i.e. the nearest blood relatives of the deceased; and *vir et uxor*, i.e. the surviving husband or wife of the deceased.

28 This collection did not survive in its original form and very little is known on the way Iulianus performed his work. Modern reconstructions are based on commentaries and interpretations of jurists from the classical period, and a few fragments incorporated in the Digest of Justinian.

29 Edicts continued to be issued until as late as the fourth century AD, but the praetors had no control over the content, as they were bound to publish the edicts in the form delivered by Iulianus.

30 The archaic *comitia curiata* was now a purely formal body.

31 The sources display a great deal of ambiguity as to when and how the *leges* and the *plebiscita* acquired the same status. According to tradition, the principle that *plebiscita* were binding on all citizens was established by two earlier legislative enactments: the *lex Valeria Horatia* of 449 BC and the *lex Publilia Philonis* of 339 BC. Probably these laws provided that the resolutions of the plebeian assembly should be regarded as binding on all citizens, subject to their ratification by the senate and/or the assembly of the centuries.

32 The *comitia centuriata* was convened usually by a consul, the *comitia tributa* by a consul or praetor, and the *concilium plebis* by a tribune of the plebs.

33 The *leges rogatae* were distinguished from the *leges datae*, i.e. the laws issued by magistrates on special occasions after obtaining the senate's permission. The category of *leges datae* embraced the various *leges coloniae* and *leges provinciae* whereby new colonies and provinces were founded.

34 It should be noted that legislative measures proposed by magistrates were normally debated in the senate before promulgation. This debate was much more important than any public discussions that might occur in *contiones*.

35 The state treasury was also known as *aerarium Saturni* because it was located in the temple of Saturn.

36 The period between the formal enactment of a law and its coming into force was termed *vacatio legis*.

37 Sometimes the preamble also included certain words indicating the subject matter of the statute. Examples include the *lex Hortensia de plebiscitis* (287 BC), providing that the resolutions of the plebeian assembly were binding on all citizens, the *lex Sempronia agraria* (133 BC), concerning the distribution of public lands (*ager publicus*), and the *lex Sempronia de provocatione* (123 BC), confirming the right of citizens convicted of capital offences to appeal to the people's assembly (*ius provocationis*).

38 For example, the *sanctio* could state that a previous law remained fully or partially in force despite the introduction of the new law.

39 An illustration is the *lex Falcidia delegatis* (40 BC) mentioned by Gaius (2. 227), which prohibited legacies from reducing the remaining property to the heir to below one-quarter of the value of the inheritance.

40 For example, consider the *lex Cincia de donis et muneribus* of 204 BC. This plebiscite prohibited the issue of gifts for the performance of tasks when such performance was regarded as a sacred duty. Gifts promised in violation of this law were not void, but the donor could raise an exception (*exceptio legis Cinciae*) if he was sued for payment. The category of *leges imperfectae* was abolished in the post-classical period (AD 439) by an enactment of Emperors Theodosius II and Valentinian III. See C. 1. 14. 5; G. Rotondi, *Leges publicae populi Romani*, Milan 1912, repr. Olms 1966, 153 ff.

41 Established by the *lex Silia*, an early statute of unknown date, and extended by the *lex Calpurnia* (passed probably after 204 BC).

42 For instance, the *legis actio per iudicis arbitrive postulationem* was extended by a *lex Licinia* (an early statute of unknown date) to the settlement of controversies between co-owners.

43 G. 3. 210. The *lex Aquilia* was divided into three chapters: the first and third chapters dealt with unlawful injury to property as such and the second chapter addressed the *adstipulator*, a particular kind of surety or joint creditor. The first chapter elaborated that when someone had wrongfully killed another person's slave or four-footed grazing animal (*pecus*), he was obliged to pay the owner the highest value of such slave or animal during the past year. The third chapter declared that when a person caused damage not encompassed by the first chapter and deriving from wrongful burning, breaking or spoiling, he would be condemned to pay the owner the value of the damaged object as existing in the

thirty days prior to the damage. And see *Inst.* 4. 3; D. 9. 2. 2. pr.; D. 9. 2. 2. 2; D. 9. 2. 27. 5.

44 It was usual to attach a qualification to the formal words that urged the magistrate to execute the wishes of the senate 'if they see fit' (*si eis videretur*). Even where such qualification was omitted, it was implied.

45 Besides playing a part in the formulation of legislative proposals, the senate indirectly exercised a law-making influence by advising the praetors and other jurisdictional magistrates to implement certain lines of policy. In such cases its recommendations would normally be incorporated in the *edictum perpetuum* issued by each magistrate at the commencement of his year of office. In this way, the senate contributed to the development of the *ius honorarium*, i.e. the law that derived its formal force from the authority of a magistrate, as opposed to the *ius civile* construed as the law that derived its formal force from *lex* and *interpretatio*.

46 It is therefore not surprising that both the *senatus consulta* and the *leges* are mentioned as sources of law by Cicero. See *Topica* 5. 28.

47 D. 1. 2. 2. 6 (Pomponius).

48 Cicero is said to have contemplated writing, or probably wrote, a work where the civil law was reduced to an art (*de iure civili in artem redigendo*). Quintilian (12. 3. 10) suggests that this work was not finished but perhaps published posthumously.

49 This seems to be the opinion of Kaser, Talamanca and Wieacker. And see M. Kaser, *Zur Methode der römischen Rechtsfindung*, Göttingen 1962, 54 ff.

50 The influence of the Aristotelian systematic thinking is stressed by several scholars. See F. Schulz, *History of Roman Legal Science*, Oxford 1946, 62 ff. Other scholars emphasized the impact of rhetoric. See J. Stroux, *Römische Rechtswissenschaft und Rhetorik*, Potsdam 1949; U. Wesel, *Rhetorische Statuslehre und Gesetzesauslegung der römischen Juristen*, Köln 1967.

51 This was a form of logical analysis that both distinguished the various concepts and subsumed those sharing the same essential elements under common heads.

52 Hermagoras of Temnos, a Greek rhetorician of the Rhodian School, introduced the distinction between *thesis* and *antithesis*. This distinction helped the jurists to discern the general principle of a case and discard the particular circumstances. The jurists were probably also influenced by Hermagoras' doctrine of stasis. Stasis theory seeks to classify rhetorical problems (declamation themes, or real forensic and deliberative situations) according to the underlying structure that each dispute involves. Such a classification will interest the practising rhetor, as it may help him to identify an appropriate argumentative strategy. For example, patterns of argument appropriate to a question of fact (did the defendant act as alleged?) may be irrelevant in an evaluative dispute (was the defendant justified in acting?). Hermagoras identified four 'questions of stasis' called conjectural, definitional, qualitative and translative (stochasmos, horos, poiotes and metalepsis). Conjectural stasis refers to disagreement over matters of fact. Definitional stasis refers to a disagreement over the meaning of a word or phrase. Qualitative stasis refers to differences in judgment as to intangible properties such as virtue. Translative stasis exists when someone thinks the topic under discussion is inappropriate for the venue. Hermagoras also identified four kinds of stasis arising from the law: where the wording and the intention of a law might clash; where laws themselves might conflict; where a law might be ambiguous; and where one claims that there is a gap in the law to be filled by analogical reasoning. Quintilian reports that the first of these was often an issue among legal consultants (Quint. 7. 6. 1). Cicero puts ambiguity first, and adds definition (problems arising from the meaning of a word) at the end (*De Inv.* 2. 116). We know that the pupils of rhetoricians customarily practised arguing for or against reliance on the letter of the law as opposed to equity. While Roman jurists may have progressed towards a more liberal interpretation of the law, largely due to the general development away from the rigidity of archaic law, some of the actual arguments they employed were probably extracted from the rhetors' arsenal.

53 See Cicero, *De Orat.* 1. 48. 212; *Topica* 17. 65–66; Aulus Gellius, *N. A.* 14. 2; D. 4. 4. 3. 1 (Ulpianus); D. 31. 47 (Proculus).

54 See W. Kunkel, *Introduction to Roman Legal and Constitutional History*, 2nd edn, Oxford 1973, 96. And see Cicero, *Pro Murena* 4. 9; *De Off.* 2. 19. 65.

55 The jurists rarely argued cases in the courts of law – this was left to advocates (*oratores*). Although trained in law, advocates often relied on the help of jurists in difficult cases to ensure that their clients' claims were properly stated according to the prescribed *formulae*. Moreover, an advocate might seek a jurist's advice when he intended to request the granting of a new form of action from a magistrate (at the *in iure* stage of the proceedings), and when he pleaded the case before the judge (*apud iudicem*).

56 The *responsa* were expressed in a casuistic form: the jurist restated the factual aspects of the case in such a way as to illuminate the legal question presented to him. By drawing on the wealth of legal principles applied in the past or encountered within his own experience he rendered a decision, only obliquely referring to the principle or rule that supported it (see, for example, D. 41. 1. 60 and D. 47. 2. 52. 13). It should be noted that the casuistic form in which the *responsa* were expressed entailed considerable differences of opinion among individual jurists with respect to certain matters. In many cases opposing points of view were adopted by contemporary or by later jurists. Many of these controversies persisted for decades or even centuries. See Cicero, *De Finibus*, 1. 4. 17.

57 Systematic instruction by professional law teachers was not introduced until the later Empire.

58 See Cicero, *De Orat.* 1. 43. 191; *Brutus* 89. 306; Aulus Gellius, *N. A.* 13. 13. 1.

59 D. 1. 2. 2. 41 (Pomponius).

60 He declared that there were five *genera* of tutorship, and that as many *genera* of possession existed as there were 'causes' for acquiring the property of others.

61 The scheme appeared in the following style: X is the essential characteristic when the choice between D or non-D must be determined; X is present in the combination of facts A; X is not present in the combination of facts B; X is the *differentia specifica* between the classes A and B, which leads to the conclusion that A→D, while B→non-D. This scheme was elaborated further by the great Augustan jurist M. Antistius Labeo. Labeo had adopted the Stoic mode of expressing Aristotelian definitions in the form of implicative statements. His 'hypotheses' (*pithana*) very much resembled legal norms: if F then D; if non-F, then non-D, and so on. Such statements were later conceived as and called norms: *regulae iuris*. They were also often designated *definitiones* or *differentia* – terms that reflect their origin in Aristotelian thought.

62 For instance, he states that to act *vi* (by violence) is to perform a forbidden act (see D. 50. 17. 73. 2). He also summarized the exceptions to the rule forbidding work on holidays by formulating them so as to cover any work, the non-performance of which would cause damage (see Macr. *Sat.* 1. 16. 11).

63 D. 35. 1. 73. And see M. Kaser, *Das römische Privatrecht*, Munich 1971, 254.

64 Cicero, *De Orat.* 1. 246; Varro, *De R. R.* 2. 5. 11; D. 1. 2. 2. 39 (Pomponius).

65 D. 1. 2. 2. 38 (Pomponius).

66 Cicero, *Pro Cluent.* 141; *De Orat.* 2. 142. 224; D. 1. 2. 2. 39 (Pomponius).

67 D. 4. 3. 1. 1 (Ulpianus). This had a far-reaching effect, as it introduced equitable considerations into determining the validity of transactions. In practice, it enabled equitable defences to be pleaded in almost any action.

68 D. 46. 4. 18 (Florentinus); *Inst.* 3. 29. 2.

69 D. 1. 2. 2. 45 (Pomponius); *Inst.* 2. 25. pr.

70 D. 1. 2. 2. 44 (Pomponius).

71 According to Cicero, Servius was the first jurist to apply the dialectic method in the study of legal problems (*Brut.* 152 ff.). And see D. 1. 2. 2. 43 (Pomponius).

72 G. 4. 35.

73 For a reconstruction of works of the late republican jurists see O. Lenel, *Palingenesia iuris*

civilis, 2 vols, Leipzig 1889, repr. Graz 1960. See also F. Bremer, *Iurisprudentiae ante-hadrianae quae supersunt*, I, Leipzig 1896.

6 THE LATE REPUBLIC: THE ADMINISTRATION OF JUSTICE

1 G. 4. 30.
2 The term *damnum infectum* referred to a damage that threatened a person's property deriving from the defective state of a neighbouring property. The owner of the threatened property had an *actio damni infecti* against his neighbour. See G. 4. 31.
3 The word *actio* denoted the right granted by the magistrate to a plaintiff to prosecute his cause before a *iudex* (and see D. 45. 1. 51; *Inst.* 4. 6. pr.). It also referred to the action of a plaintiff whereby he initiated a suit, as well as to the whole proceedings, or to the *formula* granted for a specific claim. In this last meaning, *actio* was used as a synonym for *iudicium*.
4 G. 4. 47.
5 Also sometimes referred to as *actio ad exemplum*.
6 It should be noted that the *actio utilis* and the *actio in factum* were frequently used interchangeably, without any distinction between them. Further, their respective fields of application were not subject to any precise limitations.
7 In classical law, the period of *usucapio* was two years for land and one year for movables.
8 G. 3. 92–93; *Inst.* 3. 15. pr.
9 When fraud was committed in the context of such a contract, the victim initially had no remedy against the defrauder. The only exception was that the fraud had induced a mistake on his part. In the first century BC, the action for fraud (*actio doli*) was introduced for the compensation for any loss sustained. At the same time, the *exceptio doli* was granted to prevent any action based on the contract by the defrauder. See D. 4. 3. 1. pr. (Ulpianus).
10 A further division of actions existed between temporary actions (*actiones temporales*) and perpetual actions (*actiones perpetuae*). The former were actions that could be initiated only within a fixed period and the latter were those that could be instigated without any time limitations. For example, the *actiones temporales* embraced the *actiones aediliciae* (actions introduced by the aedilician edict) that had to be instituted within a six-month period, and the *actiones praetoriae* (actions originating in the praetorian edict) that had to be presented within a year (*actiones annales*). Under the formulary system, a temporary action was transformed into a perpetual one on completion of the *in iure* phase of the lawsuit (see D. 27. 7. 8. 1). In the post-classical period it was recognized that perpetual actions were extinguished after thirty years or, in certain exceptional cases, forty years from the time the plaintiff could institute legal proceedings. The term *actiones arbitrariae* denoted actions where the judge, if he reached the conclusion that the plaintiff was right, could ask the defendant to restore (*restituere*) the claimed object to the plaintiff. The defendant was absolved if he complied; if non-compliant, the judge could condemn him to pay a sum of money. The latter event had worse results for the defendant than the immediate fulfilment of the judge's order (he might be condemned to pay a higher amount and, in some cases, be branded as an *infamis*). The term *actiones famosae* referred to actions where the condemnation of the defendant entailed infamy (*infamia*), i.e. the diminution of his social standing accompanied by certain civil disabilities (see G. 4. 182). Actions that any Roman citizen could instigate as relating to the protection of general public interests (*ius populi*) were called *actiones populares* (see D. 47. 23. 1). This category encompassed, for example, the *actio legis Laetoriae* (an action instituted against a person who exploited a minor) and the *actio de albo corrupto* (an action initiated against a person who damaged or falsified the tablet displaying the inscription of the praetorian edict). These actions had a penal character and if the defendant was condemned, the penalty was usually paid to the plaintiff. However, in

some cases the penalty was paid to the state or divided between the state and the accuser. Finally, Roman law recognized certain preliminary actions (*actiones praeiudiciales*) that were dissimilar to the ordinary actions as they were not directly associated with specific claims. A preliminary action was concerned with establishing or clarifying certain matters on which an ordinary action depended (see G. 4. 44). The distinction between *actiones in rem* and *actiones in personam* was earlier mentioned (see Chapter 3 above).

11 G. 4. 39–44.

12 It should be noted that the *demonstratio* occurred only when the relevant claim was undetermined and it was hence necessary to furnish additional details in respect thereof.

13 G. 4. 48–52.

14 G. 4. 42.

15 G. 4. 44.

16 G. 4. 131.

17 G. 4. 120.

18 G. 4. 125.

19 For example, a defendant might raise a dilatory (*dilatoria*) exception to bar the plaintiff's action on the grounds that the action was instituted prematurely, i.e. before the passing of the prescribed period (*dilatoria ex tempore*). An alternative ground was that the person who launched the action was legally incapable of so acting (*dilatoria ex persona*). In such cases, before the conclusion of the *in iure* phase of the proceedings the plaintiff could withdraw his action and institute it again later, i.e. after the prescribed period had passed, or after the impediment relating to the capacity of the person who instigated the action was removed. If the plaintiff did not withdraw his action, a dilatory exception resembled a peremptory exception as its acceptance entailed rejection of his claim. See G. 4. 116, 119, 121–22, 123–24.

20 For example, the *lex Laetoria* (192–1 BC) provided such an exception. This law aspired to protect persons under twenty-five years of age (*minores*) who were defrauded in a transaction. Although the transaction may have been *prima facie* valid, the person defrauded could bar the plaintiff's action for payment by raising an *exceptio legis Laetoriae*.

21 G. 4. 118.

22 Probably during the classical period, a further division of exceptions emerged between personal exceptions (*exceptiones personae cohaerentes*) and non-personal ones (*exceptiones rei cohaerentes*). The former could be invoked only by the defendant himself; the latter could be raised by the defendant or any other person acting on his behalf.

23 G. 4. 126; D. 44. 1. 2. 1 (Ulpianus).

24 G. 4. 127–28.

25 If the defendant failed to appear on the set date, the *vindex* was liable to the plaintiff who could initiate a praetorian *actio in factum* against him.

26 Moreover, in order to force the defendant's appearance the praetor could issue a *missio in possessionem*. This coercive measure authorized the plaintiff to acquire possession of the defendant's property. In addition, the praetor could grant the plaintiff an *actio in factum* that compelled the defendant to pay the plaintiff a sum of money. G. 4. 46 and 183.

27 A plaintiff who was denied an action could present the case before another praetor, or request a tribune to exercise his veto (*intercessio*) against the praetor's decision.

28 In the *per formulam* procedure, if the defendant raised an exception he was deemed to assume the position of a plaintiff with regard to that exception. See D. 44. 1. 1 (Ulpianus).

29 D. 42. 2. 1 (Paulus).

30 XII T. III 1.

31 It is important to remember that in preparing the *formula* the praetor was concerned with effectuating the real intentions of the parties. Initially, only the praetor prepared

the *formula*, but later the completion of this document involved consultation with the relevant parties.

32 G. 4. 90 and 114.

33 The death of the plaintiff following the *litis contestatio* did not necessarily entail the extinction of his claim. In such a case, the relevant action could be transferred to the plaintiff's heirs. This occurred even though it was impossible before the *litis contestatio* due to the personal nature of the claim. However, the rule that events transpiring after the *litis contestatio* did not affect the nature of the original claims was subject to certain exceptions. For example, it was recognized that if the object in dispute was accidentally destroyed the defendant was no longer liable. Moreover, in actions relating to property (*actiones in rem*) it was accepted that the unsuccessful defendant had to return to the plaintiff the property claimed and the fruits he collected, or should have collected, from the property.

34 This rule, also known to modern law, is expressed by the phrase *bis de eadem re ne sit actio* or, briefly, *ne bis in idem*.

35 On the effects of the *litis contestatio* see J. G. Wolff, *Die litis contestatio im römischen Zivilprocess*, Karlsruhe 1968. And see M. Kaser, *Das römische Zivilprozessrecht*, Munich 1996, 285 ff, 295 ff.

36 Judges played an important part in the development of private law, as their decisions were often scrutinized by the praetor when modifying existing *formulae* or creating new ones.

37 Although, in principle, any Roman citizen could serve as an advocate, this task was usually performed by senators or members of the equestrian class. The advocates were persons trained in the art of rhetoric, which was first taught in Rome during the second century BC. An important aspect of the relevant instruction was devoted to the selection of the arguments that must be employed in dealing with a particular legal issue. The courts provided an excellent stage for the display of a person's skills as an orator and powers of persuasion. Forensic advocacy reached its highest point of development during the later republican period when success at the law courts was a key that opened the door to a flourishing political career. Advocates usually referred to previous cases to extract support for their arguments. Their arguments often focused on the interpretation of the praetorian *formula* and the question of whether the remedy it granted was justifiable in the circumstances. Thus, their views were often considered by the praetor when altering existing *formulae* or developing new ones. In this way, the advocates played a part in the evolution of the *ius praetorium*. During the Republic advocates did not receive any remuneration for their services, although they were occasionally given gifts or small symbolic payments. See G. Kennedy, *The Art of Rhetoric in the Roman World* (300 BC–AD 300), Princeton 1972; J. A. Crook, *Legal Advocacy in the Roman World*, London 1995, M. C. Alexander, *Forensic Advocacy in the Late Roman Republic*, Toronto 1977; J. M. Kelly, *Roman Litigation*, Oxford 1966; *Studies in the Civil Judicature of the Roman Republic*, Oxford 1976.

38 The proceedings were not formally recorded, although private records could be compiled by the litigants.

39 Witnesses (*testes*) were required to swear an oath before presenting their testimony. If a witness was unable to appear in person, his testimony could be read in court after it was recorded in writing (*testimonia per tabellam dare*). The written evidence included letters (*epistolae*), memoranda (*libelli*), written declarations (*cautiones*), private account books (*tabulae accepti et expensi*), wills and other documents. When these documents were produced they were sealed in the presence of witnesses (*obsignatores*) and delivered to the judge who opened them in court. Moreover, the evidence included the results of inspections performed by experts and state officials. A confession before the judge (*confessio in iudicio*) was also relevant as evidence, but its value was determined by the judge at his discretion.

40 For example, the child of a married woman was presumed to be a legitimate child. See D. 1. 6. 6 (Ulpianus).

41 D. 42. 1. 47. pr. (Paulus). Under the Law of the Twelve Tables, if one of the parties was absent the judge had to wait until noon before he pronounced his verdict. The relevant provision probably still applied in the context of the formulary procedure. However, uncertainty prevails as to whether this provision pertained to the decision of the praetor in the *in iure* phase of the proceedings, or that of the judge in the *apud iudicem* phase.

42 In D. 4. 8. 13. 4 (Ulpianus); D. 42. 1. 36 (Paulus); Aulus Gellius, *N. A.* 14. 2. 25; Cicero, *Pro Caec.* 4.

43 In the former case, the defendant had to pay the plaintiff a certain sum of money (*condemnatio pecuniaria*) that was often determined by the judge with regard to considerations of good faith and equity.

44 In some cases, the *adiudicatio* could be accompanied by a *condemnatio pecuniaria*, when this was necessary for the fair division of the common property.

45 According to Gaius, a plaintiff might have demanded more than he was entitled to in relation to the object (*re*), the time (*tempore*), the place (*loco*) and the cause (*causa*) of the relevant action. In a *pluris petitio re* the plaintiff claimed a larger amount than was owed to him; in a *pluris petitio tempore* he requested the payment of a debt before the payment was actually due; in a *pluris petitio loco* he demanded that payment be issued to him at a place different from that originally agreed; and in a *pluris petitio causa* he claimed a specific object although the defendant was entitled to choose between two or more objects. In all the above cases, the plaintiff definitely lost his case. See G. 4. 53; *Inst.* 4. 6. 33. In some exceptional cases the praetor could grant the plaintiff a *restitutio in integrum*, a special remedy designed to reinstate the parties' former legal position. See Girard, *Textes* I, p. 285.

46 G. 4. 56 and 122.

47 G. 3. 180.

48 One of the legal consequences of declaring a person an *infamis* was his exclusion from holding public office (*turpi iudicio damnati omni honore ac dignitate privantur*). See Cicero, *Pro Cluent.* 42; *Pro Sull.* 31. 32.

49 A judicial decision might be declared invalid if a condition relating to the legality of the relevant process had not been met. For example, this occurred when the decision was issued by a judge who did not meet the prescribed age limit for eligibility.

50 See, Girard, *Textes* I, p. 345.

51 G. 4. 25.

52 See Ulpianus, *disp.* 3. 7, in Girard, *Textes* I, p. 454; also in FIRA II, p. 310.

53 Discussed in Chapter 3 above.

54 The praetor Publius Rutilius introduced the *venditio bonorum* before 118 BC and this was probably modelled on a similar procedure adopted by the quaestors for enforcing the payment of debts to the public treasury (*aerarium*). G. 4. 35.

55 See G. 3. 80.

56 G. 4. 145.

57 G. 4. 35.

58 D. 27. 10. 5 (Gaius).

59 G. 3. 78.

60 D. 42. 3. 4. pr. (Ulpianus).

61 G. 4. 91.

62 For example, a guardian (*curator*) could be ordered to promise that his administration of the property owned by the person under his protection will not diminish the property's value. See G. 1. 199.

63 D. 46. 5. 1 (Ulpianus).

64 D. 46. 5. 2 (Ulpianus).

65 D. 46. 5. 3 (Ulpianus).

66 *Minores* were persons who exceeded the age of *impuberes* (fourteen years for boys and twelve years for girls) and were under twenty-five years of age.

67 The *interdicta* and the *restitutiones in integrum* still habitually feature in modern law as adapted in accordance with contemporary requirements.

68 G. 4. 139–40; *Inst.* 4. 15. pr.

69 See, for example, the *interdictum de locis publicis* in D. 43. 8. 1 (Paulus), the *interdictum ne quid in loco sacro fiat* in D. 43. 6. 1 (Ulpianus) and the *interdictum de arboribus caedendis* in D. 43. 27. 1. pr. and 7 (Ulpianus).

70 G. 4. 140. 142.

71 Furthermore, a distinction was drawn between *interdicta simplicia* and *interdicta duplicia* (see G. 4. 156–60; *Inst.* 4. 15. 7). With respect to the former, the relevant order addressed one of the parties to a dispute. Regarding the latter, at the same time either party was defendant and plaintiff. This category enveloped, for example, the *interdicta uti possidetis* and *utrubi* that were concerned with the maintenance of an existing possessory situation (see G. 4. 139. 143).

72 Only a magistrate had the right to institute a charge against a citizen (as well as to summon the assembly), thus it was necessary for an accuser to appeal to a magistrate so that a formal accusation could be lodged against a person suspected of a crime.

73 The immense concentration of impoverished citizens in Rome during this period was accompanied by a rapid increase in crime, especially violent crime. At the same time, the lure of money tempted the greedy and malfeasance in office gained appeal with its anticipated high rewards. As no regular police force existed in Rome, the detection of criminals was usually relegated to the injured parties or common informers, and this made the prosecution of offenders very difficult. In response to the escalating threat against public order, responsibility for the prosecution and punishment of certain offences, especially offences committed by slaves, foreigners and citizens from the lower classes of society, was assigned to the *tresviri capitales*, low-ranking magistrates elected by the *comitia tributa*. See Cicero, *De Legibus* 3. 6; Sall., *Cat.* 55; Aulus Gellius, *N. A.* 3. 3. 15; Livy, 39. 14. 10; Pliny, *N. H.* 21. 8; Val. Max., 5. 4. 7; 6. 1. 10; 8. 4. 2; Varro, 50. 50. 5. 81; D. 1. 2. 2. 30.

74 However, in 123 BC a statute passed on the initiative of C. Gracchus (*lex Sempronia de capite civis*) reaffirmed the principle that no citizen could be punished for a capital crime without the sanction of the assembly. This law seems to have forbidden the establishment of special tribunals by senatorial decree alone and without the approval of the people.

75 See Livy 39. 8–19; Cicero, *De Legibus* 2. 37; and see *SC de Bacchanalibus* in FIRA I, p. 240.

76 Until the passing of the *lex Sempronia iudiciaria* in 123 BC, the *consilium* was composed exclusively of members from the senatorial class.

77 The money and other effects that were allegedly extorted, and would be restored if the prosecution proved successful, were known as *pecuniae* or *res repetundae*, or simply *repetundae*. One should note that a charge of extortion could only be instituted against a provincial magistrate after he had demitted office.

78 As in civil actions, proceedings were initiated by the injured party, in this case the aggrieved provincials.

79 In later years, the person found guilty of extortion was condemned to pay twice the value of the illegally appropriated property; other penalties that could be imposed included the expulsion of the offender from the senate and the declaration that he was an *infamis*.

80 The Romans neither shared the modern reluctance to create extraordinary or special tribunals nor did they espouse the principle enshrined in many contemporary legal systems against retroactive legislation.

81 The crime of *peculatus* was distinguished from the theft of private property, termed

furtum. The punishment for embezzlement of public funds was normally a fine that usually amounted to four times the value of the stolen property. Similar in some respects to *peculatus* was the *sacrilegium*, the theft of sacred objects (*res religiosae*). This offence entailed the death penalty, but the culprit was allowed to go into exile before the sentence was pronounced. In that event, he became subject to an *aquae et ignis interdictio*.

82 Before the enactment of this law the tribunes could still convene the *comitia* to hear charges of treason. Sulla terminated this practice by restricting the powers of the tribunes. At the same time, he broadened the definition of the *crimen maiestatis* to encompass any act performed by a Roman citizen that impaired the safety and dignity of the state. The scope of this crime then embraced wrongdoings that were previously treated as *perduellio* or *proditio*, such as sedition, unlawful attacks against magistrates, desertion and the like. Moreover the *lex Varia* of 92 BC stipulated that treason was committed by those who 'by help and advice' (*ope et consilio*) induced an allied state to take up arms against Rome. In the closing years of the first century BC, two further statutes on the crime of *maiestas* were enacted: the *lex Iulia maiestatis* of Julius Caesar (46 BC) and the *lex Iulia maiestatis* of Augustus (8 BC). Several later imperial laws were based on these statutes. The *crimen maiestatis* was punishable by death, although the person charged with the offence was usually allowed to go into exile before the court pronounced the sentence (in such a case, he was subject to an *aqua et ignis interdictio*). On the crime of treason see R. A. Bauman, *The Crimen Maiestatis in the Roman Republic and Augustan Principate*, Johannesburg 1967.

83 A series of laws devised to repress corrupt electoral practices were introduced during the second and first centuries BC, such as the *lex Cornelia Baebia* (181 BC), the *lex Cornelia Fulvia* (159 BC), the *lex Maria* (119 BC), the *lex Acilia Calpurnia* (67 BC), the *lex Tullia* (63 BC), the *lex Licinia* (55 BC) and the *lex Pompeia* (52 BC). The last law on *ambitus* was the *lex Iulia de ambitu* passed by Augustus in 18 BC.

84 An inscription attributed to C. Claudius Pulcher, consul in 92 BC, refers to his position as *iudex quaestionis veneficis*. See H. Dessau, *Inscriptiones Latinae Selectae*, Berlin 1892–1916, 45.

85 Cicero, *Pro Cluent.* 148–49. 151. 154; D. 48. 8. 1 (Marcianus); C. 9. 16.

86 This court was created by the *lex Cornelia de iniuriis* of 82 BC. Of course, *iniuria* was also a delict, and the criminal and delictual procedures operated side by side. See Cicero, *Pro Caec.* 12. 35; D. 3. 3. 42. 1 (Paulus); D. 47. 10. 5. pr. (Ulpianus).

87 This was instituted by the *lex Cornelia testamentaria* or *de falsis* of 81 BC. See Cicero, II *in Verr.* 1.

88 This court was established by the *lex Lutatia de vi* in 78 BC; that law was supplemented by the *lex Plautia de vi* passed around 63 BC. There were two kinds of violent crime, the *vis publica* and the *vis privata*. The former covered various forms of seditious conduct that fell outside the scope of the *crimen maiestatis*, as well as the organization and arming of gangs for the purpose of obstructing the activities of state organs. The punishment for such offences was banishment. On the other hand, the *vis privata* covered acts of violence against individuals and, like theft, was considered a private offence (*delictum*). The distinction between the two forms of violent crime was confirmed by two laws of Augustus, the *lex Iulia de vi publica* and the *lex Iulia de vi privata*. See D. 48. 6 and 7; C. 9. 12.

89 This court was instituted by the *lex Fabia de plagiariis* (of unknown date, but probably first century BC). D. 48. 15; C. 9. 20.

90 Established by the *lex Licinia de sodaliciis* of Crassus in 55 BC.

91 Installed by the *lex Iulia de adulteriis* of Augustus in 18 BC. See D. 48. 5; C. 9. 9.

92 In the last century of the Republic, *quaestiones extraordinariae* were still occasionally created by special statutes to deal with certain offences falling outside the jurisdiction of the permanent courts.

93 Under the *lex Pompeia* of 55 BC, the jurors were still chosen from the three groups mentioned in the *lex Aurelia* but only the richest men within each group were eligible. The *lex Iulia iudiciorum* of Caesar, passed probably in 46 BC, excluded the *tribuni aerarii* from the lists of jurors. Finally, Augustus restored the three classes of the Aurelian law and added a fourth that represented the lower classes of the community. As Augustus exercised control over the senatorial and equestrian classes, it may be safely assumed that during his time criminal courts decided cases in line with the official, that is Augustan, policies.

94 After the enactment of the *lex Calpurnia* (149 BC) that established the court of *repetundae*, the duty of presiding over the relevant proceedings was assigned to the *praetor peregrinus* as most claimants were foreigners. As the case-load increased and new standing courts were created, the number of praetors was later enlarged to eight and six of these presided over the courts. The praetors were assigned to the different courts by lot after the senate decided which courts should be presided over by a praetor. Usually praetors were allocated to courts dealing with offences of a political nature, such as extortion, electoral corruption, conspiracy against the state, treason and embezzlement. Aediles were usually assigned (also by lot) to courts addressing murder, violence and fraud. The presiding magistrate had to swear that he would abide by the statute that installed the court and could be liable to punishment if found guilty of corruption.

95 Initially, only the aggrieved party or his closest relatives were entitled to initiate an indictment, but in later times almost every citizen of good repute had the right to launch an indictment and conduct a prosecution. However, accusers motivated by the prospect of personal gain often abused the indictment procedure. Despite the possibility of a suit of slander against false accusers, some people even carved a profession from accusing wealthy fellow-citizens.

96 Cicero, *Div. in Caec.* 64; *Inst.* 4. 18. 1.

97 Where two or more persons applied at the same time for leave to institute an indictment against the same individual, a panel of jurors determined who had priority by considering the cases of all those seeking permission to prosecute (*divinatio*).

98 D. 48. 2. 3. pr. (Paulus).

99 *Calumnia* (*crimen calumniae*) was committed when a person launched charges against another knowing that the latter was innocent. False accusers were liable to severe penalties that entailed infamy and exclusion from public office. *Praevaricatio* referred to the collusion between the accuser and the accused in a criminal trial for the purpose of obtaining the latter's acquittal. A person found guilty of *praevaricatio* was harshly punished and branded with infamy. See Cicero, *Ad Fam.* 8. 8. 3.

100 See FIRA I, 7. 11. 30–35.

101 Under the *lex Acilia* the jury had to be empanelled immediately after the *nominis delatio*. But this exposed the jurors to the dangers of intimidation and corruption. Thus, subsequent to Sulla's judicial reforms, juries were empanelled after the *inquisitio* and shortly before trial day.

102 Under the *lex Acilia* (123/122 BC) the *album iudicum* comprised 450 persons, but in later years the number was increased (probably to 900). The praetor was required to publicize the list of jurors and to swear an oath that only the best men had been chosen. See FIRA I, 7. 11. 12–18.

103 Roman legal procedure was governed by the principle that a person could not be appointed as a juror without the consent of the parties concerned. The rules governing the *iudicum reiectio* were settled by the *lex Vatinia* of 59 BC.

104 On the selection of the *iudices* see A. H. M. Jones, *The Criminal Courts of the Roman Republic and Principate*, Oxford 1972, 66 ff.

105 The accused stood in a particularly strong position, as he was entitled to as many as six advocates and was granted twice the total speaking time allocated to the prosecution. It should be noted that if the accuser failed to appear in court on the day of the trial his

case was dismissed. On the other hand, the absence of the accused did not preclude the proceedings. However, in such a case it was required (under a law of Augustus) that a condemnatory verdict be unanimous. See Cassius Dio 54. 3.

106 The magistrate's role was largely formal – he did not decide points of law, summarize the evidence and so on in the manner of a modern judge sitting with a jury

107 The category of documentary evidence comprised records of various kinds, such as account books (*tabulae accepti et expensi*), letters (*epistolae*), written notices (*libelli*) and, in some cases, the account books of those entrusted with the collection of public revenues (*publicani, tabulae publicanorum*). The written evidence also included the statements of witnesses who were unable to appear in court in person for various reasons (ill health, old age, absence from Rome and so on). It also incorporated certain public statements relating to the case issued by state organs (*testimonia publica*).

108 Witnesses for the defence were often invited to speak not only about facts but also about the accused's character – those who testified to the good character of the accused were referred to as *laudatores*. Character evidence carried special weight and the absence of *laudatores* was regarded as damning in itself.

109 In such a case, jurors probably had to erase both 'A' and 'C' and scratch in the letters 'NL'. Just to erase 'A' and 'C' counted as no vote.

110 See FIRA I, 7. 11. 46–48. After the enactment of the *lex Servilia Glauciae* (*c.* 101 BC), proceedings in trials for extortion (*de rebus repetundis*) were divided into two distinct parts (*comperendinatio*). In the first part (*actio prima*), the parties elaborated their arguments and witnesses on both sides were called upon to testify. The second part (*actio secunda*) occurred after a day's interval and the parties were granted the opportunity to comment on the evidence presented and provide additional information. After this second hearing the jurors issued their verdict, which now only assumed the form of 'guilty' or 'innocent' (the 'not proven' option was not available).

111 The term *poena capitalis* (or *poena capitis*) did not refer only to the death penalty but to any penalty involving the loss of a citizen's *caput*, i.e. his personal freedom or rights as a Roman citizen. Imprisonment was not recognized as a form of punishment in the Roman criminal justice system.

112 Naturally, in times of unrest persons regarded as dangerous were ruthlessly put to death. It may have been routine practice to eliminate malefactors from the lower classes by irregular means. Moreover, it should be noted that no immunity from the death penalty was ever enjoyed by non-citizens.

113 The phrase *aquae et ignis interdictio* implies a denial of the necessaries of life to the individual in question.

114 The relevant resolution might, however, specify an extended area within which the interdiction was operative.

7 THE PRINCIPATE:
THE HISTORICAL, SOCIAL AND CONSTITUTIONAL BACKGROUND

1 As J. M. Kelly remarks, 'Augustus . . . appears to have had a genuine reverence for ancestral Roman laws and manners, and this alone might have led him to preserve everything in the old constitution which was not inconsistent with his own permanent ascendancy. But, if so, it was a course which political calculation would in any case have suggested; the soothing appearance of restoration could effectively conceal the disturbing reality of revolution'. *A Short History of Western Legal Theory*, Oxford 1992, 43.

2 The *imperium proconsulare* of Augustus differed in some important respects from that of the ordinary and extraordinary proconsuls appointed under the Republic: (i) it was universal, extending without restriction over all parts of the empire (hence its description as *imperium proconsulare infinitum*); (ii) it was not limited in time but perpetual, requiring no renewal; (iii) it remained in force both within and outside the city of Rome

(*pomerium*). Such proconsular power was referred to as *imperium proconsulare maius* to indicate its superiority over the ordinary *imperium* of the proconsuls who governed the senatorial provinces.

3 Subsequent emperors regarded their *auctoritas* as the ultimate source of their acts in the legislative, judicial and administrative fields (*ex auctoritate nostra*).

4 In the establishment and consolidation of the new political system, the Augustan ideology had a very important role. From the beginning, this ideology helped to justify and legitimate Augustus' claims, and make propaganda for his own achievements. Besides legitimizing Augustus' powers, the slogans of Augustan ideology helped to strengthen the system and make it stable and were a decisive factor in identifying the family of the *princeps* with the state. Moreover, Augustus sought to foster the mystique of imperial power by encouraging his own worship in the provinces.

5 The custom of granting the emperor the power of *imperium* by statute had its origins in the *lex curiata de imperio* by which the higher magistrates of the Republic received their *imperium*. However, with the decline and eventual disappearance of the popular assemblies and the further strengthening of imperial authority in the second century AD, the notion that the emperor's *imperium* stemmed from the will of the people became devoid of all substance.

6 In the second century AD it was established that government positions, which in the past were usually occupied by freedmen, were to be manned by equestrians.

7 The office was initially held by two, then by three or, occasionally, four individuals.

8 As they exercised their judicial functions in the name of the emperor, no appeal was allowed against their decisions.

9 The jurists Ulpianus and Paulus (third century AD) wrote extensive treatises on the powers and functions of the *praefectus urbi*, which are quoted in the Digest of Justinian.

10 The *praefectus annonae*, who was chosen from the equestrian class, had general jurisdiction in matters connected with the supply and trade of foodstuffs.

11 Like the *praefectus annonae*, the *praefectus vigilum* was chosen from the equestrian class. Over the years he acquired jurisdictional powers in cases involving offences against the public order and in certain civil cases involving disputes arising from leasing of houses.

12 In Roman private law *procurator* was a technical term referring to a legal agent entrusted with the management of another person's property. The term *procurator Caesaris* originally denoted an official who managed property belonging to the emperor. However, since no clear distinction between imperial property and state property was drawn, the procurators were in reality public officials. Although during the early Principate many freedmen were admitted to the procuratorship, the procurators were generally chosen from the ranks of the equestrians.

13 For a closer look at the development of the imperial civil service see A. H. M. Jones, 'The Roman Civil Service', in *Studies in Roman Government and Law*, Oxford 1960, 153–75; F. Jacques and J. Scheid, *Rom und das Reich in der Hohen Kaiserzeit*, Stuttgart and Leipzig 1998, 108 ff. H. G. Pflaum, *Les procurateurs équestres sous le haut-empire romain*, Paris 1950; P. C. Weaver, 'Freedmen procurators in the imperial administration', 14 *Historia* (1965), 460–69.

14 On the development of the *consilium principis* see J. A. Crook, *Consilium Principis: Imperial Councils and Counselors from Augustus to Diocletian*, Cambridge 1955.

15 Although the fiscus was not regarded as personal property of the emperor, it was controlled and administered by him through specially appointed officials, the *procuratores a rationibus* or *fisci*. In the course of time, the *fiscus* assumed a special legal personality and, from the late second century AD, it began to be represented in the courts when disputes arose between the *fiscus* and private individuals concerning debts. Distinct from the *fiscus* was the personal property of the emperor, referred to as *patrimonium Caesaris*, which was administered by officials known as *procuratores patrimonii*. Upon the emperor's death, the *patrimonium Caesaris* went to his heirs according to the rules

governing testamentary succession. The *fiscus*, by contrast, was transferred to his successor to the throne. On the imperial *fiscus* see P. A. Brunt, 'The fiscus and its development' and 'Remarks on the imperial fiscus', in *Roman Imperial Themes*, Oxford 1990, ch. 7 and 16. See also A. H. M. Jones, 'The aerarium and the fiscus', in *Studies in Roman Government and Law*, Oxford 1960, ch. 6; F. Millar, 'The fiscus in the first two centuries', 53 *JRS* (1963), 29–42.

16 Augustus reduced the number of senators from nine hundred to six hundred by expelling those persons whom he regarded as unworthy of holding the position of senator. At the same time he appointed a number of new members from among his closest friends and supporters. The right of the emperor to revise the composition of the senate (*lectio senatus*), admitting new members and excluding those whom he deemed undesirable, was connected with his censorial powers and his position as upholder of the laws and morals of the community (*cura legum et morum*). Moreover, the emperor was able to admit new members into the senate indirectly by conferring the title of ex-magistrates on persons who had not in the past held a magistracy or who had served as magistrates of a rank lower than that required for admission to the senate (*adlectio*). In this way many prominent equestrians and members of the urban aristocracy in Italy became senators. In the course of the first and second centuries AD the composition of the senate underwent a considerable change as more and more Roman citizens from the provinces were admitted to it, while the number of senators belonging to Roman and Italian families continued to decline. Augustus also passed a law, the *lex Iulia de senatu habendo* (*c.* 10 BC), introducing rules concerning the function of the senate.

17 Under certain circumstances, the senate could also issue a special decree publicly stigmatizing an emperor whose conduct was deemed disgraceful (*damnatio memoriae*). This could be done during the emperor's lifetime or posthumously.

18 Within their jurisdiction fell, in particular, cases involving the question of whether a person was a slave or a free person (*causae liberales*) and cases concerning the protection of minors.

19 Whereas during the Republic the office of consul was normally held by two persons in the course of one year, it now became common practice to appoint several pairs of consuls during one year, and this number varied according to the number of persons on whom the emperor wished to bestow the title. Under normal circumstances, the consuls remained in office for a period of two months (thus there were twelve consuls in each year). The two consuls who took office at the beginning of the year (*consules ordinarii*) gave their name to the year and were held in higher honour than those who followed (the latter were referred to as *consules suffecti* or *consules minores*).

20 During the Principate the number of praetors was increased, initially to twelve and later to eighteen. Of these, the *praetor urbanus* and the *praetor peregrinus* had general jurisdiction, while the jurisdiction of the rest was limited to certain matters only. Thus, in the Augustan era the management of the public treasury (*aerarium*) was entrusted to two praetors, referred to as *praetores aerarii*; from the time of Claudius a special praetor was appointed to deal with cases concerning trust estates (*praetor de fideicommissis*); under Nerva a special praetor was entrusted with the resolution of disputes that arose between private individuals and the imperial exchequer (*praetor fiscalis*); and in the time of the Antonine emperors the appointment of guardians and the resolution of disputes which arose between guardians were consigned to a special praetor known as *praetor tutelarius*.

21 The office of *praetor peregrinus* disappeared after the Roman citizenship was granted to all the free inhabitants of the empire in the early third century AD.

22 An important basis of the emperor's power was the *tribunicia potestas* with which he was vested for life and against which no *intercessio* could be raised either by a tribune or by any other magistrate.

23 The aedileship finally disappeared in the third century AD.

24 The quaestorship retained some significance as ex-quaestors were regularly admitted to the senate and were eligible for senior positions in the imperial administration.

25 The *comitia curiata*, Rome's oldest assembly, continued to function in a shadowy form as a gathering of thirty lictors (*lictores*) representing the thirty *curiae* into which the *populus Romanus* was divided in early times. Before them, and under the supervision of the *pontifex maximus*, took place the *adrogatio per populum*, the formal procedure through which a person *sui iuris* and his descendants passed by adoption into another family. This procedure was later superseded by the *adrogatio per rescriptum principis*, by which adoption was effected by a rescript of the emperor without further formalities.

26 Moreover, on the accession of a new emperor, the centuriate assembly passed a special law, the *lex de imperio*, by which the senate's choice was ratified and the emperor was invested with supreme powers. The republican tradition of the sovereign people as the ultimate source of political power was so deeply implanted that as late as the late second century AD the necessity of the imperial investiture by a *lex* appeared indispensable to the jurists. See, for example, Gaius, 1. 5. See also *lex de imperio Vespasiani* (AD 69), in V. Ehrenberg and A. H. M. Jones, *Documents illustrating the reigns of Augustus and Tiberius*, 2nd edn, Oxford 1955, 364.

27 In the time of Augustus, the emperor proposed the persons whom he desired to be elected to the consulship and half the number of candidates for the other magistracies, while the remaining places were, in principle, open to free competition. There were two ways in which the emperor could nominate a candidate: by simply expressing his support for a person (such an informal recommendation was termed *suffragatio* and was not regarded as binding), and by *commendatio*, a binding recommendation of a candidate. A further system was the *destinatio* that applied to the election of the consuls and praetors. Under this system, a body composed of senators and equestrians submitted to the assembly the candidates for these two offices. However, this system does not appear to have lasted for a long period. Finally, from the time of Tiberius it became customary for the emperor to nominate the consuls and a number of the lower magistrates, while the rest were chosen by the senate. The role of the *comitia* was limited to the mere confirmation of the candidates selected following the formal announcement of their names (*renuntiatio*) by the senate.

28 The last law passed by the *comitia* was a *lex agraria* enacted under Emperor Nerva (AD 96–98). This law is mentioned in the Digest of Justinian in an extract of the jurist Callistratus (D. 47. 21. 3. 1).

29 For a biographical study of the Roman emperors consider M. Grant, *The Roman Emperors: A Biographical Guide to the Rulers of Imperial Rome 31 BC–476 AD*, New York 1985.

30 Hence, the division of the Roman provinces into two categories: imperial provinces (*provinciae principis*) and senatorial provinces (*provinciae senatus*). The imperial provinces were governed by military officers termed *legati Augusti pro praetore*. The latter were appointed by the emperor and held, as his representatives, all the powers pertaining to his *imperium proconsulare*. The governors of the senatorial provinces were chosen from among those who had held the office of consul (for the provinces of Asia and Africa), or praetor (for the remaining provinces). By virtue of his *imperium*, the governor supervised the political and financial administration of his province and exercised general jurisdiction in civil and criminal matters. During the Principate, governors were more closely supervised by the central government, usually through imperial procurators. Outside the provinces but really within the empire, Augustus and his successors allowed some client kingdoms to exist (such as Pontus, Galatia, Cappadocia and Lesser Armenia.) These enjoyed internal self-government and paid no taxes to Rome, but their foreign relations were under the control of the emperor and they were bound to aid Rome militarily.

31 During the Principate, the practice of employing tax farmers (*publicani*) for the collection

of direct taxes (i.e. land and personal taxes) continued in some senatorial provinces, but in the imperial provinces the *publicani* were replaced by *procuratores* appointed by the emperor. Indirect taxes, on the other hand, continued to be collected by *publicani*, now under the supervision of imperial procurators. By the third century AD tax farming was superseded everywhere by the system of direct collection of taxes by *procuratores*.

32 In the provinces there existed many cities and towns whose inhabitants were allowed to administer their own affairs without direct interference from the Roman authorities. The various provincial communities (*coloniae, municipia, civitates peregrinorum*) had their own assemblies, magistrates and town councils. The latter were modelled on the Roman senate and consisted usually of a hundred members, termed *decuriones* or *senatores*, repre-senting the local aristocracy (*ordo decurionum*). With the progressive decline of the democratic institutions during the imperial era the *ordo decurionum* gradually came to assume the most important functions of the local assemblies.

33 In the first century AD Italy retained its privileged position in relation to the rest of the empire. Its inhabitants enjoyed all the rights of the Roman citizenship and Italian lands were exempted from taxation (*stipendium, tributum soli*) as they were subject to *dominium ex iure Quiritium*, i.e. ownership according to the rules of the Roman *ius civile*. In the course of time, however, as the centre of the empire's economic life gradually shifted from Italy to the provinces and an ever-increasing number of provincials were granted the Roman citizenship, the position of Italy came to be no different from that of the rest of the empire. As early as the time of Claudius (AD 41–54) provincials were admitted as members of the senate and, by the end of the first century AD, the office of emperor itself was opened to persons of Roman descent whose families lived in the provinces. On the administration of Italy and the provinces during the Principate see A. Lintott, *Imperium Romanum: Politics and Administration*, London and New York 1993, ch. 7–9; R. Thomsen, *The Italic Regions from Augustus to the Lombard Invasion*, Rome 1966; F. Jacques and J. Scheid, *Rom und das Reich in der Hohen Kaiserzeit*, Stuttgart and Leipzig 1998, 173 ff.

34 On the development of trade and industry see P. Garnsey and R. Saller, *The Roman Empire: Economy, Society and Culture*, London 1987; R. Duncan-Jones, *The Economy of the Roman Empire. Quantitative Studies*, Cambridge 1982; F. de Martino, *Storia economica di Roma antica* II. *L'impero*, Florence 1979.

35 A tenant was usually given a piece of land for a period of five years and was expected to pay the rent on an annual basis. From the second AD century tenants could be exempted from rent by order of the emperor if there was a poor harvest or the harvest failed due to unforeseen circumstances.

36 Membership of the *ordo senatorius* presupposed the possession of property valued at no less than one million sesterces.

37 The senatorial order included the senators and their agnate descendants up to and including the third generation.

38 But the progressive provincialization and de-Romanization of the senate had little effect on the spirit of solidarity that always characterized the *ordo senatorius*, whose members strove to retain or expand their privileges, prestige and political influence, at times even against the imperial power. On the position of the *ordo senatorius* during the Principate see G. Alföldy, *The Social History of Rome*, London 1985, 115 ff. And see R. Syme, *The Augustan Aristocracy*, Oxford 1986.

39 Membership of the equestrian order depended not so much on blood ties as on the personal success of the individual. The requisite qualifications were membership of a family which could prove free birth for at least two generations and possession of a fortune valued at no less than four hundred thousand sesterces. The emperor controlled admission to the order and had the right to elevate to the rank of senator any *equites* whose property exceeded the value of one million sesterces. The career of an equestrian followed a fixed pattern of salaried positions: after a lengthy spell as a junior army officer,

an equestrian was eligible for a procuratorship, i.e. a post in the civil service, usually the administration of public finances. After filling several procuratorships, he might finally attain one of the highest offices in the imperial administration, such as that of the *praefectus vigilum*, the *praefectus annonae*, the *praefectus Aegypti* and the *praefectus praetorio*. Moreover, *equites* often served as members of the *consilium principis* and occasionally were appointed as governors of small provinces.

40 On the role of the *equites* during the Principate see G. Alföldy, *The Social History of Rome*, London 1985, 122 ff; T. P. Wiseman, 'The definition of "Eques Romanus" in the late Republic and early Empire', 19 *Historia* (1970), 67–83; P. A. Brunt, 'Princeps and equites', 73 *JRS* (1983), 42–75; H. G. Pflaum, *Les carrières procuratoriennes équestres sous le Haut-Empire romain*, I–IV, Paris 1960–61.

41 A distinction may be drawn between the imperial governing class and the local governing class. The former comprised the most important elements of the imperial household, the senatorial and equestrian elites, and senior military officers. The latter consisted of the municipal aristocracy, to which individual members of the imperial governing class might also belong by reason of their origin or place of residence.

42 Eligible for the position of *decurio* were freeborn citizens who practised no dishonourable profession, were of good repute and possessed the minimum amount of fortune required. The minimum property qualifications varied greatly from community to community. In many larger cities, such as Carthage and Comum in northern Italy, the minimum capital required was one hundred thousand sesterces; in communities of less importance, such as in certain North African municipalities, the figure was much lower.

43 On the *ordo decurionum* see G. Alföldy, *The Social History of Rome*, London 1985, 126 ff.

44 During the later Republic manumission had become such a common practice that at the beginning of the Augustan era the number of freedmen and their offspring far exceeded the free-born Roman citizens. This was seen as a social problem by the Roman aristocracy and, under Augustus, measures were introduced aimed at reducing the number of freedmen. Manumission did not result in complete freedom for the former slave. Besides the permanent stigma of being an ex-slave, strict rules governed relations between freedmen and their former masters (*patroni*). Above all, a *libertinus* owed allegiance to his *patronus* and had no legal rights over him. Thus, it is not surprising that the great majority of freedmen held the same jobs which they had before they were freed in their masters' households. In spite of their inferior status, a minority of freedmen succeeded in acquiring considerable wealth, especially in the provinces, and came to play an important part in the empire's economic life. Of particular importance was the role of the freedmen who belonged to the imperial household. During the earlier part of the imperial era these imperial freedmen served at every level of the official bureaucracy and many of them were elevated to positions of power. On the role of freedmen during the Principate see P. R. C. Weaver, *Familia Caesaris: a Social Study of the Emperor's Freedmen and Slaves*, London 1972; A. Kirschenbaum, *Sons, Slaves and Freedmen in Roman Commerce*, Jerusalem and Washington D.C. 1987; H. Chantraine, *Freigelassene und Sklaven im Dienst der römischen Kaiser*, Wiesbaden 1967.

45 The original purpose of the institution of the *clientela*, whose roots can be traced back to early republican times, was to provide a useful social and economic relationship between the wealthy and the poor: in exchange for protection and material support from the wealthy patron, the poor client provided companionship, service and advice. But by the middle of the first century AD the institution had degenerated into a cheap parody of the oriental courts. A client was now expected to be at his patron's beck and call at all hours of the day and to escort him about the city. In return for his services the client received daily gifts of food, money or clothes and occasional favours. Although some of the clients were ex-slaves who were required to maintain a bond of allegiance to their former masters, many were men of former position and wealth who found themselves reduced, for a variety of reasons, to a way of life which they regarded as totally degrading. Indeed,

of all the forms of class hostility within the early empire none was as bitter as that embodied within the system of clientship for here, more than anywhere else, the potential of the Roman social structure to degrade and humiliate became a fact of everyday life. Although the urban *clientela* seems to have been unique to Rome itself, the social relationship implicit in the system, i.e. the humiliating deference owed by the poor to the rich, was a fact of life everywhere in the empire. Indeed, the empire itself was a system of client-states or communities with the emperor of Rome as the patron.

46 The task of feeding and entertaining the city mob was an onerous legacy left by the Republic to the Principate. The well-known slogan *panem et circenses* ('bread and games') provides the most telling description of the 'common law' rights which increasingly dominated the thoughts of the urban proletariat during the imperial era.

47 As in the late Republic, the *latifundia* (large estates owned by members of the imperial and local aristocracies) dominated agriculture in the early imperial period, but small peasant holdings persisted both in Italy and the provinces. In the course of time, however, as slave labour on the estates was gradually replaced by tenants, the number of independent farmers declined considerably. The basic complaint of the peasantry during this period was exploitation. The manner in which the peasantry was exploited followed much the same pattern as that of the urban clientship: essentially the peasant had been reduced to the position of a rural client. Instead of being an independent landholder living a free life in his rural community, the average peasant had become the tenant of an absentee landlord and, as such, was subject to the same kind of humiliating servitude and social degradation as the urban client.

48 Senators and members of the equestrian order convicted of crimes, which would have brought ordinary persons heavy sentences, were only required to withdraw into exile. See in general P. Garnsey, *Social Status and Legal Privilege in the Roman Empire*, Oxford 1970.

49 The size of the army was always limited by the financial resources available for its support and a great deal of energy was devoted by successive emperors to securing funds for its maintenance. Although, considering the size of the empire, the army was relatively small, its strict discipline, equipment and superior military tactics made it an extremely effective fighting machine.

50 Probably from as early as the mid-first century AD the auxiliaries received citizenship on the completion of their term of service (the grant of citizenship was made by the issuance of *diplomata*, official documents given to the auxiliaries at the time of discharge). The auxiliaries played an important role in extending Roman culture. Soldiers in the auxiliary units learned sufficient Latin to perform their duties, often they assumed Latin names, and as Roman citizens after discharge they tended to adopt and support the Roman way of life, as they understood it. After the extension of the Roman citizenship to practically the whole Roman world in the early third century AD, the distinction between Romans and auxiliaries disappeared and service was increasingly made similar in both types of units.

51 On the Roman army see G. Webster, *The Roman Imperial Army of the First and Second Centuries AD*, 3rd edn, London 1985; J. C. Mann, *Legionary Recruitment and Veteran Settlement during the Principate*, London 1983; G. R. Watson, *The Roman Soldier*, London 1969; J. B. Campbell, *The Emperor and the Roman Army 31 BC–AD 235*, Oxford 1984.

52 Individual awards of citizenship are attested as early as the Second Punic War (218–201 BC), but for a long time they were extremely rare.

53 Under the Empire, persons granted citizenship were not required to abandon the citizenship which they had previously held (abandoning one's former citizenship seems to have been a condition for holding the Roman citizenship during the Republic). Thus, newly admitted Roman citizens were not released from their civic duties towards the communities to which they belonged. Persons who did not belong to organized communities (*peregrini dediticii*) and who thus lacked citizenship (*nullius civitatis*) could also acquire

Roman citizenship but only after they had formally been admitted as citizens of another state.

54 D. 1. 5. 17 (Ulpianus); and see L. Mitteis and U. Wilcken, *Grundzüge und Chrestomathie der Papyruskunde* I, Leipzig 1912, 55–56; FIRA I, no. 88. Consider also C. Sasse, *Die Constitutio Antoniniana*, Wiesbaden 1958.

55 From the time of Augustus, Roman citizens had to pay five per cent tax on testamentary and intestate successions. The collection of this tax was assigned to special officers termed *procuratores hereditatium*.

56 On the manumission of a slave, the slave's master paid a tax equal to five per cent of the slave's value.

57 Cassius Dio 78. 9.

58 The transition from the concept of the city-state to that of a world state is reflected in the writings of Roman jurists of the Principate period, who speak of Rome as 'our common country' (*communis patria*). D. 48. 22. 18 (19) (Callistratus) and 50. 1. 33 (Modestinus).

59 On the extension of the Roman citizenship during the Republic and the Principate see A. N. Sherwin-White, *The Roman Citizenship*, 2nd edn, Oxford 1973; A. Lintott, *Imperium Romanum: Politics and Administration*, London and New York 1993, ch. 10.

60 An attempt to restore the senate to its previous position was made by Emperor Alexander Severus (AD 222–35) but ended in failure in the face of strong opposition by the army. By that time the most important government posts were held by members of a militarized equestrian class and the senate itself had come to consist largely of former army commanders and favourites of the emperors.

61 Under the threat of barbarian attacks some provinces, left unprotected by the central government, declared their independence from Rome. Gaul, for example, became independent for nearly ten years during this period.

62 Of the twenty-six emperors who ruled from AD 235 to 285 only one died a natural death. Almost without exception these were men who had risen from the ranks to the command of an army, and had then seized the throne or had been forced to seize it by the troops.

63 An important economic and social development of this period was the extension of the great country estates, the *latifundia*, and the expansion of the system of the colonate. As the cities were the main target of all invaders and military usurpers, they were objects of both plunder and state impositions, and thus suffered increasing damage to their economic life. On the other hand, the great estates in the country not only survived but grew still further through the acquisition by their owners of small and medium-sized properties. Thus, they developed into nearly autonomous and self-sufficient entities.

64 Among the most influential of the new philosophical schools was the mystical Neoplatonism, founded by Plotinus (AD 204–70).

8 THE PRINCIPATE: THE SOURCES OF LAW

1 As the adoptive son of Julius Caesar, Augustus bore the gentile name *Iulius*.

2 These laws were enacted in 17 BC and completed the transition from the *legis actiones* to the formulary procedure.

3 The *lex Iulia de maritandis ordinibus* was passed in 18 BC and was supplemented by the *lex Papia Poppaea* in AD 9. Both laws aspired to promote marriage and the procreation of children, and to check the decline of traditional family values. The earlier statute introduced several prohibitions on marriage (it prohibited marriages between members of the senatorial class and their former slaves, and between free-born men and women convicted of adultery). At the same time, various privileges were granted to married people who had children whereas severe social and economic disadvantages were imposed on unmarried and childless persons. The later law excluded unmarried men aged between twenty-five and sixty, and unmarried women aged between twenty and fifty from succession under a will. Both laws were referred to as *leges Iulia et Papia*

Poppaea. See Bruns, *Fontes* I, no. 23, 115 ff. And see J. F. Gardner, *Family and Familia in Roman Law and Life*, Oxford 1998, 47 ff; M. Kaser, *Das römische Privatrecht*, Munich 1971, 318 ff.

4 Under this law enacted in 18 BC, adultery (*adulterium*) was classified as a public crime (but only when it was committed by a married woman). The father of the adulteress was permitted to kill her and her partner if he caught them in his or her husband's house. A husband whose wife had committed adultery had to divorce her, otherwise he could be found guilty of match-making (*lenocidium*). He (or the woman's father) could also launch an accusation against her before a court of law within two months after the divorce. Thereafter, and for four months, any citizen could initiate a criminal charge. The punishment for a woman declared guilty of adultery was banishment, accompanied by confiscation of one-third of her property and loss of part of her dowry. Under the same enactment, the illicit intercourse with an unmarried woman or a widow (*stuprum*) was also made subject to criminal prosecution. See Bruns, *Fontes* I, no. 21; D. 48. 5. 13–14; D. 48. 5. 30. 1 (Ulpianus); D. 23. 2. 44 (Paulus). And see P. E. Corbett, *The Roman Law of Marriage*, Oxford 1930, repr. 1969, 133 ff; J. F. Gardner, *Women in Roman Law and Society*, London 1986, 117 ff; *Family and Familia in Roman Law and Life*, Oxford 1998, 121–22; M. Kaser, *Das römische Privatrecht*, Munich 1971, 319, 323, 326 ff.

5 Enacted in 18 BC.

6 This law was enacted in 10 BC and contained provisions regulating the voting procedure in the senate.

7 G. 1. 157. And see J. F. Gardner, *Women in Roman Law and Society*, London 1986, 14–20.

8 The last known *lex* was an agrarian law passed in the time of Emperor Nerva (AD 96–98).

9 As we observed earlier, in the regal and republican periods a *lex de imperio* was a statute passed by the *comitia curiata* that conferred *imperium* originally upon the king, then on the consuls and other higher magistrates of the state. That the legality of the imperial investiture was also based on an 'enabling act' is evidenced by the text of the *lex de imperio Vespasiani* (AD 69). The act styles itself as a *lex rogata*, but seems to have been a senatorial resolution submitted to the people. See P. A. Brunt, 'Lex de imperio Vespasiani', *Journal of Roman Studies* lxvii 1977, 96–116.

10 The text of the codified edict has not been preserved in its original form. Modern reconstructions are based on commentaries and interpretations of later jurists, especially those of Pomponius, Gaius, Ulpianus and Paulus. See O. Lenel, *Das Edictum perpetuum*, 3rd edn, Leipzig 1927, repr. Aalen 1956.

11 It provided that when a master of slaves was killed and the identity of the murderer or murderers remained unknown, all slaves who lived with him had to be tortured and eventually killed. A slave who revealed the identity of the killer was declared free by the praetor's order. See Tacitus, *Ann.* 14. 42–45.

12 D. 16. 1. 2. 1 (Ulpianus). The relevant transaction remained valid unless the woman sued by the creditor raised the *exceptio senatus consulti Valleiani*. She could also demand the return of the sum she had paid in fulfilment of her obligation. And see Bruns, *Fontes* I, no. 50.

13 D. 48. 10.

14 On the first of these see G. 2. 253; Bruns, *Fontes* I, no. 55. On the second see G. 2. 254. And see M. Kaser, *Das römische Privatrecht*, Munich 1971, 759 ff.

15 See Bruns, *Fontes* I, no. 60.

16 Such transactions were not invalid but the son could raise against the lender's claim an *exceptio senatus consulti Macedoniani*. See D. 14. 6. 1 (Ulpianus); C. 4. 28. See also Bruns, *Fontes* I, no. 57.

17 However, priority was accorded to the children's progeny and their father. See D. 38. 17. On this matter, consider S. Dixon, *The Roman Mother*, London and Sydney 1988, 52–55.

18 This procedure was observed during the early Principate, alongside the other form of

proposing *senatus consulta*, i.e. through a question presented to the senate by a magistrate. But by the time of the Severi, the submission of bills by magistrates had entirely ceased.

19 See M. Kaser, *Römische Rechtsgeschichte*, Göttingen 1976, 133.

20 G. 1. 5; and see *Inst.* 1. 2. 6; D. 1. 4. 1. pr. (Ulpianus).

21 As noted previously, an established principle of the republican constitution declared that the edicts of any magistrate lost their force when their author's term in office ended, although they might be renewed by his successor.

22 The majority of imperial edicts dealt with matters of public law. Moreover, it should be noted that Augustus and his successors used their power of issuing edicts sparingly. It is only during the late Principate period, when the imperial system moved closer to an absolute monarchy, that we find the emperors regularly employing edicts to achieve aims which, according to the spirit of the Augustan constitution, called for the enactment of legislation by a popular assembly or by the senate. By that time, both comitial and senatorial legislation had disappeared and the capacity of the emperor to create law directly had been recognized as an essential attribute of his office.

23 Consider also Augustus' edict restricting the torture of slaves in D. 48. 18. 8. pr. (Paulus); and refer to the edict of Emperor Claudius concerning the release of slaves abandoned by their owners because of bodily infirmity in D. 40. 8. 2 (Modestinus).

24 The *epistulae* were prepared by the imperial *scrinium ab epistulis*. See L. Mitteis and U. Wilcken, *Grundzüge und Chrestomathie der Papyruskunde*, Leipzig 1912, 373; also in Bruns, *Fontes* I, no. 196; FIRA I, no. 78.

25 W. Kunkel, *An Introduction to Roman Legal and Constitutional History*, 2nd edn, Oxford 1973, 128–29; see also W. Williams, 'The *libellus* procedure and the Severan papyri', 64 *JRS* (1974), 86–103.

26 The following are simple examples of imperial rescripts extracted from the Code of Justinian: 'The Emperors Diocletian and Maximian to Aurelius. The opinion which has prevailed is that a partnership can validly be established in which one partner contributes money and the other labour' (C. 4. 37. 1); 'The Emperor Alexander to Aurelius Maro, soldier. If your father sold the house under compulsion, the transaction will not be upheld as valid, since it was not carried out in good faith; for a purchase in bad faith is invalid. If therefore you bring an action in your own name, the provincial governor will intervene, especially since you declare that you are ready to refund the buyer the price that was paid' (C. 4. 44. 1) See also C. 9. 9. 2; 7. 61. 1; D. 48. 15. 6. pr. (Callistratus). Consider also Pliny, *Ep.* 10.

27 It should be noted that the authors of the imperial rescripts were, in most cases, the jurists who served as members of the imperial chancery. See M. Kaser, *Römische Rechtsgeschichte*, Göttingen 1976, 179–80, 188; T. Honoré, *Emperors and Lawyers*, Oxford 1994, ch. 2.

28 See, for example, the *mandatum* of Emperor Trajan stating that soldiers could form valid wills without being bound by the formalities that had to be observed by ordinary citizens in D. 29. 1. 1 (Ulpianus). Consider also D. 1. 18. 3 (Paulus); 48. 3. 6. 1 (Marcianus). And see V. Marotta, *Mandata Principum*, Turin 1991.

29 In the course of time, various compilations of imperial *mandata* were produced that were referred to as *libri mandatorum*. An important collection of imperial mandates is the *Gnomon* of the *Idios Logos*, a work dating from the second half of the second century AD. This work is partially preserved in a papyrus and contains instructions pertaining to the financial administration of Egypt; it also includes several provisions that deal with matters of private law. See FIRA I, no. 99. Consider also P. R. Swarney, *The Ptolemaic and Roman Idios Logos*, Toronto 1970; E. Seidl, *Rechtsgeschichte Ägyptens als römischer Provinz*, Verl. H. Richarz 1973, 13 ff.

30 It is germane to mention that Gaius and other classical jurists do not include the *mandata* among the imperial constitutions but mention them as a special category of imperial enactments. See G. 1. 5 and C. 1. 15. Modern writers almost invariably treat

the mandates as a form of imperial law-making, because they sometimes contained new rules of law. Consider on this N. van der Wal and J. H. A. Lokin, *Historiae iuris graeco-romani delineatio. Les sources du droit byzantin de 300 a 1453*, Groningen 1985, 10 ff.

31 The appellate jurisdiction of the emperor was explained on the grounds that, as the emperor received his powers from the people and hence acted in their name, an appeal to him was the exercise of the age-old citizen's right of appeal from a magistrate's decision to the judgment of the people in the assembly.

32 I.e. the *praetor urbanus* and the *praetor peregrinus* with respect to civil matters, and the *quaestiones perpetuae* regarding criminal matters.

33 See on this J. A. Crook, *Consilium principis*, Cambridge 1955; W. Kunkel, 'Die Funktion des Konsiliums in der magistratischen Strafjustiz und im Kaisergericht', *SZ* 84 (1967) 218–44 and *SZ* 85 (1968), 253–329; *An Introduction to Roman Legal and Constitutional History*, 2nd edn, Oxford 1973, 110, 130.

34 This branch of the law was further developed by jurisprudence and partly by senatorial legislation.

35 D. 1. 2. 2. 49 (Pomponius).

36 On the origins and scope of the *ius publice respondendi* see in general F. Wieacker, 'Respondere ex auctoritate principis', in J. A. Ankum, J. E. Spruit and F. B. J. Wubbe (eds), *Satura Roberto Feenstra Oblata*, Fribourg 1985, 71 ff; B. W. Frier, *The Rise of the Roman Jurists*, Princeton 1985, 223; R. A. Bauman, *Lawyers and Politics in the Early Roman Empire*, Munich 1989, 10 ff; F. Schulz, *History of Roman Legal Science*, Oxford 1967, 112 ff.

37 In the closing years of the Republic, the number of jurists practising in Rome had greatly increased and, as the opinions they presented all carried the same weight, it was difficult to ascertain precisely which opinions should be relied upon. As a result, the practice of law was thrown into a state of confusion that was exacerbated by the large number of complex and often controversial statutes passed during this period. It is believed that Augustus granted the *ius respondendi* to certain jurists partly to resolve this problem and partly to establish some imperial control over the jurists.

38 The first jurist of equestrian origin who was granted the *ius publice respondendi* was Massurius Sabinus. D. 1. 2. 2. 48 (Pomponius). But since most of the jurists known to us were members of the senatorial class, the designation of an equestrian must have remained an exception.

39 The jurists who had been granted the *ius publice respondendi* were referred to as *iurisconsulti* or *iurisprudentes*, although the same terms were sometimes also used to describe any prominent jurist irrespective of whether or not he enjoyed this privilege. The term *iurisperiti*, on the other hand, was used to denote less important jurists, especially jurists practising in the provinces. Such lesser jurists were particularly active in Egypt and other Roman provinces in the East. See, for example, Bruns, *Fontes* I, no. 119.

40 G. 1. 7.

41 However, composing new *formulae* for use in the *per formulam* procedure was no longer a regular task of the jurists. The reason is that, by the beginning of the Principate, the contents of the praetorian and aedilician edicts were largely fixed and adequate legal remedies existed.

42 Although the forensic speeches of jurists have not been preserved, information on the way they argued cases is derived from various historical sources, such as the *Controversiae* of Seneca the Elder, the *De Institutione Oratoria* of Quintilian and the works of Pliny the Younger (see, for example, Pliny, *Ep.* 4. 9).

43 Juristic works might be published by the jurists themselves or by their disciples and successors.

44 Sometimes responses relating to one theme were collected in one volume, e.g. the *liber singularis* of Modestinus that addressed the institution of *manumissio*, and the book of Paulus on the task of the proconsul (both these works were published in the early third century AD).

45 See P. Stein, *Regulae Iuris*, Edinburgh 1966, 79 ff.

46 Sabinus' work was divided into four parts: law of succession, law of persons, law of obligations and law of things.

47 A renowned illustration is Ulpianus' commentary on the edict (*libri ad edictum*) in eighty-three books.

48 In the Digest each extract is preceded by an *inscriptio*, which includes the name of the jurist from whose work the extract is taken. These extracts, as well as references by one jurist to another, have made it possible for modern scholars to obtain a good idea of the nature and structure of the original works. The date of the individual works is deduced largely on the basis of information in the surviving fragments, such as references to emperors, legislative enactments or events whose dates are verified by other sources. For a reconstruction of the juristic literature of the classical period see O. Lenel, *Palingenesia iuris civilis*, 2 vols, Leipzig 1889, repr. Graz 1960.

49 See D. 1. 2. 2. 47 and D. 1. 2. 2. 52 (Pomponius); Pliny, *Ep.* 7. 24; Tacitus, *Ann.* 3. 75.

50 D. 1. 2. 2. 47 (Pomponius). Compare with Tacitus, *Ann.* 3. 75; Aulus Gellius, *N. A.* 13. 12.

51 D. 1. 2. 2. 47. Labeo's *responsa* were edited and commented upon by various jurists until the third century AD.

52 Tacitus, *Ann.* 3. 75.

53 Among the members of the Proculian school were the two Nervas (father and son), Pegasus, Neratius, Priscus and the Celsi (father and son); the school of the Sabinians embraced the jurists Cassius Longinus, Iavolenus, Salvius Iulianus, Pomponius and Gaius.

54 Some scholars expressed the view that the two schools espoused different philosophical theories: the Sabinians were adherents of Stoicism, while the Proculians adopted the principles of Aristotelian (peripatetic) philosophy.

55 B. Nicholas, *An Introduction to Roman Law*, Oxford 1962, repr. 1991, 32–33. In the words of W. Kunkel, 'Roman traditionalism and the inclination to form relationships of loyalty of the most diverse kinds – or in other words, the *pietas* of the pupil towards the person and opinions of his master – were probably the principal motives which bound together many generations of jurists in consciously cultivated school traditions.' *An Introduction to Roman Legal and Constitutional History*, Oxford 1973, 2nd edn, 116.

56 On the origins and character of the law-schools see H. E. Dirksen, *Beiträge zur Kunde des römischen Rechts. Erste Abhandlung: Über die Schulen der römischen Juristen*, Leipzig 1825; F. Schulz, *History of Roman Legal Science*, Oxford 1967, 119 ff; G. L. Falchi, *Le controversie tra Sabiniani e Proculiani*, Milan 1981; R. Bauman, *Lawyers and Politics in the Early Roman Empire*, Munich 1989, 44 ff.

57 D. 1. 2. 2. 48; 1. 2. 2. 49–50 (Pomponius).

58 Although no direct reference to Sabinus' work exists in the Digest, its structure and general nature is known to us from the works of other jurists who used it as a framework for their own work, such as Pomponius, Paulus and Ulpianus. See R. Astolfi, *I libri tres iuris civilis di Sabino*, Padua 1983.

59 Aulus Gellius, *N. A.* 14. 2. 1.

60 D. 4. 8. 19. 2 (Paulus). Thus, this school is sometimes referred to as *schola Cassiana*.

61 Tacitus, *Ann.* 14. 42. 45.

62 See B. Eckhard, *Iavoleni Epistulae*, Berlin 1978; U. Manthe, *Die Libri ex Cassio des Iavolenus Priscus*, Berlin 1982.

63 Celsus is the author of the classical definition of law as 'the art of good and equitable' ('*Ius est ars boni et aequi*'). See D. 1. 1. 1. pr. (Ulpianus). And see Pliny, *Ep.* 6. 5; D. 28. 1. 27.

64 The information on his life derives from an inscription found near Tunis in northern Africa. See *Coprus Inscriptionum Latinarum*, Berlin 1863, 8. 24094.

65 D. 1. 2. 2.

66 Even his family name is unknown – Gaius is only a *praenomen*, or first name.

67 See D. 34. 5. 7. pr; G. 1. 7; 1. 193; 1. 55; 3. 134; 4. 37.

68 His works only started to be treated as authoritative in the later imperial period, many years after his death. Thus, Gaius is one of the five jurists whose authority was recognized by the Law of Citations of AD 426. In the Institutes of Justinian he is affectionately referred to as '*Gaius noster*' ('our Gaius'). See *const. Omnem* 1, *Inst.* 4. 18. 5.

69 The German historian B. G. Niebuhr discovered, in the cathedral library of Verona, a manuscript containing the epistles of St Jerome, dating from the seventh or eighth century AD. This manuscript was identified as a palimpsest, i.e. a manuscript where two or more texts are written on top of each other. Suspecting that the manuscript had some writing of special interest, Niebuhr presented his discovery to Friedrich Karl von Savigny, one of the most eminent legal historians of the time. The latter detected the text of Gaius' Institutes underneath that of St Jerome. Although about one-tenth of Gaius' text was lost or proved impossible to decipher, some of the missing parts were reconstructed after the discovery of more fragments from Gaius' Institutes in Egypt in 1927 and 1933.

70 See H. L. W. Nelson, *Uberlieferung, Aufbau und Stil von Gai Institutiones*, Leiden 1981, 78.

71 G. 1. 8. This classification of the law had probably been introduced by jurists well before Gaius' time.

72 Persons under paternal power usually included the wife (*uxor*) of the *pater familias*, provided that she had been married to him by virtue of a *cum manu* marriage; the children and further descendants of the *pater familias*, including legitimized and adopted children; and also slaves or other persons similarly dependent on the *pater familias*. The term *familia* is also used to denote the estate or assets of the *pater familias* as well as all property owned by persons under his control.

73 G. 1. 55; 1. 132.

74 As explained previously, the *res mancipi* comprised the most important forms of property that could be transferred only in a formal manner by means of *mancipatio* or *in iure cessio*. These embraced principally land and buildings situated in Italy, cattle and slaves. Other forms of property that could be passed informally by simple delivery were *res nec mancipi*. See G. 2. 15–27.

75 Corporeal objects (*res corporales*) were tangible or capable of sensory perception (e.g. an animal or a house). Incorporeal things (*res incorporales*), on the other hand, were intangible or could not be perceived by the senses (e.g. rights). G. 2. 12–14.

76 Possession implied physical control over property and the exclusion of other persons from such control. This might be enjoyed by the person who had ownership over the property – an important right arising from ownership was the right to possess (*ius possidendi*). However, ownership and possession were not synonymous. A non-owner could retain possession of property and would be deemed to have the right of possession (*ius possessionis*).

77 Gaius refers to this classification of obligations as the *summa divisio*. G. 3. 88. A later classification of obligations, also attributed to Gaius, embraced *obligationes ex contractu*, *obligationes ex delicto* (*ex maleficio*) and *obligationes ex variis causarum figuris* (obligations arising from various causes). D. 44. 7. 1 pr.

78 G. 3. 89.

79 In contrast to a personal right (*ius in personam*), a real right (*ius in rem*) was not dependent on any obligation or personal liability but was, so to speak, 'absolute' or 'unlimited'.

80 On the later influence of Gaius' work see P. H. Birks and G. MacLeod B. (trs), *The Institutes of Justinian*, London 1987 (Introduction). Recent translations of Gaius' Institutes include: Francis de Zulueta, *The Institutes of Gaius*, New York 1946, Oxford 1985; W. M. Gordon and O. F. Robinson, *The Institutes of Gaius*, London 1988.

81 See *Hist. Aug., Carac.* 8. 2.
82 He also held the office of head of the chancery *a libellis* and was a member of the *consilium principis* by virtue of his important role in the imperial administration.
83 Scholars of late antiquity, including the compilers of Justinian's codification, attribute special importance to Papinianus' works and often refer with admiration to his exceptional qualities as a lawyer. C. 6. 42. 30; 7. 45. 14; *Const. Omnem* 1.
84 Consider E. Levy, *Pauli Sententiae: A Palingenesia of the Opening Titles*, Cornel U.P. 1945.
85 About one-sixth of the Digest comprises extracts drawn from Paulus' works. See FIRA II, pp. 317–417 and pp. 419–32.
86 D. 50. 15. 1 pr. (Ulpianus).
87 On Ulpianus' contribution to Roman jurisprudence see T. Honoré, *Ulpian*, Oxford 1982.
88 D. 47. 2. 52. 20 (Ulpianus). Modestinus held the position of chief of police (*praefectus vigilum*) between AD 226 and 244. See *Lis fullonum* in Bruns, *Fontes* I, no. 188; FIRA III, no. 165.
89 On the details of this methodology see E. Bund, *Untersuchungen zur Methode Julians*, Köln, Wien and Graz, 1965.
90 As H.-J. Wolff remarks, '[the jurists'] dislike for theoretical argument went so far that the [jurists] usually hinted at the reasons for their decisions rather than fully explaining them. When they did give reasons they found them in the individual circumstances of the case rather than in the purely logical results deriving from general principles.' *Roman Law, An Historical Introduction*, Univ. of Oklahoma Press, Norman, 1951, 123.
91 As H.-J. Wolff notes, 'when we find a certain doctrinarism in the approach of the classical authorities, we must emphasize all the more that this doctrinarism did not extend to the handling of their own system. Equipped with a comprehensive knowledge of their system, they conceived it as a set of principles devised to make possible the just solution of the problems posed by the clash of conflicting interests. They kept strictly to the doctrines of their law, but rarely did they show misunderstanding of the sociological import of its rules or an unreasonable clinging to lifeless concepts. ... [I]t was the combination ... of a sure instinct for the necessities of life with the conscious application of firm principles which has given the accomplishments of these lawyers their eternal value.' *Roman Law, An Historical Introduction*, Univ. of Oklahoma Press, Norman, 1951, 115–16.
92 However, it should be noted that no systematic theory of legal interpretation was formulated by the jurists.
93 They recognized, for example, that if a legal provision is open to more than one interpretation, the most moderate interpretation should be adopted ('*in re dubia benigniorem interpretationem sequi*'). See D. 50. 17. 192. 1; 28. 4. 3 (Marcellus). On the concept of *utilitas* see D. 9. 2. 51. 2 (Iulianus); 46. 3. 95. 7 (Papinianus).
94 D. 1. 1. 1 pr. (Ulpianus); 4. 1. 7; 50. 17. 183 (Marcellus).
95 It should be noted that the term *ius naturale* does not appear in juridical literature until the time of Hadrian in the second century AD.
96 According to the jurist Ulpianus: 'Private law is threefold: it can be gathered from the precepts of nature, or from those of the nations, or from those of the city. Natural law is that which nature has taught all animals; for this is not peculiar to the human race but belongs to all animals ... From this law comes the union of male and female, which we call marriage, and the begetting and education of children ... The law of nations is that law which mankind observes. It is easy to understand that this law should differ from the natural, inasmuch as the latter pertains to all animals, while the former is peculiar to men' (D. 1. 1. 1). A few paragraphs below this quotation from Ulpianus we find the following statement of the second century jurist Gaius: 'All peoples who are governed by law and by custom observe laws which in part are their own and in part are common to

all mankind. For those laws which each people has given itself are peculiar to each city and are called the civil law . . . But what natural reason dictates to all men and is most equally observed among them is called the law of nations, as that law which is practiced by all mankind' (D. 1. 1. 9; and see G. 1. 1 and *Inst.* 1. 2. 11). In the next few paragraphs appears this definition of law attributed to Paulus: 'We can speak of law in different senses; in one sense, when we call law what is always equitable and good, as is natural law; in another sense, what in each state is profitable to all or to many, as is civil law' (D. 1. 1. 11). The divergences between these three accounts are evident: Ulpianus asserts that there is a clear difference between natural law and other human laws, the former being regarded as pertaining to the natural drives that men and animals have in common; Gaius and Paulus, on the other hand, perceive the reason for the universal validity of certain principles in their rational character and their recognition by all mankind, as well as in their inherent utility and goodness.

97 The Stoics sought to effect a reconciliation between the seemingly conflicting principles of form and matter by dialectically linking them under one principle: *Nous* or cosmic *Logos*. They perceived meaning to exist in the material world, not in a realm beyond it.

98 The idea of natural law originated from earlier Greek philosophical schools that generally distinguished between nature (*physis*) and convention, including human positive law (*nomos*). Socrates (*c.* 470–399 BC) enunciated more clearly an ethical alternative to *nomos*, even though he described it as conscience or the voice of god rather than as *physis*. Plato (427–347 BC) also devised an alternative to *nomos* in the universal forms, the transcendental archetypes that the mind alone could grasp. Aristotle (384–322 BC) did not subscribe to Plato's doctrine of forms but found orderliness in the physical world clearly independent of human judgment. From this point of view, he drew a distinction between natural and legal justice. As he elaborates in Chapter 4 of the *Nichomachean Ethics*: 'There are two kinds of political justice, one natural and the other legal. The natural is that which has the same validity everywhere and does not depend upon acceptance; the legal is that which in the first place can take one form or another indifferently, but which, once laid down, is decisive . . . [L]aws that are not natural but man-made are not the same everywhere, because forms of government are not the same either; but everywhere there is only one natural form of government, namely that which is best'. This distinction between natural and positive law implies that while human determination has decisive importance for the legal validity of positive law, natural law has the force of law independently of human determination. It is interesting that Aristotle, unlike the Stoics, regards natural law as changeable in relation to human affairs. Moreover, Aristotle related equity as a regulative principle operative in the application of positive law to natural law. Equity is construed as a virtue that, like justice, strives after natural, true law; it is only distinguished from justice on the grounds that equity does so by improving upon deficient, human positive law. However, it is important to note that the refining function of equity is limited to the community of the city-state (*polis*); like natural law, equity must be considered part of the *politikon dikaion*. The Stoic conception of natural law as a universal law of mankind is foreign to Aristotle. For elaboration on the origins and early history of natural law see: E. Barker, 'Aristotle's Conception of Justice, Law, and Equity in the Ethics and the Rhetoric', in *The Politics of Aristotle*, Oxford 1958, 362–72; H. Koester, 'The Concept of Natural Law in Greek Thought', in *Religions in Antiquity*, (ed. Jacob Neusner), Leiden 1968; F. D. Miller, 'Aristotle on Natural Law and Justice', in *A Companion to Aristotle's Politics* (ed. D. Keyt and F. D. Miller), Oxford 1991; G. Watson, 'The Early History of Natural Law', *Irish Theological Quarterly* 33, 1966, 65–74; F. H. Sandbach, *The Stoics*, London 1989; A. Erskine, *The Hellenistic Stoa: Political Thought and Action*, London 1990; R. M. Wenley, *Stoicism and its Influence*, New York 1963; C. J. Friedrich, The *Philosophy of Law in Historical Perspective*, 2nd edn, Chicago 1963, 27 ff.

99 The cultural and political background of the Stoics' cosmopolitan ideas was provided by

Alexander the Great's vast empire, which prompted the decline of the old Greek city-states as politically autonomous units.

100 It should be noted that Cicero, although sympathetic to Stoicism, was not completely a Stoic; he was an eclectic, and so other influences are apparent in his work, notably from the schools of Plato and Aristotle.

101 According to Cicero, 'True law is right reason in agreement with nature, diffused among all men; constant and unchanging, it should call men to their duties by its precepts, and deter them from wrongdoing by its prohibitions; and it never commands or forbids virtuous men in vain, while its rules and restraints are lost upon the wicked. To restrict this law is unholy, to change it illicit, to repeal it impossible; nor can we be exempt from it by the order either of senate or of popular assembly; nor need we look for anyone to clarify or interpret it; nor will it be one law at Rome and a different one at Athens, nor otherwise tomorrow than it is today; but one and the same law, eternal and unchangeable, will bind all peoples and all ages; and God, its designer, expounder and enactor, will be as it were the sole and universal ruler and governor of all things; and whoever disobeys it, because by this act he will have turned his back on himself and on man's very nature, will pay the heaviest penalty, even if he avoids the other punishments which are considered appropriate for his conduct.' *De Re Publica* 3. 22. 33. And elsewhere we are informed that 'law is the highest reason (*ratio summa*) embedded in nature, which commands what should be done and forbids the contrary. This same reason (*ratio*), when established and completed in the mind of man, is law. And so it is believed that law is wisdom (*prudentia*), which has the power to bid rightful conduct and to forbid wrongdoing'. *De Leg.* 1. 6. 18.

102 According to Cicero, '*Iustitia* is a state of mind which preserves the common good by recognizing the dignity of all men. Its conception proceeded from nature whereafter certain principles became customary by virtue of convenience. Eventually the principles arising from nature and those approved by custom were sanctioned by the fear of laws and religion.' *De Inv.* 2. 53. 161. And see *De Off.* 3. 5. 24 and 3. 6. 27.

103 *De Off.* 1. 7. 20.

104 *De Re Publica*, 3. 15. 24. *Iustitia* is closely connected with other virtues, such as good faith (*fides*) that Cicero defines as constancy and truth in respect of promises and agreements. *De Off.* 1, 7. 23. It is also the basis of honourable behaviour, 'for nothing can be honourable (*honestum*) when it is lacking in *iustitia*'. *De Off.* 1. 19. 62. Indeed, Cicero declares that *iustitia* is 'the mistress and queen of all virtues'. *De Off.* 3. 6. 28.

105 Cicero defines *ius civile* as 'the equity constituted for those who belong to the same state so that each may secure his own' *Topica*, 2. 9. It appears in diverse forms, such as statutes (*leges*), resolutions of the senate (*senatus consulta*), judicial decisions (*res iudicata*), the authority of legal experts (*auctoritas iurisperiti*), edicts of magistrates (*edicta magistratuum*), custom (*mos*) and equity (*aequitas*). *Topica*, 5. 28. Elsewhere he delineates a general division of the *ius civile* into three parts, namely *lex, mos* and *aequitas*. *Topica*, 7. 31.

106 *De Off.* 3. 17. 69.

107 *De Re Publica*, 1. 42 ff.

108 As H.-J. Wolff notes, 'the Roman jurists . . . for all their philosophical and rhetorical education, never showed more than a superficial interest in purely philosophical problems. The originality of their approach lay in their interest in, and intimate connection with, the practical application of Roman law as it was. Their efforts were directed not at building a purely theoretical jurisprudence, but at demonstrating from every possible angle the practical use to which the institutions of their law could be put'. *The Western Idea of Law*, S. C. Smith and D. Weisstub (eds), London 1983, 322.

109 As Ernst Levy observes, 'nature is here the order inherent in the conditions of life as the Romans saw it'. *Studia et Documenta Historiae et Iuris*, 15 (1949), 9.

110 In Levy's words, '"natural" was to them not only what followed from physical qualities of men or things, but also what, within the framework of that system, seemed to square

with the normal or reasonable order of human interests and, for that reason, not in need for further evidence'. Ibid. at 7.

111 *Traditio*, the most usual form for transferring ownership, involved the informal transfer of the actual control over a thing on the ground of some lawful cause, such as a contract of purchase and sale. See G. 2. 65, '[S]ome modes of alienation are titles of natural law, as delivery of possession, and others of civil law, as mancipation, surrender, usucapion, for these are titles confined to Roman citizens'. And see D. 41. 1. 9. 3.

112 According to Gaius 'another title of natural law, besides delivery of possession, is occupation, whereby things not already subjects of property become the property of the first occupant' (G. 2. 66). Objects that could be acquired in this way included wild animals, birds and fish (*Inst.* 2. 1. 12), the spoils of war (G. 2. 69), valuable objects found on the seashore (D. 1. 8. 3 and *Inst.* 2. 1. 18), objects abandoned by an owner (*res derelictae*) and hidden treasures.

113 D. 12. 6. 64; 1. 5. 4; 1. 1. 4.

114 In the words of C. J. Friedrich, 'the most that can be admitted is that there is a presumption in favor of the contention that a legal institution found in diverse *civitates* is part of the law of nature'. *The Philosophy of Law in Historical Perspective*, Chicago 1963, 32.

115 As d'Entrèves remarks, 'the real significance of natural law must be sought in its function, rather than in the doctrine itself. Because of that very function, the notion of natural law came to be as it were embodied in the Roman tradition, and was able to exert an influence which it would hardly have exerted had it remained in the regions of philosophical abstraction.' *Natural Law, An Introduction to Legal Philosophy*, London 1951, 31.

9 THE PRINCIPATE: THE ADMINISTRATION OF JUSTICE

1 One of Augustus' laws abolished the *legis actio* procedure except for cases falling within the jurisdiction of the court of the *centumviri* and for some other special cases. See G. 4. 30–31.

2 From the late second century AD, the term *edictum perpetuum* no longer referred to the edict issued by the praetor at the beginning of his year in office but was used to denote the body of the praetorian edict as codified by Julian.

3 The formulary procedure was finally abolished in AD 342. Consider C. 2. 57. 1. See also C. 3. 3. 3.

4 A praetor with special jurisdiction in matters concerning the liberty of an individual.

5 A special praetor charged with the appointment of guardians and with jurisdiction in disputes between guardians and their wards.

6 The praetor charged with jurisdiction in matters concerned with *fideicommissa*. The *fideicommissum* was a request to an heir (*fiduciarius*) to transfer part or all of an estate to another person (*fideicommissarius*), who was often not qualified to acquire property as heir or legatee. Although in republican times it was regarded as a purely moral obligation for the heir to fulfil the testator's wishes, in Augustus' era *fideicommissa* became legally enforceable by means of an extraordinary procedure. This occurred before the *praetor fideicommissarius* or, where the bequest had been made in the provinces, before the provincial governor.

7 On these officials see Chapter 7 above.

8 As the *cognitio* procedure was based largely on written communications, the state officials in charge of the proceedings were assisted by secretaries (*scribae*). Moreover, like the judicial magistrates of the Republic, they often relied on the advice of panels of experts (*consilia*).

9 The summons of the defendant by the magistrate could be made either by a letter (*evocatio litteris*) or, if the defendant's domicile was unknown, by a public announcement (*evocatio edicto*). See D. 5. 3. 20. 6d (Ulpianus).

10 If the defendant failed to appear before the judge, the judge could condemn him by default (*contumacia*). See, e.g., FIRA III, no. 169. In a formulary procedure, on the other hand, the plaintiff had to ensure that the defendant appeared before the magistrate. A judgment by default was impossible as no trial could proceed without the agreement of the defendant.

11 The term *litis contestatio* now denoted simply the moment when the judge started to hear the exposition of the case by the parties or their representatives.

12 See *Pauli Sententiae receptae*, 5, 5a, in Girard, *Textes* I, p. 345.

13 For a more detailed description of the *cognitio* procedure as it applied in the later imperial period see Chapter 12 below.

14 Offences falling within the jurisdiction of the *praefectus vigilum* included arson, robbery, burglary and theft. The most serious cases were tackled by the *praefectus urbi*. See D. 1. 15; C. 1. 45.

15 Suetonius, *Div. Aug.* 34. 1; Cassius Dio 54. 30. 4.

16 D. 48. 5; C. 9. 9.

17 D. 48. 12.

18 No doubt the rules governing the *quaestiones perpetuae* were still used as guides by magistrates exercising extraordinary jurisdiction, even though many rules were quite inadequate to serve as a basis for a mature system of criminal law.

19 During the Republic the senate did not have independent criminal jurisdiction. Its role in the administration of justice was limited to instituting, under certain circumstances, temporary courts of inquiry (*quaestiones extraordinariae*) and introducing in times of emergency any measures deemed necessary for the security of the state.

20 Similarly, Augustus is reported to have devoted much of his time to hearing cases *extra ordinem*. See, e.g., Cassius Dio 55. 7. 2; 56. 24. 7; Suetonius, *Div. Aug.* 33. 1. and 2; 51. 2.

21 A novel and, from the modern viewpoint of the Rule of Law, highly objectionable feature of the new criminal jurisdiction of the emperor was its emancipation from the general precepts of criminal law. Thus, acts that under the common criminal law were not at all punishable could be punished as crimes and trials for acts with mandatory punishments under the general criminal statutes could result in acquittal.

22 See D. 1. 12. 1. pr. and 4; Cassius Dio 52. 21. 1–2.

23 D. 1. 2. 2. 33; 1. 15. 3. 1 and 4.

24 D. 48. 12. 3. 1.

25 A number of legal restrictions were placed on the freedom of appeal, especially after the introduction of the *constitutio Antoniniana* in AD 212. In general, on appeals the governor had a degree of discretion: he could order the execution of offenders found guilty of certain grave crimes (e.g. sedition) and refuse appeals that were only initiated to delay execution when the applicant's guilt was manifest. D. 28. 3. 6. 9; 49. 1. 16; *Pauli Sent.* V. 35. 2.

26 Many of these norms had their origins in the republican period.

27 For example, it was recognized that persons accused of crimes should be duly notified of the charges and granted the opportunity to defend themselves in a court of law. See D. 48. 2. 3 (Paulus) and 7 (Ulpianus); 48. 19. 5 (Ulpianus). Further, it was accepted that criminal liability and punishment presupposed an overt act – a person could not be punished for thoughts alone. See D. 48. 19. 18 (Ulpianus). Children below the age of seven years (*infantes*) were excluded from criminal liability as they were deemed incapable of forming criminal intent. Children below the age of puberty (*impuberes* – boys under fourteen and girls under twelve) were also presumed incapable of forming such an intent, although this presumption was construed to be refutable. Consider D. 9. 2. 5. 2 (Ulpianus); 48. 8. 12 (Modestinus); 29. 5. 14 (Maecianus); 21. 1. 23. 2 (Ulpianus); 47. 12. 3. 1 (Ulpianus); 48. 6. 3. 1 (Marcianus); 48. 10. 22. pr. (Paulus); C. 9. 47. 7. Lunatics were exempted from punishment on similar grounds, although they could be

subject to restraint if they posed a threat to public safety. See D. 21. 1. 23. 2 (Ulpianus); 29. 5. 3. 11 (Ulpianus); 48. 4. 7. 3 (Modestinus); 1. 18. 13. 1 (Ulpianus); 1. 18. 14 (Macer). A person was not criminally liable if he accidentally caused a prohibited harm. D. 48. 19. 11. 2 (Marcianus); C. 9. 16. 4(5). Mistake or ignorance as to the law, contrary to mistake of fact, did not preclude culpability as it was held that citizens had a duty to know the law. D. 39. 4. 16. 5 (Marcianus); C. 9. 16. 1. The law also recognized various defences and mitigating pleas that negated or reduced culpability for a criminal act, such as self-defence (D. 48. 8. 9 (Ulpianus); 9. 2. 45. 4 (Paulus); 48. 8. 1. 4 (Marcianus)), superior orders (D. 48. 10. 5 (Julianus); 50. 17. 4 (Ulpianus); 9. 2. 37. pr. (Javolenus); 44. 7. 20 (Alfenus)), loss of self-control caused, for example, by justified anger or intoxication (D. 48. 8. 1. 5 (Marcianus); 48. 5. 39(38). 8 (Papinianus); 48. 3. 12. pr. (Callistratus); 49. 16. 6. 7 (Arrius Menander)), duress and necessity (D. 19. 2. 13. 7 (Ulpianus); Tacitus, *Ann.* 11. 36; Cassius Dio 60. 22).

28 The *honestiores* encompassed the members of the senatorial and equestrian orders together with the *curiales*, while the rest of the population ranked as *humilores* or *plebeii*.
29 See, e.g., D. 48. 13. 7(6) (Ulpianus); 48. 19. 16. 1–8 (Claudius Saturninus).
30 D. 48. 19. 8. 1 (Ulpianus).
31 D. 48. 19. 9. 11; 8. 2 (Ulpianus); 28. pr. 11–12 and 15 (Callistratus); 38. 1 (Paulus).
32 Apart from fines (*multae*), which might be imposed on anyone.
33 *Deportatio* could only be imposed by the emperor in his judicial capacity or the *praefectus urbi* with the approval of the emperor. D. 48. 19. 2. 1; 48. 22. 6. 14. And see Tacitus, *Ann.* 3. 68–69; 4. 21. 30.
34 The *relegatio* was usually imposed for only a specified period.
35 D. 48. 22. 7. 20–22 (Ulpianus); 48. 7. 1 (Marcianus).
36 D. 48. 19. 9 (Ulpianus).
37 D. 48. 19. 8. 4 (Ulpianus); 48. 19. 36 (Hermogenianus).
38 D. 48. 19. 8. 11 (Ulpianus).
39 Imprisonment (*carcer*) was used as a method for ensuring that a person would appear for trial, but it was not regarded as a legal penalty. D. 48. 3. 2. pr. (Papinianus); 3. 3 (Ulpianus). For a closer look at the forms of punishment imposed on offenders during the imperial period see B. Santalucia, *Diritto e processo penale nell'anctica Roma*, Milan 1989, 114 ff; *Studi di diritto penale romano*, Rome 1994, 239 ff; R. A. Bauman, *Crime and Punishment in Ancient Rome*, London and New York 1996, 142 ff.
40 The chief aims of criminal punishment were declared to be general deterrence, rehabilitation, retribution and the satisfaction of the victim's family. D. 48. 19. 20 (Paulus); D. 48. 19. 28. 15 (Callistratus); D. 48. 19. 16. 10 (Claudius Saturninus); 48. 19. 38. 5 (Paulus); 50. 16. 131 (Ulpianus). See on this C. Gioffredi, *I principi del diritto penale romano*, Turin 1970, 41 ff.

10 THE DOMINATE:
THE HISTORICAL, SOCIAL AND CONSTITUTIONAL BACKGROUND

1 From his capital city, Nicomedia, Diocletian ruled over Asia, Egypt and Thrace, while his Caesar, Galerius, governed the Balkan Peninsula. Maximian, whose seat of government was at Mediolanum (Milan), controlled Italy, Africa and Spain, while his Caesar, Constantius Chlorus, ruled over Britain and Gaul. Although Rome was no longer the administrative capital of the empire, it still enjoyed a privileged status and its citizens were catered for by the state.
2 Thus, legislation was always promulgated in the names of all four rulers, coins were minted by all in common, and sacrifices and other ceremonies of homage were performed before the busts of all four.
3 The trend towards the orientalization of the imperial office is reflected in the coinage of Aurelian (AD 270–75), who himself assumed the title of *deus*.

NOTES

4 Their official pantheon consisted of the Sun God, as well as Jupiter and Hercules, which were divinities still in concordance with traditional Roman beliefs. In the provinces a special clergy served the imperial cult and the emperors' statues were installed in the temples.

5 For that reason, governors were often referred to as *iudices* (judges). The title *consularis* or *corrector* was reserved for governors selected from the senatorial order, while those belonging to the equestrian order were designated *praesides*.

6 The total land tax was pronounced in an annual proclamation, called *indictio*, which also prescribed the amount assessed against each diocese and province. A general assessment of the land taxes was initially executed every five years and, from AD 312 onwards, every fifteen years (the term *indictio* also denoted the period between two assessments). It was based on a division of productive land into units called *iugera* that varied in size according to productivity. The tax paid on landed property was termed *iugatio terrena*. The *iugatio terrena* was distinguished from the *capitatio humana*, a form of poll or personal tax, and the *capitatio animalium*, a tax paid per head of cattle. The *capitatio* was assessed on the basis of the *caput* (literally, 'head'), a unit of human labour equivalent to the *iugum*. By combining the two units – *caput* and *iugum* – the tax assessors calculated all the natural physical, human and animal resources of the empire at a community, province or diocese level. The essential principle of the *capitatio–iugatio* system was the state's entitlement to demand whatever it needed from its citizens in any form. However, this right was conditional: it had to be effectuated legally and correctly on the basis of a quantified calculation of state requirements at the centre, subsequently converted into tax demands.

7 Thus, traders and craftsmen who were exempted from the *annona* paid a tax called *chrysargyrum*. The members of the senatorial order paid a tax known as *aurum oblaticium*. The *aurum coronarium*, a nominally voluntary but really compulsory contribution, was paid by municipal councillors every five years to enable the government to distribute largesse to officials and troops. From Constantine's era, a special levy, the *collatio glebalis* or *follis senatoria*, was imposed on senatorial lands, and a tax termed *aurum lustralis collatio* was paid every five years by urban merchants and corporations.

8 Besides the regular taxes, citizens were obliged to perform various public services without compensation on behalf of their home state or city. These charges (*munera*) included maintaining public buildings and roads, operating the public post system, furnishing shelter and supplies to state officials and troops and contributing transportation means for public purposes. A distinction existed between *munera personalia*, which were performed by personal work, and *munera patrimonii*, which were performed by a monetary payment as a contribution to the costs of various public works. In exacting these charges and collecting taxes and revenues in kind, government officials often practised extortions that were more onerous to citizens than the taxes themselves. On the tax system of the Later Empire see T. D. Barnes, *The New Empire of Diocletian and Constantine*, Cambridge, Mass. and London 1982, 226 ff; S. Williams, *Diocletian and the Roman Recovery*, London 1985, 115 ff; A. H. M. Jones, *The Later Roman Empire*, Oxford 1964, 462 ff; 'Over-Taxation and the Decline of the Roman Empire', in P. Brunt (ed.), *The Roman Economy. Studies in Ancient Economic and Administrative History*, Oxford 1974, 82; W. Goffart, *Caput and Colonate: Towards a History of Late Roman Taxation*, Toronto 1974.

9 As part of his coinage reform Diocletian issued new pure gold and silver coins, known as the *aureus* and the *argenteus* respectively. However, as gold and silver were so scarce, copper coins of small denominations were utilized. Despite attempts at stabilization, the copper coins suffered a continuous depreciation that exacerbated the problem of inflation.

10 This law set the maximum prices for a wide range of goods and services, and prescribed the penalties for profiteering. See M. Giacchero, *Edictum Diocletiani et Collegarum de pretiis rerum venalium*, Genoa 1974. Consider also J. Reynold in C. M. Roueche,

245

Aphrodisias in Late Antiquity, London 1989, no. 231; H. Blümner, *Der Maximaltarif des Diokletian*, Berlin 1958; S. Lauffer, *Diokletians Preisedikt*, Berlin 1971.

11 This form of 'command' economy did not emerge as a result of a preconceived plan nor was it inspired by any theories on state ownership of the means of production. It emanated from the long process of reforms initiated by Diocletian and his successors in response to practical necessities and contemporary requirements.

12 Constantine converted the gold coin devised by Diocletian and produced a new standard gold coin, the *solidus*. This formed the basis of the currency and the money of international exchange *par excellence* until the eighth century, when it shared that distinction with the gold *dinar* of the Arabs.

13 This decision became known as the 'edict of Milan', although it was not apparently expressed in the form of a general edict.

14 Clerics were exempted from personal services in AD 313 and from taxation in AD 319. Moreover, in AD 321, Constantine decreed that the Church was permitted to receive inheritances and bequests.

15 Constantine assumed the title of *pontifex maximus*, thus accepting leadership of the pagan state cult, although he generally abstained from performing the traditional sacrifices and rituals.

16 Proceedings in the Church councils closely resembled those of the Roman senate. The emperor or his representative presided over the meeting; attending bishops were entitled to express their views on the debated matter and cast their vote. Following their formal sanctioning by the emperor, the decisions of the councils were legally binding on all the parties concerned.

17 In the Donatist quarrel, the issue was the treatment of the North African Christian clergymen who yielded to the edicts of Diocletian's persecution and surrendered Christian religious works. This developed into a personal rivalry between Caecilianus, Bishop of Carthage, who advocated a pardon and restitution in office for those who repented, and a rival bishop, Donatus, who adopted a severe and intolerant stand. Enlivened by ethnic and social differences, the strife between the two parties became widespread in Roman Africa and public order was endangered. To settle the controversy, Constantine convoked the Synod of Arles in AD 314, which was a council of Western bishops that condemned the Donatists. The latter, however, refused the Synod's verdict and the conflict persisted for several decades.

18 Early in the fourth century AD Arius, bishop of Alexandria, argued that Christ was a created being – a position that contradicted the concept of the Trinity that was pivotal to Christian doctrine. Arian's doctrine attracted many followers and threatened to destroy the unity of the Church. At Nicaea, the Arian position was declared heretical and a statement of the articles of faith was proclaimed (Nicene Creed).

19 The first Christian churches were established in some major cities of the empire, such as Rome, Antioch, Alexandria, Carthage and Corinth. From these centres, branch churches were dispatched to other towns. In each town, the faithful would select a bishop, or overseer, from among themselves. The selected individual would then be consecrated by the bishops of the larger cities in the province. The latter, because of the size of their congregations, assumed a position of supremacy over the bishops of the smaller towns. Thus, a hierarchy developed within the Church that corresponded in its general divisions to the administrative hierarchy of the Roman state. At the top of this hierarchy was the emperor who was represented, in the West, by the bishops of Rome and Carthage and, in the East, by those of Constantinople, Antioch, Jerusalem and Alexandria. The lower tiers embodied the bishops of the provincial capitals who governed the bishops of the smaller towns in their provinces and the lower clergy. In the fourth century AD the bishops of the oldest and largest Christian cities (Rome, Constantinople, Jerusalem, Alexandria and Antioch) were called patriarchs, while the bishops of the chief cities in the provinces were termed metropolitans. The patriarchs and metropolitans exercised their ecclesiastical

authority over areas that corresponded in general terms with the prefectures, dioceses and provinces into which the empire had been divided for administrative purposes. But as the power and influence of the Church increased, rivalries emerged between certain episcopal sees within the Church structure, especially between those of Rome and Constantinople. Despite attempts at reconciliation, concord was not established and the divisions within the Church organization persisted throughout the later imperial period and the ensuing centuries.

20 On Constantine's religious policy see in general A. Alföldi, *The Conversion of Constantine and Pagan Rome*, Oxford 1948; N. H. Baynes, *Constantine the Great and the Christian Church*, New York 1975; R. MacMullen, *Christianizing the Roman Empire. AD 100–400*, New Haven 1984; A. H. M. Jones, *Constantine and the Conversion of Europe*, Toronto 1978; W. H. C. Frend, *The Rise of Christianity*, London 1984; M. Sordi, *I Cristiani e l' Impero Romano*, Milan 1984.

21 In the later imperial period, historical and geographical forces rendered Rome an ineffective capital. During the reign of Diocletian it ceased to exist as the imperial residence and administrative capital of the Empire. It was replaced by Milan in the West and Nicomedia in the East.

22 Rome retained its rank as a capital city, although the emperors seldom resided in the location during this period.

23 An emperor was either appointed by another emperor or elected by high military and civilian officials. After his election he was crowned before the soldiers and the populace who saluted him as *Imperator* and *Augustus*.

24 His person and everything in any way associated with him were attributed a sacred character – hence the terms *sacra constitutio* (imperial constitution), *sacrum consistorium* (imperial council), *sacrum palatium* (imperial palace) and such like.

25 Under the influence of Christian doctrine, the emperor functioned also as the supreme protector of the poor and the underprivileged against abuses by state officials and other oppressive forces.

26 So called because its members had to stand (*consistere*) in the presence of the emperor.

27 The *sacrum consistorium* developed from the earlier *consilium principis* as organized by Emperor Hadrian in the second century AD. It comprised the heads of the four main government departments, the chief of the imperial offices (*magister officiorum*), the minister of finance (*comes sacrarum largitionum*), the minister governing the administration of the imperial lands (*comes rerum privatarum*) and the minister of justice (*quaestor sacri palatii*), as well as the chamberlain of the imperial household (*praepositus sacri cubiculi* (although not as a regular member)) and several full-time councillors termed *comites consistoriani*.

28 The office of *magister officiorum* was created in AD 320.

29 In the time of Constantine, the praetorian prefects were divested of their military authority (following the disbandment of the praetorian guard) and became purely civil officials entrusted with the government of the prefectures.

30 Military authority was held by the *duces* and the *comites provinciarum*.

31 Hence provincial governors were sometimes referred to as *iudices*.

32 In AD 368, Emperors Valentinian I and Valens created the office of the *defensor civitatis* or *defensor plebis*. The *defensor civitatis* was entrusted with the protection of the lower classes within the population against abuses committed by great landowners and state officials. He supervised all provincial magistrates, advised the governors on administrative matters and exercised jurisdiction over minor disputes between citizens. He had the right to report directly to the emperor, bypassing the provincial governor. The *defensores* were chosen from among former magistrates and other persons of influence. The selectors were initially the *praefectus praetorio* and later the local councils with the participation of bishops and local clerics. The institution of the *defensor civitatis* proved largely unsuccessful, however, as many office-holders often committed abuses themselves or were manipulated through bribery or intimidation.

33 An important source of information on the administrative organization of the late empire

is the *Notitia dignitatum* ('List of Offices'), a handbook of all the officials in the imperial administration dating from the early fifth century AD. See O. Seeck (ed.), *Notitia Dignitatum*, Berlin 1876 (Eng. trans. W. Fairley, Philadelphia 1899); R. Goodburn and R. Bartholomew, (eds.), *Aspects of the Notitia Dignitatum*, Oxford 1976; J. H. Ward, 'The Notitia Dignitatum', 33 *Latomus* (1974), 397–434; G. Clemente, *La 'Notitia Dignitatum'*, Cagliari 1968.

34 The Constantinopolitan senate originally consisted of about three hundred members.

35 The senate of Constantinople was dominated by the emperor's favourites and included imperial officials and even representatives of the city trades. On the other hand, the tone of the senate in Rome was set by the representatives of the old senatorial families and landed proprietors.

36 The actual administration of Rome and Constantinople was governed by the city prefects.

37 Nevertheless, senators were often appointed as judges and it appears that the senate of Constantinople did function as a law court from time to time.

38 Eligibility for these magistracies was determined by the *censuales*, officials responsible for calculating the taxes imposed on senators and the preparation of taxation lists.

39 In the fourth century AD the distinguishing mark of this new senatorial order was the right to the title of *clarissimus*, which was acquired by inheritance, imperial grant or the attainment of certain important offices. The great increase in the number of the imperial officials during this period entailed the creation of different status groupings within the class of the *clarissimi*, such as the *spectabiles* ('respectable') and the *illustres* ('illustrious'). The title of *illustris* was assigned to some of the highest officers of the state, such as the *praefecti praetorio*, the *praefecti urbi*, the *comes sacrarum largitionum* and the *quaestor sacri palatii*. In the sixth century AD these state functionaries were referred to as *gloriosi* ('glorious'). The titles Caesar and *nobilissimus* ('most noble') were reserved for members of the imperial household.

40 Outside Rome, the most important senatorial groupings in the West were composed of senators from Spain, Gaul and North Africa, territories where very extensive senatorial estates were located. On the role of the senatorial class during the Dominate see M. Arnheim, *The Senatorial Aristocracy in the Late Roman Empire*, Oxford 1972; J. Matthews, *Western Aristocracies and Imperial Court, AD 364–425*, Oxford 1975.

41 The term is derived from *curia*, meaning senate or council.

42 The administration of a city was supervised by the *curator*, who was a fiscal official appointed by the state.

43 Under a law of AD 317, persons possessing a certain amount of property were obliged to become members of the curial order of a city, even if they were only temporary residents in that city (*C. Th.*, 12. 1. 5).

44 The son of a *curialis* could be obliged to become a member of the *curia* when he reached the age of eighteen (*C. Th.*, 12. 1. 7).

45 If a *curialis* was absent from his town for longer than five years, his property could be confiscated.

46 See, e.g., *C. Th.*, 12. 1. 6; 12. 1. 22; 12. 1. 27; 12. 1. 186; *C. Iust.*, 5. 5. 3.

47 In Rome and Constantinople corporations were supervised by the city prefects, and in the municipalities the local magistrates and provincial governors supervised these organizations.

48 See, e.g., *C. Th.*, 14. 7. 1.

49 To combat the problems of desertion and depopulation of the land, the government imposed on small landholders the obligation to cultivate, besides their own land, neighbouring lands abandoned by their owners (*agri deserti*) and to pay the relevant taxes to the state (*adiectio sterilium*). Several imperial enactments issued by Constantine and subsequent emperors pertained to the regulation of the system of *adiectio sterilium*. See *C. Th.*, 11. 1. 4; *C. Iust.*, 11. 59. 2; 1. 34. 2.

50 Although the *coloni* had the right to contract a legal marriage, a law of AD 380 prohibited them from marrying outside their class (*C. Th.*, 10. 20. 10).

51 *C. Th.*, 13. 10. 3. Pursuant to a law of Constantine, a fugitive *colonus* had to be returned by force to the estate he had left. The person who offered him shelter had to pay compensation to the state for any loss of tax (*C. Th.*, 5. 17. 1). But a fugitive *colonus* who managed to avoid capture for thirty years (or twenty in the case of women) did not have to return to the estate where he was born (*C. Th.*, 5. 18. 1).

52 More closely akin to slavery was the situation of a special class of *coloni* called *coloni adscripticii*. For closer scrutiny of the institution of the colonate see A. H. M. Jones, *The Later Roman Empire*, Oxford 1964, 795 ff; 'The Roman colonate', in P. Brunt (ed.), *The Roman Economy. Studies in Ancient Economic and Administrative History*, Oxford 1974, 293.

53 During the period AD 337–50 Constantius, the second son of Constantine, shared the rule of the empire with his brothers Constantine II (AD 337–40) and Constans (AD 337–50). After a period of civil war he became sole emperor in AD 353.

54 Christianity had experienced a remarkable expansion following the conversion of Constantine, as his successors sustained his policy of supporting and ruling the Church. Under Emperor Julian (AD 361–63) an attempt was made to revive paganism, but Julian's enforced 'Hellenism', an artificially constructed product of eclecticism, was not capable of restoring the old cults. In Theodosius' reign the victory of the Church became final with the recognition of Christianity as the state religion, while the worship of the pagan gods was declared a crime against the state. Affairs of the Church and state were now increasingly intertwined as the imperial government sought to use Christianity as a unifying force. However, the Church itself continued to be convulsed by religious controversy that fed on the spread of monasticism in the East and on the political rivalry of episcopal sees within the Church structure. At the same time, the Arian and Monophysitic heresies of the fourth and fifth centuries continued to cause divisions among the population and necessitated both government intervention and the convocation of ecumenical councils for their resolution.

55 This date is traditionally regarded as marking the end of the Roman Empire in the West.

56 South-western Gaul fell under the control of the Visigoths (AD 412–18); around this time, the Burgundians moved into south-eastern Gaul, while the Ripuarian Franks and the Alamani established their presence in northern Gaul; the Vandals invaded northern Africa where they created their own kingdom in AD 429; the Angles and Saxons moved into England around AD 430; in AD 451 the Huns, under Attila, crossed the river Rhine into Gaul, but were forced to withdraw following their defeat by the combined forces of the Romans and Visigoths at the battle of the Catalaunian Fields near Chalons (AD 451); around the middle of the fifth century, the Visigoths occupied most of Spain where they established a kingdom that endured until the Arab invasion in AD 711. In the sixth century, the eastern emperor Justinian successfully reconquered Africa (AD 533), Italy and even a part of Visigothic Spain (*c.* AD 554), but his conquests proved short-lived. Shortly after his death in AD 565, Spain fell again to the Visigoths and Italy was overrun by another Germanic tribe, the Lombards, who gradually extended their dominion over most of the country. About half a century earlier, in AD 507, Clovis, king of the Salian Franks, subdued the Visigoths of south-western Gaul and added their territory to his Frankish kingdom. In AD 531, the Franks seized the remaining Visigothic possessions in Gaul and, three years later, they overthrew the Burgundians, uniting all of Gaul under Frankish rule.

57 This partly derived from the fact that the eastern emperors had recourse to an internal supply of military manpower in the Balkans and Asia Minor.

58 His greatest architectural achievement was the construction of the church of Hagia Sophia in Constantinople. It is probably the most significant edifice in the religious architecture of Eastern Europe and the Near East, which still stands today.

59 Justinian demanded religious conformity from his subjects and steadily persecuted the followers of any other creed than the orthodox Catholic faith. Although he succeeded in

erasing what was left of paganism, his attempt to terminate the Monophysite heresy failed (this failure is related to the fact that his wife, Theodora, supported the Monophysite sect). Moreover, the religious differences between the Eastern and the Western Churches persisted throughout his reign and in the ensuing years.

11 THE DOMINATE: THE SOURCES OF LAW

1 The theoretical assumption that the emperor was also bound by the laws was nullified by the fact that he was above the law (*princeps legibus solutus*) and equally so by his legislative omnipotence (*quod principi placuit legis habet vigorem*).

2 Even after the partition of the empire, imperial constitutions were still written in Latin, although, from the fifth century AD the number of those written in Greek gradually increased.

3 H. J. Wolff remarks, 'the conservative attitude of the jurists and their self-imposed restriction to the law of the city of Rome as it had come down from republican times left comparatively little room for individual ingenuity. This limitation was bound to have a detrimental effect when, after Hadrian, the advisory practice of the jurist was in the main confined to the interpretation of the closed system of the Edict.' *Roman Law: An Historical Introduction*, Norman 1951, 127–28.

4 A last effort to preserve the fruits of the classical jurisprudence is reflected in the imperial rescripts that were transmitted to us from the reign of Diocletian (AD 284–305).

5 This type of imperial enactment is illustrated by the famous Edict of Prices (*edictum de pretiis*) created by Emperor Diocletian and issued in AD 301.

6 It should be noted, that a *lex generalis* always operated in the same way irrespective of the party to whom it was formally addressed.

7 This served to emphasize that the empire remained politically united, despite its administrative partition.

8 During Diocletian's reign, when elements of classical legal science still survived, the imperial chancery *a libellis* issued, in the emperor's name, a large number of individual case decisions in the form of rescripts that addressed diverse legal points. Approximately 1,500 of these rescripts have been conveyed to the modern world.

9 C. Th. 1. 2. 2. and 3.

10 C. Th. 1. 2. 11.

11 C. 1. 14. 3.

12 Justinian apparently endeavoured to revive the practice of issuing formal sets of instructions to officials by producing a book of instructions (*liber mandatorum*) to guide certain categories of officials in the exercise of their duties. These instructions probably had an indirect law-making effect.

13 The abandonment of precedent as a source of law and the importance attached to the formulation of abstract, general legal rules as a means of controlling decisions in individual cases exercised a great influence in medieval and modern Europe that incorporated Roman legal ideas. Thus, it is often declared that legal reasoning in countries belonging to the Roman-Civil law family is basically deductive: it proceeds from a broad rule expressed in general terms and progresses with the consideration of the facts of the particular case and the application of the rule to these facts with a view to formulating a conclusion. Employing this kind of reasoning, Civil law lawyers tend to present a legal argument as if there is only one right answer to any legal problem, and any disagreement over the application of the law to the facts is attributed to the presence of faulty logic. Under the deductive approach of the Civil law, the value of case law is limited as court decisions are perceived as particular illustrations of, or specific exceptions to, the law as expressed in a general rule or principle. In this respect, the material of law as embodied in legal codes, statutes, decrees and ordinances is construed to form an independent, closed system. In theory, all sorts of questions may be answered within this system by interpreting existing legal norms.

14 A good example of such an enactment is the *sanctio pragmatica pro petitione Vigilii* (AD 554), which embodies the response of Emperor Justinian to a petition from Vigilius, a bishop of Rome. It addressed problems concerning the legal order in Italy, which Justinian had recently recaptured from the Goths. By the same enactment, the Emperor ordered that his legislation should be in force in Italy. And see C. 1. 23. 7. 2. (Zeno).

15 Originally, the *adnotatio* seems to have been a written instruction from the emperor for the drafting of a rescript by the imperial chancery *a libellis*.

16 These were also known as *formae, programmata, praecepta* or *commonitoria*.

17 C. Th. 1. 4. 1.

18 C. Th. 1. 4. 2. It is now believed that the work known as *Pauli sententiae* was not written by Paulus himself but by an unknown author on the basis of Paulus' works.

19 C. Th. 1. 4. 3.

20 As we have discerned, the so-called 'schools' of the Sabinians and the Proculians were not formal institutions of legal learning.

21 Greg., *Orat. Paneg. ad Orig.* 5. 62.

22 The law school of Constantinople was established in AD 425. C. Th. 14. 9. 3.

23 For example, a constitution issued by Emperors Diocletian and Maximian exempted students who were studying at the law school of Beirut from compulsory services in their home town. C. 10. 50. 1.

24 C. 2. 7. 11. As the legal profession was always regarded as a form of public service, it was closely regulated by the government. Advocates had to enroll themselves in a particular court where they remained for life. Several laws issued in the late imperial period were concerned with fixing the maximum number of advocates for each bar and determining the way in which a lawyer's career progressed. In the fifth century AD, advocates progressed strictly by seniority to the position of *advocatus fisci*. A novice first enrolled himself as a supernumerary and waited for a vacant position in the establishment. He then advanced year by year. However, by the sixth century AD the legal profession tended to become hereditary: an advocate could nominate his son for a place on the establishment, while outsiders had to purchase vacancies from retiring seniors.

25 From the middle of the fourth century AD legal culture in the West exhibited a sharp downward trend – a decline precipitated by the deteriorating socio-economic conditions, political instability and the constant threat of barbarian invasions.

26 After the *constitutio Antoniniana* (AD 212) granted Roman citizenship to all the free inhabitants of the empire, knowledge of Roman law was requisite for those engaged in the practice of law, especially in the provinces where the newly admitted citizens had to conduct their affairs according to an unfamiliar system of law.

27 From the early fifth century AD, the salaries of the law professors were paid by the government. However, the official salary was only a small part of a professor's earnings, as they charged fees that varied according to their reputation and the purses of their students.

28 It is believed that the work was completed between AD 318 and 324, and that the three imperial constitutions of 330, 337 and 372 were attached later.

29 The subjects scrutinized embraced sale, usufruct, dowry, gift and legal representation.

30 For the text, see FIRA II, pp. 461–540. A critical edition of this work was produced by Th. Mommsen in 1860 – see P. Krüger, Th. Mommsen and G. Studemund, *Collectio librorum iuris anteiustiniani* III, Berlin 1927. See also B. Kübler and E. Seckel, *Iurisprudentiae anteiustinianae reliquias in usum maxime academicum compositas* a P. E. Huschke, 6th edn, Leipzig 1927.

31 The original title of this work, as found in the surviving manuscript, is *Lex dei quam praecipit dominus ad Moysen* (The divine law which the Lord gave to Moses).

32 See FIRA II, pp. 541–89. The *Collatio* was first edited in the sixteenth century but more materials were added later based on two manuscripts discovered in the nineteenth century. The standard modern edition is that of Th. Mommsen included in his *Collectio*

librorum iuris anteiustiniani III, Berlin 1927; see also B. Kübler and E. Seckel, *Iurisprudentiae anteiustinianae reliquias in usum maxime academicum compositas* a P. E. Huschke, 6th edn, Leipzig 1927.

33 C. Th. 1. 4. 2 (Constantine); 1. 4. 3 (Law of Citations).

34 See FIRA II, pp. 317–417, 419–32.

35 Some modern commentators suggested that this work was based on the Institutes of Gaius and other classical works (see, e.g., F. Schulz, *History of Roman Legal Science*, 1946, 181). However, this view was recently proved incorrect. See H. L. W. Nelson, *Überlieferung Aufbau und Stil von Gai Institutiones*, Leiden 1981, 80–96.

36 See FIRA II, pp. 261–301. And see F. Schulz, *Die Epitome Ulpiani des Codex Vaticanus Reginae 1128*, Bonn 1926.

37 See FIRA II, pp. 591–613.

38 Cujas, who taught at the University of Bourges, was a leading member of the Humanist School of the sixteenth and seventeenth centuries.

39 FIRA II, pp. 751–98. See also K.G. Bruns and E. Sachau, *Syrisch-Römisches Rechtsbuch*, Leipzig 1880, repr. Aalen 1961; P. E. Pieler, *Byzantinische Rechtsliteratur* in H. Hunger, *Die hochsprachliche profane Literatur der Byzantiner*, Bd. 2, Munich 1978, 393 ff.

40 FIRA II, pp. 635–52; P. E. Pieler, *Byzantinische Rechtsliteratur* in H. Hunger, *Die hochsprachliche profane Literatur der Byzantiner*, Bd. 2, Munich 1978, 391 ff; N. van der Wal and J. H. A. Lokin, *Historiae iuris graeco-romani delineatio. Les sources du droit byzantin de 300 a 1453*, Groningen 1985, 20–24.

41 According to the jurist Hermogenian, an established customary norm had the same force as written law because it was based on the tacit consent of the citizens ('*tacita civium conventio*'). D. 1. 3. 35; see also D. 1. 3. 32. 1 (Julianus). This view was endorsed by imperial legislation, under the condition that a customary norm did not contradict a written law and had a logical basis. C. 8. 52. (53.) 2 (Constantine).

42 For example, the institution of *abdicatio* (pertaining to the right of the head of a family to renounce a child) was still implemented during the later imperial period, despite the fact that it was abolished by a *rescriptum* of Emperor Diocletian (C. 8. 46. (47.) 6).

43 C. 6. 60. 1. Justinian finally adopted the position that a child *in potestate* could claim ownership over everything he acquired, except when he acquired property from his father. C. 6. 61. 1.

44 This procedure entailed the transfer of a person governed by the paternal power of the head of his family to the *patria potestas* of another (*pater adoptans*).

45 *Inst.* 1. 12. 8.

46 According to a law of Constantine, a wife who divorced her husband without good reason was punished by deportation and loss of her dowry. A husband who did the same was not allowed to remarry. If he did remarry, his former wife could seize the new wife's dowry. However, these penalties did not affect the validity of the divorce. See C. Th. 3. 16. 1. On Constantine's family legislation see J. Evans Grubbs, *Law and Family in Late Antiquity. The Emperor Constantine's Marriage Legislation*, Oxford 1995.

47 C. 5. 27. 10.

12 THE DOMINATE: THE ADMINISTRATION OF JUSTICE

1 A rising advocate would normally aspire to serve for some time as an assessor, and thereafter might strive for a senior position in the provincial administration.

2 The primary assignment of the governors was the administration of justice as, during the later Empire, they did not possess military powers and the size of their assigned territories had been considerably reduced.

3 The decisions of governors with proconsular rank were appealable only to the prefect or the emperor.

4 In later times, a special form of appeal (*supplicatio*) against the decisions of the prefects

could be submitted to the emperor. The petitioner requested that the emperor grant a renewed examination of a matter that normally did not permit an appeal. See C. 1. 19.

5 In the fifth century AD, soldiers who were sued on civil issues possessed the right to have their cases heard by their commanders. Moreover, all crimes other than adultery committed by members of the armed forces (including officers and commanders) were not encompassed by the cognizance of the ordinary courts, but were only tried by military courts. See C. Th. 2. 1. 2.

6 Until the time of Constantine, members of the senatorial class were deemed to be domiciled at Rome or Constantinople no matter where they actually lived. Therefore, they were regarded as falling within the jurisdiction of the prefects of the two capitals.

7 C. Th. 16. 2. 12.

8 See C. Th. 16. 2. 23 and 16. 11. 1. If a cleric's conduct constituted both an ecclesiastical and a secular offence, it would invoke two separate processes: disciplinary proceedings by the ecclesiastical authorities and a criminal prosecution by the secular authorities. A cleric's establishment of a sect advocating heretical doctrines is an illustration of such an offence.

9 The *defensor civitatis* is the first recorded instance of what is today known under the name of ombudsman, a civil commissioner entrusted with the protection of citizens against maladministration and other acts contrary to law.

10 The jurisdiction of the *defensor* pertaining to civil matters, although initially small, gradually expanded and attained considerable dimensions under Justinian.

11 1 *Cor.* 6, 1–6.

12 C. Th. 1. 27. 1.

13 C. 1. 4. 7; C. Th. 16. 11. 1 (Arcadius and Honorius).

14 It was not uncommon for bishops to appoint advocates as legal assessors. On the *episcopalis audientia* see M. Kaser, *Das römische Zivilprozessrecht*, Munich 1996, 641 ff; K. H. Ziegler, *Das private Schiedsgericht im antiken römischen Recht*, Munich 1971; G. Vismara, *Episcopalis audientia*, Milan 1937. And see J. Harries, *Law and Empire in Late Antiquity*, Cambridge 1999, ch. 10.

15 C. 2. 57. 1.

16 A similar type of procedure was adopted by the ecclesiastical courts that were first instituted by the Church during this period.

17 See, e.g., FIRA III, no. 173 (AD 338); Bruns, *Fontes* I, no. 103 (AD 361–63).

18 If the defendant could not be located he was tried *in absentia* and condemned. D. 2. 5. 2. 1 (Paulus); see also *Pauli sententiae receptae* (PS), 5. 5a. 6 in Girard, *Textes* I, p. 345.

19 *Inst.* 4. 6. 24 (Theophilus).

20 See, e.g., FIRA III, no. 177 (AD 427).

21 *Inst.* 4. 11. 2. A defendant from the *humiliores* class who failed to supply this guarantee could be detained in prison until the end of the trial; if he belonged to the class of *illustres*, he was relieved from the obligation to provide security – a formal promise under oath was deemed sufficient. C. 12. 1. 17. pr. (Zeno).

22 C. 3. 1. 13. 2–2b (AD 530); *Nov.* 112. 3 (AD 541).

23 C. 2. 59. 2 (Justinian).

24 If the defendant admitted his liability at the outset of the trial, judgment was passed against him immediately and the proceedings concluded.

25 C. 3. 9. 1 (Septimius Severus). Under the legislation of Justinian, the trial had to be completed within three years from the *litis contestatio*. C. 3. 1. 13.

26 C. 4. 20. 1 (Alexander). Documentary evidence included public records (*instrumenta publica*), such as documents retained by a public authority (*insinuatio actis*) or documents composed by a public organ at the request of the party concerned (*apud acta*), as well as private records. The latter included documents drafted by public notaries (*tabelliones*), written declarations (*cautiones*), letters (*chirographa*) and other records. In general, private records had little evidentiary weight unless they were signed by three credible witnesses attesting to their authenticity (*instrumentum quasi publice confectum*).

27 See C. Th. 11. 39. 3 (Constantine); C. 4. 20. 4 (Carus, Carinus and Numerian).

28 The judge could order one of the parties to swear an oath (*iusiurandum iudiciale*), or this oath could be imposed on one party by the other with the judge's consent (*iusiurandum in iure* or *necessarium*).

29 See, e.g., FIRA III, no. 178.

30 A presumption occurred when the existence of a fact not supported by direct evidence was logically inferred from another fact established through evidence. Some presumptions recognized under Justinian's law had the effect that certain facts were considered established in court so long as no counterproof was offered (*praesumptiones iuris*). For example, a presumption was introduced for the event that several persons died simultaneously (e.g. in a fire). It postulated that children below the age of puberty were deemed to have died before their parents, while the elder children were presumed to have died after them. In certain exceptional circumstances a counterproof was not admitted (*praesumptiones iuris et de iure*).

31 D. 42. 1. 47. pr. (Paulus); C. Th. 4. 17. 1; C. 7. 44. 3. 1 (Valens, Valentinian and Gratian).

32 C. 7. 45. 14.

33 D. 50. 17. 57 (Gaius).

34 C. 7. 62. 19 (Constantine); C. 7. 62. 32 (Theodosius and Valentinian); C. 7. 70. 1 (Justinian); *Nov.* 82. 5.

35 D. 49. 1. 5. 4 (Marcianus).

36 *Nov.* 23. 1.

37 C. 7. 62. 6. pr. 4 (Diocletian and Maximian).

38 C. Th. 4. 19. 1. pr.; C. 7. 54. 2; C. 7. 54. 3. 3.

39 D. 6. 1. 68 (Ulpianus).

40 C. Th. 9. 11. 1 (Valentinian, Theodosius and Arcadius); C. 9. 5. 2 (Justinian).

41 D. 42. 1. 15. pr. and 2. 4 (Ulpianus).

42 To avoid the infamy that the compulsory sale of his property entailed, the insolvent debtor could seek the court's permission to surrender his property to the creditors (*cessio bonorum*). D. 42. 3; C. 7. 71.

43 The *receptum arbitri* was the formal agreement whereby the nominated arbitrator assumed the task of tackling the dispute. The person who undertook to act as an arbitrator was obliged to perform his duties and could be compelled to do so by the magistrate, unless he demonstrated good reasons for his release from this obligation. D. 4. 8. 15 (Ulpianus).

44 D. 4. 8. 27. 7 (Ulpianus).

45 C. 2. 55. 5. pr. and 1 (Justinian).

46 See D. 48. 11. 1. pr. (Marcianus).

47 *Ambitus* now covered any attempt to climb faster or hold a rank longer in the imperial civil service contrary to established regulations. See C. Th. 9. 26 passim. The scope of *maiestas* now encompassed offences such as coining or maintaining a private prison. See C. Th. 9. 11. 1; 9. 21. 9 and C. 9. 24. 3.

48 C. 9. 28.

49 C. 9. 29.

50 In the field of criminal law, the distinction between *vis publica* and *vis privata* was fundamental but not always clear. The original distinction was probably based on whether an offence committed with violence affected direct interests of the state (*vis publica*) or those of a private person (*vis privata*). In the later imperial period, *vis publica* was generally understood to be committed by officials and *vis privata* by private persons. Both forms of *vis* constituted crimes against public order and were subject to severe punishment.

51 And consider C. Th. 16. 2. 31 and C. 1. 3. 10.

52 C. Th. 16. 10. 4 and C. 1. 11. 1 and 9; C. Th. 16. 9. 1 and C. 1. 10. 1; C. Th. 9. 7. 5 and C. 1. 9. 6; C. Th. 16. 5. 1 and C. 1. 5. 1; 1. 5. 20.

53 In the sphere of criminal law, the term *dolus* was used to denote the intention of the wrongdoer to commit the offence and this presupposed his knowledge of the unlawful character of the act.

54 D. 48. 19. 42.

55 D. 48. 19. 5. pr. (Ulpianus).

56 See B. Santalucia, *Diritto e processo penale nell'antica Roma*, Milan 1989, 135 ff.

57 As elaborated previously, in the republican and early imperial periods the *accusatio* procedure was adopted in trials conducted before the *quaestiones perpetuae*.

58 However, the incorporation of certain inquisitorial features substantially derogated from the presumed disinterestedness of the judge and the accusatorial nature of the proceedings. These features embraced, for example, control by the judge rather than the accuser over the questioning of the witnesses and the accused.

59 On the other hand, the practice in the Principate period was to punish only the person who accused another in full knowledge of the latter's innocence.

60 C. Th. 16. 5. 40. 8.

61 Private denunciations devised as a basis for a criminal prosecution were not generally permissible – indeed, issuing such a denunciation could be punished as a crime (see C. Th. 10. 10). However, as the gravity of the crime increased, the range of available procedures widened to include the possibility of private denunciations.

62 This was also the case in proceedings by *accusatio*, although it was customary for the judge to determine the date in consultation with the accuser.

63 Witnesses arraigned by the judge could also be secured by detention, especially in the case of witnesses destined to be examined under torture, i.e. those from the lowest strata of society, or those who were likely not to render truthful evidence of their own accord. See C. Th. 9. 37. 4.

64 A number of imperial constitutions issued during this period were concerned with the treatment of prisoners awaiting trial. It was decreed that such prisoners (as opposed to those already convicted) had to be treated humanely (according to the perceptions of the age) – this directed, for example, that prisoners could not be manacled but only lightly chained, were to be granted access to the open air during daytime, were not to be starved and that the reasons for their prolonged detention were to be regularly investigated. However, it is doubtful whether these provisions were implemented effectively, as evidenced from the recurrent references to prison malpractices in contemporary sources. Moreover, as there were always too many prisoners on remand, Justinian limited the detention period to six months for a prisoner awaiting trial (or in some cases, a year) and made provision for bail. Consider, e.g., C. Th. 9. 1. 7 and 18; C. Th. 9. 3. 6 and C. 9. 4. 5; C. 9. 4. 6; C. Th. 9. 3. 1 and C. 9. 4. 1.

65 The testimony of witnesses and the depositions of slaves were accepted as evidence only if they were factual and related to the personal experience of the witness or slave concerned. Hearsay evidence did not carry any weight, while evidence as to a person's character was permissible but accorded limited significance. The testimony of one person only was normally not admitted as proof. If there were conflicting statements before the court, their veracity was assessed by regarding the credibility of the witnesses. Congruent evidence from a number of witnesses was accorded great weight. Circumstantial evidence could probably be relied on, whether as subsidiary to other forms of evidence or as sole evidence where there were no eyewitnesses who could testify that the alleged offender actually committed the offence in question.

66 The decision whether or not to subject the accused or a witness to interrogation under torture vested in the judge, who also specified the method and degree of torture and where it would be performed. In principle, the judge could only order the accused's torture if the latter's guilt could not be proved by any other means and if a prima facie case against him had been established.

67 Persons belonging to the upper classes (*honestiores*) were exempt from interrogation under

torture. These included the members of the senatorial and equestrian nobility; all government officials of the first and second rank; senior members of municipal councils; soldiers; veterans; clerics (from the rank of priest upwards); and, to a more limited extent, ordinary members of municipal councils and their descendants.

68 As already noted, in principle a person convicted of a crime could appeal to a higher court against the judge's decision. In practice, however, the right of appeal was subject to certain limitations. For example, leave to appeal might be refused by the trial judge if he was convinced, by virtue of an admission of guilt or other cogent evidence, that there was no merit in the appeal, or that the attempt to appeal was merely a dilatory manoeuvre; leave to appeal could also be refused to those whose actions had endangered public safety. Consider C. Th. 11. 36. 1; 11. 36. 4; 9. 40. 4 and C. 9. 47. 18.

69 The term *poena capitis* (or *capitalis*) denoted not only the death penalty but any penalty that affected the condemned person's *caput*, or civil status, by depriving him of his freedom or his Roman citizenship. This consequently erased all his civil rights, including his property and family rights.

70 There was no general mandatory waiting period that had to elapse before the execution could occur. The only exception to this was when a death sentence was pronounced by the imperial court acting as a court of first instance; in this case, at least thirty days had to pass before the sentence could be executed (C. Th. 9. 40. 13). However, this limitation was not absolute as the emperor could, and often did, override this restriction.

71 Emperor Constantine abolished death by crucifixion, which was used for slaves and individuals of the lower class (*humiliores*) convicted of particularly grave crimes.

72 In practice, this amounted to a deferred death sentence as most people succumbed to the terrible living conditions in the mines. A milder form of this punishment was *damnatio ad opus metalli* (condemnation to mine labour).

73 This form of punishment was abolished in AD 399. Before this event, imperial constitutions had installed some restrictions on its imposition. A related form of punishment was *damnatio ad ludum venatorium* (a fight with wild animals), which still existed in Justinian's time.

74 This was regarded as a less severe form of capital punishment than the foregoing categories, as it did not entail enslavement as a public slave but only loss of Roman citizenship. Moreover, those subjected to this sentence were not consigned to work in a high-mortality industry. Rather, they were employed in merely ignoble, debasing works, such as road building or labour in the public bakeries, the imperial weaving establishments or one of the other compulsory guild industries. See, e.g., C. Th. 9. 40. 3. 5. 6; 9. 40. 7. 9; 10. 20. 9.

75 This was construed as the least severe form of capital punishment. It entailed the offender's retention of his free status accompanied by a deprivation of his Roman citizenship and banishment for life to a specific locality (usually, a small island or a desert oasis). The loss of citizenship meant the loss of all civil law rights and capacities and, in principle, the confiscation of the deportee's estate. However, in practice this was mitigated by the norm of conceding all or part of the estate to his family and by the custom of granting the deportee a subsistence allowance.

76 There were two forms of *relegatio*: *relegatio simplex* and *relegatio qualificata*. The former entailed banishment *from* a specific locality, while the latter (the more severe form) invoked banishment *to* a specific locality. Both forms of *relegatio* could be imposed for life or for only a certain period of time. The *relegatio* could be combined with additional punishments, such as the confiscation of the whole or a part of the condemned person's property.

77 The confiscation of an offender's estate (or a part thereof) operated mainly as a subsidiary punishment that was auxiliary to the capital punishments and to *relegatio* for life.

78 This was often imposed in cases involving minor crimes committed by slaves or by persons who were too poor to afford any fines.

79 The conditions of imprisonment were generally appalling: convicts were kept in fetters,

confined in narrow, windowless cells, never permitted into the open air and maltreated by the prison guards. The legislative reforms initiated by Emperor Constantine to improve prison conditions related only to the treatment of prisoners awaiting trial and excluded those who had already been convicted. See C. Th. 9. 3.

80 Slaves found guilty of grave crimes were usually sentenced to death (by one of the aggravated forms of execution) or condemned to the mines.

13 THE DOMINATE: THE CODIFICATION OF ROMAN LAW

1 Moreover, the Digest of Justinian references an early collection of rescripts (mainly of Marcus Aurelius and Lucius Verus) that formed part of Papirius Justus's *libri XX constitutionum*, a work that appeared in the late second century AD.

2 He is probably identified with the Hermogenianus whose *Iuris Epitomae* was a minor source for Justinian's Digest. However, the biographical evidence for the authorship of the Hermogenian and Gregorian Codes is too weak and thus imparts little benefit here.

3 For a reconstruction of the Gregorian and Hermogenian Codes see P. Krüger, *Collectio librorum iuris anteiustiniani* III, Berlin 1878–1927; FIRA II, pp. 653–65. And see A. Cenderelli, *Ricerche sul 'Codex Hermogenianus'*, Milan 1965; D. Liebs, *Hermogenians Epitomae*, Göttingen 1964, 23 ff.

4 See Chapter 11 above.

5 Only the constitutions issued since Constantine's era had to be collected in an authoritative, exclusive compendium as imperial legislation issued prior to this period already existed in the Gregorian and Hermogenian Codes.

6 Some questions have been invoked as to whether the Theodosian Code was actually promulgated in the Western Roman Empire, as required for attaining formal statutory force there. In any event, it is clear that the Code was accorded full practical effect, and was also regarded as an authoritative source of law in the West. See on this B. Sirks, 'From the Theodosian to the Justinian Code', *Atti dell'Academia Romanistica Costantiniana* (*VI Convegno Internazionale*) 1986, 275 ff.

7 C. Th. 1. 1. 6. 3.

8 Several reconstructions of the Theodosian Code have emerged since the sixteenth century. The most important early edition is that of Gothofredus (*Codex Theodosianus, cum perpetuis commentariis*), published in Lyons in 1665. Other editions of the Code were published by Hanel (Bonn 1837) and Th. Mommsen (Berlin 1905). Mommsen's edition (*Theodosiani libri XVI cum constitutionibus Sirmondianis*) is the one most widely used. For an English translation see C. Pharr (ed.) *The Theodosian Code and Novels and the Sirmondian Constitutions*, Princeton 1952. On the history and character of the Theodosian Code see T. Honoré, *Law in the Crisis of Empire*, Oxford 1998, ch. 5–7; 'The Making of the Theodosian Code', *SZ* 103, rom. Abt. (1986), 133–222; J. Harries and I. Wood (eds) *The Theodosian Code: Studies in the Imperial Law of Late Antiquity*, London 1993; J. F. Matthews, *Laying Down the Law, A Study of the Theodosian Code*, New Haven and London 2000; F. De Martini Avonzo, *La politica legislativa di Valentiniano III e Theodosio II*, Turin 1975; G.G. Archi, *Teodosio II e la sua codificazione*, Naples 1976.

9 These interpretations are clearly influenced by the *Vulgarrecht* and were probably derived from earlier sources.

10 The surviving copy of the Visigothic Code of Roman law is addressed to a Count (*comes*) named Timotheus and officially certified by Anianus, presumably a royal secretary. The aims of the code are proclaimed to be the correction of what seems unfair in the laws, the clearing up of the complexities which are present either in the written Roman laws or in the unwritten principles of ancient law, the removal of all abstruseness and the gathering within a single book of selected extracts from the works of earlier jurists.

11 In the middle of the seventh century AD, the gradual shift from the system of personal

laws to a territorial system prompted its replacement with another law book, the *Codex Legis Visigothorum* (or *Lex Visigothorum Recesvindiana*). This was intended to apply to both the Roman and Gothic subjects of the Visigothic kingdom in Spain.

12 For a modern reconstruction of the Visigothic Code of Roman law see G. Hänel, *Lex Romana Visigothorum*, Lipsiae 1849, repr. 1962. See also FIRA II, 667 ff. (appendices only). And see R. Lambertini, *La codificazione di Alarico II*, Turin 1990.

13 The order of the topics is the same as in the *Lex Condobada*, an earlier compilation issued for the Germanic part of the population.

14 For a modern reconstruction of the *Lex Romana Burgundionum*, see R. L. de Salis, MGH, *Leges* I. 2, Hanover 1892; and see FIRA II, 711 ff.

15 In the past this law code was believed to have been promulgated by Theodoric the Great (AD 493–526), ruler of the Ostrogothic kingdom of Northern Italy, for his Roman subjects.

16 See F. Bluhme (ed.), MGH, *Leges* I. 5, Hanover 1875–89; FIRA II, 681 ff.

17 In AD 530, he was minister of justice (*quaestor sacri palatii*). However, his unpopularity during the Nika riots prompted his discharge from this office and appointment as chief of the administration (*magister officiorum*). After the publication of the first parts of Justinian's codification, he once more became minister of justice. He died in AD 546 and thereafter Justinian's legal activity showed a marked decline. See Procop. *Anecd.* 13. 12. and 20. 16–17. On the life and work of Tribonian see T. Honoré, *Tribonian*, London 1978.

18 *P. Oxy.* XV 1814. See B. P. Grenfell and A. S. Hunt, *The Oxyrhynchus Papyri*, London 1898. And see P. E. Pieler, *Byzantinische Rechtsliteratur* in H. Hunger, *Die hochsprachliche profane Literatur der Byzantiner*, Bd. 2, Munich 1978, 412 ff. Consider also P. de Francisi, 'Frammento di un indice del primo Codice Giustinianeo', 3 *Aegyptus* (1922), 68–79; P. Krüger, 'Neue juristische Funde aus Agypten', 43 *SZ* (1922), 560–63.

19 No copy of the original collection has been preserved, but its content is integrated in the new Code of AD 534.

20 All the juristic works had to be considered (i.e. not only those of the five jurists mentioned in the Law of Citations) on their own merits, and no special weight was accorded to the opinions of any jurist because of his personal reputation or earlier influence. Justinian stipulated that the commission must avoid inserting matter that already existed in the *Codex* and always indicate the original source of a jurist's extract.

21 The arrangement of the materials had to adopt the divisions and subdivisions of the Commentary on the Edict.

22 *Digesta* (from *digerere*) means 'that which has been arranged or systematized'; *Pandecta* (from the Greek phrase '*pan dehesthe*') signifies 'an all-embracing work' or 'encyclopedia'.

23 See *Constitutio Deo Auctore* 1. 2. 6. 7. 12. Literal translations from Latin into Greek, short summaries (*indices*) and collections of parallel texts (*paratitla*) were permitted.

24 There is some doubt as to whether these remarks should be understood literally.

25 The earliest writers excerpted were Quintus Mucius Scaevola and Aelius Gallus. The latest was Arcadius Charisius, who apparently lived in the late third or the first half of the fourth century AD.

26 Ulpianus represented the largest contribution (about 40 per cent of the entire collection), with Paulus in second place.

27 With the exception of books 30, 31 and 32.

28 In the *constitutio Tanta* or *Dedoken* that introduced the Digest, Justinian refers to a further division of the materials into seven parts (paras 2–8). The first part, entitled 'Prota' (Books 1–4), contains general rules relating to the administration of justice (public officials, jurisdiction, the treatment of certain categories of persons and such like); the second part (Books 5–11) is entitled *De iudiciis* and deals with real actions and judicial proceedings; contracts and personal actions form the subject-matter of the third part, entitled *De rebus* (Books 12–19); the fourth part (Books 20–27) bears the title *Umbilicus Pandectarum* and is concerned with matters such as marriage, guardianship

and the rights of mortgagees; in part five (Books 28–36), various rules relating to wills, legacies and testamentary trusts are included under the heading *De testamentis*; these are followed in part 6 (Books 37–44) by rules governing the acquisition of ownership and possession of property, intestate succession, interdicts, exceptions and such like; finally, part seven (Books 45–50) covers matters such as obligations and civil injuries, local government, public works, appeals, criminal offences (included in Books 47 and 48 entitled '*libri terribiles*'), the meaning of legal terms and maxims of the law. This division seems to have been introduced mainly for instructional purposes.

29 An example of a reference taken from the ninth book of the Digest, title 2 ('On the Aquilian Law'): D. 9. 2. 11. 2 or D. 9. 2. 24 or D. 9. 2. 13. pr.

30 F. Bluhme 'Die Ordnung der Fragmente in den Pandektentiteln', *Zeitschrift für geschichtliche Rechtswissenschaft* 4 (1820), 257–472; also in *Labeo* 6 (1960), 50 ff, 235 ff, 368 ff.

31 H. Peters proposed a different hypothesis on the construction of the Digest in his work 'Die oströmischen Digestenkommentare und die Entstehung der Digesten' (*BerSachGW*, 1913, 65). Peters declared the existence of a work on the *ius* (a kind of 'pre-Digest') in the Eastern law schools that was assembled for instructional purposes, and relied on as a model by the compilers of Justinian's Digest. Although this theory attracted some attention in the past, scholars now believe that it is not adequately supported by historical evidence. For more on the construction of the Digest consider T. Honoré, *Tribonian*, London 1978, ch. 5; T. Honoré and A. Rodger, 'How the Digest Commissioners Worked', *SZ* 87 (1970), 246; D. Mantovani, *Digesto e Masse Bluhmiane*, Milan 1987; D. Osler, 'The Compilation of Justinian's Digest', *SZ* 102 (1985), 129–84.

32 One should note that the texts had probably been changed to some extent in the period that preceded the Justinianic codification. This may have derived from errors during the copying of the original manuscripts, modifications initiated during the re-editing of the works by post-classical compilers and the insertion of marginal or interlinear notes into the texts.

33 As Barry Nicholas remarks, 'in seeking to preserve the greatness of the past Justinian failed to produce a practical codification which his own subjects could use, and in seeking to present the law of his own day he distorted what he was trying to preserve'. *An Introduction to Roman Law*, Oxford 1962, repr. 1991, 44.

34 The Digest frequently cites Gaius with several quotations originating from Gaius' Institutes, a work transmitted to us through a manuscript dating from the fifth century but believed to reflect the law of the classical period. Generally, if one compares the extracts contained in the Digest with the relevant sections of the Institutes there are no major changes. However, assorted passages in the former work were evidently interpolated. For example, the Institutes 98–99 elaborates: 'Adoption takes place in two ways, either by the authority of the *people* or by the *imperium* of a magistrate, [such as the praetor]. By the authority of the *people* we adopt those who are *sui iuris* (independent); this kind of adoption is called adrogation, because the person who is adopting is asked (*rogatur*) whether he wishes to have the person adopted as his lawful son, the person who is adopted is asked whether he is consents to this, [and the people are asked whether they bid this be so].' This also appears in the Digest 1. 7. 2, but with certain changes: the phrases in brackets were omitted and word 'emperor' replaced the italicized word 'people'. Furthermore, the word '*Generalis*' (in general) has been inserted at the beginning. The comparison of these two passages clearly exhibits the kind of interpolation devised by the compilers of the Digest. In Gaius' era (second century AD), it was accepted that, theoretically, the emperor was a magistrate whose authority derived from the will of the people and that the people continued to perform all their ancient functions through their delegates. In Justinian's time, this theory was abandoned due to the transformation of the imperial power into an absolute monarchy. Moreover, in the second century AD, the praetor was still an active magistrate but in the sixth century he was merely an

honorary official divested of all his traditional powers. This explains the deletion of the reference to the praetor as a magistrate with *imperium* by the compilers of the Digest. Finally, in inserting the word '*generalis*' the compilers were simply indicating their introduction of a new topic.

35 These are known as *Litterae* or *Codices Bononienses* as they were used in the law school of Bologna, or *versio vulgata* (the 'common' or 'popular version').

36 For a photographic copy of the *Codex Florentinus* see A. Corbino and B. Santalucia (eds), *Justiniani augusti Pandectarum Codex Florentinus*, Florence 1988. The most important early editions of the Digest embrace those of Gothofredus (1583) and Spangenberg (1776–91). The most complete edition is that of T. Mommsen and P. Krüger, under the title *Digesta Iustiniani Augusti*, Berlin 1868–70, repr. 1962–63. For a shorter version, see T. Mommsen and P. Krüger, *Iustiniani Digesta* in *Corpus Iuris Civilis* I (pars 2a), 16th edn, Berlin 1954, repr. Dublin and Zurich 1973. For an English translation see A. Watson, *The Digest of Justinian*, Philadelphia 1985.

37 It has been suggested that the work on the Institutes was probably divided between Dorotheus and Theophilus, with Tribonian acting in a supervisory capacity. However, this view has been questioned by some scholars who argue that Tribonian played a more active role in the preparation of the book. See H. Ankum, 'Gaius, Theophilus and Tribonian and the Actiones Mixtae', in P. Stein and A.D.E. Lewis (eds), *Studies in Justinian's Institutes in Memory of J. A. C. Thomas*, London 1983, 4 ff.

38 Book one deals with the law of persons, except for an introductory preface on jurisprudential matters and the sources of law; the second book explores the law of property and part of the law of succession; book three addresses the remainder of the law of succession and the major part of the law of obligations; and book four concerns the remaining part of the law of obligations and the law of procedure. In book four, Gaius' discussion of the *legis actio* and the formulary procedures was replaced by a brief description of the *cognitio extraordinaria*, the procedure used in the post-classical period. It was followed by two titles on the duties of a judge (*de officio iudicis*) and on criminal law (*de publicis iudiciis*).

39 The first paragraph is the *principium* or *proemium* (pr.). Thus, to identify a citation in the Institutes one must indicate the number of the relevant book followed by the number of the title and the paragraph (or by the abbreviation 'pr.' if reference is made to the *principium*).

40 Only one fragment dating from the sixth century has been preserved.

41 The earliest printed edition of the Institutes appeared in 1468 but Cujas in 1585 produced the first scholarly edition. The definitive modern edition of the Institutes is P. Krüger's *Iustiniani Institutiones, Corpus Iuris Civilis* I (pars 1a), Berlin 1872. For English translations see J. A. C. Thomas, *The Institutes of Justinian*, Cape Town 1975; P. B. H. Birks and G. MacLeod, *Justinian's Institutes*, New York 1987.

42 Although it was provided that further enactments may be later introduced when necessary.

43 The sources of the extracted materials included the *Codices Gregorianus, Hermogenianus* and *Theodosianus*; certain collections of post-Theodosian constitutions; Justinian's own enactments; and, to some extent, the *Codex Vetus*. The Code is written in Latin; only a very small number of constitutions (mainly issued by Justinian) appear in Greek.

44 Modern scholars usually rely on the new complete edition (*editio maior*) of the *Codex Iustinianus* published last century by P. Krüger (Berlin 1877). For the *editio stereotypa* (*minor*) see P. Krüger, *Codex Iustinianus*, in *Corpus Iuris Civilis* II, 11th edn, Berlin 1954, repr. Dublin and Zurich 1970. See also T. Honoré, *Tribonian*, London 1978, 212 ff.

45 The majority of Justinian's new laws were issued in Greek, the language of business in the East. Some laws were composed in Greek and Latin, and some only in Latin (mainly those addressed to the western provinces of the empire or containing supplementary provisions to earlier enactments that had been drafted in Latin).

46 The oldest manuscript copies of this work date from the late seventh or early eighth century. For a modern reconstruction of Julian's collection see G. Hänel, *Iuliani Epitome Latina Novellarum Iustiniani*, Lipsiae 1873.

47 For a modern edition of this collection see G. E. Heimach, *Authenticum, Novellarum constitutionum Iustiniani versio vulgata*, I-II, Lipsiae 1846–51. And see P. E. Pieler, *Byzantinische Rechtsliteratur*, in H. Hunger, *Die hochsprachliche profane Literatur der Byzantiner*, Bd. 2, Munich 1978, 409 ff, 425 ff; N. van der Wal and J. H. A. Lokin, *Historiae iuris graeco-romani delineatio. Les sources du droit byzantin de* 300 a *1453*, Groningen 1985, 37–38.

48 Four constitutions of Justin II and three of Tiberius II were incorporated into this collection. It also contains some further texts that are not imperial constitutions but decrees of *praefecti praetorio*.

49 In one of these manuscripts (retained in Venice) there is an appendix containing thirteen edicts of Justinian (two of these are also traced to the other manuscript); these thirteen enactments are sometimes regarded as forming a separate collection referred to as *Edicta Iustiniani*.

50 It was one of the sources used by the compilers of the *Basilica*, the most important Byzantine law code.

51 The *Collectio Graeca* furnished the basis for the modern standard edition of the Novels produced by R. Schöll and G. Kroll in 1895 (in this edition the Novels are divided into chapters and paragraphs). See *Novellae, Corpus Iuris Civilis* III, 10th edn, Berlin 1972. For the Novels that survived in various papyri and inscriptions see M. Amelotti and L. Migliardi Zingale, *Le costituzioni Giustinianee nei papiri e nelle epigrafi*, Milan 1985.

52 In the Code, Justinian refers to his work as pertaining to the 'whole body of law' ('*in omni . . . corpore iuris*'). C. 5. 13. 1. pr.

53 The modern standard edition is that of T. Mommsen, P. Krüger, R. Schöll and W. Kroll, consisting of three volumes: Volume One contains the Institutes (ed. Krüger) and the Digest (ed. Mommsen, revised Krüger); Volume Two elaborates the Code (ed. Krüger); and Volume Three embodies the Novels (ed. Schöll and Kroll).

EPILOGUE

1 The *Basilica* is a monumental work, second only to the codification of Justinian in importance. It constitutes one of our chief sources of information on the Byzantine law and jurisprudence during the Justinianic and post-Justinianic periods. For the standard modern edition of the *Basilica* see G. E. Heimbach, *Basilicorum libri* 60, 1–6, Leipzig 1833–50 (with prolegomena, 1870); and see H. J. Scheltema, D. Holwerda, N. van der Wal, *Basilicorum libri* 60, Groningen 1953–88. Consider also P. Zepos, *Die byzantinische Jurisprudenz zwischen Iustinian und den Basiliken*, in *Ber. zum IX Intern. Byz-Kongr.*, V, I, Munich 1958, 1–27.

2 In Greece, the *Hexabiblos* remained a principal source of law until 1946 when a modern civil code was introduced. The latter was modelled on the German civil code of 1900, which also has its roots in Roman law.

3 Justinian's *Corpus* was introduced in Italy by a special enactment (the *pragmatica sanctio pro petitione Virgilii*) issued by the Emperor on 14 August AD 554 at the request of Pope Virgilius. See Nov. App. VII, 1 in R. Schöll and G. Kroll, *Novellae, Corpus Iuris Civilis* III, Berlin 1972, 799.

SELECT BIBLIOGRAPHY

Adcock, F. E., *Roman Political Ideas and Practice*, Ann Arbor, The University of Michigan Press, 1964, repr. 1975.

Albanese, B., *Il processo privato romano delle 'legis actiones'*, Palermo, Palumbo, 1987.

Alchi, G. L., *Le controversie tra sabiniani e proculiani*, Milan, Giuffrè, 1981.

Alexander, M. C., *Forensic Advocacy in the Late Roman Republic*, Toronto, University of Toronto Dept. of Classical Studies, 1977.

Alföldi, A., *The Conversion of Constantine and Pagan Rome*, Oxford, Clarendon, 1948.

Alföldy, G., *The Social History of Rome*, London and Sydney, Croom Helm, 1985.

Arangio-Ruiz, V., *Cours de droit romain (les actions)*, Naples, Jovere, 1935.

Archi, G. G., *Teodosio II e la sua codificazione*, Naples, Edizioni Scientifiche Italiane, 1976.

Arnheim, M. T. W., *The Senatorial Aristocracy in the Later Roman Empire*, Oxford, Clarendon, 1972.

Astolfi, R., *I libri tres iuris civilis di Sabino*, Padova, Cedam, 1983.

Barnes, T. D., *The New Empire of Diocletian and Constantine*, Cambridge, Mass. and London, Harvard University Press, 1982.

Bauman, R. A., *The Crimen Maiestatis in the Roman Republic and Augustan Principate*, Johannesburg, Witwatersrand University Press, 1967.

——, *Lawyers in Roman Republican Politics, A Study of Roman Jurists In their Political Setting, 316–82 BC*, Munich, Beck, 1971.

——, *Lawyers and Politics in the Early Roman Empire*, Munich, Beck, 1989.

——, *Crime and Punishment in Ancient Rome*, London and New York, Routledge, 1996.

Baynes, N. H., *Constantine the Great and the Christian Church*, New York, Haskell House, 1975.

Beard, M. and Crawford, M., *Rome in the Late Republic: Problems and Interpretations*, London, Duckworth, 1985.

Benke, N., *Juristenlatein*, Vienna, Manz, 2002.

Berger, A., *Encyclopedic Dictionary of Roman Law*, Philadelphia, APS, 1953.

Bernstein, A. H., *Tiberius Sempronius Gracchus: Tradition and Apostacy*, Ithaca and London, Cornell University Press, 1978.

Betti, E., *La crisi della Repubblica e la genesi del principato in Roma*, Rome, Pontificia universitas lateranensis, 1982.

Bleicken, J., *Staat und Recht in der Römischen Republik*, Wiesbaden, Steiner, 1978.

Boardman, J., Griffin, J. and Murray, O. (eds), *The Oxford History of the Roman World*, Oxford and New York, Oxford University Press, 1991.

Boren, H. C., *The Gracchi*, New York, Twayne Publishers, 1969.

Borkowski, J. A. and du Plessis, P., *Textbook on Roman Law*, 3rd edn, Oxford, Oxford University Press, 2005.

Bradley, K. R., *Slavery and Society at Rome*, Cambridge, Cambridge University Press, 1994.

Brunt, P. A. (ed.), *The Roman Economy: Studies in Ancient Economic and Administrative History*, Oxford, Blackwell, 1974.

——, *Italian Manpower 225 BC–AD 14*, Oxford University Press, 1987.

——, *The Fall of the Roman Republic*, Oxford, Clarendon, 1988.

——, *Roman Imperial Themes*, Oxford, Clarendon, 1990.

Buckland, W. W. and Stein, P., *A Textbook of Roman Law from Augustus to Justinian*, 3rd edn, Cambridge, Cambridge University Press, 1963, repr., 1975.

Bund, E., *Untersuchungen zur Methode Julians*, Köln, Böhlau, 1965.

Burdese, A., *Manuale di diritto pubblico romano*, 3rd edn, Turin, UTET, 1987, repr. 1994.

——, *Manuale di diritto privato romano*, 4th edn, Turin, UTET, 1993.

Bürge, A., *Römisches Privatrecht*, Darmstadt, Wiss. Buchges, 1999.

Cameron, A., *The Later Roman Empire*, London, Fontana, 1993.

Campbell, J. B., *The Emperor and the Roman Army 31 BC–AD 235*, Oxford, Clarendon, 1984.

Cannata, C. A., *Profilo istituzionale del processo privato romano*, Turin, Giappichelli, 1980.

Cary, M. and Scullard, H. H., *A History of Rome*, 3rd edn, London, Macmillan, 1975.

Chantraine, H., *Freigelassene und Sklaven im Dienst der römischen Kaiser. Studien zu ihrer Nomenklatur* (Habilitationsschrift), Wiesbaden, 1967.

Christ, K., *Krise und Untergang der römischen Republik*, Darmstadt, Wissenschaftliche Buchgesellschaft, 1979.

Corbett, P. E., *The Roman Law of Marriage*, Oxford, Clarendon, 1930.

Corcoran, S., *The Empire of the Tetrarchs*, Oxford, Clarendon, 1996.

Cornell, T. J., *The Beginnings of Rome*, London, Routledge, 1995, repr. 1997.

Crawford, M., *Coinage and Money under the Roman Republic: Italy and the Mediterranean Economy*, London, Methuen, 1985.

——, *The Roman Republic*, 2nd edn, London, Fontana, 1992.

Crifò, G., *Lezioni di storia del diritto romano*, 3rd edn, Bologna, Monduzzi, 2000.

Crook, J. A., *Consilium Principis: Imperial Councils and Counsellors from Augustus to Diocletican*, Cambridge, Cambridge University Press, 1955.

——, *Law and Life of Rome*, London, Thames & Hudson, 1967.

——, *Legal Advocacy in the Roman World*, London, Duckworth, 1995.

Daube, D., *Forms of Roman Legislation*, Oxford, Clarendon, 1956.

Declareuil, J., *Rome the Law-Giver*, London and New York, Routledge, 1996 (original edn 1927).

De Giovanni, L., *Introduzione allo studio del diritto romano tardoantico*, 4th edn, Naples, Jovene, 2000.

Delmaire, R., *Les Institutions du Bas-Èmpire romain, de Constantin à Justinien, I, Les Institutions palatines*, Paris, CERF, 1995.

De Martini Avonzo, F., *La politica legislativa di Valentiniano III e Teodosio II*, Turin, Giappichelli, 1975.

De Martino, F., *Storia economica di Roma antica*, Florence, La nuova Italia, 1979.

d'Entrèves, A. P., *Natural Law: An Introduction to Legal Philosophy*, London, Hutchinson's University Library, 1951.

Diòsdi, G., *Ownership in Ancient and Preclassical Roman Law*, Budapest, Akademia Kiado, 1970.

D'Ippolito, F., *I giuristi e la città*, Naples, Edizioni Scientifiche Italiane, 1978.

——, *Giuristi e sapienti in Roma arcaica*, Rome, Laterza, 1986.

——, *Aspetti di storia costituzionale romana*, Naples, Edizioni Scientifiche Italiane, 2001.

Dirksen, H. E., *Beiträge zur Kunde des römischen Rechts*, Leipzig, Hinrichs, 1825

Dixon, S., *The Roman Mother*, London, Croom Helm, 1988.

Dumont, J. C., *Servus: Rome et l'esclavage sous la République*, Rome, École française de Rome, 1987.

Duncan-Jones, R., *The Economy of the Roman Empire*, Cambridge, Cambridge University Press, 1982.

——, *Money and Government in the Roman Empire*, Cambridge, University Press, 1994.

Eckardt, B., *Iavoleni Epistulae*, Berlin, Duncker & Humblot, 1978.

Evans Grubbs, J., *Law and Family in Late Antiquity: the Emperor Constantine's Marriage Legislation*, Oxford, Clarendon, 1995.

——, *Law and Family in Late Antiquity*, Oxford, Oxford University Press, 1999.

Ferenczy, E., *From the Patrician State to the Patricio-Plebeian State*, Amsterdam, Hakkert, 1976.

Finley, M. I. (ed.), *Slavery in Classical Antiquity, Views and Controversies*, Cambridge, W. Heffer & Sons, 1960.

Frend, W. H. C., *The Rise of Christianity*, London, Darton, Longman & Todd, 1984.

Friedrich, C. J., *The Philosophy of Law in Historical Perspective*, Chicago and London, University of Chicago Press, 1963.

Frier, B., *The Rise of the Roman Jurists*, Princeton, Princeton University Press, 1985.

Gardner, J. F., *Women in Roman Law and Society*, London, Croom Helm, 1986.

——, *Being a Roman Citizen*, London, Routledge, 1993.

——, *Family and Familia in Roman Law and Life*, Oxford, Clarendon, 1998.

Garnsey, P., *Social Status and Legal Privilege*, Oxford, Clarendon, 1970.

Garnsey, P. and Saller, R., *The Roman Empire: Economy, Society and Culture*, London, Duckworth, 1987.

Gelzer, M., *The Roman Nobility*, Oxford, Blackwell, 1969.

Gioffredi, C., *I principi del diritto penale romano*, Torino, Giappichelli, 1970.

Giuffrè, V., *La repressione criminale nell' esperienza romana*, 4th edn, Naples, Jovene, 1998.

Goffart, W., *Caput and Colonate: Towards a History of Late Roman Taxation*, Toronto, University of Toronto Press, 1974.

Grant, M., *History of Rome*, London, Weidenfeld and Nicolson, 1978.

Gruen, E. S., *Roman Politics and the Criminal Courts, 149–78 BC*, Harvard University Press, 1968.

——, *The Last Generation of the Roman Republic*, Berkeley, University of California Press, 1974.

Guarino, A., *Storia del diritto romano*, 11th edn, Naples, Jovene, 1996.

——, *Diritto privato romano*, 12th edn, Naples, Jovene, 2001.

Gwynne-Thomas, E. H., *A Political History of the Roman Empire*, Lanham, University Press of America, 1984.

Harries, J., *Law and Empire in Late Antiquity*, Cambridge, Cambridge University Press, 1999.

Harries, J. and Wood, I. (eds), *The Theodosian Code: Studies in the Imperial Law of Late Antiquity*, London, Duckworth, 1993.

Hill, H. M. A., *The Roman Middle Class in the Republican Period*, Oxford, Basil Blackwell, 1952.

Honoré, T., *Tribonian*, London, Duckworth, 1978.
——, *Ulpian*, Oxford, Clarendon, 1982.
——, *Emperors and Lawyers*, Oxford, Clarendon Press, 1994.
——, *Law in the Crisis of Empire, 379–445 AD*, Oxford, Clarendon, 1998.
Hopkins, K., *Conquerors and Slaves*, Cambridge, Cambridge University Press, 1978.
Humbert, M, *Municipium et civitas sine suffragio*, Rome, École Française de Rome, 1978.
Jacques, F. and Scheid, J., *Rom und das Reich in der Hohen Kaiserzeit*, Stuttgart and Leipzig, B. G. Teubner, 1998.
Johnston, D., *Roman Law in Context*, Cambridge, Cambridge University Press, 1999.
Jolowicz, H. F. and Nicholas, B., *Historical Introduction to the Study of Roman Law*, 3rd edn, Cambridge, Cambridge University Press, 1972.
Jones, A. H. M., *Studies in Roman Government and Law*, Oxford, Blackwell, 1960.
——, *The Later Roman Empire*, Oxford, Blackwell, 1964.
——, *The Criminal Courts of the Roman Republic and Principate*, Oxford, Blackwell, 1972.
——, *Constantine and the Conversion of Europe*, Toronto, University of Toronto Press, 1978.
Kaser, M., *Zur Methode der römischen Rechtsfindung*, Göttingen, Nachrichten der Akademie der Wissenschaften, 1962.
——, *Das römische Privatrecht*, 2 vols, 2nd edn, Munich, Beck, 1971–74.
——, *Zur Methodologie der römischen Rechtsquellenforschung*, Vienna, Cologne and Graz, Böhlau, 1972.
——, *Römische Rechtsgeschichte*, Göttingen, Vandenhoeck & Ruprecht, 1976.
——, *Römisches Privatrecht*, Munich, Beck, 1989.
——, *Ius gentium*, Cologne, Weimar and Vienna, Böhlau, 1993.
——, *Das römische Zivilprozessrecht*, Munich, Beck, 1966; 1996 (2nd edn).
Kelly, J. M., *Roman Litigation*, Oxford, Clarendon, 1966.
——, *Studies in the Civil Judicature of the Roman Republic*, Oxford, Clarendon, 1976.
——, *A Short History of Western Legal Theory*, Oxford, Clarendon, 1992.
Kennedy, G., *The Art of Rhetoric in the Roman World (300 BC–AD 300)*, Princeton, Princeton University Press, 1972.
Kirschenbaum, A., *Sons, Slaves, and Freedmen in Roman Commerce*, Jerusalem, Magnes Press, Hebrew University; Washington, D.C., Catholic University of America Press, 1987.
Kunkel, W., *Untersuchungen zur Entwicklung des römischen Kriminalverfahrens in vorsullanischer Zeit*, Munich, Verl. der Bayer. Akad. der Wissenschaften, 1962.
——, *An Introduction to Roman Legal and Constitutional History*, 2nd edn, Oxford, Clarendon, 1973.
——, *Die Römischen Juristen*, Cologne, Weimar and Vienna, Böhlau, 2001.
Kunkel, W. and Schermaier, M., *Römische Rechtsgeschichte*, Cologne, Böhlau, 2001.
Lambertini, R., *La codificazione di Alarico II*, Turin, Giappichelli, 1990.
Lambiris, M. A., *The Historical Context of Roman law*, Sydney, LBC Information Services, 1997.
Levick, B., *The Government of the Roman Empire: a Sourcebook*, 2nd edn, London and New York, Routledge, 2000.
Lévy-Bruhl, L., *Recherches sur les actions de la loi*, Paris, Publications de l'Institut de droit romain de l'Université de Paris. no. 19, 1960.
Lewis, A. D. E. and Ibbetson, D. J. (eds), *The Roman Law Tradition*, Cambridge, Cambridge University Press, 1994.
Lintott, A., *Judicial Reform and Land Reform in the Roman Republic*, Cambridge, Cambridge University Press, 1992.

——, *Imperium Romanum: Politics and Administration*, London and New York, Routledge, 1993.

——, *The Constitution of the Roman Republic*, Oxford, Clarendon, 1999.

Lintott, A. W., *Violence in Republican Rome*, Oxford, Clarendon, 1968.

MacMullen, R., *Roman Government's Response to Crisis. AD* 235–337, New Haven, Yale University Press, 1976.

——, *Christianizing the Roman Empire (AD* 100–400), New Haven, Yale University Press, 1984.

Mann, J. C., *Legionary Recruitment and Veteran Settlement During the Principate*, London, University of London Institute of Archaeology, 1983.

Manthe, U., *Die Libri ex Cassio des Iavolenus Priscus*, Berlin, Duncker & Humblot, 1982.

Mantovani, D., *Digesto e masse bluhmiane*, Milan, Giuffrè, 1987.

Marotta, V., *Mandata principum*, Turin, Giappichelli, 1991.

Matthews, J., *Western Aristocracies and Imperial Court, AD* 364–425, Oxford, Clarendon, 1975.

——, *Political Life and Culture in Late Roman Society*, London, Variorum Reprints, 1985.

——, *Laying Down the Law: a Study of the Theodosian Code*, New Haven, Yale University Press, 2000.

Merryman, J. H., *The Civil Law Tradition*, Stanford, Stanford University Press, 1969.

Metzger, E., *A New Outline of the Roman Civil Trial*, Oxford, Clarendon, 1997.

——, *Litigation in Roman Law*, Oxford, Oxford University Press, 2005.

Millar, F., *The Emperor in the Roman World*, Ithaca, New York, Cornell University Press, 1977.

Mitchell, R.E., *Patricians and Plebeians: The Origins of the Roman State*, Ithaca and London, Cornell University Press, 1990.

Mommsen, Th., *Römisches Staatsrecht* I, Leipzig, Duncker & Humblot, 1887, repr. Graz, Akademische Druck-und Verlaganstalt, 1952.

——, *Römisches Strafrecht*, Leipzig, Duncker & Humblot, 1899, repr. Graz, Akademische Druck-und Verlaganstalt, 1955, and Darmstadt, Wissenschaftliche Buchgesellschaft, 1961.

Monier, R., *Manuel élémentaire de droit romain*, Aalen, Scientia, 1977.

Mousourakis, G., *The Historical and Institutional Context of Roman Law*, Burlington, Ashgate, 2003.

Nelson, H. L. W., *Überlieferung, Aufbau und Stil von Gai Institutiones*, Leiden, Brill, 1981.

Nicholas, B., *An Introduction to Roman Law*, Oxford, Clarendon, 1962, repr. 1991.

Nicolet, C., *L'ordre équestre à l'époque républicaine*, Paris, Éditions E. de Boccard, 1966.

——, *The World of the Citizen in Republican Rome*, London, Batsford, 1980.

Nippel, W., *Public Order in Ancient Rome*, Cambridge, Cambridge University Press, 1995.

Noailles, P., *Du droit sacré au droit civil*, Paris, Publications de l'Institut de Droit Romain de l'Université de Paris, no. 4, 1949.

Olechowski, T. and Gamauf, R., *Rechtsgeschichte und Römisches Recht*, Vienna, Manz, 2006.

Pflaum, H.-G., *Les carrières procuratoriennes équestres sous le Haut-Empire romain*, Paris, Adrien Maisonneuve, 1950.

Pugliese, G., *Il processo civile romano*, Milan, Giuffre, Rome, Ricerche, 1962-1963.

Rainer, J. M., *Einführung in das römische Staatsrecht*, Darmstadt, Wiss. Buchges., 1997.

Richard, Jean-Claude, *Les origines de la plèbe romaine: essai sur la formation du dualisme patricio-plébéien*, Rome, École Française de Rome, 1978.

Riggsby, A. M., *Crime and Community in Ciceronian Rome*, Austin, University of Texas Press, 1999.

Robinson, O. F., *The Criminal Law of Ancient Rome*, London, Duckworth, 1995.

——, *The Sources of Roman Law*, London and New York, Routledge, 1997.

Salmon, E. T., *Roman Colonisation under the Republic*, London, Thames & Hudson, 1969.

Santalucia, B., *Diritto e processo penale nell' antica Roma*, Milan, Giuffrè, 1989, 2nd edn 1998.

——, *Studi di diritto penale romano*, Roma, 'L'Erma' di Bretschneider, 1994.

Scevola, R., *La responsabilità del iudex privatus*, Milan, Giuffrè, 2004.

Schiller, A. A., *An American Experience in Roman Law*, Göttingen, Vandenhoeck & Ruprecht, 1971.

——, *Roman Law: Mechanisms of Development*, The Hague and New York, Mouton, 1978.

Schulz, F., *Classical Roman Law*, Oxford, Clarendon, 1951.

——, *History of Roman Legal Science*, Oxford, Clarendon, 1967 (original edn 1946).

Seidl, E., *Rechtsgeschichte Ägyptens als römischer Provinz*, St Augustin, Richarz, 1973.

Sherwin-White, A. N., *The Roman Citizenship*, 2nd edn, Oxford, Clarendon, 1973.

Sinnigen, W. G. and Boak, A. E. R., *A History of Rome to AD 565*, 6th edn, New York, Macmillan, 1977.

Smith, J. C. and Weisstub, D. N. (eds), *The Western Idea of Law*, London, Butterworth, 1983.

Sordi, M., *I cristiani e l'impero romano*, Milan, Jaca Book, 1984.

Staerman, E. M., *Die Blütezeit der Sklavenwirtschaft in der römischen Republik*, Wiesbaden, Steiner, 1969.

Stein, P., *The Character and Influence of the Roman Civil Law*, London, Hambledon, 1988.

——, *Roman Law in European History*, Cambridge, Cambridge University Press, 1999.

Stein, P. C., *Regulae Iuris: From Juristic Rules to Legal Maxims*, Edinburgh, Edinburgh University Press, 1966.

Stein, P. G. and Lewis, A. D. E. (eds), *Studies in Justinian's Institutes in Memory of J. A. C. Thomas*, London, Sweet & Maxwell, 1983.

Stockton, D. L., *The Gracchi*, Oxford, Clarendon, 1979.

Strachan-Davidson, J. L., *Problems of the Roman Criminal Law* I, Oxford, Clarendon, 1912, repr. Amsterdam, Rodopi, 1969.

Stroux, J., *Römische Rechtswissenschaft und Rhetorik*, Potsdam, E. Stichnote, 1949.

Sutherland, C. H. V., *Roman Coins*, London, Barrie & Jenkins, 1974.

Swarney, P. R., *The Ptolemaic and Roman Idios Logos*, Toronto, A. M. Hakkert, 1970.

Syme, R., *The Augustan Aristocracy*, Oxford, Clarendon, 1986.

——, *The Roman Revolution*, Oxford, Clarendon, 1939; Oxford University Press, 2002.

Talamanca, M. (ed.), *Lineamenti di storia del diritto romano*, 2nd edn, Milan, Giuffrè, 1989.

Tamm, D., *Roman Law and European Legal History*, Copenhagen, DJOF, 1997.

Taylor, L. R., *Party Politics in the Age of Caesar*, University of California Press, 1949.

——, *Roman Voting Assemblies*, Ann Arbor, The University of Michigan Press, 1966.

Tellegen-Couperus, O. E., *A Short History of Roman Law*, London and New York, Routledge, 1993.

Thomas, P. J., *Introduction to Roman Law*, Deventer, London, Kluwer Law and Taxation, 1986.

Thomsen, R., *The Italic Regions from Augustus to the Lombard Invasion*, Rome, 'L'Erma' di Bretschneider, 1966.

Treggiari, S., *Roman Freedmen During the Late Republic*, Oxford, Oxford University Press, 2000.

Urch, E. J., *The Evolution of the Inquisitorial Procedure in Roman Law*, Chicago, Ares Publishers, 1980.

Van der Wal, N. and Lokin, J. H. A., *Historiae iuris graeco-romani delineatio*, Groningen, Forsten, 1985.

Vinogradoff, P., *Roman Law in Medieval Europe*, Oxford, Clarendon, 1929.

Vismara, G., *Episcopalis audientia*, Milan, Vita e Pensiero, 1937.

Watson, A., *The Law of the Ancient Romans*, Dallas, Southern Methodist University Press, 1970.

——, *Law Making in the Roman Republic*, Oxford, Clarendon, 1974.

——, *Rome of the XII Tables*, Princeton, Princeton University Press, 1975.

——, *Roman Slave Law*, Baltimore, Johns Hopkins University Press, 1987.

——, *Roman Law and Comparative Law*, Athens, University of Georgia Press, 1991.

——, *The State, Law and Religion: Pagan Rome*, Athens, University of Georgia Press, 1992.

——, *The Spirit of Roman Law*, Athens, University of Georgia Press, 1995.

Watson, G. R., *The Roman Soldier*, London, Thames and Hudson, 1969.

Weaver, P. R. C., *Familia Caesaris: a Social Study of the Emperor's Freedmen and Slaves*, London, Cambridge University Press, 1972.

Webster, G., *The Roman Imperial Army of the First and Second Centuries AD*, London, Black, 1985.

Wells, C., *The Roman Empire*, 2nd edn, London, Fontana, 1992.

Wenger, L., *Die Quellen des römischen Rechts*, Vienna, Holzhausen, 1953.

Wesel, U., *Rhetorische Statuslehre und Gesetzesauslegung der römischen Juristen*, Köln, C. Heymann, 1967.

Westbrook, R., *Zeitschrift der Savigny Stiftung für Rechtsgeschichte* 105, 1988, 74–121

Westermann, W. L., *The Slave Systems of Greek and Roman Antiquity*, Philadelphia, American Philosophical Society, 1955.

Whittaker, C. R., *Frontiers of the Roman Empire: A Social and Economic Study*, Johns Hopkins University Press, 1994.

Wieacker, F., *Römische Rechtsgeschichte* I, Munich, Beck, 1988.

Williams, S., *Diocletian and the Roman Recovery*, London, Batsford, 1985.

Wolf, J. G., *Die litis contestatio im römischen Zivilprozess*, Karlsruhe, Müller, 1968.

Wolff, H.-J., *Roman Law: An Historical Introduction*, Norman, University of Oklahoma Press, 1951.

Ziegler, K. H., *Das private Schiedsgericht im antiken römischen Recht*, Munich, Beck, 1971.

INDEX

punishments 94, 134, 176, 178,
203n25, 256n77
Pyrrhus, King of Epirus 9

quaesitor 79
quaestio de adulteriis 78, 130
quaestio de annona 130
quaestio de falsis 78
quaestio de plagiariis 78
quaestio de sicariis 78
quaestio de sodaliciis 78
quaestio de veneficis 78
quaestio de vi 78
quaestio repetundarum 77–9
quaestiones 113
quaestiones extraordinariae 77
quaestiones perpetuae: abolition 86;
chairmen 13, 79; creation and types
of 77–8, 130; deficiencies 130;
membership 79–80; penalties 81;
procedure 80–1
quaestor sacri palatii 143, 160, 183
quaestores militares 15
quaestores parricidii 36, 37, 208n42
quaestores provinciales 201n44
quaestores urbani 15
quaestorship 11, 14–15
quinquaginta decisiones (Fifty Decisions)
184, 188

Reception of Roman law 194
receptum arbitri 254n43
recuperatores 32
regal period *see* Monarchy
regimen morum 14
regium consilium 7
regulae 113
relegatio 134
religion: contrast between Diocletian
and Constantine 140; *see also*
Christianity; *fas*
replicationes 68–9
Republic: crisis and fall 43–8; dates of
1; expansion in Italy 9, 198n22;
expansion into Mediterranean world
39–40; late Republic 41–3
republican constitution 10
res corporales 238n75

res incorporales 238n75
res mancipi 54–5
res nec mancipi 54–5
rescripta 102, 108, 160–1, 179
respondere 30, 62, 101, 112
responsa 51–2, 62–3, 112, 113, 158,
218n56
restitutiones in integrum 75
Revival of Roman law 187, 193
revocatio in duplum 73
rex see king
rhetoric 60–1
rogatio 38, 58; *see also leges rogatae*
Roman legal history: overview 1–2;
post-Justinian developments 192–5
Rome: founding of 3–4; recapture of
154; sack of 153
Romulus 4
Romulus Augustulus, Emperor of the
West 153
Rutilius Rufus, P. 64

Sabines 3
Sabinian mass 185
Sabinians (Cassians) 113, 114–15
Sabinus, Massurius 113, 115, 236n38;
see also Sabinians
sacer homo 36
sacramentum 33
sacrilegium 176
sacrum consistorium 143, 160, 247n26
Samnites 9
sanctio 58
sanctio pragmatica 161
sanctio pragmatica pro petitione Vigilii
251n14
Savigny, Friedrich Karl von 238n69
Saxons 153
Scaevola, Q. Mucius 63–4, 113
scholae palatinae 143
Scholia Sinaitica 167
Scipio Aemilianus 212n19
Scipionic circle 212n19
scrinia 143–4
scrinium a libellis 112
scrinium ab epistulis 111–12
scrinium dispositionum 144
scrinium epistularum 144